CONTRACT BRIDGE:

THE PLAY OF
THE CARDS

By

FRED L. KARPIN

Introduction by ALFRED SHEINWOLD

BRIDGE QUARTERLY PUBLISHING COMPANY
CHESTNUT HILL 67, MASSACHUSETTS

Library of Congress Catalog Card Number 58-13418

Printed in the United States of America

INTRODUCTION

Fred Karpin put his finger on the sorest spot in bridge when he observed that millions know how to bid acceptably but that only a few thousand can play the cards up to a similar level.

You might think that this condition can easily be corrected. "After all," you might argue, "the millions of good bidders had to learn from books. Why can't they learn to play the cards from other books?"

There's a difference. It's easy to know when you're bidding badly. You keep landing in silly contracts, and you can see for yourself that something is wrong. If you don't, your partner will usually point it out.

Bad play isn't so obvious.

What happens if you make the wrong play on ten hands in a row? On one hand, perhaps, the "wrong" play happens to work, while the "right" play would fail. On another hand, the cards are so miserably placed that any play at all is sure to fail. On perhaps two hands your luck is so good that any play will work. That leaves six hands on which your wrong play costs you one or more tricks — perhaps the contract.

This is a terrible state of affairs — to drop tricks on six hands out of ten. *But who notices it?*

Your opponents? They're busy taking credit for their brilliant defense. This probably means that they followed suit without revoking.

Your partner? Only a very advanced player can sit across the table from declarer and see what should have been done as well as what actually was done.

What about you, yourself? If you could see the error, you wouldn't have made it in the first place.

As a result, you practically never have your errors drawn to your attention. For all you know, you're the world's best card player!

Now that you have this book, you can improve your play and can learn to spot an error when it takes place. It won't be painful, for Fred Karpin is a born teacher and a pleasant companion as well as a first class analyst.

Don't let it end there. Get somebody else to read this book, even if you have to sit on him until he has read the first few pages. (From that point, he'll read on without further persuasion.)

That's the best way to make good players out of our nation's thirty million so-called "bridge players." Otherwise, it might well be that the current ratio of about three thousand good players to 29,997,000 card pushers will be maintained for quite a while to come.

— ALFRED SHEINWOLD

CONTENTS

PART I

Declarer's Play

iv

PART II

Defenders' Play

FOREWORD

During the past nine years, as a direct consequence of the introduction, development, and the manifold refinements of the point-count method of bidding, there was a tremendous over-emphasis on bidding. In these circumstances it was rather natural that the study and mastery of the technique of play became de-emphasized and relegated to a secondary role — the forgotten man of bridge, as it were.

As a result of this inordinate stress on bidding technique, the general standard of play declined appreciably; and through either lack of time to devote to a more thorough understanding of the play, or plain lethargy, an unhealthy atmosphere of unbalance was created. To borrow a phrase from our psychologists, the majority of our bridge players lapsed into a condition of "arrested development": as their bidding ability spiralled upward toward greater heights, their playing ability simultaneously descended toward lower depths. In my opinion, the disparity of development between proper bidding and proper play has currently become so pronounced that the plane of average bridge living has retrogressed to a mere survival level.

That this inverse state of affairs should exist is most lamentable and, actually, paradoxical, for surely bidding should be subordinate to the play of the hand. After all, when one stops to consider it, bidding is nothing more than a contractual estimate of the number of tricks that one hopes to win in the play. This prevailing state of affairs — of the cart being before the horse — is doubly unfortunate for the new generation of bridge players who were attracted to the game as an avocation because it was sold to them as the most fascinating and mentally-stimulating of all the card games. Through expert guidance, they learned how to bid authoritatively, to arrive at the optimum contract — and were then abandoned and left to their own resources to wend their way via the path of trial and error towards the fulfillment of their contract.

Viewing the situation from a pedagogic point of view, there is nothing more frustrating to aspiring bridge players and nothing more conducive to the shattering of their confidence, than the too-frequent arrival at a game or slam contract which goes down to defeat. Unless these misguided ones can be made to see that they have played the hand incorrectly, the cumulative impact of their defeats must ultimately make them feel that they have bid too optimistically. And, psychologically, from having been burned so often, they will then tend to tread too cautiously in the future, and approach their bidding in unduly pessimistic fashion; they will now embark on the path of underbidding, with the desired effect being to obtain at least a little profit, instead of showing a loss. The inevitable result will be that instead of trying to elevate their standard of play to their higher standard of bidding, they will lower their standard of bidding to the level of necessary survival. All of which can be summed up in one word: degeneration.

The purpose of this book is to assist in re-establishing the correct relationship between bidding and play: to bring the play of the cards to the fore, where it properly belongs. It is the hope of your author that in the not-too-distant future there will come about a resurgence of interest in the play of the cards, leading to a renaissance of playing ability. Only then will the healthy and normal balance between bidding and play become restored, and accurate bidding will achieve its just reward — the fulfillment of the contract.

Throughout this book there are included approximately 250 complete illustrative deals, embodying the major themes of offensive and defensive play. A large proportion of these deals arose in actual competition. The reader will find that five or six of them are repeated in different chapters. Since there undoubtedly will be those who will notice this repetition, I should like to state that its reason is not that I ran out of illustrative deals. Rather it is because in each of these deals there are two or three major phases of play which, if analyzed simultaneously, might result in the reader losing sight of the one specific subject being discussed within that chapter. Hence the duplication, in order that each vital point can be viewed in its proper topical perspective.

To the many expert bridge players whose names are mentioned in this book, I owe a debt of gratitude. Although they had nothing to do with the actual writing of this book, some of the hands which confronted them in combat have been assimilated into this book as illustrations of technically-accurate, highly imaginative, and brilliant play of the hand. As a result of their real-life contributions, I was spared the time and effort of "building up" hands to describe many of the most important features of the play. My appreciation and thanks are hereby recorded.

FRED L. KARPIN

September, 1958.

CHAPTER I

THE FINESSE

Y OU and your partner have just arrived at a vulnerable *seven notrump* contract. West opens the *Jack of Spades* and you hold your breath while waiting for the dummy to be put down. A few anxious moments go by, and the dummy comes into full view:

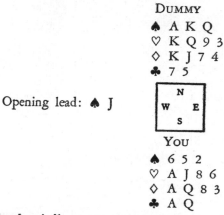

DUMMY

♠ A K Q
♡ K Q 9 3
◇ K J 7 4
♣ 7 5

Opening lead: ♠ J

YOU

♠ 6 5 2
♡ A J 8 6
◇ A Q 8 3
♣ A Q

You hurriedly count your sure winning tricks: three in Spades, four in Hearts, four in Diamonds, and one in Clubs, a total of twelve. Depending on your bridge personality, evolved from past experiences, you either like or dislike your position: your thirteenth trick can be made only if East has the King of Clubs, only if the club finesse is successful, a 50-50 proposition. Some of you are undoubtedly thinking of a few choice words to say to your partner for putting you into a grand slam contract which hinges on a finesse; others of you have probably convinced yourselves that the finesse will be unsuccessful, for have not these finesses always lost for you in similar crucial situations?

But whatever your attitude, sooner or later you lead the five of clubs off dummy, East follows with the deuce, and you hopefully put up your Queen, closing your eyes as you do, while silently and entreatingly supplicating the gods of chance to come to your immediate aid. You then open your eyes, and with your heart fluttering you turn to see what West has played. If it's a low club, then joy is unbounded, and you have just realized that "all is for the best in this best of all possible worlds." But if it is the King of Clubs that West has played, then the thought may come to mind that Dante's statement with respect to Hell, "All hope abandon, ye who enter here," applies equally well to the taking of finesses.

Emotions analogous to the above have occurred in every bridge game that has ever been played, or ever will be. On virtually every single deal that is encountered, there will be at least one finesse to take, sometimes two, or even three or four. There are those days when every finesse that you take turns out to be successful; and there are those other days — that Mother warned you about — when all finesses are losing ones. On any given day you find yourself in some game contract. You take three finesses, each one of them loses, and you are down a trick; or you take the same three finesses, they all win, and you make twelve tricks.

What I am trying to do, in introducing the above attitudes with respect to the finesse, is to point out and emphasize that the most important and most frequently-occurring single play in bridge is the finesse. Although the finesse is a fairly elementary play, without understanding it and without mastering its various aspects, no bridge player can ever hope to become an expert, or even a "good" player. Just as it is said that the poor and taxes will always be with us, so the finesse will always be a most necessary and vital weapon in declarer's arsenal of aggressive warfare.

This chapter is devoted to presenting the different types of finesses, how and when they should be taken, *and when they should not be taken.* Let's start at the beginning, and proceed from the very simple, to the less simple, and ultimately, to the more complex.

Defined formally, a finesse might be described as *an attempt to win a trick with a card when there is a higher card (or cards) outstanding.* In effect the finesse is really wishful thinking put into action. That is, you figuratively put the card that you are looking for where you want it to be, and proceed to surround it by putting the "holder" in the middle and trapping him. In other words, you create the condition which must exist if your finesse is to succeed. The following examples illustrate this wishful-thinking aspect:

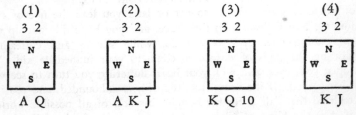

(1)	(2)	(3)	(4)
3 2	3 2	3 2	3 2
A Q	A K J	K Q 10	K J

On each of the four preceding illustrative hands, the suit is diamonds, and the deuce is led from the North hand, East following with the *four-spot*.

In (1), as you play your Queen, you are indulging in wishful thinking — you "put" the King of Diamonds in the East hand and then play on that assumption.

In (2), you play your Jack of Diamonds, finessing East for the Queen (hoping he has it). If he does not, your wishful thinking has not materialized.

In (3), you insert your ten of Diamonds with the hope that East has the Jack. If he does, you will have two sure diamond tricks for yourself. An alternative wishful-thinking play would be to put up the King, playing East for the Ace. If he has it, then the King will win, after which dummy will be re-entered via another suit, and another diamond led toward the Queen. If East had the Diamond Ace before, he still has it, and the Queen will become your second winner.

In (4), you make up your mind as to whether you desire East to possess the Ace or the Queen. If it is the Ace that you "put" in his hand, then you play your King; if it is the Queen you "give" to East, then you put up your Jack. And 50% of the time your wishful thinking will develop as hoped for.

The finesse, as you can see, is always a 50-50 proposition. The card you are finessing for is either in the hand you want it to be, or in the hand of the other opponent. Unfortunately, too many of our "conservative" bridge players consider the finesse as a gamble, and as such do not want to have anything to do with it, for gambling is a reflection on one's character, a sign of weakness, etc., etc. Somehow the idea was developed — and promulgated — that if you take the "gambling" finesse you may lose something. Actually if one stops to think about it, unless there is a better play available, *the finesse stands to gain everything and lose nothing*. Let us go back for a moment to the first illustration:

♢ 3 2

♢ A Q

You lead the two of diamonds, East plays the four, and you put up the Queen. The Queen will win 50% of the time, and it will lose 50% of the time. A gamble, you might say. Well, in the sense that one tosses a coin in the air, calling "heads I win, tails I lose," the finesse is a gamble, since the result is based on pure luck as opposed to skill. *But what is the alternative* in the above situation, as opposed to finessing the Queen? It is to play the Ace, hoping to catch the King. Let me say that with the opponents having the nine missing diamonds, the odds against your catching West with a singleton King are about 1500 to 1. In other words, by playing the Ace, you will capture West's singleton King once out of every 1500 times that you try it. By taking the 50-50 finesse you will get your second diamond trick 750 times out of 1500 (50%). Is it not true that the gambling play is to lay down the Ace, and that the correct orthodox play is to take the finesse?

Incidentally, many of the players who point the finger of scorn at a finesse use as their justification the fact that experts tend to spurn finesses. Let me say first that if an expert never took a finesse, he would be a losing bridge player in every session in which he played. It is true that an expert does not particularly care for a finesse as a first-choice play, but that is because he is always looking for a line of play which offers better than a 50% chance of success. This aspect of whether to take a finesse, or to search for a superior line of play, will be illustrated in the latter part of this chapter.

The four illustrations of the finesse thus far presented were each characterized by the play of a high card *third hand*— that is, the next to the last card played to the trick. Of course, a finesse may also take place when the high card is led first. Again — and at all times — wishful thinking is the determining factor.

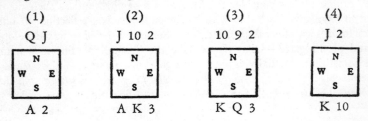

(1)	(2)	(3)	(4)
Q J	J 10 2	10 9 2	J 2
A 2	A K 3	K Q 3	K 10

Hearts is the suit in each of the above examples.

In (1), you lead the Queen of Hearts, and when East plays low you do too, with the hope that East has the King of Hearts. Of course, if East plays the King on the Queen, you breathe a sigh of relief and take it with your Ace. Dummy's Jack has now become promoted into a winning trick.

In (2), as you lead the Jack of Hearts, you "put" the Queen in the East hand, and accordingly finesse. If your wishful thinking materializes, the Jack will win the trick.

In (3), one fond hope is for East to possess the Jack of Hearts so that you can finesse against it. Therefore, dummy's ten-spot is led, and when East plays low, you play your three-spot. An alternative hope would be to play East for the Ace of Hearts instead of the Jack. If this is the case, a low heart will be led off dummy and your Queen will win, after which dummy will be re-entered via some other suit, and another heart led toward the King. And, again, if East had the Ace of Hearts before, he still has it, and your King of Hearts will produce a second heart trick.

In (4), you again put on your "wishful thinking" shoes, and decide whether you want East to have the Ace of Hearts or the Queen of Hearts. If you "place" the Ace of Hearts in East's hand, then when you lead the Jack from dummy and East plays low, you put up your King; if you hope that East has the Queen of Hearts instead, then when dummy's Jack is led, upon which East follows with a low one, you play your ten-spot and finesse East for the Queen. If East does have the Queen, then your King will become a sure winner.

In all of the simple finessing situations which have been presented up to this point, there were two fundamental characteristics: third hand (declarer) always had a higher card than did first hand (dummy), and in each situation the original lead was from the hand that held the lower card or cards toward the one that held the high card or cards. The purpose behind this was to get second hand — holding the card that you were looking for — to make his play before you (third hand) made your play. Thus you were "over" second hand, lying in ambush, waiting for him to make his move before you made yours. In bridge literature these finesses are known as *direct*, or attacking, *finesses*.

There is another type of simple finesse, known as the *"indirect"* finesse. This indirect finesse arises very frequently, and is quite often mishandled by the non-expert bridge player.

I should like to interject at this point a statement that may appear to be absurdly naive: when you take a direct finesse, *the sole object is to gain a trick*. This is accomplished by "putting" the card you are finessing against in the hand where you want it to be, and proceeding to encircle or trap it. In the "indirect" finesse, instead of surrounding the missing high-card you get it at "long-range," thereby promoting one of your own high cards into a winner.

The following is the most important, and most frequently encountered, "indirect" finesse:

1.

♡ Q 3 2

```
        N
    W       E
        S
```

♡ A 5 4

If your original heart lead is the Queen, *you can never gain a trick.*
Should East have the King, he will play it (cover) on your Queen,
forcing you to take your Ace. As far as the heart suit is concerned,
you will then never make another trick. If it is West, instead of East,
who possesses the King of Hearts, then he will capture your Queen,
and all you will ever make will be your Ace, which was always a winner.
Putting the above in diagram form:

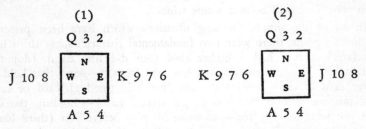

(1)   (2)

Q 3 2   Q 3 2

```
        N                            N
J 10 8  W   E  K 9 7 6    K 9 7 6  W   E  J 10 8
        S                            S
```

A 5 4   A 5 4

In both diagrams (1) and (2), if you lead the Queen all you will
ever make will be your Ace. But if, on diagram (2), you lead *the
four-spot toward dummy's Queen,* can you see that your Queen is bound
to win a trick, either now (if West plays low), or on the next round
of the suit (if West wins the first trick with the King)? This is the
"indirect finesse," the concession of a trick to the King, and the subsequent
establishment of your Queen as a winning trick without wasting one of
your high cards.

What this specific situation boils down to is the following: whenever
West possesses the King, then by leading toward the Queen you will
establish your Queen as a winner; whenever East has the King, you
will never gain a trick no matter which way you play it. Putting it
another way, when you take this indirect finesse, you again indulge in
wishful thinking: the hope that the hand in front of the Queen possesses
the King, and that, therefore, the Queen will be created into a winner.

Let us now look at an actual deal where the improper use of the
"indirect" finesse resulted in a slam contract being defeated:

♠ Q 5 3
♡ 8 7
◇ A Q J 4
♣ 10 6 5 3

```
   N
 W   E
   S
```

♠ A 6 2
♡ A Q
◇ K 7 5
♣ A K Q J 2

Against South's *six notrump* contract West opened the ten of diamonds, declarer's King winning. South now counted 11 sure winners: five in clubs, four in diamonds, one in hearts, and one in spades. The twelfth trick had to come from either a direct heart finesse, or an indirect spade finesse. In declarer's mind it was a simple 50-50 guess as to whether to hope that the Spade King was in the West hand or to hope that the Heart King was in the East hand.

Electing to take the indirect finesse, declarer then laid down the Ace of Spades, and with a fervent hope led the deuce of spades towards dummy's Queen. As you can see from the four hands which follow, declarer went down two tricks:

♠ Q 5 3
♡ 8 7
◇ A Q J 4
♣ 10 6 5 3

♠ 9 8 7   ♠ K J 10 4
♡ J 5 4   ```   ♡ K 10 9 6 3 2
◇ 10 9 8 2   N   ◇ 6 3
♣ 9 8 4   W   E   ♣ 7
                S
              ```

♠ A 6 2
♡ A Q
◇ K 7 5
♣ A K Q J 2

Concerning the fact that declarer needed either the "indirect" spade finesse or the "direct" heart finesse in order to fulfill his contract, there is no doubt. But he could have availed himself of both finesses at no extra cost.
              ```

At trick two, he should have led the deuce of spades towards dummy's Queen, instead of first laying down his Ace of Spades. If West had the King, then the Queen would become declarer's slam-going trick. If East had the King, he would, of course, capture dummy's Queen. Whatever he then returned, declarer would be able to capture that trick, and then still have the time to take the heart finesse. As the reader can see, the latter finesse would have worked.

2. A second standard situation in which the indirect finesse becomes the proper play is the following rather frequent holding:

♠ J 3 2

♠ A K 5 4

If the Jack is led from the North hand, should East possess the Queen, he will play it on the Jack, forcing South to win the trick; now the ten-spot (in the possession of an opponent) will become an established trick; if, when the Jack of Spades is led from dummy, East plays low and South takes the "finesse," should West have the Queen, he will capture the Jack. In other words, if North's Jack is led originally, *that card will never win a trick.* Illustrating this in diagram form:

(a)

♠ J 3 2

♠ 9 6   ♠ Q 10 8 7

♠ A K 5 4

(b)

♠ J 3 2

♠ Q 10 8 7   ♠ 9 6

♠ A K 5 4

If you take the "indirect" finesse, cashing the Ace of Spades first (in case one of the opponents has a singleton Queen), and then leading South's four-spot towards North's Jack, *whenever West has the Queen, the Jack will win a third trick for you in that suit.*

In diagram (a), you can *never* win more than two spade tricks, no matter how you play the suit.

In diagram (b), by leading towards the Jack (away from the AK), your Jack will win a third trick; by leading the Jack originally, you restrict yourself to two winning tricks. In summary then, the "indirect" finesse — leading towards the Jack — is the only correct play, since it will gain a trick 50% of the time. The original lead of the Jack from dummy will *never* gain a trick.

A deal in which the knowledge of the proper application of the indirect finesse resulted in a fulfilled small slam contract is the following:

♠ J 8 3
♥ 9 7 5 4
♦ A K 7 5
♣ K 2

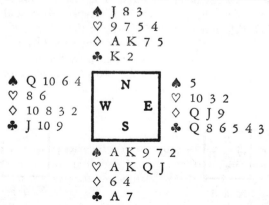

♠ A K 9 7 2
♥ A K Q J
♦ 6 4
♣ A 7

South arrived at a *six spade contract,* against which West opened the Jack of Clubs, dummy's King winning. A low spade was then led to declarer's Ace, both opponents following suit. The normal impulse now would be to cash the King of Spades — but if declarer had done this he would have lost his contract.

Declarer was perfectly willing to lose one spade trick — since he had no losers in the other suits — but he couldn't afford to lose two tricks. If he cashed the King of Spades, and it turned out that one of the opponents happened to have started with the Q 10 x x of spades, two spade tricks would inevitably have been lost.

So after cashing the Ace of trumps, our declarer led a low spade towards dummy's Jack — and his reward was a well-deserved one:

♠ J 8 3
♥ 9 7 5 4
♦ A K 7 5
♣ K 2

♠ Q 10 6 4   ♠ 5
♥ 8 6   ♥ 10 3 2
♦ 10 8 3 2 ♦ Q J 9
♣ J 10 9   ♣ Q 8 6 5 4 3

♠ A K 9 7 2
♥ A K Q J
♦ 6 4
♣ A 7

As the reader can see, had declarer cashed the Ace and King of Spades in the hope that spades were divided 3-2, he would have lost his slam.

It is virtually impossible to categorize the many specific finessing situations that are constantly presenting themselves. That is, one cannot say to the reader: "Study these groupings: these are Class 'A' finesses, these are Class 'B' finesses, these are Class 'C' finesses, etc.". Up to this point there has been a general breakdown of finesses into what we called (1) the direct finesse, and (2) the indirect finesse — and that is about as far as we can go in classifying finesses.

From here on, the various standard, specific, and frequently-arising finessing situations will be introduced and discussed on an individual basis, each to be looked at as an entity unto itself. By studying each one, the reader will understand the logic underlying its practical application. Let us look at these finesses one by one, never losing sight of the fundamental fact that the object of each finesse is to *gain a trick*.

1.

```
        A J 2
      ┌───────┐
      │   N   │
      │ W   E │
      │   S   │
      └───────┘
        K 4 3
```

This is a most elementary situation. You lead the King first, and then the three-spot, finessing the Jack if West plays low, and 50% of the time the Jack will win — and 50% of the time it will lose. But if you had played the Jack originally, *it would never have won,* for if East had the Queen he would have covered your Jack, forcing you to take your King. In diagram form, here are the two possible situations:

```
          A J 2                           A J 2
        ┌───────┐                       ┌───────┐
        │   N   │                       │   N   │
Q 10 9 8│ W   E │ 7 6 5         7 6 5   │ W   E │ Q 10 9 8
        │   S   │                       │   S   │
        └───────┘                       └───────┘
          K 4 3                           K 4 3
```

Where either North or South also holds the ten-spot, it is an out-and-out guess as to which way to finesse:

A J 10

```
┌─────────┐
│    N    │
│ W     E │
│    S    │
└─────────┘
```

K 4 3

The only thing that can guide you in the above situation is a good "hunch." Lacking that, you "put" the Queen in either East's hand or in West's hand and finesse, accordingly.

2.

♠ K J 10

```
┌─────────┐
│    N    │
│ W     E │
│    S    │
└─────────┘
```

♠ 4 3 2

The correct play to win two tricks is to lead the deuce and insert North's ten-spot. Whenever West has the Queen, either the ten-spot will win the trick, or it will be captured by the Ace. Whichever of the two happens, the South hand will then be re-entered via some other suit, and the three-spot will be led, dummy's Jack being finessed. And just as surely as West had the Queen originally (your ten-spot either having won or having been captured by East's Ace), so he will still have the Queen.

If, instead, you had led the deuce of spades and put up dummy's King, even if the King had won, you would have had to lose two tricks in this suit (unless your King play dropped East's singleton Queen, a most unlikely possibility). Here are the situations in diagram form:

(a)	(b)
K J 10	K J 10

```
          (a)                      (b)
        K J 10                   K J 10
      ┌─────────┐              ┌─────────┐
      │    N    │              │    N    │
Q 9 7 6 │ W   E │ A 8 5   A Q 9 6 │ W   E │ 8 7 5
      │    S    │              │    S    │
      └─────────┘              └─────────┘
        4 3 2                    4 3 2
```

(c)

K J 10

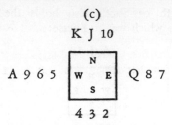

A 9 6 5   Q 8 7

4 3 2

In (a) and (b), the play of the ten-spot third-hand ultimately wins you two tricks. In (c), you can never win two tricks no matter how you play it.

3. ♣ Q 10 9

♣ 4 3 2

The proper finesse here is to lead the deuce and play North's nine-spot, finessing against West's hypothetical Jack. This is strictly a 50-50 proposition. If instead of putting up the nine-spot, you play the Queen, you will win a trick only if West had played low from an A K x or A K x x combination. "Mathematics" tell us that it is much more likely for West to have just the Jack of Clubs (50%) than it is for him to have both the Ace and King of Clubs. Here are the possibilities:

(a)   (b)

♣ Q 10 9   ♣ Q 10 9

♣ K J 6 5   ♣ A 8 7   ♣ J 8 6 5   ♣ A K 7

♣ 4 3 2   ♣ 4 3 2

(c)   (d)

♣ Q 10 9   ♣ Q 10 9

♣ A 8 6 5   ♣ K J 7   ♣ A K 7   ♣ J 8 6 5

♣ 4 3 2   ♣ 4 3 2

In (a) and (b), the finesse of the nine-spot (against the Jack) is the winning play. In (c), you can win no club tricks no matter how you play your club combination. In (d), if you finesse the nine-spot, you will lose to the Jack. But I will bet dollars to doughnuts that when you lead a low club from the South hand, West, holding the A K x, will play his King. Next time you re-enter the South hand you will then lead another club, playing West for the Ace — and you will wind up making a club trick. It would take a truly clairvoyant West player, holding the A K x, to play the low one on your lead of the deuce, especially if the Q 10 9 were in the concealed hand.

4.

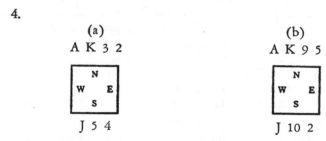

(a)
A K 3 2

J 5 4

(b)
A K 9 5

J 10 2

In the illustrations of the "indirect finesse," (example (a) was discussed earlier) — the proper play is to lead away from the A K and towards the Jack. Whenever East has the Queen, the Jack will become a winner.

But when the ten-spot is held, (b), in combination with the Ace, King, and Jack, the correct play to make *all* the tricks is to lead the Jack and finesse West for the Queen. This applies when you have 5, 6, 7, or 8 cards of the suit, between the two hands. Where nine or more cards are held, the proper play is to lead the Ace and King in the hope of dropping the Queen. A more detailed discussion of this latter situation is presented in the Chapter on "The Percentage Play" (Page 67).

5.

Q 10 2

K 4 3

To win two tricks, the right play is to finesse West for the Jack. The three-spot is led and when West follows with a low card, North's ten-spot is inserted. In diagram form:

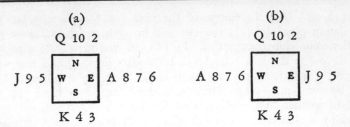

    (a)   (b)

In (a), finessing North's ten-spot will yield you two tricks.

In (b), you cannot make two tricks on your own power even if the opponents place their cards face up on the table for you to see.

Just a reminder at this point, in case you have forgotten: any finesse is nothing more than wishful thinking; that is, putting a "key" card where you would like it to be, and then finessing through it. In the above situation if you "put" the Jack in the East hand, you cannot finesse through it, since it is not "finessable." So "put" it in the West hand, where you can handle it with consummate ease.

When the nine-spot is added to the combination just given, it becomes a pure guess as to the winning play. That is:

Q 10 2

K 9 3

The winning of two tricks with the above combination depends on your "ability" to guess which of the opponents holds the Jack. If you think that West has it, you lead the three-spot and put up North's ten; if you think that East possesses the Jack, then you lead the deuce from the North hand and play South's nine.

6.   ♠ A J 10

♠ 4 3 2

The above is a standard finessing situation, of frequent occurrence, known to the trade as "the double finesse" (finessing against two missing high cards). The object here is to win two tricks.

Proper play is to lead the deuce and if West follows with a low card, you put up North's ten-spot. This will in all probability lose to East's Queen (or King), but when you re-obtain the lead, you will lead the three-spot and finesse dummy's Jack, which will probably win. This might be the situation described:

A J 10

K 9 6 5   W N E   Q 8 7
              S

4 3 2

The theory behind the double finesse is that West figures to have been dealt at least *one* of the two missing high cards, *either the King or the Queen*. So, whenever you double-finesse, you will lose the first trick, but then your A J will be sitting over West's K x or Q x, and on the next lead your finesse of the Jack will be successful.

A word of advice to the pessimistic is in order at this point. When your first finesse loses, do not get frantic and lay down the Ace on the second lead. Get back to the South hand and finesse again. This double-finesse is an expert play, and will lose only when East was dealt precisely the K Q doubleton:

A J 10

9 8 7 6 5   W N E   K Q
                S

4 3 2

In the above illustration, had you laid down the Ace of Spades first, you would have caught East's Queen, thereby guaranteeing two tricks in the suit. But the odds against East having been dealt the K Q doubleton in the above situation are 34 to one. So, if you cash North's Ace of Spades first, you will be making the winning play only 3 out of 100 times.

If the thought is going through the reader's mind, "What if East has the K Q x, or K Q x x?", the answer to this question is that you must lose two tricks no matter how you play it — and you can then charge your failure to "circumstances beyond your control."

So what it boils down to is this: the double-finesse will fail to win a second trick only in the extreme case where East was dealt precisely the K Q doubleton; it will win a second trick whenever West was dealt either the King or Queen, any number of times (that is, K x, K x x, K x x x, K x x x x x; or Q x, Q x x, Q x x x, Q x x x x, Q x x x x x; or K Q x, K Q x x, etc.).

7.
A Q 10

4 3 2

The above is another frequently arising "double-finesse" situation. The logic underlying the correct play is identical to that given in the preceding type of double-finesse (A J 10 opposite x x x).

The proper play of the above combination is based on the mathematically-sound assumption that West was dealt either the King or Jack. Your first lead is the deuce, and when West plays low, you play North's ten-spot. If this should lose to the King, you have just created a winner out of the Queen. Should the ten lose to the Jack, when you later return to the South hand, you will lead the three-spot and finesse dummy's Queen. As in the previous illustration, this will be a losing play *only* if East started with exactly the doubleton K J. Putting the above in diagram form:

(a)   (b)

(c)

Actually, it is possible that you may win three tricks in this suit by "double-finessing." This would be the case if West were dealt *both* the King and Jack.

♡ A Q 10

♡ K J 9 7   [N W E S]   ♡ 8 6 5

♡ 4 3 2

When the finesse of the ten-spot wins, you return to the South hand and lead another low heart, to successfully finesse dummy's Queen.

8. A variation of the double-finesse is found in this commonly-encountered situation:

♠ J 3 2

[N W E S]

♠ A Q 9

As the reader can perceive, two spade tricks can always be won by merely conceding the Queen, thereby establishing the Jack. But the expert player will, on occasion, win three tricks. Most players, however, would never make three tricks, for they would lead North's deuce and finesse South's Queen. Let us assume that the finesse works. Here it is in diagram form:

♠ J 3 2

♠ 8 7 6 4   [N W E S]   ♠ K 10 5

♠ A Q 9

East must now eventually obtain a spade trick, since he has the K 10 remaining against North's Jack and declarer's Ace.

Proper play of the above combination is to lead the Jack from the North hand. If East should play low, then the Jack will win the trick, after which it will be routine play for declarer to lead a low spade and again finesse East for the King. If, however, East covers the Jack with the King, declarer will re-enter dummy via some other suit to lead the deuce of spades, finessing East's ten-spot. The evolution of this can be observed from the following diagram:

(a)

♠ *J* 3 2

♠ 8 7 6 4̲ |N W E S| ♠ *K̲* 10 5

♠ *A* Q 9

(b)

♠ 3 2̲

♠ 8 7 6̲ |N W E S| ♠ 10 5̲

♠ Q 9̲

The ability to win three tricks assumes East's possession of both the King and ten, with declarer finessing for both of these cards. If *West* has the King or the ten, then three tricks cannot be made (except where West was dealt a singleton King, an almost impossible distribution to either exist, or to be diagnosed correctly). So, if you are to obtain three tricks, your most practical hope is to indulge in the "wishful thinking" assumption that East holds both the King and ten.

9. Although the following finessing situation may sound quite complex, it is actually nothing more than an extension of the double finesse just presented. This particular type of finesse is known as a "triple-finesse" (finessing against three high cards). The occasions for utilizing this triple finesse are of frequent occurrence:

◇ A J 9

|N W E S|

◇ 4 3 2

The object is to make two tricks on the above combination, with the opponents possessing the King, Queen, and ten.

The expert (proper) play is to lead the deuce from the South hand, putting up dummy's nine-spot if West plays low. This will produce two tricks whenever West was originally dealt either the Q 10 or K 10, regardless of how many cards in that suit he was dealt:

◇ A J 9

◇ Q 10 8 6 |N W E S| ◇ K 7 5

◇ 4 3 2

The deuce is led, and North's nine-spot is captured by West's King. On re-entering the South hand, declarer then leads the three-spot, and North's Jack is finessed, winning the trick.

The original play of the nine-spot will lose whenever West started
with the K Q x or K Q x x, etc., and East started with the 10 x,
10 x x, etc. That is:

◊ A J 9

◊ K Q 8 6   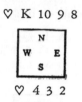   ◊ 10 7 5

◊ 4 3 2

In the above case, the nine-spot will lose to the ten, and later on West
will capture North's Jack. But, relying on our mathematical geniuses
— and the approval of the expert bridge player — the original play of
the nine-spot will win about twice as often as will any other play.

10. Another "triple finessing" situation is the following. Although
the occasion for its use does not occur as frequently as the one just
presented, it nevertheless arises often enough for the reader to study it
and earmark it for future employment.

♡ K 10 9 8

♡ 4 3 2

The best play to obtain two tricks in this suit is to make the
mathematically-sound assumption that West was dealt *either* the Queen
or Jack of Hearts.

Your proper lead is the deuce of hearts, upon which West plays low,
and you insert North's eight-spot, which, let us say, is captured by
East's Jack. When you re-obtain the lead, you lead the three of hearts,
and if West again plays low, you play North's nine-spot. If West
were dealt either the Queen or Jack, two heart tricks are now guaranteed.
The situation as it normally might be:

♡ K 10 9 8

♡ A Q 6 5   ♡ J 7

♡ 4 3 2

As the reader can see, by assuming that West has either the Queen or Jack, declarer makes two heart tricks. If declarer puts up North's King of Hearts at trick one, he will capture that trick, but the opponents will win the next three tricks with the Ace, Queen and Jack.

11. The "Backward" Finesse.

The "backward" finesse is so called because it is taken in an unnatural way rather than in the way that most players would consider natural, or normal. Generally speaking, this "backward" finesse might be considered as an expert play, for it is used in two special situations:

(1) When "card-reading" proves that the normal way of finessing will lose, and

(2) When the finesse is taken, it is taken in such a manner that a "dangerous" opponent will be kept out of the lead.

Let us examine these two situations:

(1) When "card-reading" proves that the normal way of finessing will lose.

The following deal was played many years ago by the late Ely Culbertson, the "father" of contract bridge in this country.

♠ K Q J
♡ Q 6 4 3
◇ 8 7 5
♣ A 9 8

```
        N
    W       E
        S
```

♠ A 10 5
♡ K J 10 9 8
◇ 6 2
♣ K J 6

The bidding:

WEST	NORTH	EAST	SOUTH
One Diamond	Pass	Pass	One Heart
Pass	Two Hearts	Pass	Four Hearts
Pass	Pass	Pass	

West opened the King of Diamonds after which the Ace was cashed. The Queen of Diamonds was then led, declarer trumping. Mr. Culbertson now laid down his King of trumps, *East* winning with the Ace. East then played back a spade, dummy's Jack capturing the trick.

Declarer next led his Jack and ten of trumps, picking up the adverse pieces. He then paused to take inventory.

It was perfectly obvious to the expert Mr. Culbertson that West possessed the Queen of Clubs, for surely East, with the Ace of Hearts *and* the Queen of Clubs would not have passed the opening one diamond bid (remember, East has shown up with the Ace of Hearts). The normal finesse would be to lead a club to the Ace, then return a little one, put up the Jack, and finesse East for the Queen. But, since *West had to have* the Queen of Clubs, the normal way of finessing would then lose to West's Queen. So, declarer took the "backward" finesse, in this fashion:

He led the Jack of Clubs out of his own hand. Had West played low to this trick, declarer would have let the Jack ride, winning the trick. But West covered the Jack with the Queen, dummy's Ace winning. The nine of clubs was then led off the board, and when East played low, so did declarer, finessing East for the ten-spot. When West followed with a low club, dummy's nine-spot was a winner. The contract was now fulfilled. The deal was:

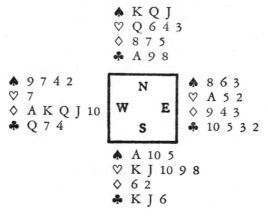

♠ K Q J
♥ Q 6 4 3
♦ 8 7 5
♣ A 9 8

♠ 9 7 4 2
♥ 7
♦ A K Q J 10
♣ Q 7 4

N W E S

♠ 8 6 3
♥ A 5 2
♦ 9 4 3
♣ 10 5 3 2

♠ A 10 5
♥ K J 10 9 8
♦ 6 2
♣ K J 6

(2) When the "backward" finesse is taken, it is taken in such a manner that a "dangerous" opponent will be kept out of the lead.

In this second type of backward finesse, although the prime purpose is to keep one of the opponents from obtaining the lead, as opposed to the gaining of a trick which is usually the purpose of a finesse, the backward finesse will often gain a trick which would have been lost by the natural approach.

The following deal illustrates the above points:

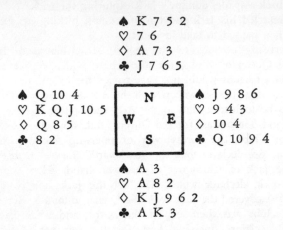

♠ K 7 5 2
♡ 7 6
◊ A 7 3
♣ J 7 6 5

♠ Q 10 4   ♠ J 9 8 6
♡ K Q J 10 5   ♡ 9 4 3
◊ Q 8 5   ◊ 10 4
♣ 8 2   ♣ Q 10 9 4

♠ A 3
♡ A 8 2
◊ K J 9 6 2
♣ A K 3

You are South playing a *three notrump* contract against which West opens the King of Hearts which is permitted to win the trick. [1] The Queen of Hearts then follows, which wins, after which the Jack of Hearts is led, and you take this trick with the Ace.

Upon observation, it becomes apparent that in order to fulfill your contract you must obtain four diamond tricks. Therefore you should be perfectly willing to give up one diamond in order to make four diamond tricks — provided you do not give it up to West who figures to have the established hearts.

The "natural" way of attacking the diamond suit would be to lead a diamond to dummy's Ace, and then finesse the Jack on the way back. But to finesse in this manner would risk losing to West — and that would be no good.

So, the unnatural "backward" finesse is tried. You lead the Jack, with the full intention of passing it by if West plays low. You are perfectly willing to lose the trick to East, if the latter has the Queen, since East is out of hearts. [2]

What actually develops can be seen by looking at all four hands. If West plays low on the lead of the Diamond Jack, you make five diamond tricks. If West covers with the Queen, dummy's Ace wins, and East's ten-spot falls on the second round, after which you also make five diamond tricks.

---

[1] This particular play, known as the "hold-up" is the theme of Chapter V.
[2] This point is discussed at length in Chapter V, "The Hold-Up Play."

Let us briefly consider the possible adverse diamond distributions to see why the "backward" finesse was mandatory on this deal. To begin with (and hurriedly dispense with) West might have held the Q 10 x, or Q 10 x x, in which case declarer would have been defeated. Of course, West could have held the Q 10 doubleton, and that would have been fine, as the King would then have dropped the ten on the second round. The reader might, at this point, raise the question: "But would we not have finessed East for the ten-spot on the second round if West had covered the Jack with the Queen?" The answer is that the ten-spot would not have been finessed, as that play would have run the risk of losing to West. On the second lead of the suit declarer's King would have been cashed, since declarer was perfectly willing to give up a trick *to East* if the latter had the ten-spot. If East held the Q x x, or the 10 x x, then a diamond trick would be lost — but it would be lost to the "safe" East (no more hearts), and not to the "dangerous" West (lots of established hearts).

So much, then, for the expert play of the "backward" finesse.

Let us now look at some finessing positions that arose in actual combat, and see how they were handled:

1.

♠ J 7 5 2
♡ 8 4 3
◇ A Q 9 2
♣ K Q

♠ A Q 6 3
♡ J 10 6
◇ K J 4
♣ A 7 5

South arrived at a *four spade contract,* against which the opponents quickly cashed three heart tricks and then shifted to a club, dummy's Queen winning.

Declarer next led the deuce of spades out of dummy, successfully finessing his Queen. Then came the Ace of Spades, dropping East's King. A spade to dummy's Jack now picked up West's remaining trump, and the contract was fulfilled. The deal was:

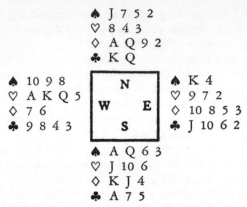

♠ J 7 5 2
♥ 8 4 3
♦ A Q 9 2
♣ K Q

♠ 10 9 8   ♠ K 4
♥ A K Q 5   ♥ 9 7 2
♦ 7 6   ♦ 10 8 5 3
♣ 9 8 4 3   ♣ J 10 6 2

♠ A Q 6 3
♥ J 10 6
♦ K J 4
♣ A 7 5

On the face of it, there may appear to be absolutely nothing to the play of this hand. However, it contains a "pat" situation which is very often mishandled by most bridge players. I refer to the given trump combination:

♠ J x x x

♠ A Q x x

Just one combination of the five outstanding trumps can exist where declarer will be able to avoid the loss of a trick. This combination is the K x doubleton in the East hand. So the only hope for declarer is to finesse the Queen, and then optimistically lay down the Ace to drop East's King. *Do not originally lead the Jack from dummy.* If you do, you *must* lose at least one trick.

(a)   (b)

♠ J x x x   ♠ J x x x

♠ 10 9 x   ♠ K x   ♠ 9 x   ♠ K 10 x

♠ A Q x x   ♠ A Q x x

The reader, looking at the above illustrations, may echo my point that in (b) whether you lead the Jack, or a low card, you have to lose a spade trick. Granted. But you can *never* gain by leading the Jack, and *you will* lose a trick if (a) exists.

2. I think it is agreed that the taking of finesses will always be with us, and that in taking finesses the usual object is to gain a trick. Very often, however, a finesse is "on the house", as it were: even if it loses, you gain a trick and tend to promote lower cards in that suit into a winner or winners. For instance:

♠ A Q J
♡ 8 3 2
◇ A Q J 5
♣ 9 7 3

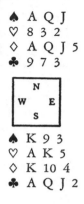

♠ K 9 3
♡ A K 5
◇ K 10 4
♣ A Q J 2

South is playing a *six notrump contract,* West opening the Queen of Hearts, declarer capturing the trick with the King.

Taking inventory, declarer counts nine sure winning tricks in spades, hearts, and diamonds. He further perceives that he can get no more and no less than nine tricks in these three suits, and that to fulfill his contract three club tricks must be obtained.

At trick two declarer enters dummy via a spade, and hopefully leads a low club, putting up his Queen. If the finesse wins, then the King of Clubs will be "marked" as being in the East hand, and it will now become a routine matter to re-enter dummy to finesse the Jack of Clubs, which will win just as surely as the Queen had won the preceding club finesse.

But, as it turns out, declarer's Queen of Clubs is captured by West's King, after which West returns another heart, declarer's Ace winning.

In losing the Queen of Clubs to the King, declarer's Jack has become promoted into a winning trick, and declarer now has eleven certain winners. Where is the twelfth trick coming from? Only from the hoped-for establishment of the two of clubs.

So, in the course of play, South cashes his Ace of Clubs, everybody following suit as they did to the first club trick. Then comes the Jack of Clubs and again everybody follows suit. Twelve clubs have now been played — and that little "pain-in-the-neck," the deuce of clubs, is promoted into declarer's slam-going trick. The deal was:

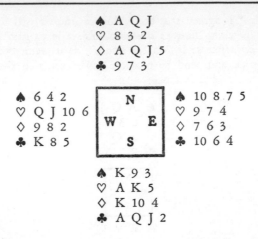

♠ A Q J
♡ 8 3 2
◇ A Q J 5
♣ 9 7 3

♠ 6 4 2
♡ Q J 10 6
◇ 9 8 2
♣ K 8 5

♠ 10 8 7 5
♡ 9 7 4
◇ 7 6 3
♣ 10 6 4

♠ K 9 3
♡ A K 5
◇ K 10 4
♣ A Q J 2

The above deal is an elementary one, but the reader should not lose sight of the two points previously mentioned: (a) that a finesse, even in losing, very often creates a trick by promotion (the Jack); and (b) that the finesse, in losing, often tends to establish a low card (or cards) in that suit as a potential and hoped-for winner (the deuce of clubs). Stating this latter point as a fact, as each high-ranking card is played, every lower card moves up one step in rank. A four can become a "high card" if the only other card of the suit remaining in circulation is the three-spot. Or, as on the deal just presented, a deuce can become the highest-ranking card if it is the sole surviving card of that suit.

3. Almost all finesses are taken against high cards — Aces, Kings, Queens, Jacks, and sometimes ten-spots. But a finesse can also be taken (and is) against lower-ranking cards when it becomes apparent that it is the correct thing to do. In a certain sense, these finesses against low cards fall into the category of "expert plays." The reason for this is that the expert, through years of experience, has developed the knack of observing the cards as they fall, and paying attention to the "spots" on the cards. If the reader has not acquired this knack of close observation, and is apprehensive of his ability to do so, let me reassure him. It will come to you as you learn to look for it.

As an illustration of finessing against "teeny-weeny" cards, take a look at the following deal. The declarer, South, was Albert H. Morehead, one of the nation's top ranking players, and for years the Bridge Editor of "The New York Times."

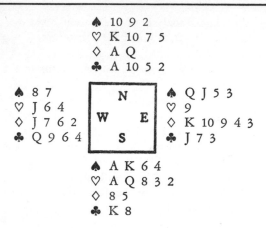

♠ 10 9 2
♡ K 10 7 5
◇ A Q
♣ A 10 5 2

♠ 8 7   ♠ Q J 5 3
♡ J 6 4   ♡ 9
◇ J 7 6 2   ◇ K 10 9 4 3
♣ Q 9 6 4   ♣ J 7 3

♠ A K 6 4
♡ A Q 8 3 2
◇ 8 5
♣ K 8

Against Mr. Morehead's *six heart* contract, West opened the eight of spades, dummy's nine was put up, East covered with the Jack, and declarer's King captured the trick. Three rounds of trumps were then drawn, ending up in dummy. The ten of spades was then led, East played the Queen, and declarer took the trick with his Ace. On this trick West followed with the *seven of spades.*

It was now clear to declarer that East had the five and three of spades remaining, for surely if West had either of these cards he would not have dropped the seven-spot which was the *highest-ranking spade left.*

Dummy was then re-entered via the Club Ace, and the deuce of spades was led. When East followed with the three-spot, declarer's four-spot was played, successfully finessing against East's five-spot.

The six of spades was then played, and on it dummy's Queen of Diamonds was discarded. All thirteen tricks were now taken, declarer ruffing out his losing diamond.

To Finesse — or Not to Finesse

Lest the reader has developed the opinion that finesses are compulsory whenever a finessing position exists, let me correct — and revise — that opinion.

Generally speaking, a finesse is taken to gain a trick. Speaking more specifically, there are three major situations where a finesse should be avoided:

(1) When the taking of the finesse places the contract in needless jeopardy.

(2) When the logical analysis of a situation makes it apparent that the finesse cannot succeed, and that, therefore, it must be a losing play to attempt it.

(3) When a line of play exists which is superior to the 50% chance of a successful finesse.

The five actual deals which follow serve to illustrate the three above situations. Throughout this book, especially in Chapter III on "The Percentage Play", the reader will find several additional deals covering the question of "to finesse or not to finesse." Also, in the chapter on "The Percentage Play," the reader will discover a fourth type of situation when a finesse should not be taken. This fourth situation, based on the mathematics of suit distributions, will not be illustrated in this section. [3]

(1) When the taking of a finesse places the contract in needless jeopardy — do not take the finesse.

(a)

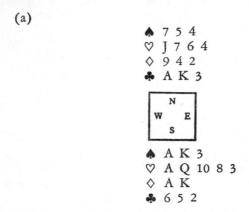

♠ 7 5 4
♡ J 7 6 4
◊ 9 4 2
♣ A K 3

♠ A K 3
♡ A Q 10 8 3
◊ A K
♣ 6 5 2

South arrives at a *four heart contract,* against which West opens the Jack of Clubs, dummy's King is put up, and East follows with *the Queen.*

Examination of the combined hands will make it obvious that declarer has just three losers: one spade, one heart, and one club. That is, he has just three losers unless one of the opponents gets to trump something that declarer had not counted on — and East's Queen looks ominous, as if it were a singleton.

Can you see that if declarer now takes a heart finesse he is placing his contract in jeopardy, for if West has the King of Hearts he will return a club for East to trump? (After all, West is not blind! He, too, saw East's Queen of Clubs fall on the opening lead).

---

[3] Discussed and illustrated in Chapter III, "The Percentage Play," page 55.

So, at trick two, declarer leads a heart to the Ace, and then plays another heart, conceding a trick to whomever has the King. Victory is now his. Had the finesse been taken — the reader can see for himself. The deal was:

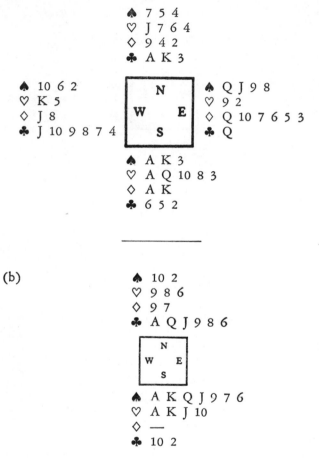

```
                    ♠ 7 5 4
                    ♡ J 7 6 4
                    ◇ 9 4 2
                    ♣ A K 3
  ♠ 10 6 2              N        ♠ Q J 9 8
  ♡ K 5                          ♡ 9 2
  ◇ J 8         W         E      ◇ Q 10 7 6 5 3
  ♣ J 10 9 8 7 4         S       ♣ Q
                    ♠ A K 3
                    ♡ A Q 10 8 3
                    ◇ A K
                    ♣ 6 5 2
```

(b)

```
                    ♠ 10 2
                    ♡ 9 8 6
                    ◇ 9 7
                    ♣ A Q J 9 8 6
                        N
                   W         E
                        S
                    ♠ A K Q J 9 7 6
                    ♡ A K J 10
                    ◇ —
                    ♣ 10 2
```

You are in a *six spade contract,* West opening the Ace of Diamonds, which you trump. Four rounds of trumps are now drawn, removing West's four pieces. The ten of clubs is then led, and it wins when everybody follows with low clubs.

If you now let the lure of a potential overtrick overrule your judgment, and take another club finesse, you will be sorry. Why take it again? Is not your contract now guaranteed? Lead a club to the Ace, take a heart finesse, and whether it wins or loses is of no importance. As it actually turns out, this latter line of play will net you all 13 tricks.

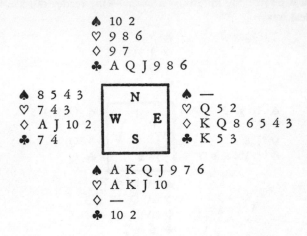

♠ 10 2
♡ 9 8 6
◇ 9 7
♣ A Q J 9 8 6

♠ 8 5 4 3   N   ♠ —
♡ 7 4 3   W   E   ♡ Q 5 2
◇ A J 10 2   S   ◇ K Q 8 6 5 4 3
♣ 7 4   ♣ K 5 3

♠ A K Q J 9 7 6
♡ A K J 10
◇ —
♣ 10 2

(c) The reader probably has not reached this stage as yet, but when one gets burned a few dozen times by taking needless finesses which result in contracts being defeated, he becomes unduly pessimistic about every finesse. As a result, he shies away from finesses, and justifies his position by always prefacing his apology with, "But, partner, if I took the finesse and it lost, had the adverse distribution been such and such, the opponents would have returned so and so, and I would have gone down . . ." (which he did, anyway). A deal portraying this pessimistic point of view was observed by me a few years ago:

♠ Q J 8 2
♡ A Q J
◇ 5 2
♣ A Q J 10

N
W   E
S

♠ A K 10 4 3
♡ 10 9 5
◇ 7 6
♣ 6 5 3

Against declarer's *four spade contract,* West opened the King of Diamonds, and followed with the Queen. He then shifted to the seven of clubs — and an apprehensive South got panicky.

South undoubtedly thought to himself: *"If* the seven of clubs is a singleton, and I take the finesse, East will win with the King, return a club for West to trump, and I'll be down." Having convinced himself that the seven-spot was a singleton, declarer won the club lead with dummy's Ace, and drew trumps. He then staked everything on a heart finesse. When it lost, declarer went down one. The deal:

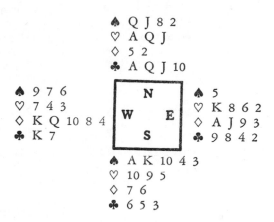

♠ Q J 8 2
♥ A Q J
♦ 5 2
♣ A Q J 10

♠ 9 7 6   ♠ 5
♥ 7 4 3   ♥ K 8 6 2
♦ K Q 10 8 4   ♦ A J 9 3
♣ K 7   ♣ 9 8 4 2

♠ A K 10 4 3
♥ 10 9 5
♦ 7 6
♣ 6 5 3

It is granted that the seven of clubs might have been a singleton, but there was another consideration that declarer should have taken into account. Having taken two diamond tricks, what option did West have when he looked at the dummy? Either to play a club or a heart. In other words, West's club lead was, in a certain sense, a lead that it was apparent he did not "love," but he had little leeway in his choices. So declarer should have taken the club finesse.

Let me say that if the contract were *three spades* (instead of four spades), then declarer should not run the risk of the club finesse, since his contract would be guaranteed even if he lost a club and a heart. But at a four spade contract, to immediately give up a 50% chance of fulfillment figured to be a losing policy.

(2) When the logic of a situation makes it apparent that the finesse cannot succeed and that, therefore, it must be a losing play to attempt it — do not finesse.

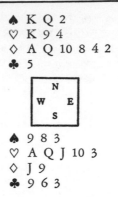

♠ K Q 2
♡ K 9 4
◇ A Q 10 8 4 2
♣ 5

♠ 9 8 3
♡ A Q J 10 3
◇ J 9
♣ 9 6 3

The bidding:

EAST	SOUTH	WEST	NORTH
One Club	Pass	Pass	Double
Two Clubs	Two Hearts	Pass	Four Hearts
Pass	Pass	Pass	

West opened the Ace of Clubs, and then shifted to a low spade, on which dummy's Queen was played and East's Ace captured the trick. East now returned the Jack of Spades, taken by dummy's King.

Declarer now drew three rounds of trumps, ending up in the South hand. He then led the Jack of Diamonds, West played low — and do you finesse or not?

The answer is NO. West had shown up with the Ace of Clubs. Surely if he also had the King of Diamonds he would not have passed out East's opening one club bid. The diamond finesse, therefore, *had to lose*. So you, and our declarer, put up dummy's Ace — and catch East's singleton King!

Did I hear someone say that declarer sure was "lucky" to catch a singleton King? I concur. But I wonder how many players would have caught that singleton King? From a business point of view, if declarer took the diamond finesse, *he would never win*. If he played the Ace, he would, on occasional days, catch East not with a tripleton King, nor a doubleton King, but with a singleton King. And today was one of those days. The complete deal was:

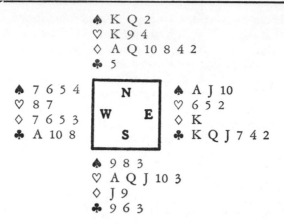

♠ K Q 2
♡ K 9 4
◇ A Q 10 8 4 2
♣ 5

♠ 7 6 5 4   ♠ A J 10
♡ 8 7   ♡ 6 5 2
◇ 7 6 5 3   ◇ K
♣ A 10 8   ♣ K Q J 7 4 2

♠ 9 8 3
♡ A Q J 10 3
◇ J 9
♣ 9 6 3

(3) When a line of play exists which is superior to a straight 50% chance of a successful finesse, do not go taking the finesse because it is "the path of least resistance." Look around for an alternative line of play which may offer you better than a 50% chance.

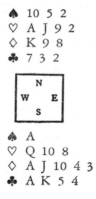

♠ 10 5 2
♡ A J 9 2
◇ K 9 8
♣ 7 3 2

♠ A
♡ Q 10 8
◇ A J 10 4 3
♣ A K 5 4

You are South playing a *three notrump* contract, against which West opens the King of Spades which you capture with your Ace. Of course you feel quite uncomfortable about the whole thing, knowing that if either opponent ever gets the lead again, lots of spades will be cashed against you.

On counting your sure winners you perceive that you have six: one in spades, one in hearts, two in diamonds, and two in clubs. Two suits each offer the opportunity of acquiring the three additional needed tricks: (1) if the King of Hearts is in the West hand, then repeated heart finesses will yield the three required tricks; (2) if the Queen of

Diamonds can be located, then by successfully finessing for it the entire diamond suit can be brought home without loss of a trick, thereby picking up the three needed tricks. Of course, it is apparent that whichever finesse you elect to take offers you a 50% chance of success. But if you misguess the location of the key card you are finessing against, then you are down, for the opponents, upon obtaining the lead, will run their established spades.

Most players would leave it at that, and putting their faith in their ability to guess, would take one finesse or the other. Some would guess right and some would guess wrong.

The expert player, however, would fulfill his contract much more than 50% of the time, for he would recognize that it was not a question of one finesse or the other (which is strictly a 50-50 proposition). He would first cash the Ace and King of Diamonds, on the chance that one or the other of the opponents had the Q x doubleton of diamonds. If it should come to pass that one of them did, then the three additional tricks would be forthcoming in the diamond suit. If the Queen of Diamonds did not drop on the first two rounds of the diamond suit, then declarer, *as a last resort, and not as a first choice,* would still have available the 50% chance that West held the King of Hearts, and he would finesse against it.

Mathematically speaking, only 25% of the time would one of the opponents be holding the Q x of Diamonds. However, the "experts" are what they are because they look for — and often find — that extra 25% chance which their competitors do not find. The actual deal was:

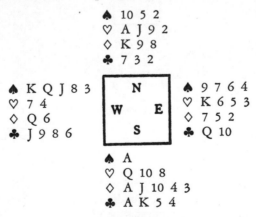

	♠ 10 5 2	
	♡ A J 9 2	
	◊ K 9 8	
	♣ 7 3 2	
♠ K Q J 8 3	N	♠ 9 7 6 4
♡ 7 4	W E	♡ K 6 5 3
◊ Q 6	S	◊ 7 5 2
♣ J 9 8 6		♣ Q 10
	♠ A	
	♡ Q 10 8	
	◊ A J 10 4 3	
	♣ A K 5 4	

STANDARD CARD COMBINATIONS

T HOSE of you who have played bridge for more than a dozen sessions know that there are many specific card combinations which repeat themselves time after time even in one session of play. To the expert, these various repetitive standard card combinations have become second nature; through years of experience he has learned to recognize immediately which "type" a particular combination is, and instinctively to react correctly. As a result, when these varied combinations confront him, he is spared the trouble, mental effort, and time, of working them out at the table.

For example, the different types of finesses — which are actually standard card combinations — that were illustrated in the preceding chapter, are all in the expert's arsenal of *attacking weapons,* always close at hand, and available for immediate use when the occasion so demands. There are other card combinations, however, *not of an attacking nature,* which are continually encountered by declarer in his every day struggle. These "pat" combinations are created when *the opponents make an attacking lead,* placing you either in a defensive position, or in a counter-attacking one.

Let us see then how declarer should properly handle certain standard combinations when an opponent has attacked.

♣ Q 3

♣ A 1 2

The situation was presented in the preceding chapter on "The Finesse." Declarer, on his own power, would take an indirect finesse: that is, he would lead the deuce of clubs from the South hand, in the hope that West possessed the King. If this hope materialized, then North's Queen would develop into a winner.

But what if West *opens* a low club? In the above illustration, declarer's play is exactly the same. He indulges in wishful thinking, and hopes that West has led away from the King. North's Queen is put up — and if East does not cover with the King, then the Queen has won the trick, just as the Queen would have been a winner had declarer taken an indirect finesse.

A situation somewhat similar to the above is the following:

I.

♣ Q 3

```
+---+
| N |
|W E|
| S |
+---+
```

♣ A 2

If declarer elected to *lead* the club suit himself, he could never win more than one club trick. If he originally led the deuce of clubs, then if West possessed the King, he would take it, and declarer's Queen and Ace would fall together on the second round of the suit; or, if East held the King, then he would capture North's Queen when declarer led the suit.

Or, if the Queen were led from dummy originally, then East, holding the King, would cover the Queen, restricting declarer to just one trick, the Ace; and, of course, if West held the King, then it would capture the Queen. Presenting the above in diagram form:

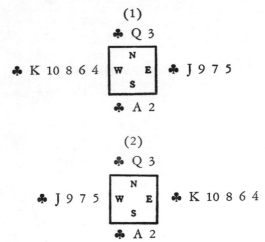

(1)

♣ Q 3

♣ K 10 8 6 4   ♣ J 9 7 5

♣ A 2

(2)

♣ Q 3

♣ J 9 7 5   ♣ K 10 8 6 4

♣ A 2

But if West opens a low club, you have a *free chance* to win a second club trick. With the club opening you hopefully put up North's Queen. If West has led away from the King (as in the first illustration), then your Queen will win; if West has not led away from the King (as in the second illustration) then all you could ever win would be one trick, the Ace.

In this specific case, then, if left to your resources, you will capture just one trick; but if the opponents open the suit, you have a chance "on the house" to capture a second trick with the Queen.

The same situation would exist if this were the set-up:

♣ A 2

♣ Q 3

West opens a little club and you play the deuce from dummy, for therein lies your sole hope of ever winning two club tricks. If West has led away from the King, South's Queen will win this trick; if East has the King, then you never can make more than your Ace of Clubs, whether you attack the suit yourself, or whether the opponents attack it.

Two situations that are related to the above are the following:

(1)   (2)
Q 4 3   Q 4 3

A 5 2   A 2

On his own power, declarer would take the indirect finesse by leading the deuce towards dummy's Queen. But if West leads the suit, the three-spot should be played from dummy in both (1) and (2), there being no hurry about putting up the Queen. After all, if you play low, East *may* put up the King, and now you will have two sure tricks in the suit. To illustrate, using (1) as the example:

(a)   (b)
Q 4 3   Q 4 3

J 9 8 6   K 10 7   K J 9 8   10 7 6

A 5 2   A 5 2

In (a), when dummy plays low, *if* East plays the King, dummy's Queen will be promoted into a winner. What does it cost declarer to give East the chance to go wrong?

In (b), when dummy plays low on the opening lead, East's ten will force declarer's Ace. But on the next lead of the suit, will not declarer be able to take the indirect finesse by leading towards dummy's Queen, establishing that card as a winner?

II.

The two following standard situations are "distant relations" of the positions which have just been presented:

(A)   (B)

◊ Q 10 2   ◊ Q 10 9

◊ A 4 3   ◊ A 4 3

West opens the six of diamonds.

In (A), your best play is to put up North's ten-spot, in the hope that it will force the King from the East hand. If it does, your Ace will capture the trick, and North's Queen will become promoted into a winner. Should East cover the ten-spot with the Jack, you will win the trick with the Ace. Later on, you will lead the three-spot toward the Queen, taking an "indirect" finesse. If West has the King, all is well, for your Queen then becomes an ultimate winner; if East has the King, (in addition to the Jack), then you can never make two diamond tricks. In diagram form, here are the possibilities:

(1)   (2)

Q 10 2   Q 10 2

J 9 7 6   K 8 5   K 9 7 6   J 8 5

A 4 3   A 4 3

(3)

Q 10 2

9 7 6 5   K J 8

A 4 3

In (B), once West has opened a diamond you have two sure tricks no matter what you play from the North hand. But it is possible that you might make three tricks if you put up the nine-spot from dummy — *and East covers it with the King.* If this happens, you of course will take the King with the Ace, and later on successfully finesse West for the "marked" Jack of Diamonds (if East had the Jack he would have played it originally instead of playing the King):

$\diamondsuit$ Q 10 9

$\diamondsuit$ J 8 7 6 $\diamondsuit$ K 5 2

$\diamondsuit$ A 4 3

If, instead of putting up the nine-spot you play the Queen, you automatically restrict yourself to two tricks no matter what the adverse distribution is:

(1)	(2)

(1)

$\diamondsuit$ Q 10 9

$\diamondsuit$ J 8 7 6 $\diamondsuit$ K 5 2

$\diamondsuit$ A 4 3

(2)

$\diamondsuit$ Q 10 9

$\diamondsuit$ K 8 7 6 $\diamondsuit$ J 5 2

$\diamondsuit$ A 4 3

III.

(A)

$\spadesuit$ K 5 4

$\spadesuit$ Q 3 2

(B)

$\spadesuit$ K 4

$\spadesuit$ Q 3 2

West opens a low spade. In (A), the correct play is to play the four-spot from the North hand, the hope being that East will win the trick with the Ace, thereby giving you two future tricks with your King and Queen. If, instead, you put up North's King, you can never win more than one trick:

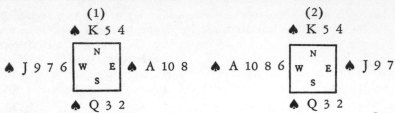

(1)

♠ K 5 4

♠ J 9 7 6 [W E] ♠ A 10 8

♠ Q 3 2

(2)

♠ K 5 4

♠ A 10 8 6 [W E] ♠ J 9 7

♠ Q 3 2

In (2), if you put up the King, it will win, but later on your Q 3 will be trapped by West's A 10.

In (B), West again opens a low spade. Here your proper play is to put up the King in the hope that West is leading away from the Ace. If, instead, you play the four-spot from dummy, even if East has the Ace, he will wait to capture the King. In putting up the King, if West is leading away from the Ace your King will win the trick. If West ever again obtains the lead, he will be unable to lead that suit without promoting your Queen into a winner. Here are the illustrations of the above:

(1)

♠ K 4

♠ A 10 8 5 [W E] ♠ J 9 7 6

♠ Q 3 2

(2)

♠ K 4

♠ J 9 7 6 [W E] ♠ A 10 8 5

♠ Q 3 2

The above explanations apply equally well, of course, to the following, the Queen and King being interchanged.

(C)

♠ Q 5 4

[N W E S]

♠ K 3 2

(D)

♠ Q 4

[N W E S]

♠ K 3 2

In (C), on the lead of a small spade from West, the four-spot is played; in (D), the Queen is hopefully put up.

IV.

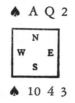

♠ A Q 2

♠ 10 4 3

If *you* had to lead this suit from either the North or South hand, it would be impossible to obtain more than two tricks and possibly only one trick. But if West opens a small spade, you have a chance of making three tricks, and an excellent chance of securing two tricks.

On West's lead of a low spade, your proper play is to follow with the deuce from dummy. Let us look at what can happen: (a) should East play low, your ten-spot will win after which you will subsequently finesse West for the King, (b) should dummy's deuce be captured by East's King, then North's Ace and Queen will become two winners, (c) if East plays the Jack on the opening lead, winning the trick, then you later finesse West for the King, and, (d), if East has both the King and Jack, then you could never have made more than one trick in spades.

Presenting the above in diagram form:

(a)

♠ A Q 2

♠ K J 7 5   ♠ 9 8 6

♠ 10 4 3

(b)

♠ A Q 2

♠ J 9 7 5   ♠ K 8 6

♠ 10 4 3

(c)

♠ A Q 2

♠ K 7 6 5   ♠ J 9 8

♠ 10 4 3

(d)

♠ A Q 2

♠ 9 7 6 5   ♠ K J 8

♠ 10 4 3

V.

♠ A J 4

♠ 9 3 2

Here, too, if *you* were compelled to lead this suit yourself, you would make just one trick except in the one unlikely situation where West started with both the King and Queen. But if West opens a low spade you stand a good chance of winning two tricks by playing the four-spot from dummy. If West started with either the K 10 or Q 10, you will win two spade tricks:

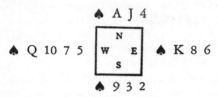

♠ A J 4

♠ Q 10 7 5   ♠ K 8 6

♠ 9 3 2

The first trick will be lost to East's King, but later on you will successfully finesse West for the Queen, dummy's Jack becoming a winner.

VI.

The following combination is a most important one, for it occurs very frequently. The expert player has learned *to avoid* leading from this combination, for if he does he will win only two tricks in it. But if he can get the opponents to lead into it, he will, in most cases, obtain three tricks:

♡ A 3 2

♡ K 10 9

If *you* lead either the Ace or King originally, you will wind up winning two tricks. But if West (or East) leads a heart, you will be able to make three tricks:

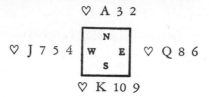

♡ A 3 2

♡ J 7 5 4   N   ♡ Q 8 6
             W   E
                 S

♡ K 10 9

Should West lead the four-spot, East's Queen will be captured by South's King. Then the ten of hearts will be led, and West's Jack will be successfully finessed.

This handling of the above type of combination is based on the mathematically-sound assumption that, much more often than not, one of the opponents will hold the Queen, and the other will hold the Jack, as opposed to the Queen and Jack being in the same hand.

VII.

◇ J 2

N
W   E
S

◇ A 9 3

Playing the above combination on your own power, you can never win more than the Ace. But if West leads a low diamond, you have a slight chance of obtaining two tricks — *if West has led away from the KQ.* So you hopefully put up the Jack, for if you do not, you will never win two tricks. If the King is in one opponent's hand, and the Queen is in the other, then you never could have won more than one trick.

(a)   ◇ J 2

◇ K Q 7 4   N   ◇ 10 8 6 5
             W   E
                 S

◇ A 9 3

(b)   ◇ J 2

◇ K 10 7 4   N   ◇ Q 8 6 5
              W   E
                  S

◇ A 9 3

VIII.

Here is another frequently arising combination that is often mishandled.

♣ J 2

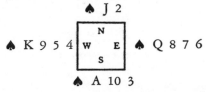

♣ A 10 3

If *you* were compelled to make a lead from either the North or South hand, the chances are that you would win but one trick (except if East possessed both the King and Queen).

But if West leads this suit, *two tricks are guaranteed* by playing the deuce from dummy. Should East put up the Queen or King, your Ace will win, after which your Jack and ten will eventually create another trick for you. Of course, if East plays low, your ten-spot will produce the second trick. Do not make the mistake of putting up North's Jack on the lead of the suit by West. If you do, it may cost you a trick:

♠ J 2

♠ K 9 5 4   ♠ Q 8 7 6

♠ A 10 3

As the reader can see in the above illustration, if North's Jack is inserted, East will cover with the Queen and South's Ace will win. Now South's 10 3 will be trapped by West's K 9. But if, instead, the deuce is played from dummy, East will be compelled to play the Queen anyway (otherwise South's ten will win), leaving North-South with the J 10 against West's King.

IX.

Q 2

A 10 3

This is exactly the same as (VIII) above. Do not make the mistake of putting up North's Queen on West's lead in order to win a trick "in a hurry." By playing the deuce, you are guaranteeing yourself two tricks:

(a)   (b)

Q 2   Q 2

J 8 6 4 [N W E S] K 9 7 5   K 9 7 5 [N W E S] J 8 6 4

A 10 3   A 10 3

As the reader can see, by playing North's deuce exactly two tricks will be made, no more and no less, regardless as to the location of the King and Jack. By putting up the Queen in (a), covered by East's King and taken by South's Ace, South restricts himself to that *one trick*. In (b), declarer makes two tricks whether he plays the Queen (incorrectly) or the deuce.

X.

♡ J 2

[N W E S]

♡ Q 4 3

West opens a low heart, and the only proper play is to automatically follow with the *deuce* from the North hand. This will guarantee the procurement of a trick, since East, to win the trick must put up the Ace or King. And, once he does, you will have the Queen and Jack remaining, to take care of the high honor outstanding.

♡ J 2

♡ K 10 7 5 [N W E S] ♡ A 9 8 6

♡ Q 4 3

If, instead, the Jack is played from dummy, East's Ace will win, and South's Queen will then be trapped by West's K 10.

On the play of any combination of the Jack facing the Queen, the expert has learned to avoid leading from it, for if he should make the initial lead, he will virtually never win a trick in that suit. That is, holding the following combinations, the purpose in life is to get the *opponents* to attack the suit, as opposed to declarer attacking it himself:

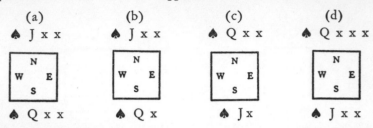

(a) ♠ J x x — ♠ Q x x
(b) ♠ J x x — ♠ Q x
(c) ♠ Q x x — ♠ J x
(d) ♠ Q x x x — ♠ J x x

If declarer tries to establish a winner in any of the above combinations by leading the suit himself, he will usually discover the following, or a reasonable facsimile thereof, to exist:

♠ J x x

♠ A 10 x x   ♠ K 9 x

♠ Q x x

When he leads low from the South hand, West will also play low, and North's Jack will be captured by East's King. Now South's Q x will be trapped by West's A 10, and declarer will win no spade tricks.

If, on the other hand, *either* East or West leads the suit originally, declarer will not be compelled to waste his Queen or Jack to force out the opponents' Ace or King. And, as a result, he will still retain the Queen and Jack at trick two, to knock out the opponents' remaining high card, thereby establishing a trick for himself.

The "principle" of avoiding the initial lead from the above combinations is based on the fact that when the opposition possesses both the Ace and King, these two cards will usually be divided in their hands, as opposed to both of them being in the same hand.

XI.

◇ J 2

◇ A K 3

West opens the four of diamonds — and your best chance of winning three tricks is to put up North's Jack. If West has led away from the Queen, you have just "found" a third trick. If East has the Queen, then "luck" is against you.

J 2

Q 9 7 4   10 8 6 5

A K 3

J 2

9 8 6 4   Q 10 7 5

A K 3

XII.

♣ Q 2

♣ 10 9 3

The contract is *notrump,* against which West opens the five of clubs — and your only correct play is to put up *North's Queen.* If you do not, you will never make a trick whether East puts up the Jack, the King, or the Ace.

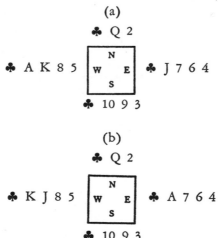

(a)

♣ Q 2

♣ A K 8 5   ♣ J 7 6 4

♣ 10 9 3

(b)

♣ Q 2

♣ K J 8 5   ♣ A 7 6 4

♣ 10 9 3

In (a), by putting up the Queen, you "steal" a trick. In (b), you are inevitably doomed to lose four club tricks.

XIII.

This final play is not one in which the defenders make an attacking lead. But every declarer who has ever had to attack in the following standard combination has always wished that the opponents had attacked it.

♠ Q 7 6 5

The problem is how to make three tricks in the above combination. Let us say that you have a "hunch" that West possesses the Ace of Spades. In this case you would lead the five of spades and put up North's King, which would win if your hunch was correct. You would then return the spade deuce, and no matter what East puts up, a low spade would be played from the South hand. If West started with the A x of spades originally, he will be compelled to win the trick with the Ace. The entire suit will now belong to you:

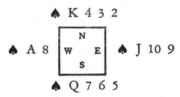

♠ Q 7 6 5

The reader may raise the question: "But what if West started with the A J 8 or the A 10 8, or the A 9 8?" If this were the distribution, then declarer *could not avoid* the loss of two tricks, no matter how he played it.

The procurement of three tricks in this situation depends on two specific things: (1) guessing where the Ace is located, and (2) the hope — and the fact — that the Ace must be part of a doubleton.

Let us take a look at the above situation again. This time, however, you have a different "hunch" or feeling: that *East* has the Ace of Spades.

♠ K 4 3 2

N
W   E
S

♠ Q 7 6 5

You would first get to the North hand via some other suit. Then the deuce of spades would be led and the Queen played, which would win the trick. Now the five of spades would be returned, and no matter what West would put up, you would play low from the North hand. *If* East originally held the A x, then he would be compelled to capture this trick with the Ace — and the rest of the suit would be yours. If East held three spades headed by the Ace, you could not avoid the loss of two tricks. Here are the two situations just discussed:

The above play has been known through the years as "The Obligatory Finesse," although actually it is not a finesse within the strict meaning of the word "finesse." In the sense that the play is an attempt to gain a trick by "wishful thinking" — putting a card where you would like it to be and playing accordingly — it does bear some remote resemblance to the normal finesse.

An illustration of this Obligatory Finesse in actual play is presented in the following deal:

$$
\begin{array}{c}
\spadesuit \ 4\ 3 \\
\heartsuit \ K\ 10\ 5\ 2 \\
\diamondsuit \ K\ 8\ 6 \\
\clubsuit \ K\ Q\ 3\ 2
\end{array}
$$

$$
\begin{array}{c}
\text{N} \\
\text{W} \qquad \text{E} \\
\text{S}
\end{array}
$$

$$
\begin{array}{c}
\spadesuit \ A\ K\ 5 \\
\heartsuit \ J\ 7\ 6 \\
\diamondsuit \ Q\ 7\ 5\ 4\ 2 \\
\clubsuit \ A\ 5
\end{array}
$$

Against South's *three notrump* contract, West opens the Queen of Spades, which is captured by South's Ace. A moment's reflection makes it clear to South that in order to fulfill his contract, he must establish the diamond suit.

To this end, South leads the deuce of diamonds, putting up North's

King when West plays low. With the King capturing the trick —
East following with the nine-spot — the Ace is now "marked" as being
in the West hand. The six of diamonds is then returned, East playing
the ten-spot.

At this point, there are just two diamonds outstanding: the Ace and
the Jack. If West has both of these cards, then South *must lose* two
diamond tricks no matter what he plays. The hope, therefore, is that
East has the Jack, and West has the now-singleton Ace.

So South follows with a low diamond — and luck is on his side when
West is forced to win the trick with the Ace. The contract is now
guaranteed, for South can win four diamond tricks, two spade tricks, and
three clubs. The deal was:

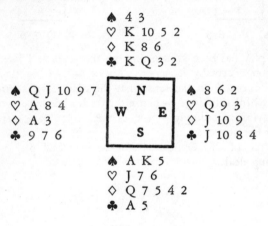

```
                    ♠ 4 3
                    ♡ K 10 5 2
                    ◇ K 8 6
                    ♣ K Q 3 2

  ♠ Q J 10 9 7         N          ♠ 8 6 2
  ♡ A 8 4                         ♡ Q 9 3
  ◇ A 3         W         E       ◇ J 10 9
  ♣ 9 7 6               S         ♣ J 10 8 4

                    ♠ A K 5
                    ♡ J 7 6
                    ◇ Q 7 5 4 2
                    ♣ A 5
```

Chapter III

THE PERCENTAGE PLAY

NOTE WELL: The theories presented in this chapter, except where otherwise stated, do not take into consideration the bidding of the opponents or other clues which develop at the table. The illustrations show you the proper thing to do in the absence of external influences.

A "PERCENTAGE PLAY" (or, as it is called in the lexicon of the gambling profession, 'playing percentages') is nothing more than the selection from a choice of two or three different and optional lines of play, the one which offers the greatest chance of success. In a certain sense, it is directly comparable to this situation: you meet some magnanimous soul who says: "I'll give you a present absolutely free of charge, and you have your choice of two things, either 50¢ in cash or 36¢ in cash. Which do you want?" I assume your answer is the obvious one — at least I hope it is, for otherwise you will have trouble with "percentage plays." However, since I have yet to meet anyone who chose the 36¢, I shall take it for granted that each reader selected the 50¢, and proceed on that assumption.

In case the reader has developed the feeling that the preceding paragraph was intended to "soften you up" before introducing you to a lengthy dissertation on "Mathematics and Contract Bridge," you can promptly dispel those fears for all time. While mathematics is the foundation upon which "percentage plays" are based, we, as bridge players, have nothing to do with mathematics. And, contrary to popular belief, very few successful bridge players know any more about mathematics than does the average person. Ordinary common sense, the ability to count to thirteen, and past situations remembered for application to similar future situations, will make you an excellent player.

Let us take a look at a few "mathematical" situations. How would you play each of the following hands, sitting South as declarer at a *three notrump contract?*

1.

♠ 6 5 2
♡ A K Q
◊ A Q 4
♣ A K Q 6

```
        N
    W       E
        S
```

♠ A
♡ 9 7 5 3
◊ 8 6 5 3 2
♣ 4 3 2

West opens the Jack of Spades against your *three notrump* contract, which trick you win with your Ace. You are now in your own hand for the first and last time.

You take inventory and can see eight sure tricks: one in spades, three in hearts, one in diamonds, and three in clubs. Where can you obtain your ninth trick? In one of two places: (1) either by taking a successful diamond finesse, or (2) by establishing dummy's fourth club, which can be done if the six adverse clubs are divided 3-3. And, as is apparent, you get just one chance, for you can attack one suit or the other, but not both. That is, if you take the diamond finesse, and it loses, the opponents will cash their established spade suit. If, instead, you elect to attack the club suit, and the suit is not favorably divided, you are, as before, doomed to defeat.

Well, since you all have received your Ph.D. degree in mathematics at the various universities here and abroad, you know that the finesse gives you an exact 50-50 chance (50%) for your ninth trick. With respect to the alternative play of attacking the club suit, the mathematicians who came before us — and are still with us — have stated that when six cards of a suit are missing, they will be divided 3-3, just *36%* of the time. So, what would you rather have, 50¢ or 36¢?

Consequently, you take the finesse in diamonds as opposed to playing for the adverse clubs to be divided 3-3, for the finesse has become the "percentage play."

2. Let us now change the hands a wee bit:

♠ 6 5 2
♡ A K Q
◇ A Q 4
♣ A K Q 6

♠ A
♡ 9 7 5 3
◇ 8 6 5 3
♣ 5 4 3 2

Again, you are South playing a *three notrump* contract, West opening the Jack of Spades which your bare Ace captures. The same problem now exists: (a) the diamond finesse for the ninth trick, or (b) a 3-2 break of the five adverse clubs, which will then create a winner out of declarer's fourth club.

Here again we must take refuge in "higher mathematics": the diamond finesse offers a 50% chance of success; a 3-2 division of the five missing clubs (as opposed to a 4-1 or 5-0 division) will occur 68% of the time.

The "percentage play" therefore, is to forsake the diamond finesse, and instead promptly to attack the clubs. No guarantee is forthcoming, of course, but since the findings of the mathematicians have been checked and double-checked, who are we not to accept a 68% chance instead of a 50% chance?

For those who might be interested in all of the mathematics pertaining to the division of the missing cards in a suit (when 2 cards are missing, or 3, 4, 5, 6, etc.), a table giving every significant mathematical probability relating to the division of suits is presented on page 83. But, with *three important exceptions,* the memorizing of this table is wasted effort as far as the improvement of one's game is concerned. Here are the three situations which are most important to know, two of them having already been introduced in this chapter.

1. When you and your partner have *seven cards* of a given suit, the six which the opponents hold in that suit will be divided 3-3 only 36% of the time (a little over ⅓ of the time).

2. When you and your partner have *eight cards* of a suit, the five which the opponents possess will be divided 3-2 about 68% of the time (over ⅔ of the time).

3. When you and your partner have *nine cards* of a suit, the missing four will be divided 2-2 only 40% of the time (this situation will be illustrated in a moment).

Actually, the figures themselves are not important except insofar as academic learning is concerned. The thing to remember is that when you have seven of a suit, the six missing ones do not figure to be divided 3-3; similarly, when you have nine of a suit, do not expect the four missing ones to be divided 2-2, for they will not break that way. But when you have eight of a suit, you can be optimistic about your chances of developing one winner or more out of the low cards (depending on whether your suit is divided 4-4; 5-3; 6-2; 7-1; or 8-0), for you now know that the five adverse cards in the suit will be divided 3-2 over two-thirds of the time.

Why these three "suit division" situations are so vital can be realized when it is pointed out that on *every* deal that you will ever get to play, you and partner will have between you at least two seven-card suits or one eight-card, or longer, suit (or suits). It is, of course, important to know what your chances are of developing winners out of the low cards in your long suit, since the necessity of creating tricks is an ever-present situation. And, in virtually every deal, there will be a finesse available, a 50-50 proposition.

As has been demonstrated, you will frequently be confronted with the option of either taking a finesse to establish a much needed trick, or of attacking your long suit to create that trick. Which you will do wil depend on your suit. You will pit the "mathematics" presented against the 50% chance of a finesse, and you will accept the one that offers you a better proposition, or as we say in the vernacular, "better odds."

Let us now look at the nine-card situation, where the four missing ones do not figure to be divided 2-2. In my opinion, more bridge players than not have the feeling that when their partnership has nine of a suit, they are living in tough luck when the missing four turn out to be divided 3-1. It is not hard luck. It is those darn mathematicians who are pointing their collective finger at you and stating "I told you so."

To illustrate:

♣ A K 7 3 2

N
W   E
S

♣ 9 6 5 4

You find yourself in a *seven club* contract with the above trump suit. You have no losers in the other suits, and all you have to worry about is this trump suit. Take my word for it, either start worrying, start hoping, or get ready to take it out on your partner. You figure to make your contract just *40%* of the time, and no more.

3.

The question of whether to attack the nine-card suit in the hope of creating a winner out of a low card in the suit for the game-going trick, or to take a finesse instead, is the theme of the following deal:

```
          ♠ A K Q J
          ♡ A Q
          ◊ 8 4
          ♣ A K 8 7 4

              ┌─────────┐
              │    N    │
              │ W     E │
              │    S    │
              └─────────┘

          ♠ 9 7 5
          ♡ 10 6 5 3 2
          ◊ A
          ♣ 6 5 3 2
```

South arrives at a *three notrump* contract (a five club or even a six club contract is much superior) against which West opens a low diamond, East's ten-spot being captured by declarer's Ace. As in the two preceding deals, South is in his own hand for the first and last time.

Upon observation, South perceives 8 sure winners: 4 spades, 1 heart, 1 diamond, and 2 clubs. The ninth trick is available (in theory) in one of two places — either by a successful heart finesse, or by a 2-2 break in the adversely-held clubs.

As you now know, the adverse clubs will be divided 2-2 just 40% of the time. The heart finesse will work 50% of the time. Ergo, you take the "percentage play" of the heart finesse, although you may not like only a 50-50 chance. But as you know, not only is half a loaf better than none, but half a loaf is better than two-fifths (40%) of a loaf.

As a brief digression, I should like to mention probably the most important single element in bridge, namely "luck." On any given deal, or on any given "percentage play," a rank beginner may obtain a better result than will a top-flight expert. That is, on any one hand, proper play might fail and incorrect play will succeed. However, as you play more carefully, and more understandingly, you will discover that the "hard luck" which always seemed to hound you has either gone on to hound someone else, or has diminished appreciably. The knowledge and the application of the proper play is the most effective antidote against "finesses always losing," "suits never breaking," and "hard luck" in general.

There have thus far been presented three deals illustrating the 50-50 chance of a finesse for a needed trick versus the play for the development of a low card in a 7, 8, or 9-card suit. The reader should scrutinize these situations, as the opportunity for their usage is very frequent. Here they are again, in summary:

(1)	(2)	(3)
♠ 6 5 2	♠ 6 5 2	♠ A K Q J
♡ A K Q	♡ A K Q	♡ A Q
◇ A Q 4	◇ A Q 4	◇ 8 4
♣ A K Q 6	♣ A K Q 6	♣ A K 8 7 4

N	N	N
W E	W E	W E
S	S	S

(1)	(2)	(3)
♠ A	♠ A	♠ 9 7 5
♡ 9 7 5 3	♡ 9 7 5 3	♡ 10 6 5 3 2
◇ 8 6 5 3 2	◇ 8 6 5 3	◇ A
♣ 4 3 2	♣ 5 4 3 2	♣ 6 5 3 2

On (1) playing a *three notrump* contract, against an opening spade lead, South takes the diamond finesse as opposed to playing for the adverse clubs to be divided 3-3.

On (2), same contract, same lead, South plays for clubs to be divided 3-2, as opposed to taking a diamond finesse.

On (3), against South's *three notrump* contract, West opens a diamond, South winning. The percentage play here is to take the heart finesse, as opposed to playing for the four adverse clubs to be divided 2-2.

Let us revise each of these hands a bit. The proper "percentage play" now becomes completely different.

1a.

♠ 6 5 2
♡ A K Q
◇ A Q 4
♣ A K 6 4

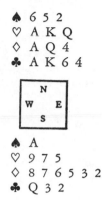

The Queen and four of Clubs have been interchanged; and South has been given a sixth diamond instead of the fourth heart.

♠ A
♡ 9 7 5
◇ 8 7 6 5 3 2
♣ Q 3 2

The contract is *three notrump*. West opens the Jack of Spades, South's Ace winning. The ninth trick can be made by either (1) a successful diamond finesse, or by (2) a 3-3 break of the six missing clubs. How do you play the hand?

It is no longer a question of one or the other, for declarer has an additional entry in the Queen of Clubs. South can now avail himself of *both* the finesse and the break in clubs, and the percentage (odds) in favor of his obtaining the ninth trick has increased tremendously.

Proper play is to cash the Ace and King of Clubs, and then to lead a club to the Queen. If the adverse clubs are divided 3-3, South will know it at this point (having counted the clubs as they fell). He will, in this case, get to the North hand to cash the thirteenth club. If the clubs are not divided 3-3, South will then try the diamond finesse for his ninth trick. Played in this manner South has first the 36% chance that clubs are divided 3-3; if they are not, then as a last resort, he has the 50% chance of a diamond finesse. If neither play works, then he can consider himself "unlucky," or he can charge it to "percentages." But, whatever the result, his conscience will be clear: he played the hand exactly as the world's best players would have played it.

2a.

♠ 6 5 2
♡ A K Q
◇ A Q 4
♣ A K 6 5

The Queen and Five of Clubs have been interchanged; and South has been given a Fifth Diamond instead of the Fourth Heart.

♠ A
♡ 9 7 5
◇ 8 7 6 5 3
♣ Q 4 3 2

Again the contract is *three notrump,* and West's spade opening is captured by declarer's Ace. With the Queen of Clubs now in the South hand, declarer has acquired a second entry.

Proper play now is to cash the Ace, King and Queen of Clubs. If the five adverse clubs are divided 3-2 (68%), then the contract is guaranteed; if not, then South will take the diamond finesse (50%). If neither works, then South is really running in "hard luck" — and he would be entitled to our sympathy.

3a.

♠ A K Q J
♡ A Q
◇ 8 4
♣ K 8 7 6 4

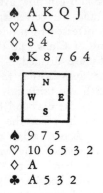

The Ace and Six of Clubs have been interchanged.

♠ 9 7 5
♡ 10 6 5 3 2
◇ A
♣ A 5 3 2

The contract is *three notrump,* West's diamond opening lead being captured by South's Ace. As in the two previous deals, South has acquired an additional entry, and he now has the time to test the adverse distribution of the club suit. If it is unfavorable, then the heart finesse will be taken.

At trick two a club is led to the King, followed by a club to the Ace. If the four adverse clubs are divided 2-2 (40%), then the contract is guaranteed; if not, the 50% chance of a successful heart finesse is still available. And, whatever the result, South has played it correctly, according to "percentages."

The deal which follows illustrates how the expert subconsciously lives (and plays) in the world of "percentages." It is a simple deal from declarer's point of view, and yet it possesses a certain logic of thinking which many bridge players can neither comprehend nor apply. Make the assumption as you read through the deal, that you are kibitzing the South declarer, and that you temporarily possess the ability to look into his mind to see how it is functioning as he is playing the hand. Declarer is thinking aloud, and you are listening:

♠ K 8 4
♡ A 6 5
♢ A K J 2
♣ 7 4 3

```
      N
  W       E
      S
```

♠ A 7 5
♡ K 3 2
♢ 7 5 3
♣ A Q J 2

The bidding:

SOUTH	WEST	NORTH	EAST
One Club	Pass	One Diamond	Pass
One Notrump	Pass	Three Notrump	Pass
Pass	Pass		

Opening lead: Queen of Spades.

"A good contract . . . seven tricks right off the top . . . if the King of Clubs is 'right,' I have nine tricks . . ." (The opening spade lead is therefore captured by dummy's King, and a club finesse is taken, losing to West's King. Declarer now counts eight sure winners, the Jack of Clubs having been promoted into a trick. West returns the Jack of

Spades) . . . "Well, so the club finesse didn't work . . . now to test the clubs . . . but if they don't break, I'll have to go after the diamonds, so I think I'd better 'hold up' on the Jack of Spades to eliminate East's spades" . . . (The Jack of Spades is permitted to win the trick, after which a spade continuation is captured by South's Ace. The Ace and Jack of Clubs are then played, but West shows out on the third round. Clubs did not break). "Nothing is working so far . . . probably the diamond finesse will lose too. We'll know in just a moment" . . . (the Diamond Jack is finessed, losing to East's Queen. East then cashes his high club. East, out of spades, returns the heart Queen, dummy's Ace winning) . . . "My last chance now . . . come on, you diamonds, be nice boys and break 3-3 . . . Well, what do you know, they broke 3-3! Oh, you lovely deuce of diamonds . . ."

The actual hands were:

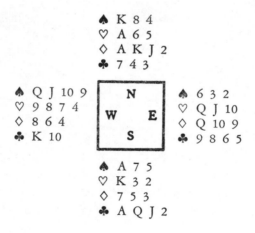

```
              ♠ K 8 4
              ♡ A 6 5
              ◇ A K J 2
              ♣ 7 4 3

♠ Q J 10 9        N        ♠ 6 3 2
♡ 9 8 7 4                  ♡ Q J 10
◇ 8 6 4      W       E     ◇ Q 10 9
♣ K 10            S        ♣ 9 8 6 5

              ♠ A 7 5
              ♡ K 3 2
              ◇ 7 5 3
              ♣ A Q J 2
```

Declarer's reasoning on this hand was perfect. First he attacked the club suit because he stood to develop two additional winners (Q J of Clubs) if the King were favorably located, as opposed to attacking the diamond suit where if the Queen were favorably located he would gain but one trick. Or, stating it another way, even if the club finesse of the Queen lost, declarer would have gained a trick (the Jack). If the diamond finesse lost, declarer would have gained nothing.

When the club finesse lost, declarer still had the club suit going for him if the six adverse clubs broke 3-3. But if they did not, he had the foresight to realize that he would have to attack the diamond suit, which meant that East might well obtain the lead via the Queen of

Diamonds. Hence the 'hold up' play, so that if East obtained the lead he would be unable to return a spade. And when the diamond finesse lost to the Queen, East's communication with his partner had been destroyed, so East played back a heart. Declarer then laid down dummy's Ace and King of Diamonds, and the diamonds broke 3-3. Dummy's deuce of diamonds had now become declarer's game-going trick.

Look at the "percentages" going for declarer as he played the hand:

1. The club finesse 50%
2. A 3-3 break in clubs 36%
3. The diamond finesse 50%
4. A 3-3 break in diamonds 36%

All he needed was *one* of the four above conditions to be favorable, and he was able to test each of them. Mathematically (pardon the word) he had approximately a 90% chance of making his contract. If nothing were "right" for him, he would have gone down a trick. But you will agree with me that nobody could be that unlucky, and that proper use of "percentage plays" will (almost) always pay off.

Very briefly summarizing what has been presented up to this point, let me put it this way:

On a majority of deals you, as declarer, will be confronted with an option of two lines of play, of "either this or that." You now know what the answer is with respect to taking a finesse as opposed to playing for a favorable adverse division of a suit which you would like to develop. But always go one step further: look to see whether you can avail yourself of both lines of play as opposed to just one or the other, and if you can, then take advantage of the situation.

THE STANDARD PERCENTAGE PLAY IN FREQUENTLY
OCCURRING COMBINATIONS WITHIN A SUIT
(Usually the Trump Suit)

In each of the situations which follows, the idea is to play *the suit* in such a manner as to avail yourself of the best "percentage play" to hold the losses in a given suit to a *minimum,* or to avoid the loss of any tricks in the suit. No guarantees are given here, but the percentage plays to be presented offer you the best chance of not losing any tricks. Bear in mind as you go through these plays, that no information with respect to the opponents' distribution has been divulged in either the bidding, or in the play to the previous tricks.

I.

A.

♠ x x x
♡ x x x
◊ K J x x
♣ A Q x

♠ A K J x x
♡ x x x
◊ A Q x
♣ K x

You are South, playing a *four spade* contract, and the defenders take the first three heart tricks, after which a club is played which you win with the Queen.

Proper percentage play in the trump suit is to lay down the Ace of Spades, then get to dummy via a club or diamond. A spade is now led out of dummy, and the Jack is finessed with a prayer.

As was mentioned at the outset of this chapter, the mathematics of the situation do not concern us. But, from a superficial mathematical point of view, the finesse for the Queen is taken because East will hold the Q x x more often than West will hold (specifically) the Q x. If you elect to lay down the Ace and King in the hope of dropping the Queen, you will succeed less often than if you finesse the Jack to trap the Queen.

B.

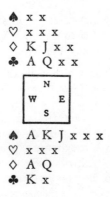

♠ x x
♡ x x x
◊ K J x x
♣ A Q x x

♠ A K J x x x
♡ x x x
◊ A Q
♣ K x

Here the play of the *four spade* contract is exactly the same. After the opponents cash three heart tricks and declarer obtains the lead, he lays down the Ace of Spades, then gets to dummy and finesses the Jack. And, as the mathematicians have told us, the finesse will succeed more often than will the play of the Ace and King in the hope of dropping the Queen.

C.

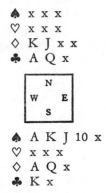

♠ x x x
♡ x x x
♢ K J x x
♣ A Q x

N
W E
S

♠ A K J 10 x
♡ x x x
♢ A Q x
♣ K x

The play of the trump suit here is exactly the same as in the two above illustrations. The Ace of Spades is cashed, dummy is entered, and a spade finesse is taken.

But on the following deal, where the combined eight-card trump suit is identical to the above, the "percentage play" is different.

D.

♠ x x
♡ x x x
♢ K J x x
♣ A Q x x

N
W E
S

♠ A K J 10 x x
♡ x x x
♢ A Q
♣ K x

The contract is again *four spades,* with the opponents cashing three hearts and then shifting to a club. Correct play is to get to dummy and *take the spade finesse immediately,* and not lay down the Ace first. The reason is this, according to our mathematical friends: East will have the Q x x x more often than West will have the singleton Queen. If you cash the Ace first, then, your ultimate finesse for the Spade Queen will be successful, but you will still have to lose a trick if East started with Q x x x. But, if you finesse the Jack at once, and it wins, you can then get to dummy again to finesse the ten-spot. You will now avoid the loss of a trick if East originally held the Q x x x.

In a tournament which took place some years ago, a famous expert slipped up on this particular percentage play situation, and it cost him and his team a National Championship.

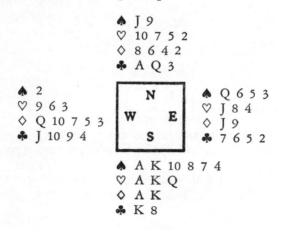

The contract was *seven spades,* against which West opened the Jack of Clubs, South's King winning. South cashed the Ace of Spades, led a club to dummy's Queen of Clubs, and then laid down the Jack of trumps, finessing for the Queen. The Jack, as you can see, won the trick — but East still had the Q x left and eventually made a spade trick.

Proper percentage play was to capture the opening club lead with dummy's Queen and promptly to lead the Jack of Spades, which would win. The nine of spades would be led next — and East's Queen would never win a trick.

Of course, if West held a singleton Queen of Spades, the story would be a different one. But percentage is percentage — and East figured to have the Q x x x of spades more often than West figured to have the singleton Queen.

II.

♠ x x x x
♡ x x x
◇ K J x
♣ A Q x

♠ A K J x x
♡ x x x
◇ A Q x
♣ K x

The contract is *four spades,* against which the defenders cash three heart tricks and shift to a club, declarer's King winning. Proper percentage play with the combined holding of *nine* cards in a suit headed by the A K J is to *lay down the Ace and King to drop the Queen,* as opposed to finessing the Jack. Here again we accept the word of the mathematicians: the Queen will drop more often than the finesse will succeed.

Where the holding is A K J x x x opposite x x x or the A K J x x x x opposite x x, the play is the same: lay down the Ace and King to drop the Queen, instead of finessing for the Queen.

III.

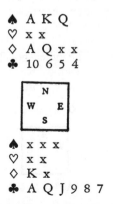

♠ A K Q
♡ x x
◇ A Q x x
♣ 10 6 5 4

♠ x x x
♡ x x
◇ K x
♣ A Q J 9 8 7

The contract is *five clubs.* The opponents cash the two heart tricks, and then shift to a diamond, dummy's Queen winning.

Many bridge players, holding ten cards in a suit headed by A Q, tend to cash the Ace in the hope of catching the singleton King. This is incorrect. Proper "percentage" play is to finesse the Queen. If there happens to be a singleton King in back of the Queen, then your "percentage" will have backfired. Nevertheless, the finesse is proper. Let's look at it logically. Whenever *East* originally holds the K 2, K 3, or K 3 2, the finesse will win; whenever *West* holds the singleton King the finesse will lose. It is much more probable for East to hold either the K 2, K 3, or K 3 2, than it is for West to have the specifically singleton King. (All of the other possible distributions of the three adverse clubs do not enter into consideration. That is, if *West* has the K x, then no play will prevent the loss of a club trick; or, if *East* has the singleton King then no matter how declarer plays the suit, he will not lose a trick).

IV.

On occasion, the following trump situation will present itself:

◇ Q 9 8 5

```
  N
W   E
  S
```

◇ A 10 6 4 3 2

If you can afford to lose one trick, then you take the safety play of leading a low diamond away from the Ace towards the Queen. This is guaranteed to lose no more than one trick (see page 122).

But if you cannot afford to lose a trick, the percentage play is to lay down the Ace, with the fervent hope that one of the opponents was dealt the singleton King. The other possibility is to enter the North hand and lead the Queen, hoping that West was dealt the singleton Jack, in which case no tricks will be lost. That is:

◇ Q 9 8 5

◇ J
```
  N
W   E
  S
```
◇ K 7

◇ A 10 6 4 3 2

By simple reasoning, it is more likely for *either* East or West to have been dealt the singleton King than it is for *West* to have been dealt the singleton Jack (with any other distribution of the three missing diamonds declarer must lose at least one diamond trick).

V.

The final standard, frequently occurring, and most annoying situation, is the following:

$\heartsuit$ K 10 6 3 2

$\heartsuit$ 5 N W E S $\heartsuit$ Q

$\heartsuit$ A 9 7 4

You cannot afford to lose any heart tricks. The Ace is led, West follows with the five and East drops the Queen. Should you now finesse West for the Jack, making the assumption that East's Queen was a singleton; or should you cash dummy's King in the hope that East's original holding was the Q J doubleton?

There is no guaranteed answer to this situation. On some days East was dealt a singleton Queen, on other days he was dealt a doubleton Q J.

Oswald Jacoby, one of the world's top-ranking players, has this to say on the subject, and it seems to offer a better chance than a pure guess:

"When East drops the Queen, it's either a singleton, or from the Q J doubleton. Whenever East is dealt the Q J doubleton, roughly half the time he will play the Jack and half the time he will deceptively play the Queen. So, when he drops the Queen he is either telling the truth (a singleton), or a half-truth (maybe singleton, maybe doubleton). I therefore finesse West for the Jack, and I think I'll be right about 75% of the time: when East had no choice (a singleton); and when East, having held the Q J doubleton, would have played *the Jack!*"

The above may be difficult to interpret, but I suggest that when the Queen is dropped on the first lead, finesse for the Jack; also, if the Jack is dropped on the first lead, finesse for the Queen as opposed to believing the Jack to be part of the Q J doubleton.

Let us now look at some "percentage plays" as they were developed on the field of battle:

Percentage Plays in Actual Competition

A.

     ♠ 8 5 4
     ♡ A J 9 2
     ◊ K 5 2
     ♣ 7 3 2

```
      N
  W       E
      S
```

     ♠ A 2
     ♡ Q 10 8
     ◊ A J 10 9 3
     ♣ A K 4

South arrives at a *three notrump* contract, against which West opens a low spade and East plays the Queen which is permitted to win. A spade is played back, South's Ace winning.

Declarer has six sure tricks. The possibility of obtaining the three additional tricks exists in either of two places: (a) the heart suit, if the King of Hearts is in the West hand, and (b) the diamond suit, if declarer can guess where the Queen is. Which finesse to take?

Actually, proper play will enable you to test *both* the diamonds and the hearts instead of restricting yourself to a choice of one or the other!

The King and Ace of Diamonds should be cashed first, there being quite a decent chance that one or the other of the opponents was dealt specifically the Q x of diamonds. If the Queen does not drop, then declarer, as a last resort, will still have available the 50-50 chance of the heart finesse. Surely two chances for the same price are better than one. The hands were:

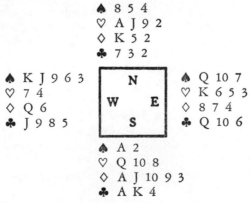

                 ♠ 8 5 4
                 ♡ A J 9 2
                 ◊ K 5 2
                 ♣ 7 3 2

♠ K J 9 6 3   N   ♠ Q 10 7
♡ 7 4   ♡ K 6 5 3
◊ Q 6   W   E   ◊ 8 7 4
♣ J 9 8 5   S   ♣ Q 10 6

                 ♠ A 2
                 ♡ Q 10 8
                 ◊ A J 10 9 3
                 ♣ A K 4

It is surprising to me how many people go wrong on the above hand by selecting to take one finesse or the other, instead of availing themselves of the proper percentage play. Yet, if the following hand had been held by them, they would have had no trouble:

```
              ♠ 8 5 4
              ♡ A J 9 2
              ◊ K 5 4 2
              ♣ 7 3

              ┌─────────┐
              │    N    │
              │ W     E │
              │    S    │
              └─────────┘

              ♠ A 2
              ♡ Q 10 8
              ◊ A J 10 9 3
              ♣ A K 4
```

Here with *nine* diamonds, they would confidently play the Ace and King of Diamonds, and if they did not catch the Queen they would (properly) be disappointed. Holding eight diamonds, the play is the same, except that the odds in favor of catching the Queen are not so good.

B.

```
              ♠ 10 7 4 2
              ♡ 8 4 2
              ◊ A 7
              ♣ 10 8 7 5

              ┌─────────┐
              │    N    │
              │ W     E │
              │    S    │
              └─────────┘

              ♠ A K 3
              ♡ A Q 7
              ◊ K 9 6 5
              ♣ A K 9
```

Against South's *three notrump* contract a heart is opened, East's King being captured by declarer's Ace. Declarer counts eight tricks and perceives that the ninth trick can be obtained in spades or clubs, by the establishment of the fourth card in either suit. Which suit to attack?

Whether to attack the spade suit in the hope that the six adverse spades are divided 3-3, or whether to attack the club suit for the same reason, appears to be a pure guess. Actually it is not a guess — there is a definite percentage play on the hand.

Suppose, for example, you play the Ace and King of Spades, and on the latter trick West drops the Jack. Are you out of the woods? The answer is "no," for East might still have the remaining Q 9. But suppose you play the Ace and King of Clubs, with West dropping the Jack on the latter trick. Your contract now becomes guaranteed, for you next play your nine of clubs which one of the opponents will capture with the Queen. Dummy's ten-spot has just been developed into your ninth trick.

In other words, if you cash the Ace and King of Clubs, and either opponent plays the Queen or the Jack on the second round of the suit, dummy's ten of clubs becomes your game-going trick. But if you play the Ace and King of Spades, catching an honor on the second lead of the suit, you are no nearer home than when you started. The hands were:

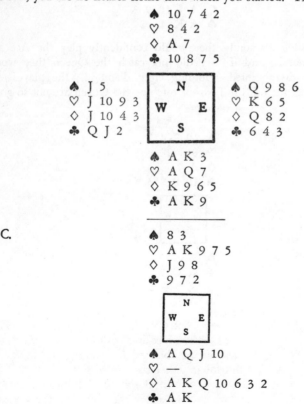

C.

There will be those days when you find yourself in a grand slam in diamonds on hands similar to the above. Whatever complaint you have against your partner for *his* bad bidding should, of course, be reserved until after the completion of the hand. After all, if you fulfill your contract, it is hardly the wise thing to chastise him for bidding too much.

The Queen of Clubs is the opening lead, captured by your King. A cursory inventory reveals that you can discard two of your spades on dummy's Ace and King of Hearts, after which a spade finesse can be taken for your thirteenth trick.

But more intensive examination will indicate that an additional line of play is available which may eliminate the necessity of taking a finesse (and nobody likes to take a finesse to fulfill a grand slam contract). If the eight adverse hearts are divided 4-4, then dummy's fifth heart can become established as a winner, and on it declarer can then discard his Queen of Spades.

At trick two declarer leads a low diamond and takes it with the Jack. He then plays a low heart off dummy, ruffing it with a high trump (let us say the Ace) just to make sure that it cannot be overruffed. Another trump is then led to the nine-spot, and a second heart is trumped high. Dummy is then re-entered via the last trump. The Ace and King of Hearts are now cashed and declarer discards two spades. With each of the opponents having followed suit four times, dummy's fifth heart is now the sole surviving heart, and on it declarer discards his Queen of Spades. No finesse is necessary, which is just as well, for West held the King of Spades. The complete deal was:

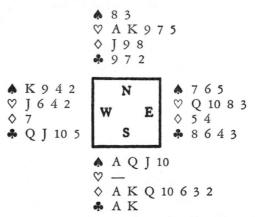

```
              ♠ 8 3
              ♡ A K 9 7 5
              ◇ J 9 8
              ♣ 9 7 2
♠ K 9 4 2        N          ♠ 7 6 5
♡ J 6 4 2    W     E        ♡ Q 10 8 3
◇ 7              S          ◇ 5 4
♣ Q J 10 5                  ♣ 8 6 4 3
              ♠ A Q J 10
              ♡ —
              ◇ A K Q 10 6 3 2
              ♣ A K
```

Admittedly the odds were against the eight adverse hearts being divided 4-4, (only 33%, according to the table). But it cost you absolutely nothing to ascertain whether they were divided favorably or not. If they were not split 4-4, you would have discovered it upon cashing the Ace and King of Hearts; and then, as a last resort as opposed to an only choice, you could still take the spade finesse. And, believe me, there is no bridge player in the world who can ever afford to turn up his nose at an additional 33% chance of fulfilling his contract.

D.

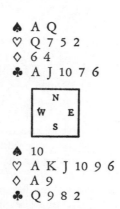

♠ A Q
♡ Q 7 5 2
◇ 6 4
♣ A J 10 7 6

♠ 10
♡ A K J 10 9 6
◇ A 9
♣ Q 9 8 2

South is playing a *six heart* contract, against which West opens the Diamond King, declarer's Ace winning. The Ace and King of trumps are then cashed, picking up the adverse trumps. Which finesse to take, the spade or the club?

If whichever finesse you take happens to lose, the opponents will then cash a diamond. Is it strictly a 50-50 proposition? The answer is "no."

The percentage play is to cash the Ace of Clubs first, with the outside hope that one of the opponents was dealt the singleton King. This is not too remote a possibility when you consider that only four clubs are missing. Should you drop the singleton King on this play, then there will be no problem. If you fail to drop the King, you then return to your own hand via a trump, and take the spade finesse. If it wins, then on the Ace of Spades you will discard your losing diamond. When you then concede a trick to the club King, the remainder of the tricks will be yours.

If the club King does not fall, and the spade finesse does not work, then declarer will be down two tricks instead of one. But surely the possibility of losing an extra 50 points should not influence your "percentage play" when the fulfillment of a small slam is at stake.

The actual deal was:

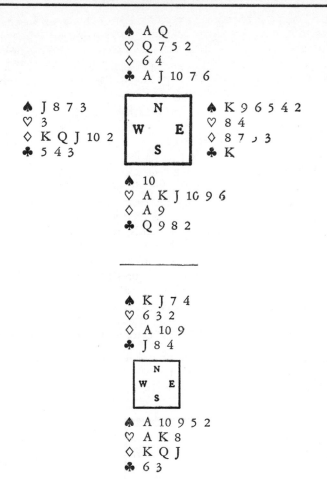

♠ A Q
♥ Q 7 5 2
♦ 6 4
♣ A J 10 7 6

♠ J 8 7 3
♥ 3
♦ K Q J 10 2
♣ 5 4 3

♠ K 9 6 5 4 2
♥ 8 4
♦ 8 7 ، 3
♣ K

♠ 10
♥ A K J 10 9 6
♦ A 9
♣ Q 9 8 2

E.

♠ K J 7 4
♥ 6 3 2
♦ A 10 9
♣ J 8 4

♠ A 10 9 5 2
♥ A K 8
♦ K Q J
♣ 6 3

The bidding:

South	West	North	East
One Spade	Two Clubs	Two Spades	Pass
Four Spades	Pass	Pass	Pass

Constant reference has been made in this chapter to "percentage plays" made without any clues having been derived from either the opponents' bidding or their play. Let us look at a deal where the opponents' play dictated that a normal percentage play should not be taken.

West opened the King of Clubs against South's *four spade* contract, then continued with the Ace of Clubs, East discarding a low diamond. West then shifted to the Queen of Hearts, declarer's King winning.

The normal play of a nine-card suit headed by the A K J is to play the Ace and King in the hope of catching the Queen (as opposed to finessing the Jack). But on this deal West had shown up with *seven clubs,* and was almost certainly sure to have the Q J of hearts for his shift to hearts. So nine of his cards were accounted for. The odds against his having exactly the Q x of spades were therefore remote. Putting it conservatively, East had started with twelve cards in spades, hearts and diamonds (he had but one club). West had started with only six cards in spades, hearts and diamonds. Take these 18 cards, shuffle them up, give West six of them (without looking) and give East the other 12 cards. Where does the Queen of Spades figure to be? The answer is: in the hand of 12 cards, just as if I took the pack of 52 cards, pulled one out face downward, and asked you: "In which pack is the Queen of Spades? Is it in the 51 remaining cards, or is it the card I pulled out?" Obviously it figures to be with the 51. Similarly (though the odds are not nearly so good), when the ratio is 6 to 12, the Queen figures to be with the 12 cards, and not with the six cards.

On this reasoning, at trick four, declarer led a spade to dummy's King, and then finessed East for the Queen. The complete deal was:

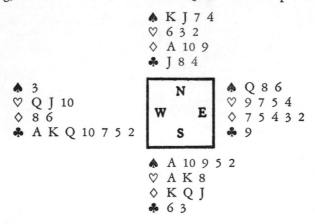

```
                 ♠ K J 7 4
                 ♡ 6 3 2
                 ◇ A 10 9
                 ♣ J 8 4

♠ 3                              ♠ Q 8 6
♡ Q J 10          N             ♡ 9 7 5 4
◇ 8 6          W     E          ◇ 7 5 4 3 2
♣ A K Q 10 7 5 2     S          ♣ 9

                 ♠ A 10 9 5 2
                 ♡ A K 8
                 ◇ K Q J
                 ♣ 6 3
```

F.

On the following deal, an "abnormal" percentage play almost exactly the same as on the preceding deal became the proper play, based on both the bidding and play by the opponents.

♠ K 9 6 3
♡ 6
◇ K J 8 6
♣ Q 10 8 3

♠ A J 10 8
♡ A 3
◇ A Q 10 2
♣ 7 6 4

The bidding (both sides vulnerable):

SOUTH	WEST	NORTH	EAST
One Diamond	One Heart	Two Diamonds	Pass
Two Spades	Four Hearts	Four Spades	Pass
Pass	Pass		

Against declarer's *four spade* contract West opened the King of Clubs, East playing the nine, and followed up with the Ace, East dropping the deuce. West then played a third round of clubs, East trumping.

East now returned a heart, South winning with the Ace. Since East had trumped a club, there were just four spades remaining in the opponents' hands and the normal play seemed to be to play the Ace and King to drop the Queen. But this was not the percentage play.

West's vigorous vulnerable bidding had clearly indicated at least a six-card suit, perhaps even a seven-card suit (no player in his right mind would jump to four hearts by himself on a five-card suit missing the Ace). The play to the first three club tricks proved that West had originally started with four clubs. So West had, at most, three cards in *both* diamonds and spades. East, on the other hand, had exactly two clubs, and at most four hearts. So East had at *least* seven cards in spades and diamonds. Again, if you take those 10 cards in spades and diamonds, give East seven of them and give West the remaining three, where would the Queen of Spades figure to be? No guarantee, of course, but East would be more likely to have it.

On this logic, after capturing East's heart return, declarer led a spade to dummy's King, and then finessed East for the Queen of Spades on the way back. The complete deal was:

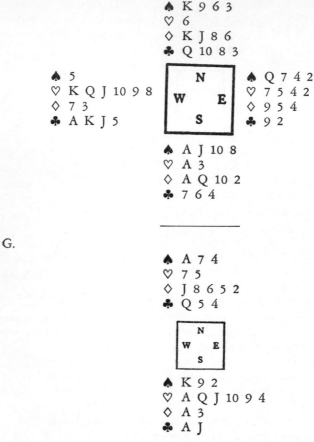

♠ K 9 6 3
♡ 6
◇ K J 8 6
♣ Q 10 8 3

♠ 5
♡ K Q J 10 9 8
◇ 7 3
♣ A K J 5

♠ Q 7 4 2
♡ 7 5 4 2
◇ 9 5 4
♣ 9 2

♠ A J 10 8
♡ A 3
◇ A Q 10 2
♣ 7 6 4

G.

♠ A 7 4
♡ 7 5
◇ J 8 6 5 2
♣ Q 5 4

♠ K 9 2
♡ A Q J 10 9 4
◇ A 3
♣ A J

This deal is one which, after you get through reading about it, might cause you to say: "Thank goodness every deal isn't like this. If it were, I wouldn't last out the evening." Actually, the deal is not a complex one, but it is most annoying since at trick one you have to decide which of several lines of play is the proper percentage play.

West opens the Queen of Spades against your *four heart* contract. Let us assume for the moment that you elect to capture the trick with dummy's Ace. Do you take the trump finesse or the club finesse? There is a 50% chance that East has the King of trumps and there's also a 50% chance that East has the King of Clubs. But, as between one or the other, the club finesse is the right play. If you take the heart finesse and it wins, you may not have gained anything since East might have held the K x x or the K x x x of Hearts originally and there then would be no way of avoiding the loss of a heart trick (you can not get back to dummy to finesse again). But if you take the club finesse and it wins, that is final: you have gained a trick. So the club finesse offers you a 50% chance of success (of winning a trick); the heart finesse less than 50%, since not only does the king have to be in the East hand, but it also has to be specifically a doubleton (K x) for South to avoid the loss of a heart trick.

There is available, however, a third line of play which is much superior to the 50% chance of a successful club finesse.

Why not win the opening lead *in your own hand with the King of Spades,* and then play the Ace of Clubs, followed by the Jack of Clubs, which the opposition will win with the King? Will you not now have the established Queen of Clubs in dummy, with the Spade Ace as an entry? And, when you later get to dummy, then on the Queen of Clubs you will discard the losing spade or the losing diamond.

The reader may raise the question: what if the Queen of Clubs is trumped? The answer is that for the Queen of Clubs to be trumped, the adverse clubs would have to be divided 6-2. If they are divided 4-4 or 5-3, will not the Queen of Clubs live? Take a look at the table on page 83. You will see there that when you and partner have five cards in a suit, the eight missing ones figure to be divided 4-4 about 33% of the time and 5-3 about 47% of the time. So 80% of the time your Queen of Clubs will not be trumped.

On this deal, then, it is not a matter of finding the perfect play. It is a matter of selecting the best of what's available — and I think the reader will agree that 80% is better than 50%. The actual deal was:

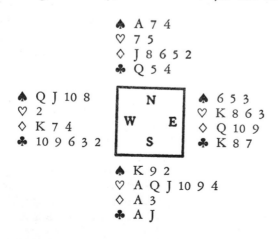

H.

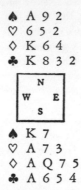

♠ A 9 2
♡ 6 5 2
◇ K 6 4
♣ K 8 3 2

♠ K 7
♡ A 7 3
◇ A Q 7 5
♣ A 6 5 4

One of the factors responsible for the "retarded" development of many bridge players is their reluctance to give up a trick even when necessity so demands. As an illustration, witness the above deal.

South arrived at a *three notrump contract* against which West opened the King of Hearts, which you permitted to hold the trick. The Queen of Hearts was then led, also winning, and the third round of the suit was captured by declarer's Ace. Everybody followed suit to these three rounds of hearts. (South's "hold-up" play is the theme of Chapter V.)

Declarer now perceived that he had eight tricks: two spades, one heart, three diamonds, and two clubs. He also saw that if the six missing diamonds were divided 3-3, his fourth diamond would be promoted into the ninth trick. He therefore promptly attacked the diamond suit, but East showed out on the third round of the suit. West now had himself a diamond trick, and when he ultimately obtained the lead with his Queen of Clubs, he also cashed the high diamond and the established heart:

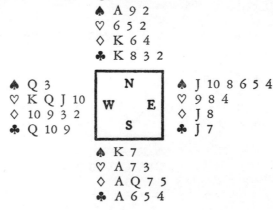

♠ A 9 2
♡ 6 5 2
◇ K 6 4
♣ K 8 3 2

♠ Q 3
♡ K Q J 10
◇ 10 9 3 2
♣ Q 10 9

♠ J 10 8 6 5 4
♡ 9 8 4
◇ J 8
♣ J 7

♠ K 7
♡ A 7 3
◇ A Q 7 5
♣ A 6 5 4

Declarer's play of attacking the diamond suit immediately was ill-advised, and was certainly not the percentage play. If the adverse diamonds were divided 3-3, they would still be divided 3-3 later, and declarer would always make his fourth diamond. He had nothing to create in the diamond suit.

Proper play was to attack his eight-card club suit first, playing for the probable 3-2 break. If this normal distribution existed, then his fourth club would become his ninth trick. There was absolutely no danger in giving away a club trick — there was just one heart outstanding, since everybody had followed to three rounds of that suit. But, for some reason, declarer was either unwilling or afraid to relinquish the lead in the club suit.

If the clubs had not broken 3-2, then declarer could always revert back to the diamond suit and hope that the adverse diamonds were divided 3-3. But when he played diamonds *first*, he established a diamond trick for West and it caused his downfall.

I.

The following is a deal which is simple — in retrospect only. I have used it frequently in teaching "play of the hand," and very few people ever play it correctly. Superficially, it appears that there is just one right way to play the hand — but on further examination it becomes evident that this "right" play can never win, and that a much superior line of play is available.

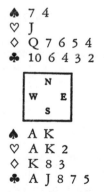

```
             ♠ 7 4
             ♡ J
             ◊ Q 7 6 5 4
             ♣ 10 6 4 3 2
                ┌─────────┐
                │    N    │
                │  W   E  │
                │    S    │
                └─────────┘
             ♠ A K
             ♡ A K 2
             ◊ K 8 3
             ♣ A J 8 7 5
```

Against South's *three notrump contract* West opens the six of spades, declarer's King capturing East's Jack.

The "automatic" play now is to lay down the Ace of Clubs, and then play another club to establish the suit. And the clubs do break 2-1, according to "percentage." A spade will then be played back, declarer's Ace winning, and his last stopper is gone.

If declarer now stops for reflection, it will suddenly dawn on him that he is facing imminent doom. He has eight tricks — two in spades, two in hearts, and four in clubs. But as soon as he leads a diamond to try for his ninth trick, whichever one of the opponents has the Ace will take it, and their established spade suit will be cashed for sufficient tricks to defeat declarer.

Had declarer been experienced enough to look ahead, he would have foreseen that by attacking clubs he would never have the time to develop nine tricks. Let us look at the deal before proceeding to the correct play.

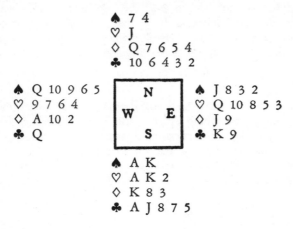

Proper play was to lead a diamond towards the Queen at trick two! If the Queen won, then declarer, in a certain sense, would have "stolen" a trick. Now he would switch to the club suit, and bring in his contract, making two spades, two hearts, one diamond and four clubs. If, on the diamond lead, West hopped up with his Ace, declarer would at that moment have his nine tricks: two spades, two hearts, *four* diamonds, and one club.

You may now be asking two questions: (1) What if East had the Ace of Diamonds, and (2) what if diamonds broke 4-1 instead of 3-2? In these cases, declarer would go down one trick. But the point is this, as a "percentage" situation: if declarer attacks the clubs first, *he can never make his contract*. By attacking diamonds first, the contract will be made if diamonds break 3-2 with West having the Ace, or if West has the Ace and does not take it on the lead toward the Queen.

How Any Suit Figures to be Divided

When the Combined Partnership Holding in a Suit is:	The Division of that Suit in Opponents' Hands Will Be:	Percentage of Time
5 Cards	4–4	33%
	5–3	47%
	6–2	17%
	7–1	3%
	8–0	0
6 Cards	4–3	62%
	5–2	30%
	6–1	7%
	7–0	1%
7 Cards	3–3	36%
	4–2	48%
	5–1	15%
	6–0	1%
8 Cards	3–2	68%
	4–1	28%
	5–0	4%
9 Cards	2–2	40%
	3–1	50%
	4–0	10%
10 Cards	2–1	78%
	3–0	22%
11 Cards	1–1	52%
	2–0	48%

NOTE WELL: These Percentages Apply Only When No Clues Relevant to the Distribution of the Opponents' Cards Have Been Divulged During Either the Bidding or Play.

THE SAFETY-PLAY

In a broad sense, a "safety-play" would be a play in which declarer is attempting to reduce to a minimum the risk of losing his contract. If defined in this manner every hand would naturally be reduced to finding the safety-play.

However, as the term "safety-play" is actually used in bridge, it refers specifically to *the play of a suit,* as opposed to the play of the entire hand. A safety-play is the play of a suit in such a manner as to either (1) protect against an abnormal or bad break in that suit, or (2) to avoid losing too many tricks in that suit. Where, for example, declarer can afford to lose *one* trick in a suit, but cannot afford to lose two tricks (which would mean the defeat of the contract), he will seek the safety-play to restrict his losers to but one trick. On occasion, declarer cannot afford to lose any tricks in a suit — and, again, he will try to find the perfect safety-play in the suit, if one exists. In most of these safety-play situations, declarer sacrifices a possible overtrick to attain his objective. And, when this is done, declarer is in effect taking out "insurance" against a bad break that would defeat his contract. The cost of the insurance is the payment of a possible overtrick.

Still speaking generally, the motive behind the quest for the safety-play — as far as the better players are concerned — is the recognition of one fact: *the fulfillment of the contract is the sole consideration,* and it is never jeopardized for the sake of an overtrick. Why the above is a *must* can be observed from the following scoring situation:

We	They
100	

On the previous deal "We" fulfilled a three notrump contract, accounting for the above score. Now, on the next deal, "We" find ourselves in a *six heart* contract, which, if made, will give us the game, rubber, and this score:

We	They
750	
700	
100	
180	

84

By addition, this totals to 1730 points. But suppose we play a bit optimistically, hoping to get an overtrick. And, upon receiving a "bad break" in a suit (to which we had not given even a passing thought), we now go down a trick. The score will then look like this:

We	They
	100
100	

The difference between the two results is 1730 points — which we have just lost. And why did we lose them? To pick up a possible 30 points, the value of an overtrick! The overtrick was not even the equivalent of interest on a principal — and we gambled away the principal to pick up the interest. That is certainly bad business — and equally bad bridge.

The recognition of when a safety-play is to be executed is not at all difficult. It does not require any special knowledge of card distribution, nor does it necessitate the ability to recognize certain specific-type situations (as for example, a squeeze or end-play). What the recognition does require, however, above all else, is the simple ability *to count your winning tricks* in order to see how many you have for sure, as related to how many you need. That is, if you have contracted for ten tricks and have ten tricks, you will not try for overtricks if in so doing you jeopardize your contract; if you have contracted for ten tricks and can count only nine sure winners, but can obtain the tenth trick by employing a safety-play, then common sense will tell you to avail yourself of the safety-play. As you will see from the deals that follow, the recognition of the safety-play necessitates nothing more than counting your winners and applying your powers of observation.

Getting more specific, the precise nature of a safety-play becomes quickly apparent when one examines the two principle types:

(1) The deliberate sacrifice of a possible extra trick in order to eliminate or minimize the risk of losing the contract.

(2) The handling of standard honor combinations *(especially in the trump suit)* in such a manner that the worst possible distribution of the opponents' cards in that suit can be taken care of without losing the contract.

The deals which follow, illustrating the safety-play, all arose in actual competition:

1.

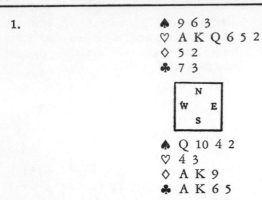

♠ 9 6 3
♡ A K Q 6 5 2
◇ 5 2
♣ 7 3

♠ Q 10 4 2
♡ 4 3
◇ A K 9
♣ A K 6 5

South is playing a *three notrump contract* against which West opens the Queen of Clubs, declarer's King winning. If South counts his winners, he will perceive that he needs *five* heart tricks to fulfill his contract. He therefore leads a low heart — and plays low from dummy! When everybody follows suit the contract is guaranteed no matter how the five adverse hearts were originally divided, for South's remaining heart will serve as an entry to cash dummy's hearts. The actual deal was:

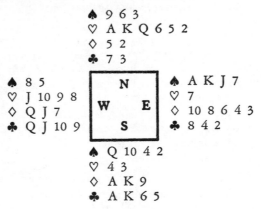

♠ 9 6 3
♡ A K Q 6 5 2
◇ 5 2
♣ 7 3

♠ 8 5
♡ J 10 9 8
◇ Q J 7
♣ Q J 10 9

♠ A K J 7
♡ 7
◇ 10 8 6 4 3
♣ 8 4 2

♠ Q 10 4 2
♡ 4 3
◇ A K 9
♣ A K 6 5

As is apparent, if the first heart lead is captured in dummy, when the second round of hearts is led and East shows out, none of dummy's low hearts can ever be cashed since dummy has no entry, and the game goes out of the window.

Admittedly, the five missing hearts figured to be divided 3-2. Had they been so distributed, declarer's play of "giving away" a heart trick would have cost an overtrick. But surely the insurance against a 4-1 break in hearts was worth the "sacrifice" of an extra 30 points.

2.

♠ 7 5 4
♡ Q 9 6 4
◇ A 8 4
♣ A K 3

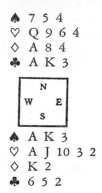

♠ A K 3
♡ A J 10 3 2
◇ K 2
♣ 6 5 2

You are South, playing a *four heart* contract. West opens the Jack of Clubs, dummy's King winning, and East drops the *Queen of Clubs*. How do you play the hand?

If you count your winners, you will see ten of them: two spades, four hearts, two diamonds, and two clubs. Or, if you elect to count losers, you have three of them, one spade, one heart, and one club. Your contract is therefore guaranteed unless something "unforeseen" happens — and the only "unforeseen" thing that ever happens at a suit contract is when an opponent suddenly trumps a sure winner.

So, with the safety of the contract being the *sole* consideration, you play a low trump, take it with the Ace, and return a trump. Nothing short of a hurricane can now prevent you from taking ten tricks no matter how the adverse hearts are divided. But, if you had taken the heart finesse, you would not have enjoyed the future of the hand:

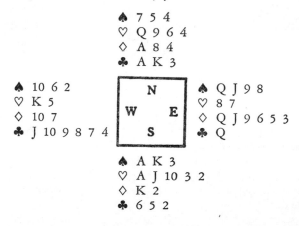

♠ 7 5 4
♡ Q 9 6 4
◇ A 8 4
♣ A K 3

♠ 10 6 2
♡ K 5
◇ 10 7
♣ J 10 9 8 7 4

♠ Q J 9 8
♡ 8 7
◇ Q J 9 6 5 3
♣ Q

♠ A K 3
♡ A J 10 3 2
◇ K 2
♣ 6 5 2

From South's point of view, when East played the Queen of Clubs on the opening lead, South should have been forewarned — the Queen was a singleton! If declarer then took the "normal" heart finesse, and it lost, West would surely return a club for East to ruff dummy's Ace (unless West did not see the Queen fall). Consequently, as far as declarer was concerned, the heart finesse was a pitfall to be avoided, since it endangered the safety of the contract.

As you get to be an expert player, even if East had played the deuce of clubs on the opening lead (instead of the Queen), you would not have taken the heart finesse, just in case something "unforeseen" might have happened if the finesse lost. As you will learn from bitter experience, whenever you relinquish the lead to the opponents while they still have trumps, dire consequences sometimes result.

It now being obvious that the heart finesse is to be avoided, here is the way the expert player would play it. He would lead the Queen of Hearts from dummy in order to entice East into "covering an honor with an honor." After all, the expert has no objection to making overtricks. But if the Queen is not covered, the expert would win it with his own Ace, and promptly return a heart, making haste to get rid of trumps — and, again, guaranteeing his contract.

3.

      ♠ A J 10 6 2
      ♡ 8 3 2
      ◊ 7 5
      ♣ 6 4 3

```
        N
      W   E
        S
```

      ♠ Q 5
      ♡ A K 5
      ◊ A K 4
      ♣ A 9 8 5 2

The contract is *three notrump* against which West opens the Jack of Diamonds, South's King winning. Upon examination, declarer sees that he needs *four* spade tricks to fulfill his contract.

At trick two he leads the Queen of Spades, West puts up the King — and a low spade is played from dummy! The contract is now fulfilled. Here is the deal:

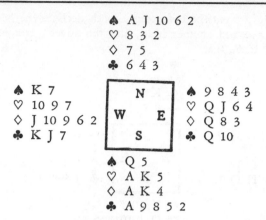

♠ A J 10 6 2
♡ 8 3 2
◇ 7 5
♣ 6 4 3

♠ K 7
♡ 10 9 7
◇ J 10 9 6 2
♣ K J 7

♠ 9 8 4 3
♡ Q J 6 4
◇ Q 8 3
♣ Q 10

♠ Q 5
♡ A K 5
◇ A K 4
♣ A 9 8 5 2

If dummy's Ace of Spades were to take West's King, then South could make but three spade tricks. By conceding a trick to the King, the contract is fulfilled whether the adverse spades break 3-3 or 4-2; by capturing the King with the Ace, the success of the contract *depends on spades breaking 3-3* — which they do not.

4.

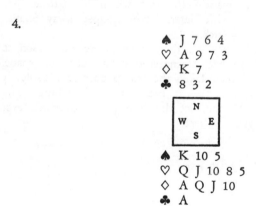

♠ J 7 6 4
♡ A 9 7 3
◇ K 7
♣ 8 3 2

♠ K 10 5
♡ Q J 10 8 5
◇ A Q J 10
♣ A

The bidding:

SOUTH	WEST	NORTH	EAST
One Heart	One Spade	Two Hearts	Pass
Four Hearts	Pass	Pass	Pass

After West has overcalled in spades, he opens the King of Clubs, South's Ace winning. Looking at the combined hands, South sees just *three* losers: two spades and one heart — unless something "unforeseen" happens. So, to prevent the unforeseen, South declines the heart finesse. He plays the Ace and another heart, and the adverse trumps are now removed. And that's that.

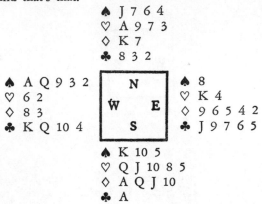

♠ J 7 6 4
♡ A 9 7 3
◊ K 7
♣ 8 3 2

♠ A Q 9 3 2
♡ 6 2
◊ 8 3
♣ K Q 10 4

♠ 8
♡ K 4
◊ 9 6 5 4 2
♣ J 9 7 6 5

♠ K 10 5
♡ Q J 10 8 5
◊ A Q J 10
♣ A

It is obvious what would have happened had declarer decided to try for an overtrick by taking the heart finesse. East, upon winning, would have returned his singleton spade — the suit which his partner had bid — and he would, a few tricks later, have trumped away South's King of Spades, for the setting trick.

Suppose West had not overcalled, there then being no reason to assume that East might have had a singleton or a doubleton spade. Should declarer, in this case, have taken the trump finesse? Absolutely not, for the contract was guaranteed if the risk of something being trumped were eliminated. Do not let the lure of an overtrick ever trap you into jeopardizing your contract.

5.

♠ K 6 5
♡ A 8 4
◊ Q J 10 9 3
♣ 8 3

♠ A Q 4
♡ K 7 2
◊ A 7 4 2
♣ A 7 6

You are South, playing a *three notrump contract*. West opens a low club, East puts up the Queen, and it wins the trick. The ten of clubs is then returned, you again hold-up, after which a third round of the suit is captured by your Ace. (South's "hold-up" play is the theme of Chap. V.)

It becomes quickly apparent that in order to fulfill the contract, you must make three diamond tricks. The "normal" play is to get to dummy, lead the Queen of Diamonds, and stake everything on the 50-50 chance of the finesse. But if it loses, West will then cash his established clubs.

You should avail yourself of some insurance on this deal. If West has the King of Diamonds protected (K x, K x x, K x x x) then nothing can prevent him from obtaining the lead and cashing his established clubs. But if he happens to have a singleton King, why give him a trick with it?

Therefore at trick four, you should lay down the Ace of Diamonds. If the Ace should happen to catch the King, then it is smooth sailing; if it does not, then you play another diamond. Should East have the King, then everything is fine, for East has no more clubs to return. If West still has the King, then you can attribute your defeat to "circumstances beyond your control." The complete deal was:

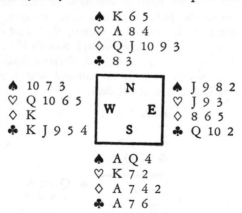

```
                    ♠ K 6 5
                    ♡ A 8 4
                    ◇ Q J 10 9 3
                    ♣ 8 3
♠ 10 7 3                              ♠ J 9 8 2
♡ Q 10 6 5          N                 ♡ J 9 3
◇ K              W     E              ◇ 8 6 5
♣ K J 9 5 4         S                 ♣ Q 10 2
                    ♠ A Q 4
                    ♡ K 7 2
                    ◇ A 7 4 2
                    ♣ A 7 6
```

The reader may question my statement, that "should East have the King, then everything's fine, for East has no more clubs to return." It is possible, of course, that East had four clubs originally, instead of three. If that were the case, then West had only four clubs to start with, and the contract would be assured. The point of this deal is the recognition of the fact that declarer should do everything in his power to prevent *West* from obtaining the lead. Hence the "insurance" or safety-play of the *Ace of Diamonds*.

6.

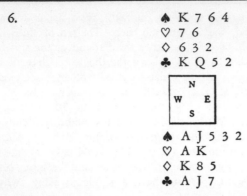

♠ K 7 6 4
♡ 7 6
◊ 6 3 2
♣ K Q 5 2

♠ A J 5 3 2
♡ A K
◊ K 8 5
♣ A J 7

Against South's *four spade contract*, West opens the Queen of Hearts, declarer's Ace winning. Potentially, South has four losers — three in diamonds and one in spades. But, if East can be kept out of the lead, then after trumps are drawn declarer can discard one of his losing diamonds on dummy's fourth club.

The normal play of a nine-card suit containing A K J in the combined hands is to play the Ace and King in the hope of catching the Queen, as opposed to finessing the Jack. [1] On this deal, however, if the plays of the Ace and King fail to drop the Queen, then East — should he have the Queen — may play a diamond through South's King.

So, after winning the opening heart lead, declarer leads a spade to dummy's King, after which a spade is returned and South's Jack is finessed. Let us now look at the actual deal:

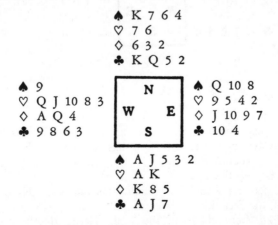

♠ K 7 6 4
♡ 7 6
◊ 6 3 2
♣ K Q 5 2

♠ 9
♡ Q J 10 8 3
◊ A Q 4
♣ 9 8 6 3

♠ Q 10 8
♡ 9 5 4 2
◊ J 10 9 7
♣ 10 4

♠ A J 5 3 2
♡ A K
◊ K 8 5
♣ A J 7

---

[1] See Chapter III, "The Percentage Play."

When South's Jack of Spades wins, it now becomes routine to play the Ace and drop the Queen, after which South also is able to discard a diamond on dummy's fourth club, thereby making an overtrick.

Suppose, however, that when South finessed the Jack of Spades, it lost to West's (hypothetical) Queen. Would not South now be assured of making his contract, since East could never obtain the lead, and South could always discard one of his diamonds on dummy's fourth club?

On the deal the "safety-play" involved giving up a trump trick *to West* — if the latter held the Queen — in order to safeguard the contract. In a sense, the proper play of a suit was dispensed with in the interests of the proper play of the entire hand. The trick which, hypothetically, might deliberately have been given away to West, would always be regained by being able to discard a losing diamond on North's fourth club.

7.

♠ 10 9 4
♡ A Q J
◊ A J 8 6 3
♣ 5 4

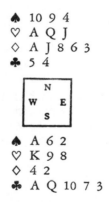

♠ A 6 2
♡ K 9 8
◊ 4 2
♣ A Q 10 7 3

South is playing a *three notrump contract,* West opening a low spade, with East's Queen being permitted to hold the opening lead. East returns a spade, West winning with the Jack and returning a spade, South capturing the trick with his Ace. On this trick, East fails to follow suit, discarding a low heart.

South's problem is a simple one: he must bring home four club tricks without permitting West to obtain the lead. He therefore gets to dummy, and leads a low club, putting up his Queen which holds the trick (If West has the King, South's defeat would — as on Deal 5 — be attributed to "circumstances beyond his control"). The dummy is then re-entered via the Ace of Hearts, to lead dummy's remaining club. Here is the deal in its entirety:

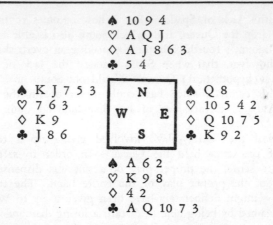

♠ 10 9 4
♡ A Q J
◇ A J 8 6 3
♣ 5 4

♠ K J 7 5 3
♡ 7 6 3
◇ K 9
♣ J 8 6

♠ Q 8
♡ 10 5 4 2
◇ Q 10 7 5
♣ K 9 2

♠ A 6 2
♡ K 9 8
◇ 4 2
♣ A Q 10 7 3

If on the second club lead East plays low, South's Ace wins, after which a third club is played, East's King winning. Declarer is now "home," for his two low clubs have become established.

If on the second club lead East puts up the King, he will be permitted to hold the trick. Now, no matter what East returns, South's Ace will drop the outstanding clubs, and again he will have his four club tricks.

If East had put up his club King on the *first* club lead, that too would have been permitted to win the trick. And, again, South would now bring home the suit without West ever obtaining the lead.

After South had successfully finessed the Club King on the first club lead, had he then laid down the Ace, East would have had it in his power to throw the King on the Ace, thereby establishing West's Jack as an entry. Hence the necessity of South getting to dummy to make the second club lead — to keep West out of the lead.

8.

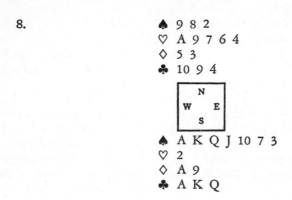

♠ 9 8 2
♡ A 9 7 6 4
◇ 5 3
♣ 10 9 4

♠ A K Q J 10 7 3
♡ 2
◇ A 9
♣ A K Q

The fact that South found himself in a *six spade* contract (rather than six notrump) after West had opened the bidding with *three hearts,* does not concern us. He probably was affected by his 150 honors.

Against the six spade contract West opened the King of Hearts, dummy's Ace was played — and East trumped! The defenders ultimately obtained a diamond trick to inflict a one-trick set on declarer.

Had South looked closely at both hands prior to playing to the first trick, or if he had recalled the bidding, he undoubtedly would have "played it safe." The King of Hearts should have been permitted to win the first trick (since the bidding had indicated that the danger did exist of East being void of hearts). The heart continuation by West would then have been trumped by declarer, after which the three missing trumps would have been drawn, ending up in dummy. Now, on the Ace of Hearts, the losing diamond would have been discarded with no danger of the trick being trumped. The actual deal was:

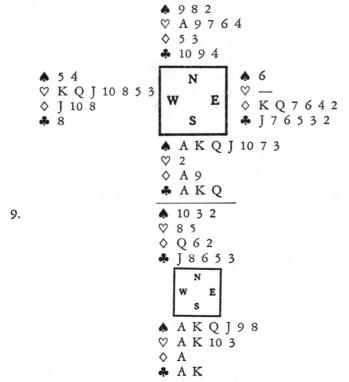

9.

The contract is *six spades* by South, against which West opens the seven of hearts, East's Jack falling to South's King. Can you find the safety-play on this hand? A clue is in order, since the hand is a difficult one: if you cash your Ace of Hearts, it will be ruffed — and you will ultimately go down one trick.

Proper play at trick two is to lead *a low heart,* which either of the opponents can, in theory, capture. No matter what they return they will be powerless to prevent you from ruffing the ten of hearts with dummy's ten of spades. After that trumps will be drawn, and the Ace of Hearts can then be cashed with complete safety. The reader might call this "highly-fancy" play, but on detailed examination he will recognize that it is merely a matter of playing a slam contract as safely as possible. The hands were:

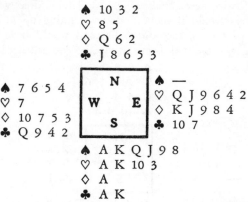

♠ 10 3 2
♡ 8 5
◇ Q 6 2
♣ J 8 6 5 3

♠ 7 6 5 4
♡ 7
◇ 10 7 5 3
♣ Q 9 4 2

W E

N

S

♠ —
♡ Q J 9 6 4 2
◇ K J 9 8 4
♣ 10 7

♠ A K Q J 9 8
♡ A K 10 3
◇ A
♣ A K

If South tries to cash the heart Ace at trick two, West will ruff. Later, when South tries to ruff a low heart in dummy, West will ruff again, forcing dummy's ten-spot to overruff. Now declarer will have a losing heart which he will be unable to ruff out since West's remaining trumps will be higher than dummy's.

10.

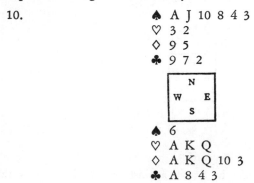

♠ A J 10 8 4 3
♡ 3 2
◇ 9 5
♣ 9 7 2

N

W E

S

♠ 6
♡ A K Q
◇ A K Q 10 3
♣ A 8 4 3

You are sitting South, playing a *three notrump contract,* against which West opens the Jack of Hearts, taken by your Queen. How do you plan to play the hand?

The correct approach is to cash the Ace of Diamonds, and then lead the three-spot toward the nine. Whatever happens from here in, you are assured of one spade trick, three hearts, four diamonds and one club.

If instead, you cash the Ace and King of Diamonds, you might lose your contract — as our actual declarer did. Here is the deal:

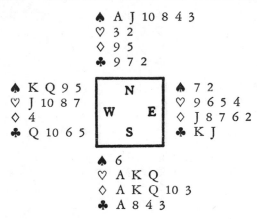

```
                ♠ A J 10 8 4 3
                ♡ 3 2
                ♢ 9 5
                ♣ 9 7 2

  ♠ K Q 9 5          N          ♠ 7 2
  ♡ J 10 8 7                     ♡ 9 6 5 4
  ♢ 4           W        E       ♢ J 8 7 6 2
  ♣ Q 10 6 5         S          ♣ K J

                ♠ 6
                ♡ A K Q
                ♢ A K Q 10 3
                ♣ A 8 4 3
```

The above safety-play is designed to protect against either hand holding five diamonds headed by the Jack. Admittedly this distribution is not likely to exist — but then, safety plays are used to take care of improbable distributions.

11.

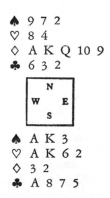

```
                ♠ 9 7 2
                ♡ 8 4
                ♢ A K Q 10 9
                ♣ 6 3 2

                    N
                W        E
                    S

                ♠ A K 3
                ♡ A K 6 2
                ♢ 3 2
                ♣ A 8 7 5
```

Three notrump is the final contract, against which West opens the heart Queen. The safety-play on this hand is to find the line of play which will offer the best chance of cashing four diamond tricks. Normally, with the above hand, by playing the Ace, King, and Queen of Diamonds, you figure to drop the Jack. But in this case, since dummy has no entry, correct play at trick two is to lead a low diamond, putting up dummy's nine-spot when West follows suit. No matter how the adverse diamonds were distributed originally, four diamond tricks are now guaranteed. The complete deal was:

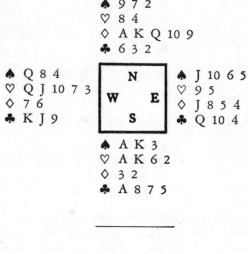

```
                 ♠ 9 7 2
                 ♡ 8 4
                 ◇ A K Q 10 9
                 ♣ 6 3 2
    ♠ Q 8 4          N          ♠ J 10 6 5
    ♡ Q J 10 7 3   W   E        ♡ 9 5
    ◇ 7 6              S         ◇ J 8 5 4
    ♣ K J 9                      ♣ Q 10 4
                 ♠ A K 3
                 ♡ A K 6 2
                 ◇ 3 2
                 ♣ A 8 7 5
```

12.

```
                 ♠ A 6
                 ♡ K 10 8 3
                 ◇ 6
                 ♣ A Q 10 9 6 3
                      N
                   W     E
                      S
                 ♠ Q 10 8 4 3
                 ♡ A 5 2
                 ◇ A J 2
                 ♣ K 8
```

South arrives at a *three notrump contract,* against which West opens the diamond five, East's King being taken by declarer's Ace. It is apparent that if East ever gets the lead and returns a diamond through South's J x, South will be in sad shape.

To prevent East from obtaining the lead, declarer gets to dummy via the King of hearts, and leads a low club, putting up *the eight* from his own hand. If the eight-spot wins, both opponents following suit, the contract is now guaranteed. If West wins the trick with the Jack, whatever he returns cannot harm declarer, since the J x of diamonds constitutes protection against West. (If West returns a spade, dummy's Ace wins, and the Ace of Clubs is then played, South's King falling, after which North takes the remainder of the clubs.) Here are all four hands:

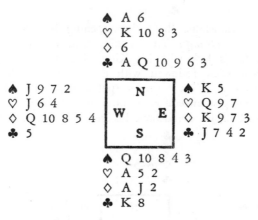

At this point, permit me to remind the reader again that the safety-play will very frequently lose a trick which normally need not be lost. Remember, however, that the safety-play is insurance against a bad break in that suit, and the payment is quite often a trick. On the previous deal, for example, there is no question but that the normal division of the five adverse clubs figured to be 3-2, in which case, by playing the King, Queen and Ace of Clubs, declarer would capture all the adverse clubs without loss of a trick. But to protect against East having the J x x x of clubs, declarer was willing to concede a trick to guarantee his contract.

The extreme use to which a safety-play is on occasion employed can be evidenced from the following deal which arose some years ago at the Cavendish Club in New York City. The South declarer was Peter Leventritt, one of the nation's top-ranking players:

13.

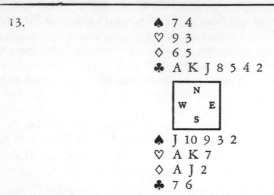

♠ 7 4
♡ 9 3
◊ 6 5
♣ A K J 8 5 4 2

♠ J 10 9 3 2
♡ A K 7
◊ A J 2
♣ 7 6

After North's vulnerable three club opening bid, South contracted for game at *three notrump.* The opening lead was a low heart, and Peter captured East's Jack with his King. He then led the seven of clubs, and when West followed with the three-spot, *the deuce was played from dummy!* When the seven-spot won the trick, East showing out, ten tricks were guaranteed. Had South put up the Jack from dummy on the first club lead, he would have lost his contract! The deal was:

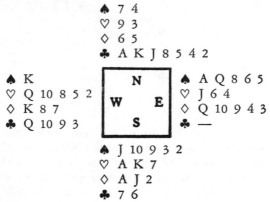

♠ 7 4
♡ 9 3
◊ 6 5
♣ A K J 8 5 4 2

♠ K
♡ Q 10 8 5 2
◊ K 8 7
♣ Q 10 9 3

♠ A Q 8 6 5
♡ J 6 4
◊ Q 10 9 4 3
♣ —

♠ J 10 9 3 2
♡ A K 7
◊ A J 2
♣ 7 6

The reader may wonder what South would have done had West put up the ten (or the Queen) on the opening lead. Knowing Mr. Leventritt as I do, I can assure you that he would have permitted West to win the trick, to protect against West having started with all four clubs. He needed six club tricks (not seven) to fulfill his contract, and he would have been perfectly happy to give one club trick away, if in so doing he were able to guarantee his contract.

All the safety-plays which have been presented up to this point have been plays in which declarer did not necessarily have to lose a trick in a particular suit, but he voluntarily chose to sacrifice a possible trick in order to increase his chances of fulfilling his contract. The reader should have no difficulty applying the above type of safety play once he learns *to count his tricks*.

The two "safety-play" deals which follow are of a type frequently encountered, and are actually quite fundamental and simple. Nevertheless, the average bridge player too often tends to go wrong in his play of these rather obvious situations. The type of play referred to is in a suit where it is apparent that *one trick must be lost for sure*, no matter how favorably the adverse cards in that suit are distributed. The point of the safety-play on these deals is *to avoid the loss of two tricks*.

14.

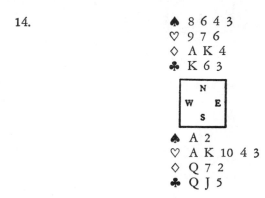

♠ 8 6 4 3
♡ 9 7 6
◇ A K 4
♣ K 6 3

♠ A 2
♡ A K 10 4 3
◇ Q 7 2
♣ Q J 5

Against South's *four heart contract*, West opens the Queen of Spades, declarer's Ace winning. Declarer then lays down the Ace of Hearts, everybody following suit. The "normal" play now (which is wrong) is to next lay down the King, since mathematics say that when five of a suit are missing, they will be divided 3-2 in the hands of the opponents. [2] If that is done, declarer will go down on this deal — and the fault will be his.

When everybody follows to the first lead of hearts, three hearts are still missing: the Q J x. Is it not obvious that one heart trick *must* be lost? Why then not get to dummy via the King of Diamonds, and lead a low heart. If East plays low, then South's ten-spot will be inserted. The ten-spot will either win (if East originally started with Q J x x), or it will be captured by West with the Queen or Jack. If the latter occurs, then will not there be just one heart now outstanding — and will not declarer's King drop it as soon as he obtains the lead?

---

[2] See Chapter III, "The Percentage Play."

The safety-play is designed to guard against East having started with Q J x x. If the hearts are divided 3-2, then nothing has been lost and nothing gained by conceding the second heart trick instead of the third. If West has the Q J x x, then nothing could ever have prevented West from winning two heart tricks. The complete deal was:

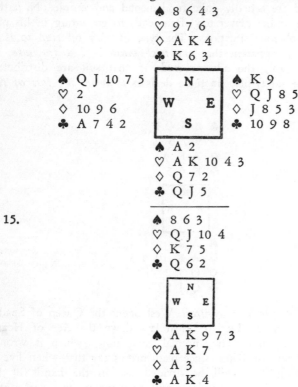

	♠ 8 6 4 3	
	♡ 9 7 6	
	◇ A K 4	
	♣ K 6 3	
♠ Q J 10 7 5	N	♠ K 9
♡ 2	W E	♡ Q J 8 5
◇ 10 9 6	S	◇ J 8 5 3
♣ A 7 4 2		♣ 10 9 8
	♠ A 2	
	♡ A K 10 4 3	
	◇ Q 7 2	
	♣ Q J 5	

15.

```
              ♠ 8 6 3
              ♡ Q J 10 4
              ◇ K 7 5
              ♣ Q 6 2
                 N
              W     E
                 S
              ♠ A K 9 7 3
              ♡ A K 7
              ◇ A 3
              ♣ A K 4
```

South is declarer at a *six spade contract*, with West opening the ten of clubs, South's King winning. Surveying the combined hands, declarer perceives that things look good; that the spades figure to be divided 3-2, in which case one spade trick will be conceded, and declarer's slam will then be guaranteed.

Declarer therefore starts drawing trumps — and on the lead of the Ace, West drops the *Queen!* If West started with the Q J or the Q J 10, then it makes no difference what trump declarer plays next, for he will lose no more than one trump trick; but if the Queen is a singleton, and declarer follows up by leading the King of trumps, then two tricks will inevitably be lost to East's J 10.

So, to protect against East having started with the J 10 x x, declarer next leads a low spade to dummy's eight spot. Here is the deal:

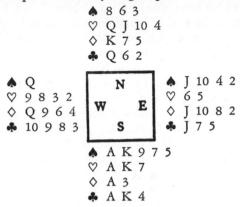

♠ 8 6 3
♡ Q J 10 4
♢ K 7 5
♣ Q 6 2

♠ Q
♡ 9 8 3 2
♢ Q 9 6 4
♣ 10 9 8 3

♠ J 10 4 2
♡ 6 5
♢ J 10 8 2
♣ J 7 5

♠ A K 9 7 5
♡ A K 7
♢ A 3
♣ A K 4

As the reader can perceive, East will win the trick with the ten-spot, but now his J 4 will be hopelessly trapped by declarer's K 9, and the defenders will get no more tricks in this suit.

The same effect could have been achieved if, after seeing West drop the Spade Queen, declarer had entered dummy via a side suit, and led a low spade off dummy toward his nine-spot. Although this would have been a reasonably safe line of play, it involved the slight risk of East possibly trumping your side suit lead to dummy.

16.   The following deal presents a situation not too often encountered, in which declarer was faced with the certainty of losing *two trump tricks,* but he could not afford to lose three trump tricks. If you, on occasion, find yourself playing a hand in a bad trump suit (and who hasn't?), it is worthwhile earmarking this play for future availability.

♠ A
♡ A 8 6 3
♢ A K 9 7 2
♣ A 8 4

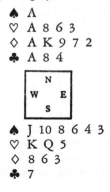

♠ J 10 8 6 4 3
♡ K Q 5
♢ 8 6 3
♣ 7

Against South's *four spade contract* West opened the Club Jack, dummy's Ace winning, after which dummy's Ace of trumps was cashed. South then got to his hand via the King of Hearts, and led the *Jack of Spades*. He went down a trick, losing three spades and a diamond.

South's mistake came at trick four, when he led the Jack of Spades. He should have led a low spade, preserving the J 10. The low spade lead would limit his trump losers to but two if either opponent held the K x or Q x. If the original spades which the opponents held were divided 3-3 (K x x . . . Q x x, etc.), then whether South led a low spade or the Jack would be immaterial since he would automatically lose no more than two spade tricks. To protect against a 4-2 break, however, with the K x or Q x in either hand, the low spade lead was the only correct play since it had everything to gain and nothing to lose.

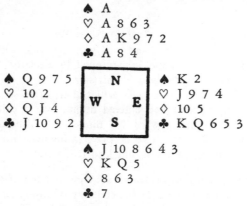

On Page 85, the two principal types of safety-plays were given:

(1) The deliberate (and willing) sacrifice of a possible trick to eliminate, or minimize, the risk of losing one's contract.

(2) The handling of standard honor combinations (especially in the trump suit) in such a way that the worst possible distribution of the opponents' cards in that suit can be taken care of without losing the contract.

Type (1) has been presented pretty much in detail on Deals 1-13, inclusive. On Deals 14 and 15 were illustrated two additional situations, in which declarer had to inevitably lose a trick in the suit he was trying to establish, but could not afford to lose two tricks in that suit; and it became a matter of *when* he should lose that trick. On Deal 16, the problem was really an extension of the situation on Deals 14 and 15: declarer had two sure losers in his trump suit, and it became a question of finding a safety-play which would minimize the danger of losing three tricks in that suit.

We now come to the discussion and illustration of the second-type of safety-play, namely, the handling of *standard honor combinations,* especially in the trump suit, in such a way as to obtain the desired result if it is humanly possible to do so. In the six deals which follow, standard safety-plays pertaining to *nine-card suits only* is discussed.

THE HANDLING OF STANDARD HONOR COMBINATIONS

Deal 17, which follows, arose in a rubber bridge game. The number of points lost by declarer because he failed to employ the safety-play was a staggering amount.

17.
♠ A 9 4
♡ A Q 5
◇ 10 7 3 2
♣ A 8 6

```
        N
    W       E
        S
```

♠ K Q 10 7 6 3
♡ K 9 8
◇ A
♣ K Q 3

South's contract was *seven spades,* against which West opened the King of Diamonds, which declarer's Ace captured. Declarer then led a trump to dummy's Ace — and when East showed out, declarer was down a trick. Let us look at the score as it would have been had he fulfilled his absolutely-guaranteed contract, and what the final score was after he went down, and the opponents ultimately won the rubber by making a small slam.

	(1)			(2)	
We	They		We	They	
				750	
1500				500	
700				100	
120			120		
210				100	
				180	

The difference between winning and losing the rubber was 4040 points! "We" lost those points because "We" took it for granted that the four missing spades would be divided normally; "We" forgot to think about whether a safety-play could be found to take care of the extreme situation where trumps were divided 4-0, instead of 3-1 or 2-2.

Proper play of the trump suit was to play the King (or Queen) first. *If* either opponent had the J x x x originally, he would be discovered when his partner failed to follow suit; and he would then be finessed out of his Jack. If trumps were divided 2-2, or 3-1, then declarer could never lose a trump trick, even if he were the world's worst player . . . 4040 points! Ouch!

The actual deal was:

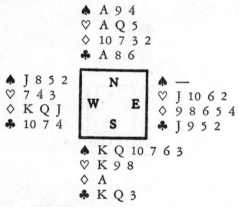

The exact same safety-play is available for use on all of the following honor-card combinations:

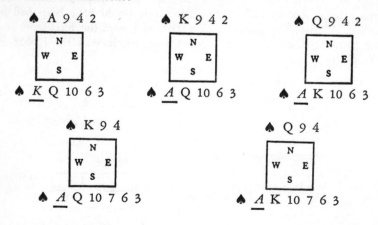

In each of the above situations the underlined honor is the correct play, with no danger of ever losing a trick in the suit. The reader will do well to study these illustrations and earmark them for future reference, since they arise very frequently.

18. The safety-play employed on this deal might be called a variation of the one used on Deal 17. However, in this situation, the ten-spot is missing — and it makes a world of a difference.

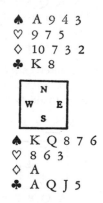

    ♠ A 9 4 3
    ♡ 9 7 5
    ◊ 10 7 3 2
    ♣ K 8

    ♠ K Q 8 7 6
    ♡ 8 6 3
    ◊ A
    ♣ A Q J 5

Against South's *four spade* contract, West cashes the A K Q of hearts and then shifts to a diamond, declarer's Ace winning.

If the four missing trumps are divided 2-2, or 3-1, it makes no difference whether the King is led first, or the Ace from dummy, for with the "normal" distribution existing South will never lose a trump trick. Therefore the "safety-play-conscious" declarer raises the question: what if one of the opponents has the four missing trumps: J 10 5 2?

On analysis of the above — which from now on should become a "pat" situation — if *West* has the four missing trumps, *he will always make a trump trick,* no matter how declarer plays it, since West's ten-spot can always force out dummy's Ace. But if East has the J 10 5 2 of spades, then by leading to the Ace first, East's J 10 5 2 can be finessed through twice, and declarer avoids the loss of a spade trick. Therefore *the lead to the Ace is the only correct play:* it will gain whenever East has the missing trumps; it will never be a losing play, since if West has the four missing trumps declarer could never have done anything about it. If the King is led originally, a trick will be lost if East has the four missing spades. Here are the four hands:

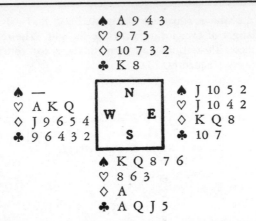

♠ A 9 4 3
♡ 9 7 5
◇ 10 7 3 2
♣ K 8

♠ —
♡ A K Q
◇ J 9 6 5 4
♣ 9 6 4 3 2

♠ J 10 5 2
♡ J 10 4 2
◇ K Q 8
♣ 10 7

♠ K Q 8 7 6
♡ 8 6 3
◇ A
♣ A Q J 5

As is readily apparent, if we interchange the Ace with the King or Queen, the situation remains the same: with the J 10 x x in the opponents' hands, the first lead is made *towards* the single honor.

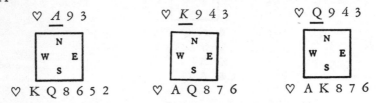

♡ *A* 9 3

♡ K Q 8 6 5 2

♡ *K* 9 4 3

♡ A Q 8 7 6

♡ *Q* 9 4 3

♡ A K 8 7 6

In each of the above illustrations, the underlined card is the correct card to play on the first lead.

19.

♠ 7 4 2
♡ K 9
◇ 6 5 3
♣ A Q 10 7 6

♠ A K Q 3
♡ A 5
◇ A J 8
♣ 9 8 5 3

West, on lead against South's *three notrump contract*, opens the seven of hearts, East's Jack being taken by South's Ace. Declarer then leads a club, West follows with a low club — and declarer deliberates: should he finesse the Queen or the Ten? Let us say he finesses the Queen, which loses to East's King, and a heart is then returned, dummy's King winning. Again a problem for declarer arises: shall he lay down the Ace of Clubs, to drop the Jack? Or shall he return to his own hand and finesse dummy's ten-spot? If he guesses right he will make his contract; if he guesses wrong, the opponents will obtain the lead to run their established hearts.

The above situation in the club suit is a standard type of "safety-play" which is employed to give declarer his maximum chance of obtaining four tricks in a suit. The correct play is first to lay down the Ace in the hope of catching the King or a Jack in the East hand. If he does catch an honor, four tricks are assured. If he does not, then he returns to his own hand and leads a low one towards the Queen. The only time declarer will not make four tricks in the suit is when East started with the K J x or K J x x, in which case four tricks could *never* have been made. The deal was:

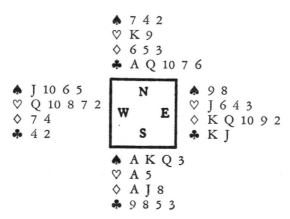

Let us examine this specific situation in a little more detail, since it is a very frequent trump holding in the combined hands:

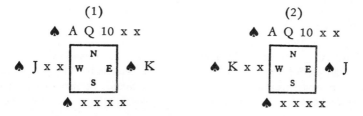

(3)

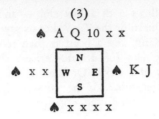

As the reader can perceive in the three above situations, if declarer guesses right in finessing he will make four or more spade tricks; if he does not, he will make but three tricks. If *four tricks are needed, then by playing the Ace, first, instead of finessing, declarer will always make them if they are makable.* That is, East will never make either a singleton King, a singleton Jack, or both the King and Jack if he holds the K J doubleton.

You may wonder as to what happens when the Ace is cashed if East shows out. Nothing, except momentary fright — and then the realization that four tricks can still be made. To illustrate:

♠ *A* Q 10 x x

♠ K J x x   ♠ —

♠ x x x x

South now returns to his own hand via some other suit, and leads towards the remaining Q 10 x x, trapping West's Jack. Later on, South again returns to his own hand to finesse West out of his Jack — and he makes four spade tricks.

When the above combination exists and all *five tricks* are needed, the superior play is to finesse the Queen immediately, and hope that West originally started with K x and East with the J x. With five tricks needed, there is no safety-play; mathematically, however, the finesse of the Queen is superior to all other plays.

Precisely the same situation develops when the nine cards of a suit headed by A Q 10 are divided either 6-3 or 7-2, instead of 5-4, and declarer can afford to lose *only one trick* in the suit. These are also relatively normal trump distributions, and should be earmarked for future reference:

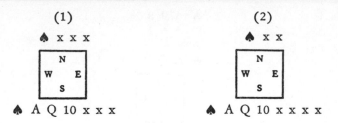

Play the Ace first in (1) and (2) to drop a singleton Jack or King in the West hand. If no honor drops, return to the North hand to lead a low one:

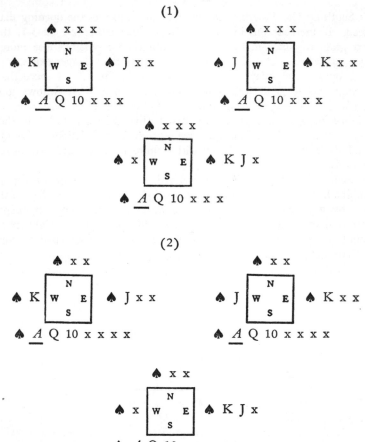

20.

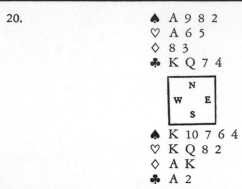

♠ A 9 8 2
♥ A 6 5
♦ 8 3
♣ K Q 7 4

♠ K 10 7 6 4
♥ K Q 8 2
♦ A K
♣ A 2

South arrives at a *six spade contract,* and captures the opening diamond lead. If the four missing spades are divided either 2-2 or 3-1, there is no problem, since in these cases South cannot possibly lose more than one spade trick. But if they are divided 4-0, then danger exists.

Proper "safety-play" technique — to avoid the loss of more than one trump trick — is to lead a low one, and when West follows low, the *eight-spot* is played from dummy. Either the eight will win, or the eight-spot will be captured by East's (hypothetical) Jack. If the Jack wins, then there remain but two spades in circulation — the Q x — and declarer's Ace and King will capture them on the two succeeding rounds.

South's concern, as was mentioned, was that one of the opponents might have started with the four missing trumps. When West followed to the first spade lead, then *he alone* became the only opponent who might have held four spades. Hence the play of the eight-spot from dummy, as protection against West having held four spades originally.

The hands were:

♠ A 9 8 2
♥ A 6 5
♦ 8 3
♣ K Q 7 4

♠ Q J 5 3
♥ J 4
♦ J 10 9 5 2
♣ J 6

♠ —
♥ 10 9 7 3
♦ Q 7 6 4
♣ 10 9 8 5 3

♠ K 10 7 6 4
♥ K Q 8 2
♦ A K
♣ A 2

The reader might raise the point that the same result could be obtained by first laying down the King, and observing that East has no spades, West would be held to just one spade trick. All well and good on this deal, but what if *West* showed out on the lead of the King, thereby marking East with an original holding of Q J x x? With either of the following, if it is essential to win *four tricks:*

(1)

♠ A 9 8 2

(2)

♠ K 9 8 2

♠ K 10 7 6 4

♠ A 10 7 6 4

proper play is to lead low from either hand, and if second hand also plays low, to play either the nine or ten third-hand. Of course, if second hand puts up the Queen or Jack, the winning of four tricks becomes routine.

21.

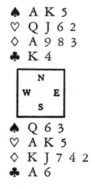

♠ A K 5
♡ Q J 6 2
◇ A 9 8 3
♣ K 4

♠ Q 6 3
♡ A K 5
◇ K J 7 4 2
♣ A 6

The contract is *six notrump.* West opens the Queen of Clubs which you win with the King. How would you play the diamond suit, needing three diamond tricks to guarantee the contract? . . . If you elect to play the Ace first, you will lose a slam!

Here again, as on the previous deal, your "worry" is that somebody might have the four missing diamonds (Q 10 x x). The reader can see what will happen if the Diamond Ace is led first and West started with the Q 10 x x of diamonds — two tricks will have to be lost in the suit. The deal was:

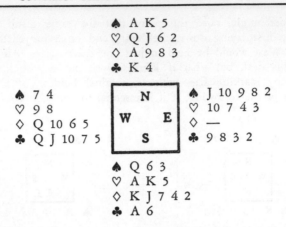

```
              ♠ A K 5
              ♡ Q J 6 2
              ◇ A 9 8 3
              ♣ K 4
♠ 7 4           ┌─────────┐        ♠ J 10 9 8 2
♡ 9 8           │    N    │        ♡ 10 7 4 3
◇ Q 10 6 5      │ W     E │        ◇ —
♣ Q J 10 7 5    │    S    │        ♣ 9 8 3 2
                └─────────┘
              ♠ Q 6 3
              ♡ A K 5
              ◇ K J 7 4 2
              ♣ A 6
```

With three diamond tricks being needed, correct play is to lay down the diamond *King* first. This will guarantee four tricks in the suit, no matter who has all the missing diamonds.

Suppose West does not follow on the lead of the Diamond King? South's next play will be a diamond to dummy's Ace, and a third round will then be led off dummy. All East can ever make will be his Queen:

```
            ◇ A 9 8 3
                ┌───────┐
◇ —             │   N   │      ◇ Q 10 6 5
                │ W   E │
                │   S   │
                └───────┘
            ◇ K J 7 4 2
```

Interchanging the Ace and King, the "safety-play" of leading the top honor from the hand that contains two honors remains the same: that is, the Ace is led.

```
            ◇ K 9 8 3
                ┌───────┐
                │   N   │
                │ W   E │
                │   S   │
                └───────┘
            ◇ A J 7 4 2
```

22.

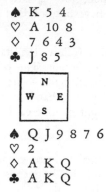

♠ K 5 4
♡ A 10 8
◇ 7 6 4 3
♣ J 8 5

♠ Q J 9 8 7 6
♡ 2
◇ A K Q
♣ A K Q

When this deal was actually played, South arrived at a *six spade contract*, against which West opened the Jack of Diamonds, South's Queen winning. A low spade was then led to dummy's King — and East showed out. Declarer now had to lose two trump tricks, since West had started with A 10 x x.

Had South been "safety-play-conscious," he would have protected against West (or East) having held the four missing spades. This could have been accomplished by leading the Queen first. Then, if it were revealed that either opponent held the four outstanding spades, that opponent would have been finessed out of his ten-spot. The complete deal was:

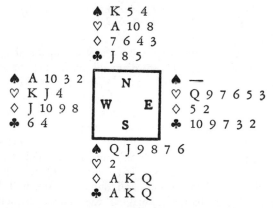

♠ K 5 4
♡ A 10 8
◇ 7 6 4 3
♣ J 8 5

♠ A 10 3 2
♡ K J 4
◇ J 10 9 8
♣ 6 4

♠ —
♡ Q 9 7 6 5 3
◇ 5 2
♣ 10 9 7 3 2

♠ Q J 9 8 7 6
♡ 2
◇ A K Q
♣ A K Q

If South had played the Queen first, for a "look-see," then whether West took his Ace or not, South's second trump lead would have been the nine-spot, trapping West's ten. Had East been the one to show up with four spades, then, too, a later lead of a low spade from dummy would effectively have finessed East out of his ten-spot.

On the four deals which follow, the standard safety-plays pertaining to 8 *card suits only* are presented. The occasions for the utilization of these plays — as with nine-card suits — are quite numerous in occurrence, since whenever one is playing a hand in a trump suit, he usually finds that his trump suit is of eight or nine card length.

23.   All the cards in this deal are virtually the same as in Deal 21, except that the North-South holding consists of eight diamonds rather than the nine previously discussed.

♠ A K 5
♥ Q J 6 2
♦ A 9 8 3
♣ K 4

♠ Q 6 3
♥ A K 5
♦ K J 4 2
♣ A 6 2

Against South's *six notrump* contract, West opens the Club Queen, declarer's Ace winning. Three diamond tricks are needed to fulfill the contract — and they are *absolutely guaranteed* if the suit is properly played.

At trick two, the King of Diamonds is laid down, both opponents following suit. Then comes a low diamond, West following low — and the nine-spot is put up from dummy! Either the nine-spot will win, in which case it becomes declarer's third diamond winner; or the nine-spot will be captured by East's ten or Queen, in which case diamonds will have broken 3-2, and dummy's Ace will later pick up the opponents' last diamond, making the fourth diamond a winner. The safety-play here is designed to protect against West having the Q 10 x x or the Q 10 x x x of diamonds, in which case an original play of the Ace from dummy will lose two tricks. The deal was:

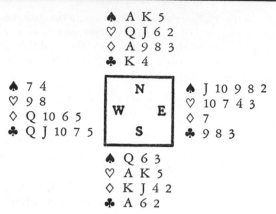

```
              ♠ A K 5
              ♡ Q J 6 2
              ◇ A 9 8 3
              ♣ K 4
♠ 7 4          ┌─────────┐    ♠ J 10 9 8 2
♡ 9 8          │    N    │    ♡ 10 7 4 3
◇ Q 10 6 5     │ W     E │    ◇ 7
♣ Q J 10 7 5   │    S    │    ♣ 9 8 3
              └─────────┘
              ♠ Q 6 3
              ♡ A K 5
              ◇ K J 4 2
              ♣ A 6 2
```

Again, if East were the one who held the Q 10 x x or Q 10 x x x of diamonds, three tricks would be guaranteed on the original play of the King, for West would show out on the first or second round of the suit, dummy's Ace winning the second lead, after which a third round of the suit would now be led from dummy. Declarer's Jack would then become his third winner in the suit.

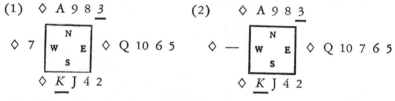

(1)   ◇ A 9 8 *3*

◇ 7   ┌ N ┐   ◇ Q 10 6 5
      │W E│
      └ S ┘
      ◇ *K J* 4 2

(2)   ◇ A 9 8 *3*

◇ —   ┌ N ┐   ◇ Q 10 7 6 5
      │W E│
      └ S ┘
      ◇ *K J* 4 2

24.   This safety play is virtually the same as on the preceding deal, the situation being that declarer is willing to lose one trick in his suit, but cannot afford to lose two tricks.

```
              ♠ A 8 4
              ♡ K Q 6
              ◇ 7 5 3 2
              ♣ A Q 7
              ┌─────────┐
              │    N    │
              │ W     E │
              │    S    │
              └─────────┘
              ♠ K J 9 7 5
              ♡ A J 2
              ◇ A K
              ♣ K 8 3
```

Against South's *six spade contract,* West opens the Jack of Diamonds, declarer's King winning. The "normal" play is to lead a spade to the Ace, followed by a spade off dummy, with the probable intention of finessing the Jack. And if East fails to follow to the second round of spades, declarer will go down.

To digress for a brief moment, I should like to point out that safety-plays were not invented by some theoretician who sat down at his desk and decided to invent them. Safety-plays arose out of the experience — and errors — of the better players, who, upon making a mistake as our "normal" declarer might have just done, discovered their error and analyzed it. They did not make the same error again, for out of the understanding of their mistake they learned to take out insurance against the improbable (distribution) happening. Thus safety-plays were born.

On the above deal, after winning the opening diamond lead, proper play would be to lay down the King of Spades, everybody following. Then a low spade would be led, and dummy's eight-spot inserted. The eight would either win (if West started with the Q 10 x x) or it would be captured by East's ten or Queen. In the latter case, the opponents would have but one spade remaining, which dummy's Ace would pick up. The actual deal was:

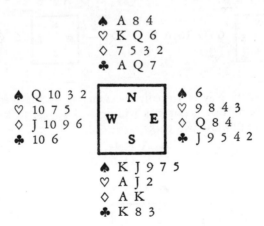

```
              ♠ A 8 4
              ♡ K Q 6
              ◇ 7 5 3 2
              ♣ A Q 7

  ♠ Q 10 3 2     N        ♠ 6
  ♡ 10 7 5                ♡ 9 8 4 3
  ◇ J 10 9 6   W   E      ◇ Q 8 4
  ♣ 10 6         S        ♣ J 9 5 4 2

              ♠ K J 9 7 5
              ♡ A J 2
              ◇ A K
              ♣ K 8 3
```

Of course, if West fails to follow to the second round of spades, then dummy's Ace will capture this trick. Now dummy's remaining spade will be led and all declarer will lose will be one trick to East's Queen. An easily-makable contract — if one does not get careless.

25.

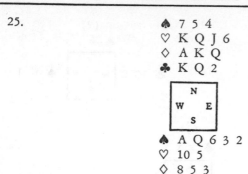

♠ 7 5 4
♡ K Q J 6
◊ A K Q
♣ K Q 2

♠ A Q 6 3 2
♡ 10 5
◊ 8 5 3
♣ A 6 5

South arrives at a *four spade contract,* against which West opens the Jack of Diamonds. It is apparent that there are no losers in either clubs or diamonds, and one loser in hearts. Declarer's concern, therefore, is to avoid the loss of three trump tricks.

Probably 95% of all bridge players would now finesse the Spade Queen — and, on this deal, they would go down at their contract. The remaining 5% would first lay down the trump Ace — and they would make their game.

Here are the four hands:

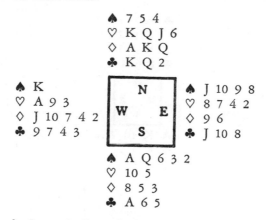

♠ 7 5 4
♡ K Q J 6
◊ A K Q
♣ K Q 2

♠ K   ♠ J 10 9 8
♡ A 9 3   ♡ 8 7 4 2
◊ J 10 7 4 2   ◊ 9 6
♣ 9 7 4 3   ♣ J 10 8

♠ A Q 6 3 2
♡ 10 5
◊ 8 5 3
♣ A 6 5

If the spade Queen is finessed, declarer must lose three spade tricks.

The proper play of the *trump Ace* will gain whenever West has a singleton King. Admittedly this distribution is unlikely to exist, but is not the play of the Ace nevertheless the proper play? South *must* lose at least one spade trick no matter how the adverse spades are divided:

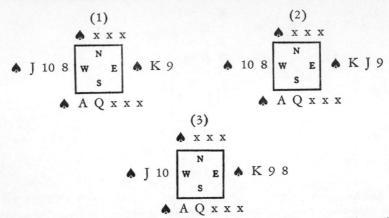

(1)

♠ x x x

♠ J 10 8   N / W E / S   ♠ K 9

♠ A Q x x x

(2)

♠ x x x

♠ 10 8   N / W E / S   ♠ K J 9

♠ A Q x x x

(3)

♠ x x x

♠ J 10   N / W E / S   ♠ K 9 8

♠ A Q x x x

In each of the above, when the Ace fails to drop the King, the North hand is entered via some side suit, and a low spade led towards the Queen. Just as the finesse would have succeeded by finessing directly, so by now playing the Queen (assuming East to play low) the "delayed" finesse will also succeed. But, as the reader can see, the original play of the Ace safeguards declarer against a singleton King being in the West hand.

26.

♠ A 8 4
♡ Q 9 2
◇ K 7 5
♣ 8 6 4 2

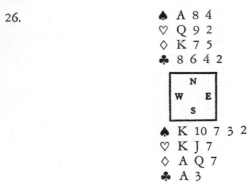

N / W E / S

♠ K 10 7 3 2
♡ K J 7
◇ A Q 7
♣ A 3

The contract is *four spades,* and West opens the King of Clubs which declarer's Ace captures. A trump is then led to dummy's Ace, and the four of trumps is returned, East playing the nine-spot. At this moment, the opponents have two trumps remaining, the Queen and the Jack. To protect against East holding both of them, declarer should put up his ten of spades on the second spade lead. Should West win the trick with the Jack or Queen, declarer's King will pick up the remaining trump. The actual deal was:

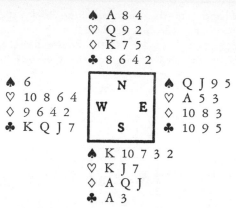

♠ A 8 4
♡ Q 9 2
◇ K 7 5
♣ 8 6 4 2

♠ 6
♡ 10 8 6 4
◇ 9 6 4 2
♣ K Q J 7

♠ Q J 9 5
♡ A 5 3
◇ 10 8 3
♣ 10 9 5

♠ K 10 7 3 2
♡ K J 7
◇ A Q J
♣ A 3

There are precisely two ten-card safety-play situations that arise often enough to warrant their presentation. On these two, the average player quite often plays incorrectly, yet escapes unscathed because the three adverse cards are distributed nicely and evenly. It is worthwhile studying these two plays, for if you know them, you will be spared the trouble (and time) of working them out as they arise at the bridge table.

27.

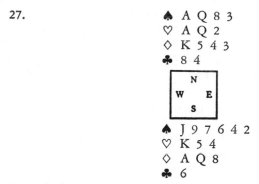

♠ A Q 8 3
♡ A Q 2
◇ K 5 4 3
♣ 8 4

♠ J 9 7 6 4 2
♡ K 5 4
◇ A Q 8
♣ 6

South finds himself in a *six spade contract* against which West opens the King of Clubs and then follows with the Ace, declarer ruffing. With a prayer, most declarers would now lead a low spade and finesse dummy's Queen. Should the finesse win they would breathe a sigh of relief unless East shows out, in which case they would bemoan their "hard luck," because, since West would have started with the K 10 x of spades, the loss of a spade trick would now become inevitable.

Proper play on this hand *is to take the finesse,* but not by leading a low card to dummy's Queen. The correct play is to lead *the Jack* from declarer's hand. If the Jack wins the trick, it then becomes routine to lead another spade, finesse dummy's Queen, and pick up the entire suit without losing a trick. (If the finesse loses, what difference whether East's King captures the Jack or the Queen?) Let us look at the deal:

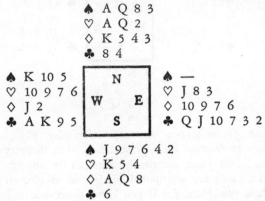

♠ A Q 8 3
♥ A Q 2
♦ K 5 4 3
♣ 8 4

♠ K 10 5
♥ 10 9 7 6
♦ J 2
♣ A K 9 5

♠ —
♥ J 8 3
♦ 10 9 7 6
♣ Q J 10 7 3 2

♠ J 9 7 6 4 2
♥ K 5 4
♦ A Q 8
♣ 6

The safety play here is to take out insurance against West holding the K 10 x. If the Queen is finessed at trick one it will win, but West will still have the K 10 remaining with dummy holding the A x, and declarer the J 9. West will now automatically make a spade trick.

But if the Jack is led first, declarer has a cinch. Should West cover, the Ace will win, East showing out. Now declarer will return to his own hand, lead the nine-spot, and finesse West for the "marked" ten-spot.

28.

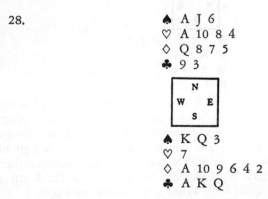

♠ A J 6
♥ A 10 8 4
♦ Q 8 7 5
♣ 9 3

♠ K Q 3
♥ 7
♦ A 10 9 6 4 2
♣ A K Q

The contract is *six diamonds*. West leads the Heart King, which is taken by dummy's Ace. Do you now lead a low diamond, and put

up the Ace when East plays low? Or do you lead the Queen? . . .
If you make *either* of these two leads you are 100% wrong!

On observation, it becomes apparent that your only concern is to
avoid the loss of two diamond tricks. If the three adverse diamonds
are divided 2-1, then there is no problem. But if the East has the
K J x, the play of the Ace will give East two diamond tricks. If West
has the K J x, the lead of the Queen will give West two diamond tricks.

The safety-play here is to lead a low diamond from dummy, and
when East plays low, declarer puts up his ten-spot. This will guarantee
the loss of no more than one diamond trick if East started with the
three missing diamonds. Of course, should East show out on the first
diamond lead, then the Ace will win, after which a low diamond will be
led towards the board's Queen, and all West will ever make will be his
King. By leading low from dummy, and playing low from his own
hand when East follows with a low diamond, declarer is assured of the
loss of no more than one diamond trick.

(1)   (2)

◇ Q 8 7 5   ◇ Q 8 7 5

```
       ┌─────────┐                         ┌─────────┐
       │    N    │                         │    N    │
◇ —    │ W     E │  ◇ K J x      ◇ K J x   │ W     E │  ◇ —
       │    S    │                         │    S    │
       └─────────┘                         └─────────┘
```

◇ A 10 9 6 4 2   ◇ A 10 9 6 4 2

The complete deal was:

♠ A J 6
♡ A 10 8 4
◇ Q 8 7 5
♣ 9 3

```
♠ 9 7 4          ┌─────────┐          ♠ 10 8 5 2
♡ K Q J 6 3      │    N    │          ♡ 9 5 2
◇ —              │ W     E │          ◇ K J 3
♣ 10 8 7 5 2     │    S    │          ♣ J 6 4
                 └─────────┘
```

♠ K Q 3
♡ 7
◇ A 10 9 6 4 2
♣ A K Q

The assorted safety-plays which follow, occur not nearly so often as
do those which have already been presented in this chapter. Nevertheless,

during any given year of a bridge player's "career", all of them will come up a few times, if not more often. These safety-plays are embodied in seven-card suits, eight-card suits, and nine-card suits.

29.

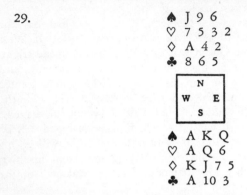

♠ J 9 6
♡ 7 5 3 2
◇ A 4 2
♣ 8 6 5

♠ A K Q
♡ A Q 6
◇ K J 7 5
♣ A 10 3

Against South's *three notrump* contract, West opens the Jack of Hearts, East puts up the King, and South captures the trick with the Ace. Upon observation, it becomes evident that to make his contract South must develop a diamond trick. The normal (but incorrect) play would be to lead a diamond to the Ace, and then finesse the Jack of Diamonds on the way back.

Proper play is to lead the King of Diamonds first, followed by a diamond to dummy's Ace. A third diamond is then led off dummy, and if East has the Queen, will not declarer's Jack be promoted into a winner, and declarer's ninth trick?

Here are the four hands:

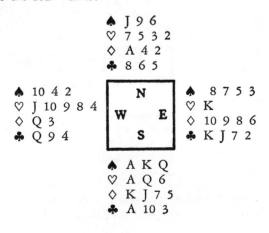

♠ J 9 6
♡ 7 5 3 2
◇ A 4 2
♣ 8 6 5

♠ 10 4 2
♡ J 10 9 8 4
◇ Q 3
♣ Q 9 4

♠ 8 7 5 3
♡ K
◇ 10 9 8 6
♣ K J 7 2

♠ A K Q
♡ A Q 6
◇ K J 7 5
♣ A 10 3

The safety play in the above deal is designed to prevent West from making a trick out of a doubleton Queen. As was stated, whenever *East* has the Queen, South's Jack will always make a trick. Conversely, whenever West has the Queen protected (Q 10 x, or Q 10 x x, etc.), he cannot be prevented from making his Queen. But why give him the Queen "for free" when he is not entitled to it? Some day it may be very costly, as will be evidenced on the next deal, which is but a slight variation of this one.

30.

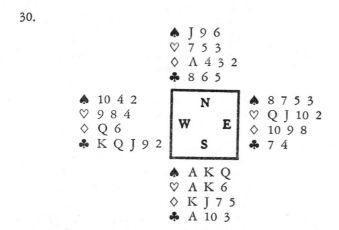

♠ J 9 6
♡ 7 5 3
◇ A 4 3 2
♣ 8 6 5

♠ 10 4 2
♡ 9 8 4
◇ Q 6
♣ K Q J 9 2

♠ 8 7 5 3
♡ Q J 10 2
◇ 10 9 8
♣ 7 4

♠ A K Q
♡ A K 6
◇ K J 7 5
♣ A 10 3

Against South's *three notrump* contract, West opened the club King, and then continued with the Queen and Jack, South holding up his Ace until the third round, East discarding a spade.

On taking inventory declarer counted eight tricks and realized that the ninth could be made only in the diamond suit. If the diamonds were to be played normally, — a low diamond to the Ace and then a finesse of the Jack on the way back — should the finesse lose, West would obtain the lead to cash his established clubs.

Our "safety-play conscious" declarer, realizing that an all-out effort had to be made to keep West out of the lead, first cashed his King, and then led to the Ace. With the Queen dropping, South easily fulfilled his contract. Had the Queen not dropped, a third round of diamonds would have been led off dummy. Whenever East held the Queen, declarer's Jack would have yielded him his ninth trick. And, if West had the Queen (Q 10 9 or Q 10 9 6), then there was never anything declarer could have done about fulfilling his contract.

31.

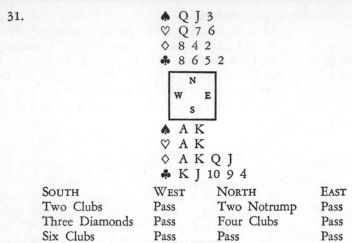

♠ Q J 3
♡ Q 7 6
◇ 8 4 2
♣ 8 6 5 2

♠ A K
♡ A K
◇ A K Q J
♣ K J 10 9 4

SOUTH	WEST	NORTH	EAST
Two Clubs	Pass	Two Notrump	Pass
Three Diamonds	Pass	Four Clubs	Pass
Six Clubs	Pass	Pass	Pass

As is apparent, the contract is quite an optimistic one, but can you blame South for hoping that North, for the four club bid, had the Queen of Clubs? How would you play the hand with West opening the Jack of Hearts?

If the four missing clubs are divided 2-2, South will lose two club tricks, regardless as to how he plays the suit, losing one trick to the Ace, the other to the Queen. If either opponent has the Q x x of clubs while the other has a singleton Ace, then whether declarer lays down the King or the Jack he must lose two club tricks. But if one of the opponents has *the singleton Queen* while the other has the A x x, then by playing the King immediately, declarer will lose just one trick. In other words, by leading the King, South stands to gain and can never lose unless he were lost before he started. Here is the deal:

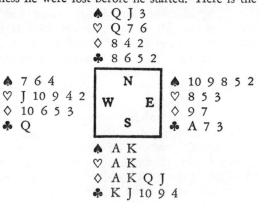

♠ Q J 3
♡ Q 7 6
◇ 8 4 2
♣ 8 6 5 2

♠ 7 6 4
♡ J 10 9 4 2
◇ 10 6 5 3
♣ Q

♠ 10 9 8 5 2
♡ 8 5 3
◇ 9 7
♣ A 7 3

♠ A K
♡ A K
◇ A K Q J
♣ K J 10 9 4

32.

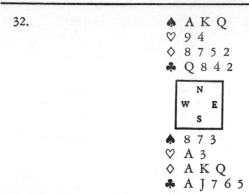

♠ A K Q
♡ 9 4
◊ 8 7 5 2
♣ Q 8 4 2

♠ 8 7 3
♡ A 3
◊ A K Q
♣ A J 7 6 5

You are South, playing a *five club contract,* against which West opens the Queen of Hearts, which you capture with the Ace. Since a heart trick has to be lost, you are trying to find some "safety-play" in the club suit to try to avoid the loss of two club tricks. How do you play the suit?

It is obvious that if the four adverse clubs are divided 2-2 or 3-1 then no more than one club trick will ever be lost. But what if one of the opponents has the K 10 9 x? *If that opponent is West, then declarer will lose two club tricks no matter how he plays the suit.* If East has the K 10 9 x, however, then South can limit his loss to but one trick by playing the Queen off dummy to the first club lead.

Declarer therefore gets to dummy via the Spade Queen, leads the Queen of Clubs which East covers with the King, and declarer takes the trick with the Ace, West showing out. Declarer then returns to the board by playing another spade, leads the eight of clubs, and loses just one club trick. The actual cards were:

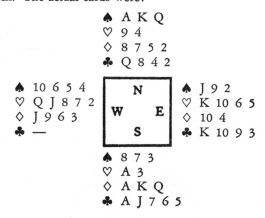

♠ A K Q
♡ 9 4
◊ 8 7 5 2
♣ Q 8 4 2

♠ 10 6 5 4
♡ Q J 8 7 2
◊ J 9 6 3
♣ —

♠ J 9 2
♡ K 10 6 5
◊ 10 4
♣ K 10 9 3

♠ 8 7 3
♡ A 3
◊ A K Q
♣ A J 7 6 5

Exactly the same line of reasoning (and play) applies to each of the following:

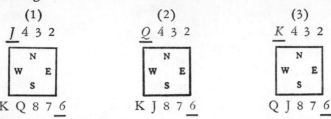

On all three of the above, the honor is led from the North hand. Whenever East has the A 10 9 5, North's first play of the honor will hold the loss to one trick (assuming North has re-entries).

33. On occasion you will find yourself in a *notrump contract*, confronted with the following situation in which you *must obtain two tricks:*

◇ A J 5 4

```
        N
    W       E
        S
```

◇ 10 6 3 2

Assuming you have plenty of entries to either hand, how do you play the above combination to *assure* two tricks? If you lead the ten-spot originally, you might be held to one trick; if you lead a low card and finesse the Jack, you might also be held to but one winner in the suit. That is:

(1)	(2)
◇ *A* J 5 4	◇ A *J* 5 4
◇ *Q* [N W E S] ◇ K 9 8 7	◇ Q 9 8 7 [N W E S] ◇ K
◇ 10 6 3 *2*	◇ *10 6 3 2*

Of course, whenever the five missing diamonds are divided 3-2, declarer can always establish a winner out of the fourth diamond. But if the opponents' five diamonds are divided 4-1 or 5-0, improper play will cost declarer a trick (either a low one from the South hand to finesse the Jack, or the ten-spot from the South hand).

The correct play to obtain *two tricks* is to lay down the Ace, then to lead a low card towards the ten-spot. No matter how the adverse diamonds are divided, declarer will obtain another trick in the suit.

(1)   (2)

◇ A J 5 4   ◇ A J 5 4

◇ K Q 9 8 7   [N/W/E/S box]   ◇ —   ◇ —   [N/W/E/S box]   ◇ K Q 9 8 7

◇ 10 6 3 2   ◇ 10 6 3 2

In (1), after the second lead towards the ten is captured by West's Queen, the South hand is re-entered via some other suit and a third round is led towards the Jack. In (2), East will capture the second lead with the Queen, but declarer will still possess the Jack and ten to force out East's King, and will thereby create a second diamond winner for himself.

To conclude this section on safety-plays, I should like to introduce five deals which arose in actual combat.

1.

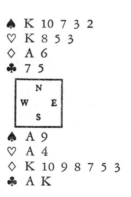

♠ K 10 7 3 2
♡ K 8 5 3
◇ A 6
♣ 7 5

♠ A 9
♡ A 4
◇ K 10 9 8 7 5 3
♣ A K

The contract was *six diamonds*. The South declarer was Alphonse (Sonny) Moyse, Jr., of New York City. The opening lead was the Jack of Clubs, which declarer's King captured.

At trick two the three of diamonds was led, West played the deuce, the six-spot was put up from the North hand — and it captured the trick when East showed out! From here in it was smooth sailing. Here is the deal:

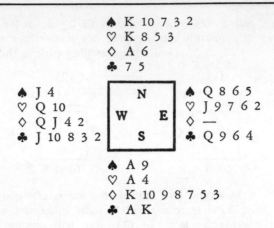

♠ K 10 7 3 2
♡ K 8 5 3
◊ A 6
♣ 7 5

♠ J 4
♡ Q 10
◊ Q J 4 2
♣ J 10 8 3 2

♠ Q 8 6 5
♡ J 9 7 6 2
◊ —
♣ Q 9 6 4

♠ A 9
♡ A 4
◊ K 10 9 8 7 5 3
♣ A K

Was declarer's play of the six-spot a "fancy" play? Not at all. He was merely taking out insurance against West holding the four missing diamonds. He really did not expect the six-spot to win the trick, feeling reasonably certain that East would take the trick with the Queen or Jack. If the latter did happen, then declarer would still have the Ace and King of Diamonds to pick up the two remaining cards of that suit. Sonny's insurance play paid a very handsome dividend.

2.

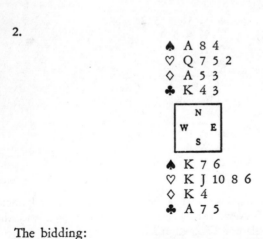

♠ A 8 4
♡ Q 7 5 2
◊ A 5 3
♣ K 4 3

♠ K 7 6
♡ K J 10 8 6
◊ K 4
♣ A 7 5

The bidding:

SOUTH	WEST	NORTH	EAST
One Heart	Two Clubs	Three Hearts	Pass
Four Hearts	Pass	Pass	Pass

West's opening lead is the Queen of Clubs. What do you play from dummy?

Let us analyze. West has overcalled in clubs, so he has at least a five-card suit, and probably a six-card suit since he lacks both the Ace and King of Clubs. Looking at the combined deck, it is almost certain that West has the Ace of Hearts as part of his overcall.

Declarer's major worry is that when he draws trumps at trick two, West, upon winning the Ace, will play back a club for East to trump.

So declarer wins the opening club lead with *dummy's King,* and leads a trump, West's Ace winning. West does return a club, East trumps — and declarer has not lost a thing since he had a sure club loser anyway, and he still retains the Ace of Clubs. Here is the deal:

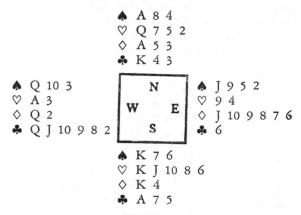

Declarer's play of the King of Clubs on the opening lead was in the nature of a safety-play; he had one sure loser in the suit but could not afford to lose two tricks. By taking the King immediately, he rendered the ruff harmless.

The reader can see what would have developed if declarer had won the opening club lead with his own Ace. West, upon winning the trump Ace, would return the Jack of Clubs, the King would be played from dummy — and East would trump declarer's sure winner. Declarer would then still have a losing club and a losing spade.

3. In the following deal, there is presented a "spur of the moment" safety-play which only a top-flight expert could conceive of and execute at the bridge table (many of us might conceive of it a few hours later, while we are dunking in our coffee or eating a sandwich).

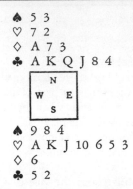

```
        ♠ 5 3
        ♡ 7 2
        ◇ A 7 3
        ♣ A K Q J 8 4
```

```
        ♠ 9 8 4
        ♡ A K J 10 6 5 3
        ◇ 6
        ♣ 5 2
```

West opened the diamond King against South's *four heart contract,* dummy's Ace winning. The natural (orthodox) play now would be to lead a trump to the Ace and — too late! If you take the Ace of Hearts, West will show out, leaving East with the Q x x, and you will wind up losing three spades and a heart. The deal was:

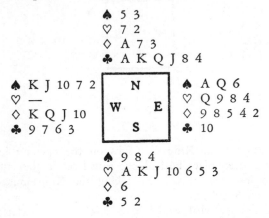

```
                    ♠ 5 3
                    ♡ 7 2
                    ◇ A 7 3
                    ♣ A K Q J 8 4

♠ K J 10 7 2                      ♠ A Q 6
♡ —                               ♡ Q 9 8 4
◇ K Q J 10                        ◇ 9 8 5 4 2
♣ 9 7 6 3                         ♣ 10

                    ♠ 9 8 4
                    ♡ A K J 10 6 5 3
                    ◇ 6
                    ♣ 5 2
```

At trick two, our declarer, Edward Hymes, Jr., led the two of hearts and finessed his ten-spot What if it lost to West's (hypothetical) Queen? Then the defenders could take two spades and a heart at most.

A difficult safety-play? It sure was. But then, that is why an expert is an expert.

4. Another brilliant "spur-of-the-moment" safety-play can be observed in the deal which follows. The South declarer was Gloria Turner of Chicago, one of the nation's top-ranking players. I am willing to wager that if the deal were encountered in actual combat

(as opposed to being presented as a "problem"), not one out of five of our expert players would come up with the right answer:

♠ A 7 6 4 2
♡ K 8 6
◇ Q 7
♣ 10 8 5

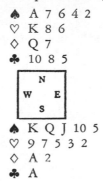

♠ K Q J 10 5
♡ 9 7 5 3 2
◇ A 2
♣ A

The bidding:

SOUTH	WEST	NORTH	EAST
One Spade	Double	Four Spades	Pass
Pass	Pass		

West opened the Ace of Hearts, everybody following suit, after which the Queen of Hearts was led. The absolutely "normal" play at this point would be to automatically put up the King — which East would trump! And, if East now shifted to a diamond, the contract would be defeated, for West would eventually cash another heart and the Diamond King.

On West's lead of the Queen of Hearts at trick two, Gloria played low from dummy — and East showed out, discarding a low club. A third heart was now led, dummy's King being trumped by East. East then switched to a diamond, declarer's Ace winning, after which trumps were drawn. It was routine play from here in, declarer trumping her fourth heart. On the fifth heart she discarded a diamond from dummy, and was then able to ruff out her losing diamond.

How did Gloria know enough not to put up dummy's Heart King on the second heart lead? Well, she knew when East followed to the first heart lead that the adverse hearts were divided no worse than 4-1 — and that her fifth heart had the potential of becoming established. On it she could dispose of dummy's losing diamond.

In playing low at trick two, declarer was sacrificing a potential overtrick, which would have been the case had hearts been divided 3-2. In this situation, of course, the King of Hearts would have won the second trick. But, reasoned Gloria, if the Queen of Hearts were not covered with the King, then West would still have the lead. Whether or not East followed to the second heart was immaterial, for West, by leading a third heart, would remove dummy's remaining heart (East trumping). As was stated, it would then be a simple matter for declarer to ruff her fourth heart, thereby establishing the fifth one for a diamond discard.

The reason why this highly-imaginative play would be such a difficult one for most players to make would be because it requires the fluidity of thought which embodies the willingness to give up a trick to safeguard one's contract. But to one who has been trained in "safety-first," it would become less difficult, for "safety-first" necessitates taking out insurance against the improbable — and the premium is usually the payment of a potential overtrick. The deal was:

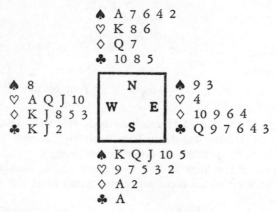

5. The last "safety-play" deal is a simple one. Yet I know that many bridge players would play it incorrectly.

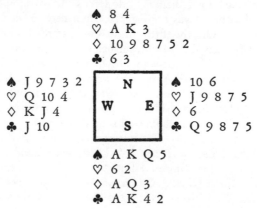

West, on lead against South's *three notrump contract,* opened the three of spades, declarer's Queen winning. South's next lead was a heart to dummy's King after which he returned a low diamond, finessing his Queen which lost to West's King. West then played his Queen of Hearts, knocking out dummy's Ace. It now became impossible for declarer to establish and cash dummy's diamonds.

As was stated, this is a simple hand — for one who has learned to count his winning tricks. All declarer needed was to pick up an extra trick in diamonds. At trick two the Ace of Diamonds should have been played, followed by the Queen, West winning (or East, had *he* held the King). Whatever was then returned South would capture, concede his remaining diamond to the Jack — and claim the remainder of the tricks. Played in a simple, straight-forward, common-sense manner, declarer would have taken three spade tricks, two heart tricks, four diamonds, and two clubs, for a total of eleven tricks.

In conclusion, I should like to make a brief observation. The expert bridge player takes chances only when he has to, as a last resort, never as a first choice. He looks for "safe investments," and if there is any way of avoiding risks on a hand, he will seize the opportunity of playing it safely. The perpetual quest for safety-plays is the first step towards becoming an excellent bridge player — and it is to the attainment of this objective that this chapter has been dedicated.

THE HOLD-UP PLAY

T HE "hold-up" play consists of the refusal to win a trick in order to maintain *control* of the suit which an opponent has led until such time as the control can be relinquished with comparative safety. Although there are various reasons for the desire and necessity of maintaining control, one primary motive stands out above all others: to break the communication between the opponents' hands — that is, to eliminate from the leader's partner's hand, the suit which the leader has led, so that if the leader's partner subsequently obtains the lead, he will be unable to return his partner's suit.

Putting the above into more specific terms, when you have just one "stopper" (controlling card) in the suit which an opponent has led, that suit will ultimately become *established* despite anything you can do if they keep on leading that suit. But you can diminish the danger of their *cashing* that suit if you can restrict a future lead to just *one* opponent, instead of to both of them, and hope that he is the one who does not hold any cards in the then-established suit. The question of how to restrict a future lead to the opponent who has been rendered void in their established suit, is the major theme of this chapter.

The hold-up play is most frequently employed by declarer in *notrump contracts,* although there are many situations where it is also used to good advantage in suit contracts. Why this is so will become self-evident in a moment.

It is a universally-accepted fact that against notrump contracts the opening lead is made from the leader's *longest* suit. The world's best players do it, you and I do it, and your opponents do it. And it is just as much of a fact that almost always the leader will have more cards in the suit which he has led than will his partner. So, if you can get rid of the "few" from the leader's partner's hand, leader's partner will be rendered "non-dangerous." *The hold-up play is designed to eliminate the suit that is led from the hand of the leader's partner,* thereby destroying their line of communication within that suit. To illustrate:

♢ 7 3

♢ Q 10 8 6 4 | N W E S | ♢ K J 9

♢ A 5 2

The contract is *three notrump,* against which West opens his fourth best diamond, and East puts up his King. Declarer now employs the "hold-up" play — that is, he declines to take his Ace. Can you see what the effect would be if he took it, and East subsequently obtained the lead? East would return the Jack of Diamonds, followed by the nine-spot, and the defenders would cash four diamond tricks.

When declarer "holds-up" on the King of Diamonds, East will, of course, return the Jack of Diamonds to trick two. And again declarer will "hold-up" his Ace. Now East's remaining diamond will be led, declarer being forced to win it. Should East ever again obtain the lead, *he will be unable to return a diamond* — and West will never cash his two established diamonds.

There is no compromise with the hold-up play. That is, in the above situation, after declarer declines to win with the Ace on the opening diamond lead, when the Jack is led on the second round, declarer again declines to capture the trick. He does not say, at trick two, "Well, I've made my token contribution to the hold-up play. I'll take my Ace now." If he takes it, East will still have one diamond left, and upon obtaining the lead later, he will lead it — and West will cash his established diamonds. You go all the way, holding back the taking of your Ace until you are compelled to take it.

The general principle of the hold-up play can be stated in this fashion:

In a *notrump contract,* whenever an opponent opens a suit in which you have precisely *one* "stopper," defer winning a trick with it until you are absolutely compelled to. In so doing, you will effectively tend to disrupt the communication between the enemies' hands — that is, you will make it impossible for one hand to reach the other via that suit.

In a suit contract, of course, there is no necessity of employing the hold-up play in the attempt to prevent the opponents from ultimately establishing and *cashing* their suit. Your trumps, *the controlling cards,* will effectively destroy their established suit.

In the deals which follow, illustrating the hold-up play, its necessity and advantages, there will be featured the frequent situations where declarer is enabled to "maneuver" his play of the hand in such a manner that if he must lose a trick, he is able to lose it to what we call the "non-dangerous" hand. The "non-dangerous" hand is the one which has no cards remaining in the suit that was led and established — and he cannot hurt you if he obtains the lead since he is unable to play back partner's suit.

Although the hold-up play is applied most frequently at notrump contracts, there will be presented those situations where the hold-up play is properly employed in a suit contract.

The reader will do himself and his future partners a great service if he carefully scrutinizes the various applications of the hold-up play, for one cannot ever learn to play notrump contracts correctly unless he can master this play. Actually, the "hold-up" is a fairly simple play. Yet too many players have never been familiar with the logic behind the play, and so have never been able to completely understand how and when to apply it — which is unfortunate, since the opponents have a knack of leading the suit in which you are weakest, the suit in which you have just one "stopper." And, when you relinquish control too quickly, you become a doomed man if either of the opponents ever obtains the lead again.

Let us now look at the "hold-up" play in action:

1.

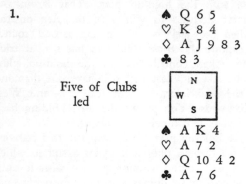

Five of Clubs
led

♠ Q 6 5
♡ K 8 4
◇ A J 9 8 3
♣ 8 3

♠ A K 4
♡ A 7 2
◇ Q 10 4 2
♣ A 7 6

You are the South declarer at a *three notrump contract,* West opening the five of clubs, with East putting up the Queen. How do you play the hand?

The automatic, and proper, play is to employ the "hold-up," permitting East to win the trick. East then continues with the ten of clubs, and again you do not take your Ace. When a third round of clubs is led, you of course have no choice but to capture it.

By counting your winners, it becomes apparent that you need three diamond tricks to fulfill your contract. So you take the diamond finesse — and your Queen loses to East's King. And now your contract is guaranteed, since East has no club to return to partner. The deal was:

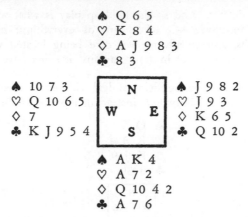

♠ Q 6 5
♡ K 8 4
◇ A J 9 8 3
♣ 8 3

♠ 10 7 3
♡ Q 10 6 5
◇ 7
♣ K J 9 5 4

♠ J 9 8 2
♡ J 9 3
◇ K 6 5
♣ Q 10 2

♠ A K 4
♡ A 7 2
◇ Q 10 4 2
♣ A 7 6

I think it is obvious as to what would have happened had you won either the first club lead or the second. East, upon subsequently obtaining the lead, would have returned a club, and the defenders would have taken four clubs and a diamond to defeat the contract. But, with the hold-up play, each time declarer declined to take his Ace, East's club length was reduced by one card, until East reached the point where he had none left — and at that moment, he had become "non-dangerous." When declarer lost the diamond finesse to East at trick four, his worry about the opponents' established club suit had ceased to exist.

The reader might well ask: "But what if East had another club to return?" The answer is that if East had another club, then West would have had one club less — and the clubs would have been divided 4-4. If this were the case, then declarer would have lost just *three* clubs and a diamond, fulfilling his contract.

The hold-up play is designed to protect you in all situations where the adversely-led suit is divided either 6-2, or 5-2, or 5-3, with the opening leader having the greater number. Where the suit that is led is divided 4-4, you require no protection, whether you are the world's best player, the world's worst player, or anything in between. When the suit is divided 4-4, you will lose three tricks in the suit whether you capture the first, second or third round of that suit. In effect, then, the hold-up play is insurance at no cost whatsoever, and is protection against what is usually the normal thing: that the opening leader has more of the suit led than does his partner.

The question might also arise: "If the King of Diamonds were favorably located, then was not the hold-up play a wasted effort?" The answer is "yes." But we all know that finesses sometimes work, and sometimes do not. And so the hold-up play is what we might call comprehensive insurance — it takes care of everything: both the bad divisions of suits, and an adverse key card being located where it can hurt you unless you take out insurance against it being adversely located.

2. Let us now examine the identical deal with one card being changed: dummy has the *King of Diamonds* instead of the Ace of Diamonds.

♠ Q 6 5
♡ K 8 4
◇ K J 9 8 3
♣ 8 3

♠ A K 4
♡ A 7 2
◇ Q 10 4 2
♣ A 7 6

Again the contract is *three notrump,* with West opening the five of clubs and East putting up the Queen. How about the hold-up play now?

The answer is a most positive *yes.* As a matter of fact, in virtually every notrump contract, when a suit is led and you have just one stopper in that suit, do not take it until you are forced to — or unless you can prove that it should be taken earlier (for instance, if you are in a *seven notrump* contract, to employ the hold-up play would be ridiculous).

On the above deal if you fail to employ the hold-up play you will go down unless the eight adverse clubs are divided 4-4, for upon relinquishing the lead to the opponents' Ace of Diamonds (which you must do), they will cash at least four clubs. I should estimate that if you immediately take the club Ace, you will go down at your contract at least 80% of the time — that is, you will make your contract perhaps 20% of the time.

But suppose you hold-up your club Ace until the third round, exhausting East of clubs, except if the original club distribution was 4-4, in which case it does not matter what you do since you will then always make your contract. What next? You hopefully lead a diamond, and if East has the Ace, all is well. If West has the Ace, he will cash his clubs.

As is apparent, there is no guarantee on this hand. But as you can see, the employment of the hold-up play increases your chances of making the contract from 20% to 50% (the 50-50 chance of East holding the Diamond Ace, as opposed to West). The deal was:

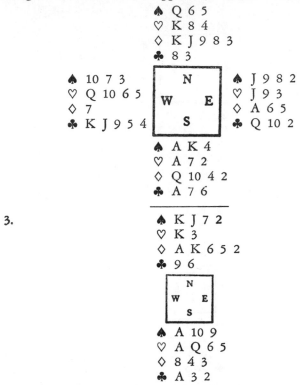

♠ Q 6 5
♡ K 8 4
◊ K J 9 8 3
♣ 8 3

♠ 10 7 3
♡ Q 10 6 5
◊ 7
♣ K J 9 5 4

N
W   E
S

♠ J 9 8 2
♡ J 9 3
◊ A 6 5
♣ Q 10 2

♠ A K 4
♡ A 7 2
◊ Q 10 4 2
♣ A 7 6

3.

♠ K J 7 2
♡ K 3
◊ A K 6 5 2
♣ 9 6

N
W   E
S

♠ A 10 9
♡ A Q 6 5
◊ 8 4 3
♣ A 3 2

South arrives at a *three notrump contract* without any adverse bidding. West opens the King of Clubs, which is permitted to win the trick. The Queen of Clubs is then led, after which comes the Jack of Clubs, declarer's Ace capturing the third round of the suit.

By "holding-up" South has eliminated clubs from the East hand. Declarer now leads the Ace of Spades, after which the ten of spades is led and finessed. *Whether the ten wins or loses, declarer's Jack of Spades has become promoted into his ninth trick!*

If East has the Queen of Spades, he will capture the ten, but he will have no clubs to return (if he has one, then clubs were originally divided 4-4). If West has the Queen, then declarer's play of the ten will be a successful finesse. But if declarer failed to employ the hold-up play, in order to make his contract he would be forced to guess the location of the spade Queen. The deal was:

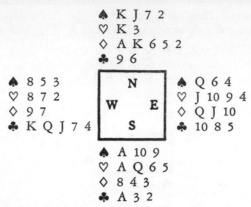

♠ K J 7 2
♡ K 3
◇ A K 6 5 2
♣ 9 6

♠ 8 5 3   ♠ Q 6 4
♡ 8 7 2   ♡ J 10 9 4
◇ 9 7   ◇ Q J 10
♣ K Q J 7 4   ♣ 10 8 5

♠ A 10 9
♡ A Q 6 5
◇ 8 4 3
♣ A 3 2

Using the same hands, I should like to introduce a variation in the bidding to show how declarer would be influenced:

♠ K J 7 2
♡ K 3
◇ A K 6 5 2
♣ 9 6

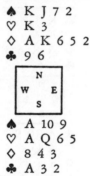

♠ A 10 9
♡ A Q 6 5
◇ 8 4 3
♣ A 3 2

The bidding:

NORTH	EAST	SOUTH	WEST
One Diamond	*Two Clubs*	Two Hearts	Pass
Two Spades	Pass	Three Notrump	Pass
Pass	Pass		

West, in response to his partner's club overcall, opens the eight of clubs, East overtaking with the ten-spot, which is permitted to win. South then holds up his club Ace for another round, and on the third round takes his Ace, West following to all three rounds of clubs.

Now the shoe is on the other foot. East, with the established clubs, has become the "dangerous" hand, and he must be kept out of the lead. So South enters dummy via a heart or a diamond, and takes a finesse in spades in such a manner that if it loses, it will lose only to West (the "non-dangerous" hand, since West has no more clubs).

After entering dummy, a low spade is led and declarer's ten-spot put up. If it wins, then it has become declarer's ninth trick; if it loses, to the "non-dangerous" West, then dummy's Jack of Spades has become declarer's ninth trick. What were the adverse hands? Put the Queen of Spades wherever you want it to be, and you will see that the play as has been presented guarantees the fulfillment of the contract:

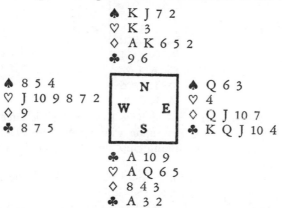

```
                    ♠ K J 7 2
                    ♡ K 3
                    ◇ A K 6 5 2
                    ♣ 9 6
  ♠ 8 5 4            N           ♠ Q 6 3
  ♡ J 10 9 8 7 2               ♡ 4
  ◇ 9           W       E        ◇ Q J 10 7
  ♣ 8 7 5            S           ♣ K Q J 10 4
                    ♣ A 10 9
                    ♡ A Q 6 5
                    ◇ 8 4 3
                    ♣ A 3 2
```

4. The hold-up play is employed not only when the Ace is possessed, but also with the King when that card has become the "top banana." As an example, witness the following deal:

```
                    ♠ K 8 7
                    ♡ K 8 3
                    ◇ A Q J 9 4
                    ♣ 10 2
                        N
                    W       E
                        S
                    ♠ A Q 4
                    ♡ A J 2
                    ◇ 10 7 6 5
                    ♣ K 7 3
```

Against South's *three notrump contract*, West opens the five of clubs, East's Ace winning. East returns the Jack of Clubs — and you employ the hold-up play, declining to take the King. A third round of clubs is then led, your King capturing the trick.

A diamond finesse is now tried, losing to East's King. And it is smooth sailing from here, since East has no club left to return:

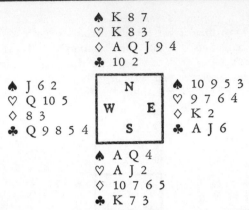

♠ K 8 7
♡ K 8 3
◊ A Q J 9 4
♣ 10 2

♠ J 6 2
♡ Q 10 5
◊ 8 3
♣ Q 9 8 5 4

♠ 10 9 5 3
♡ 9 7 6 4
◊ K 2
♣ A J 6

♠ A Q 4
♡ A J 2
◊ 10 7 6 5
♣ K 7 3

It is quite apparent what would have happened if declarer had taken the Club King at trick two. East, upon winning with his Diamond King, would have returned his remaining club, and West would have enjoyed himself tremendously.

To repeat, the purpose of the hold-up play is to break the communication between the adverse hands. So hold on to your stopper — the controlling card — just as long as you can when the opponents have opened a suit in which that stopper is your only measure of protection.

5.   If a title were required for the following deal, it would be "fools rush in where angels fear to tread." The deal took place in actual combat.

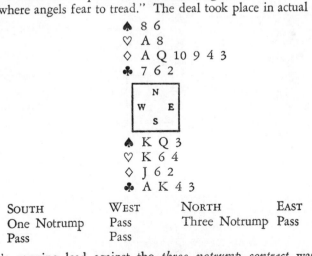

♠ 8 6
♡ A 8
◊ A Q 10 9 4 3
♣ 7 6 2

♠ K Q 3
♡ K 6 4
◊ J 6 2
♣ A K 4 3

SOUTH	WEST	NORTH	EAST
One Notrump	Pass	Three Notrump	Pass
Pass	Pass		

West's opening lead against the *three notrump contract* was a low spade, on which East played the ten-spot, declarer's Queen winning.

The diamond finesse was then hopefully attempted, but a carnage developed when East won the trick with his King of Diamonds, returned a spade — and West cashed five spade tricks. He went down two on a hand that should have produced ten tricks. The deal was:

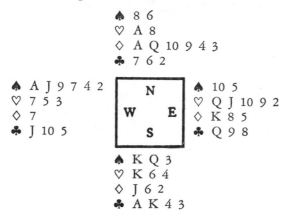

```
              ♠ 8 6
              ♡ A 8
              ◇ A Q 10 9 4 3
              ♣ 7 6 2
♠ A J 9 7 4 2       N        ♠ 10 5
♡ 7 5 3                      ♡ Q J 10 9 2
◇ 7          W       E       ◇ K 8 5
♣ J 10 5            S        ♣ Q 9 8
              ♠ K Q 3
              ♡ K 6 4
              ◇ J 6 2
              ♣ A K 4 3
```

From South's point of view, he needed five diamond tricks to fulfill his contract, even if he never obtained a spade trick. What was his hurry to win the first spade lead? Why not retain the spade stopper as long as possible, in accordance with the principle of the hold-up play?

When East played his ten of spades at trick one, he should have been permitted to win the trick. As the reader can see, upon a spade return South would put up the Queen — and West could establish his spades but he could never obtain the lead to cash them.

Had declarer taken stock of the situation at trick one, he would have recognized that the diamond finesse was to be taken in such a manner that if it lost, it could lose only to East; and that, therefore, every effort had to be made to eliminate spades from East's hand, so that if he obtained the lead, he would be unable to return a spade. Hence, the refusal to win the opening spade lead was the only proper play.

The reader may raise the question: "What if East had three spades? Then when he returned a spade at trick two, upon which declarer would play his Queen, couldn't West 'hold up' his Ace? Later, when East obtained the lead via the Diamond King, he would return his third spade, declarer's King falling to West's Ace, and West would cash the remaining spades." That is, if the distribution of the spade suit had been the following, would not the defenders, by astute defense, have defeated declarer whether he employed the hold-up play or he did not?

♠ *8* 6

N
♠ A J 9 *7 4*   W   E   ♠ *10* 5 2
S

♠ K Q *3*

The answer is "yes." If the above 5-3 division of the opponents' spades existed, then no matter whether declarer did or did not employ the hold-up play, he was doomed to defeat, *provided that* West made the excellent play of refusing to take the second spade lead, thereby maintaining communication with his partner. *If this were the distribution, then declarer's ultimate defeat (if* it happened) *could be attributed to circumstances beyond his control.*

But, by employing the hold-up play, declarer was taking out insurance at no cost against a 6-2 distribution of the adverse spades. And, as was stated, you seldom get guarantees in bridge, and the winning bridge players are those who do the right thing more often than do their competitors.

The above type of hold-up play is also utilized when the King and Queen are split between the North and South hands:

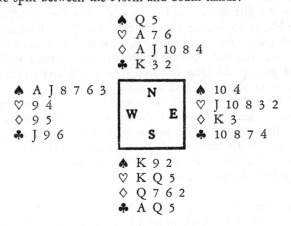

♠ Q 5
♡ A 7 6
◇ A J 10 8 4
♣ K 3 2

♠ A J 8 7 6 3   ♠ 10 4
♡ 9 4   N   ♡ J 10 8 3 2
◇ 9 5   W   E   ◇ K 3
♣ J 9 6   S   ♣ 10 8 7 4

♠ K 9 2
♡ K Q 5
◇ Q 7 6 2
♣ A Q 5

West opens a low spade against South's *three notrump contract* — and declarer's concern should not be how he can best get two spade tricks, but rather how he can most effectively prevent West from establishing and cashing the latter's spade suit.

Since it is apparent that a diamond finesse must be taken, and that if East has the King he cannot be kept out of the lead, declarer's approach should be to eliminate spades from the East hand. To this end he plays a low spade from dummy, and when East puts up the ten-spot, he is permitted to win the trick.

As the reader can see, West will henceforth never be able to cash his spade suit, for when East returns his remaining spade at trick two, he will have been rendered "non-dangerous."

If declarer had won the opening spade lead with either the King or Queen, he would be doomed to defeat. For East, upon later obtaining the lead via the Diamond King, would then have returned a spade, enabling West to cash five spade tricks.

Let me vary the North-South hands a bit in order to introduce a standard situation where the hold-up play should *not* be employed at trick one, and where declarer has the option as to which hand should capture the opening lead:

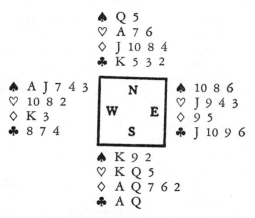

Again the contract is *three notrump,* with West opening the four of spades. If South wins the trick with his King, then declarer will lose his contract should the diamond King be adversely located, for the spade Ace will drop dummy's Queen, and West will then cash his remaining spades.

The proper play is to put up dummy's Queen of Spades at trick one, in the hope that West has the Ace of Spades. Should the Queen win, a diamond finesse can then be taken with safety, for if it loses it will lose only to West. And, in this case, declarer will still have the K 9 of spades as a stopper against West.

If declarer allows the opposition to win the opening spade lead, the suit will then become established upon continuation — and if West possesses the diamond King, declarer will lose his contract.

6.

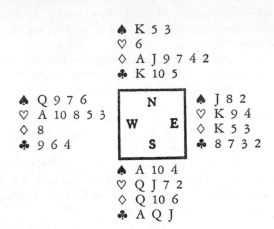

♠ K 5 3
♥ 6
♦ A J 9 7 4 2
♣ K 10 5

♠ Q 9 7 6
♥ A 10 8 5 3
♦ 8
♣ 9 6 4

♠ J 8 2
♥ K 9 4
♦ K 5 3
♣ 8 7 3 2

♠ A 10 4
♥ Q J 7 2
♦ Q 10 6
♣ A Q J

Against South's *three notrump contract* West opened the five of hearts, and East played the King which won the trick. He then returned the nine of hearts, declarer put up the Jack — and West employed a defensive "hold-up" play, permitting declarer's Jack to win. West's play was based on the hope that East had another heart and an entry in some outside suit. If East did not, then the contract figured to be unbeatable. Had West taken his heart Ace at trick two, and returned a third heart, establishing the suit, he could never have regained the lead to cash the established hearts.

Declarer, upon winning the second trick with the heart Jack, then took the diamond finesse, losing to East's King. East now returned his remaining heart, and declarer's Q 7 was trapped. All in all, the defenders took four heart tricks and one diamond.

While the type of hold-up that declarer should have employed on this deal does not occur too frequently, it is nevertheless accepted as being a standard hold-up situation.

At trick two, on East's lead of the nine of hearts, declarer should have played low, retaining his Q J combination! Now East would play back his remaining heart, declarer would put up his Jack — and all West could ever make would be his Ace of Hearts.

From declarer's point of view he should have realized that he was going to take a diamond finesse, and that if East had the diamond King, there would be no way of preventing him from obtaining the lead. But he could be prevented from returning a heart — if his hearts were eliminated before he obtained the lead via the King of Diamonds. Hence the proper hold-up play with Q J x x, to render East "non-dangerous."

7. Let us now look at three types of situations where the hold-up play is utilized in a *suit* contract:

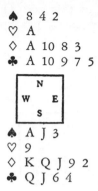

♠ 8 4 2
♡ A
◇ A 10 8 3
♣ A 10 9 7 5

♠ A J 3
♡ 9
◇ K Q J 9 2
♣ Q J 6 4

South is playing a *five diamond contract* against which West opens the King of Spades, which declarer declines to win. If West now continues with a spade, South will win two spade tricks with the A J. Whatever else West now shifts to, at trick two, declarer will not lose any more than one additional trick (in clubs). The deal was:

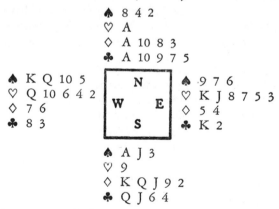

♠ 8 4 2
♡ A
◇ A 10 8 3
♣ A 10 9 7 5

♠ K Q 10 5
♡ Q 10 6 4 2
◇ 7 6
♣ 8 3

♠ 9 7 6
♡ K J 8 7 5 3
◇ 5 4
♣ K 2

♠ A J 3
♡ 9
◇ K Q J 9 2
♣ Q J 6 4

Had declarer captured the opening spade lead, when he ultimately took the club finesse, losing to East, a spade return would have given the defenders two spade tricks.

By refusing to win the opening spade lead, declarer retained control of the suit. After drawing trumps, and then taking the club finesse, he was able to discard his Jack of Spades on dummy's fifth club.

The hold-up with the A J x against first hand's lead of the King is known as "The Bath Coup." The purpose of this type of hold-up play is not to break the communication between the opponents' hands, but rather to force first hand to abandon leading the suit, thereby enabling declarer to retain control of that suit. Of course, if first hand elects to lead that suit again, declarer will pick up an extra trick.

8.

♠ 10 9 7 6
♡ K 5
◊ J 5
♣ A Q 9 6 2

	N	
W		E
	S	

♠ A K Q J 5
♡ 6 4 3
◊ A 10
♣ J 10 4

You are sitting South, playing a *four spade contract*. The opening lead is a low diamond, East putting up the Queen. Do you take your Ace or "hold-up?"

When you have reached the "expert" stage, you will have learned to look ahead. What is the danger on this hand? Is it not that West may later obtain the lead, which might result in declarer losing two heart tricks?

To prevent this, you permit East's Queen of Diamonds to win the opening lead! No matter what East now returns, it will be impossible for West to ever obtain the lead to play a heart through dummy's King. Let us look at the complete deal before discussing this point any further.

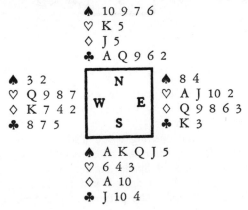

                    ♠ 10 9 7 6
                    ♡ K 5
                    ◊ J 5
                    ♣ A Q 9 6 2

♠ 3 2   ♠ 8 4
♡ Q 9 8 7   ♡ A J 10 2
◊ K 7 4 2   ◊ Q 9 8 6 3
♣ 8 7 5   ♣ K 3

                    ♠ A K Q J 5
                    ♡ 6 4 3
                    ◊ A 10
                    ♣ J 10 4

Let us assume that East, upon winning the diamond Queen at trick one, returns a diamond, declarer's Ace winning (no other return by East would serve the defenders any better). Declarer then takes the club finesse, losing to East's King. From here in all the defenders can make is the Ace of Hearts, for declarer will discard two of his hearts on dummy's fourth and fifth club.

Had declarer won the opening diamond lead with his Ace, after drawing trumps he would have taken a club finesse, losing to East's King. East would then have entered West's hand by leading a diamond to his partner's King. And West, perceiving the futility of leading either a diamond or a club, would automatically have shifted to a heart enabling the defenders to take two heart tricks, inflicting a one-trick set on declarer.

9.   Let us now examine the final type of situation where the hold-up play is employed at a suit contract. In this situation declarer frequently has to guess whether or not to hold-up.

```
                     ♠ 9 5 2
                     ♡ A J 10 6
                     ◇ 8
                     ♣ K Q 7 5 3
                      ┌─────────┐
                      │    N    │
                      │  W   E  │
                      │    S    │
                      └─────────┘
                     ♠ A 7 3
                     ♡ Q 9 3
                     ◇ A 4
                     ♣ A J 10 6 4
```

The bidding:

SOUTH	WEST	NORTH	EAST
One Club	One Spade	Two Hearts	Pass
Two Notrump	Pass	Four Clubs	Pass
Four Hearts	Pass	Five Clubs	Pass
Pass	Pass		

West, having overcalled in spades, opens the King of Spades and

South has a rough problem. Shall he take the King, or shall he "hold-up?" If West has the King of Hearts, then no matter what declarer elects to do, he will come out all right, since he will then have no losers in hearts, diamonds or clubs. But if East has the King of Hearts, then the success of declarer's contract depends on whether East started with one or two spades.

With *East* possessing the King of Hearts, if he started with a singleton spade, then the winning play by declarer would be to capture the opening spade lead, draw trumps, and take the heart finesse. Should this lose, declarer will be able to discard one of his spades on dummy's fourth heart, since East will have no spade to return. But if East started with a doubleton spade, then the winning play would be to "hold-up" on the opening spade lead, and capture the second spade lead, thereby exhausting East of spades. Now when the losing heart finesse is taken, East will have no spade to return, and declarer will be able to discard his remaining spade on dummy's established fourth heart.

As you can see, whether to win the first or second spade lead depends on whether you think West started with five spades or with six spades. On this deal, it is an out-and-out guess. On other deals it will not be a guess, especially where no overcall was made, in which case you can assume that the leader has a five-card suit and not a six-card one. The deal, or rather two deals as they might have been, follow:

(a)

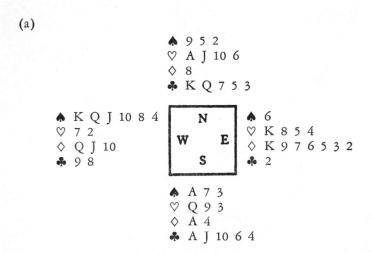

```
                        ♠ 9 5 2
                        ♡ A J 10 6
                        ◇ 8
                        ♣ K Q 7 5 3
   ♠ K Q J 10 8 4    ┌─────────┐    ♠ 6
   ♡ 7 2             │    N    │    ♡ K 8 5 4
   ◇ Q J 10          │ W     E │    ◇ K 9 7 6 5 3 2
   ♣ 9 8             │    S    │    ♣ 2
                     └─────────┘
                        ♠ A 7 3
                        ♡ Q 9 3
                        ◇ A 4
                        ♣ A J 10 6 4
```

(b)

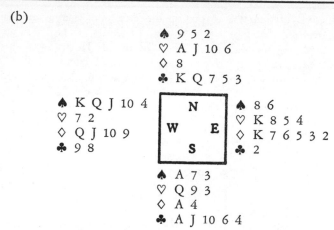

```
              ♠ 9 5 2
              ♡ A J 10 6
              ◇ 8
              ♣ K Q 7 5 3
♠ K Q J 10 4      N      ♠ 8 6
♡ 7 2                    ♡ K 8 5 4
◇ Q J 10 9   W      E    ◇ K 7 6 5 3 2
♣ 9 8            S       ♣ 2
              ♠ A 7 3
              ♡ Q 9 3
              ◇ A 4
              ♣ A J 10 6 4
```

On (a), the hold-up will lose, for East will trump the second spade lead, and ultimately win a heart trick. On (b), the hold-up wins, for on the spade continuation, declarer's Ace wins, eliminating spades from the East hand. When the heart finesse subsequently loses, East will have no spade to return and declarer will then discard his losing spade on dummy's fourth heart.

10. The occasions for employing the specific type of hold-up play which the following deal portrays, will occur rather infrequently. The deal is introduced to illustrate the imaginative element which has become ingrained in the expert players' arsenal of winning plays.

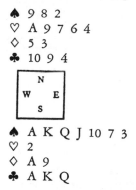

```
              ♠ 9 8 2
              ♡ A 9 7 6 4
              ◇ 5 3
              ♣ 10 9 4
                  N
              W       E
                  S
              ♠ A K Q J 10 7 3
              ♡ 2
              ◇ A 9
              ♣ A K Q
```

After West had opened the bidding with *three hearts,* South arrived at a *six spade contract,* against which West's opening lead was the King of Hearts.

The instinctive reaction was to put up the Ace. But South, recalling the bidding, realized that East might be void of hearts, so he "held-up" the Ace — and East showed out! The Queen of Hearts was then continued, declarer trumping. He then led the Ace of trumps, followed by a trump to dummy's nine-spot. With trumps having been removed, it now became safe to lead the Ace of Hearts, upon which declarer discarded his losing diamond. The deal was:

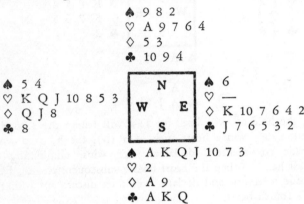

```
                    ♠ 9 8 2
                    ♡ A 9 7 6 4
                    ◇ 5 3
                    ♣ 10 9 4
  ♠ 5 4                              ♠ 6
  ♡ K Q J 10 8 5 3     N             ♡ —
  ◇ Q J 8          W       E         ◇ K 10 7 6 4 2
  ♣ 8                  S             ♣ J 7 6 5 3 2
                    ♠ A K Q J 10 7 3
                    ♡ 2
                    ◇ A 9
                    ♣ A K Q
```

By not putting up the heart Ace at trick one, declarer lost a heart trick immediately instead of losing a diamond trick ultimately. Putting it another way, he saved the Ace of Hearts until it was safe to play it.

11.

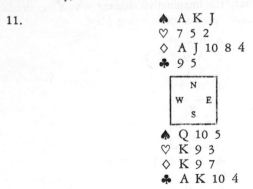

```
                    ♠ A K J
                    ♡ 7 5 2
                    ◇ A J 10 8 4
                    ♣ 9 5
                       N
                    W     E
                       S
                    ♠ Q 10 5
                    ♡ K 9 3
                    ◇ K 9 7
                    ♣ A K 10 4
```

Against South's *three notrump contract,* West opened the Queen of Hearts and declarer made what may appear to be a most dangerous play: he declined to win the trick! West then continued with the Ace, followed by a third round of hearts, declarer's King winning. On this trick East failed to follow suit.

From here in the play was routine, declarer taking the diamond finesse through West — that is, in such a manner that if it lost it would lose only to the "non-dangerous" East hand. The deal was:

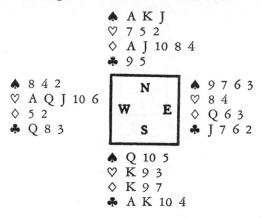

```
              ♠ A K J
              ♡ 7 5 2
              ◇ A J 10 8 4
              ♣ 9 5

 ♠ 8 4 2          N          ♠ 9 7 6 3
 ♡ A Q J 10 6                ♡ 8 4
 ◇ 5 2        W     E        ◇ Q 6 3
 ♣ Q 8 3          S          ♣ J 7 6 2

              ♠ Q 10 5
              ♡ K 9 3
              ◇ K 9 7
              ♣ A K 10 4
```

As the reader can see, if declarer had won the opening heart lead with the King, the success of his contract would have depended on whether he guessed correctly the location of the Diamond Queen. If he misguessed, then the opponents would cash four heart tricks. By "holding-up" and subsequently eliminating hearts from the East hand, he was enabled to finesse with safety. Even if the finesse lost, declarer was sure of making three spade tricks, four diamonds, and two clubs.

The reader may raise the question: what if West, upon winning his heart Queen, now shifted to a spade? In this case, dummy's King would win, and declarer would lead the four of diamonds from dummy, finessing his nine-spot. *Even if this finesse lost* (which it would not have), *West would again have the lead* — and he would be back to the same position as at trick two, except that in the interim declarer would have established his diamond suit.

One last possible "loophole" to the suggested line of play might be raised. What if after the Queen of Hearts was permitted to hold the first trick, West had then played his Jack of Hearts? Declarer, of course, would now take his King. He would then finesse the diamonds in such a manner that only East could win the trick. This line of play would be guaranteed to fulfill the contract: if East had no more hearts, then there would be no problem. If East did have a third heart, then the original distribution of the adverse hearts had to be 4-3, and all declarer could ever lose would be three hearts and one diamond.

12. A situation comparable to the theme of the preceding deal is the following, in which the extent to which the hold-up play is utilized is determined by considering the distribution of the opponents' suit.

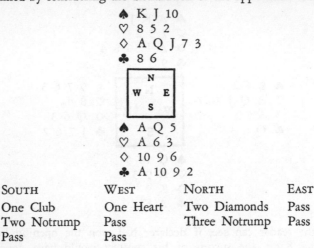

♠ K J 10
♡ 8 5 2
◇ A Q J 7 3
♣ 8 6

♠ A Q 5
♡ A 6 3
◇ 10 9 6
♣ A 10 9 2

SOUTH	WEST	NORTH	EAST
One Club	One Heart	Two Diamonds	Pass
Two Notrump	Pass	Three Notrump	Pass
Pass	Pass		

West opens the King of Hearts, South holding-up. The Queen of Hearts is then continued — *and declarer should take it!* Declarer now leads the ten of diamonds, and finesses, East's King winning the trick. If East is then able to return a heart, does not that mean that the adverse hearts were divided 4-3, and that all declarer will lose will be three hearts and a diamond? Of course, if hearts were divided 5-2, then East, upon winning with the diamond King, will have no heart to return.

If you do not capture the second round of hearts, you will be very unhappy, for at trick three West will shift to the King of Clubs:

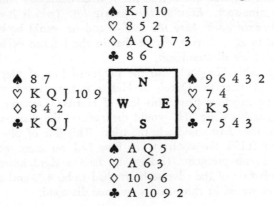

♠ K J 10
♡ 8 5 2
◇ A Q J 7 3
♣ 8 6

♠ 8 7
♡ K Q J 10 9
◇ 8 4 2
♣ K Q J

♠ 9 6 4 3 2
♡ 7 4
◇ K 5
♣ 7 5 4 3

♠ A Q 5
♡ A 6 3
◇ 10 9 6
♣ A 10 9 2

13. On occasion, it is difficult to differentiate a single stopper from a double stopper. As an illustration of this point, witness the following deal:

♠ 5 3
♡ A 9 7
◇ A 8 7 2
♣ 10 9 6 3

```
      N
  W       E
      S
```

♠ A J 4
♡ K Q 10
◇ K 3
♣ A Q J 8 4

Against South's *three notrump contract* West opens a low spade, and East puts up the Queen. Should you take it or "hold-up?"

If you examine the hand closely, you will perceive that you are going to take the club finesse in such a manner that if the finesse loses it can lose *only to West*. That is, if East has the Club King he can never obtain the lead with it.

Since West, then, is the only one who can ever get the lead via the Club King, you should capture the spade Queen with your Ace, after which you get to dummy to take the club finesse. Now you still have the J x of spades left, as protection against West's K x. Should West obtain the lead via the King of Clubs, if he cashes his Spade King, he will establish your Jack. If he abstains from leading any more spades, you have ten sure tricks: one spade, three hearts, two diamonds, and four clubs. The deal was:

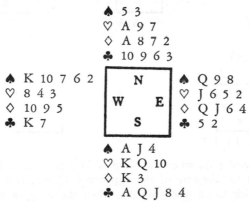

♠ 5 3
♡ A 9 7
◇ A 8 7 2
♣ 10 9 6 3

♠ K 10 7 6 2   ♠ Q 9 8
♡ 8 4 3   ♡ J 6 5 2
◇ 10 9 5   ◇ Q J 6 4
♣ K 7   ♣ 5 2

♠ A J 4
♡ K Q 10
◇ K 3
♣ A Q J 8 4

If you decline to capture the spade Queen, with the Ace, East will continue spades. No matter what you do from here in, West will establish his spades. And when he obtains the lead via the Club King, he will cash sufficient spade tricks to defeat your contract.

14.   As can be evidenced from the preceding deal, it is most important to be able to distinguish a single stopper from a double stopper. This may appear to be rather a naive statement — that is, anybody can tell the difference between A x x and A K x, etc. But there are certain types of situations — as on the previous deal — where the possession of a double stopper is not clearly discernible to the naked eye, and where the untrained observer has occasional difficulty in differentiating one from the other.

There is another type of situation, somewhat analogous to the above, where it is not readily apparent whether two stoppers are possessed, or one. This is the case when a lead by an opponent has *created* a second stopper for you in a suit where there was but one stopper originally. And, *where you have a double-stopper in a suit which an opponent has led, as a principle you do not hold-up generally,* since the second stopper still preserves your control of the suit. To illustrate:

West has opened the *King of Hearts* against each of the following combinations. On each of them you will take your Ace, since the King of Hearts lead has established a second stopper for you.

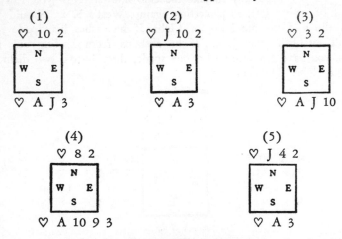

(1) ♡ 10 2
N
W   E
S
♡ A J 3

(2) ♡ J 10 2
N
W   E
S
♡ A 3

(3) ♡ 3 2
N
W   E
S
♡ A J 10

(4) ♡ 8 2
N
W   E
S
♡ A 10 9 3

(5) ♡ J 4 2
N
W   E
S
♡ A 3

In (1), (2), and (3), when the King of Hearts is taken by the Ace, the J 10 are left to take care of the opponents' Queen, one trick to be won, and one trick to be lost. In (4), when the King is captured by the Ace, the 10 9 8 combination must win one future trick against the opponents' Q J combination. In (5), since West's opening lead denotes the K Q, upon taking the King with the Ace, then later leading the three-spot toward the Jack, the Jack will become promoted into a winner.

Let us take a brief look at a simple deal illustrating the correctness of not holding-up when a second stopper has been created for you:

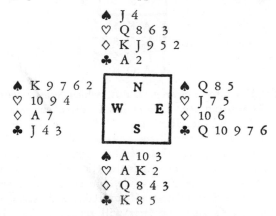

♠ J 4
♡ Q 8 6 3
◇ K J 9 5 2
♣ A 2

♠ K 9 7 6 2
♡ 10 9 4
◇ A 7
♣ J 4 3

♠ Q 8 5
♡ J 7 5
◇ 10 6
♣ Q 10 9 7 6

♠ A 10 3
♡ A K 2
◇ Q 8 4 3
♣ K 8 5

Against your *three notrump* contract West opens his fourth best spade, and East puts up the Queen. If you "hold-up" your Ace, spades will be continued until you take your Ace. Then, when you attack the diamond suit, West will take his Ace, and you will lose your contract, the defenders making four spades and one diamond.

But if you properly take your spade Ace at trick one, your contract is guaranteed. You then lead a diamond — and you still have the J 10 of spades left to take care of their King.

15. There is a specialized type of situation where the hold-up play is employed in notrump contracts despite the fact that you originally held *two sure stoppers* in the suit led. It is a not infrequent situation, and the principle upon which it is based is this:

Whenever you have *two key cards to drive out of the opponents' hands,* and you have a double-stopper in the suit which they have led, "hold-up" on the *first* lead of their suit. In so doing, you will ultimately break the communication between their hands, and effectively prevent the leader from cashing his suit. To illustrate:

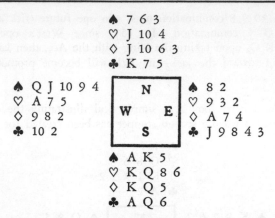

The contract is *three notrump*, against which West opens the Queen of Spades. As you can see, declarer has to drive out two "key" cards: the Diamond Ace and the Heart Ace. And, as you will understand in a moment, declarer should permit the Queen to win the opening lead.

Let us assume, however, that declarer wins the Queen of Spades with his King, and that he now leads the King of Diamonds, East's Ace winning. East will then return a spade, and even if declarer now holds up, it will be too late, for West will overtake, and lead another spade, driving out declarer's Ace. Declarer will sooner or later have to lead a heart, and West will take his Ace to cash his established spades.

The reader may raise the point: "But what if declarer, at trick two, had played a heart instead of a diamond, knocking out *West's* Ace? Then West could never re-obtain the lead to cash his to-be-established spades." Quite right. As I played the hand in the preceding paragraph, had declarer guessed to knock out the Heart Ace first (instead of East's Diamond Ace), then he would have made his contract. The hold-up play, holding a double-stopper, with two key cards to knock out, *will always eliminate the guess as to which of the two key cards to knock out first.*

So let us now play the hand correctly. The Queen of Spades is permitted to win the first trick, and the second spade lead is captured by declarer's King. Can you see that the contract is now guaranteed whether declarer leads a heart or a diamond? If he leads a diamond, East will win it, but he will have no spade to return; if declarer leads a heart instead, West will win it, play another spade to establish his suit — but he will never again obtain the lead to cash the suit.

Two more questions may come to mind: (1) what if East had three spades and (2) what if West had both red Aces?

On (1), if East had a third spade to return whenever he obtained the lead, then the original spade distribution would have been 4-3 (instead of the actual 5-2), in which case declarer could not have lost more than two spades, a heart, and a diamond no matter how he played the hand.

On (2), if West had both the Ace of Hearts and the Ace of Diamonds (with the spades being divided 5-2), then the contract would have been predestined to defeat, for nobody on earth could have fulfilled it against a spade opening.

Whenever the two missing key cards are split in the hands of the opponents, the hold-up with a double stopper in a notrump contract will assure success.

16. This is the final "hold-up" hand, and as on Deal 15, it illustrates the situation where a hold-up is employed with a double-stopper when two of the opponents' key cards are to be driven out (in notrump contracts only).

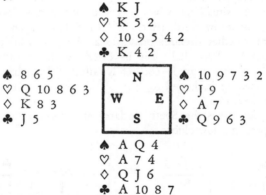

♠ K J
♡ K 5 2
◊ 10 9 5 4 2
♣ K 4 2

♠ 8 6 5
♡ Q 10 8 6 3
◊ K 8 3
♣ J 5

♠ 10 9 7 3 2
♡ J 9
◊ A 7
♣ Q 9 6 3

♠ A Q 4
♡ A 7 4
◊ Q J 6
♣ A 10 8 7

The contract is *three notrump,* and West opens the six of hearts.

As declarer views the combined North-South hands, it becomes apparent that he must drive out the Ace and King of Diamonds to establish that suit.

Let us say that declarer plays it incorrectly and wins the opening heart lead. He now leads a diamond, which *East* captures with his Ace. East then returns a heart, and even if declarer now holds up, West will overtake and drive out declarer's last stopper (dummy's King) by continuing the heart suit. When West subsequently obtains the lead with the Diamond King, he will then cash his established hearts. All in all, the defenders will make two diamond tricks and three heart tricks.

But if declarer holds up on the opening lead by playing low from both hands, East's Jack will win the trick. East will now return his remaining heart — and declarer has smooth sailing from here in. He leads a diamond: if East wins his Ace, he has no heart to return; if, instead, West takes his King, he knocks out declarer's last stopper in hearts. Another diamond is then led, East's Ace winning — but East has no heart to return and dummy's diamond suit is established and cashable.

As mentioned in the previous illustration, if East had another heart (three of them), then the original heart distribution would have been 4-3, guaranteeing the fulfillment of the contract. Had West held both the Ace and King of Diamonds (and *five* hearts), then the contract would be doomed to defeat owing to circumstances beyond declarer's control.

There were presented some pages back five specific situations in which an opponent's lead created a second stopper for declarer, where but one sure stopper had existed originally. There are also a few comparable stock situations where, as the opponent's lead is made, declarer does not know until after *third hand* has played (the partner of the leader) whether declarer possesses a single or double stopper in the suit which has been led. Let us briefly examine these situations to see how declarer's play is concretely affected by what third hand plays on the opening lead, and to understand what motivates declarer in playing as he does.

You find yourself as the South declarer at a *three notrump contract,* with West opening a low club.

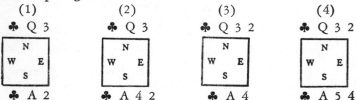

In (1) and (2), your correct play is to put up the Queen. If third hand plays low, meaning West has led away from the King, then your Queen will capture the trick, and the Ace will still control the suit. If the Queen is covered by third hand's King, then you will allow the King to win, "holding-up" your Ace as long as possible. In (1), it can be only until the second round; in (2), you will hold up until the third round.

If you do not put up dummy's Queen at trick one, you will never be able to win more than one trick, regardless as to the location of the

King. Should you play low, East will play either the nine, ten, or Jack, which will capture the trick (unless you take your Ace), and their King, regardless of its location, will capture dummy's Queen on the next round.

In (3) and (4), the better play generally is to play a low card from dummy, winning the trick in your own hand with the Ace. Thereafter you should try to keep West out of the lead, for the Q x in dummy constitutes protection should East obtain the lead. That is, if East leads a club, North's Queen will be promoted into a future winner. But if West leads a club, and East has the King, dummy's Queen will be trapped. Should it develop that West cannot be prevented from subsequently obtaining the lead, and he then plays a club, you will put up dummy's Queen and fervently hope that West is leading away from the King.

What then is the difference between (1) and (2) as opposed to (3) and (4)? In the former, if the Queen is not played to the first trick, it gets left alone in dummy and is of no value. Therefore, you play it at once, gaining a trick if West has led away from the King, while still retaining control of that suit. In (3) and (4), if you play low from dummy and capture the trick with your Ace, you will still be retaining the *guarded* Queen in dummy, and consequently the Queen will be a control with respect to that suit — that is, it will at least temporarily prevent the opponents from running through you in that suit.

CHAPTER VI

ENTRIES

IT is much easier for declarer to play his cards intelligently and correctly than it is for the defenders. The obvious reason for this is that declarer sees 26 cards, his own and dummy's, *and can plan the play of these cards*. After all, it is simpler to look at 26 cards and know what the precise problems are in relation to the fulfillment of any given contract than it is to look at just 13 cards and guess as to what your partner's 13 cards might be.

One of declarer's major problems in planning his campaign is the question of "communication" between his own hand and dummy. For example, suppose declarer is playing a four spade contract. He looks at his combined 26 cards and takes inventory: "I have nine sure tricks. *If I can get to dummy* to take a successful club finesse, I'll have my tenth and game-going trick." So he looks around to see how *he can get to dummy*. And this brings him — and us — to the subject of "entries," or "communication."

In order to get to dummy, declarer needs what is called "an entry card." An entry card is a card which enables a player to get to the hand from which he wishes to lead. In other words, *an entry card is a winner which puts the hand containing it into the lead whenever that winner is cashed*. The most direct example of an entry card would be an Ace, a sure winner; or a King of a suit when partner holds the Ace of the same suit. Many other types of entries are not so easy to see, or to find, or to create, such as low cards which have not as yet been developed into future entries, or high cards which are just possible entries, depending on the location of adversely-held high cards.

One of the prime attributes of the better bridge player is his ability to move gracefully and easily from one hand to another, *as necessity demands*. Without this fluidity of movement it becomes impossible to accomplish the various things which are mandatory for the attainment of winning play.

This chapter is devoted to giving the reader the key which will open the door, and which will provide access to and from one hand or the other. The solving of this "entry" problem will also serve to maintain communication between both hands, a most vital weapon in conducting aggressive warfare. In bridge, "access" and "communication" are synonymous with the word "entry."

Now let us see what all the fussin' is about.

You are in a *six notrump contract* with the following cards:

♠ K J 10 2
♥ 6 4
♦ J 10 9 7 3
♣ 5 3

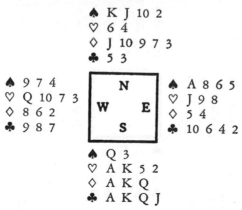

♠ Q 3
♥ A K 5 2
♦ A K Q
♣ A K Q J

West opens the nine of clubs, which you capture with the Jack. You now stop to take inventory: four club tricks, five diamond tricks, two heart tricks, and one spade — if you can enter dummy to cash the Jack and ten of diamonds.

But you had better give serious consideration to the question of entering dummy. Only the spade suit is a possibility. Should you elect to play the Queen of Spades immediately, playing low from dummy when West plays low, you will go down, if your Queen is not captured! You will eventually be compelled to lose both a spade and two hearts.

Proper handling of this hand requires the cashing of the Ace, King and Queen of Diamonds first. Then the Queen of Spades is led *and overtaken by dummy's King*. Whether East (or West) takes his Ace is immaterial, for an entry to dummy is certain, either now via the King or later via the Jack. There is now no way of preventing declarer from cashing his twelve tricks. The deal was:

♠ K J 10 2
♥ 6 4
♦ J 10 9 7 3
♣ 5 3

♠ 9 7 4   ♠ A 8 6 5
♥ Q 10 7 3   ♥ J 9 8
♦ 8 6 2   ♦ 5 4
♣ 9 8 7   ♣ 10 6 4 2

♠ Q 3
♥ A K 5 2
♦ A K Q
♣ A K Q J

Let us look at another entry situation, the type which occurs at more or less frequent intervals, and is most annoying especially when you can do nothing but leave it to the gods of chance:

♠ J 10 4 2
♡ Q J 10 6 3
♢ 10 4
♣ 8 5

♠ A K Q
♡ A K
♢ K 8 7 2
♣ A K 9 2

You are in *three notrump,* against which West opens a low diamond and East's Queen is captured by your King. On "paper," you have 12 tricks; four spades, five hearts, one diamond, and two clubs. It is quite obvious, however, that these twelve tricks are on paper only, since there is just no way of entering dummy to cash the Jack of Spades and the Q J 10 of Hearts. As a matter of fact, all you can hope to take for sure are eight tricks: three spades, two hearts, one diamond, and two clubs.

So you win the opening diamond lead, cash the three top spades, the two top hearts, and the Ace and King of Clubs. Then you lead a diamond — and hope that somehow or other the opponents will put you into the dummy. Here is the deal:

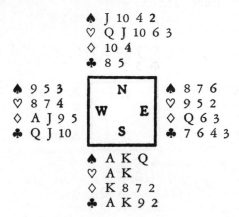

♠ J 10 4 2
♡ Q J 10 6 3
♢ 10 4
♣ 8 5

♠ 9 5 3
♡ 8 7 4
♢ A J 9 5
♣ Q J 10

♠ 8 7 6
♡ 9 5 2
♢ Q 6 3
♣ 7 6 4 3

♠ A K Q
♡ A K
♢ K 8 7 2
♣ A K 9 2

As you can see, all the defenders can cash will be three diamonds and one club, after which they must put you in dummy by leading a heart, for your ninth trick. You wind up, then, by making your contract — but it is a moot question as to whether the aggravation and annoyance throughout the play of the hand was worth the ultimate fulfillment. If only the Queen and Jack of Spades had been interchanged to the Q 10 4 2 opposite the A. K. J! How easy it would then have been to cash four spade tricks (by overtaking the Jack with the Queen), five heart tricks, one diamond and two clubs. As you know, however, wishful thinking is of no practical assistance in a bridge game. You have to make the best of what is dealt you.

Here is another hand where the question of an entry to dummy became the issue of the day. As you will see, declarer sacrifices a possible winning trick in order to create a much needed entry — and it pays off.

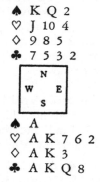

♠ K Q 2
♡ J 10 4
◇ 9 8 5
♣ 7 5 3 2

♠ A
♡ A K 7 6 2
◇ A K 3
♣ A K Q 8

Against your *six heart* contract West opens the Queen of Diamonds which is captured by your King. On superficial examination you have three possible losers: one in hearts, one in diamonds, and one in clubs.

At trick two you lay down the Ace of trumps, both opponents following suit. Your impulse now may be to play the King, hoping to drop the Queen — but this impulse would be wrong. Isn't it better to now cash the Ace of Spades, and then lead a low trump towards dummy's J 10, conceding a trick to the Queen, and establishing the ten-spot as an entry to dummy? Will it then not be routine to discard your low diamond and your low club on dummy's King and Queen of Spades? Why gamble on dropping the Queen of trumps when there is no reason for gambling? In conceding a trick to the Queen, you create two tricks for yourself in the King and Queen of Spades, plus an entry to cash them. If you had cashed the Ace *and* King of Hearts, you would not have fulfilled the slam. The deal was:

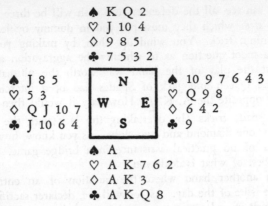

♠ K Q 2
♡ J 10 4
◇ 9 8 5
♣ 7 5 3 2

♠ J 8 5
♡ 5 3
◇ Q J 10 7
♣ J 10 6 4

♠ 10 9 7 6 4 3
♡ Q 9 8
◇ 6 4 2
♣ 9

♠ A
♡ A K 7 6 2
◇ A K 3
♣ A K Q 8

The three hands which have just been presented illustrate the subject of entries. Now let us look at a few deals that arose in actual play, and see how some of our top-flight "name" players handled the various entry problems that confronted them at the table. We shall proceed from the simple to the more complex, so please do not be offended if the first two deals appear to be too easy.

1. The following deal was once played by Bruce Gowdy, of Toronto, Canada. I know that he would not think that there was anything "expert" to the play of the hand, but the fact is that many players would probably go wrong because the hand was "too simple."

♠ A K 6 3
♡ 10 9 4 3
◇ 7 5 4
♣ 6 3

♠ 7 5
♡ A Q 2
◇ A J 9 2
♣ A K Q J

The contract was *three notrump,* with West's opening lead of the club ten being captured by declarer's Jack. Bruce then led the Ace of Hearts and followed up with the Queen, East's King winning. The contract now became a cinch, another heart being given up to West's Jack, with dummy's ten of hearts being promoted into declarer's ninth trick.

When I say that many players would go wrong on this hand, I speak from experience, since I have used this hand frequently for teaching purposes. The average student, upon winning the opening club lead, tends to lead a spade to dummy's Ace, and then he finesses the Queen of Hearts, West's King winning. *What if West now returns a spade, knocking out dummy's King?* Would not dummy's last entry then be removed? How can you ever get to dummy to cash the to-be-established ten of hearts? You can't — and you never make your ninth trick.

I will concede that West, upon winning the heart King, may not play back a spade, thereby preserving dummy's entry. But why risk it when you can automatically make nine tricks by leading the Ace, Queen, and a third heart from your own hand? The deal was:

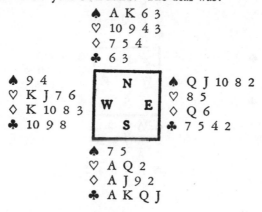

♠ A K 6 3
♡ 10 9 4 3
◇ 7 5 4
♣ 6 3

♠ 9 4
♡ K J 7 6
◇ K 10 8 3
♣ 10 9 8

♠ Q J 10 8 2
♡ 8 5
◇ Q 6
♣ 7 5 4 2

♠ 7 5
♡ A Q 2
◇ A J 9 2
♣ A K Q J

2. Years ago I saw this simple hand below played by Harold S. Vanderbilt, of New York City. There is nothing to it, and yet if you give it to one of your less experienced friends to play, you may discover that the *losing play* will be made at trick one:

♠ Q J
♡ 8 7 6
◇ K Q J 10 9 4
♣ 8 3

♠ A K 2
♡ A J 3 2
◇ A
♣ K J 6 4 2

Mr. Vanderbilt arrived at a *three notrump* contract, against which West opened the ten of spades, dummy's Jack was put up, East followed with the three spot — and if you elect to win the trick "cheaply" with the Jack, you will be sorry. There will now be no way to enter dummy to cash the diamonds.

When the deal was actually played, the Jack of Spades was overtaken by declarer's King. Now the Ace of Diamonds was laid down, after which the deuce of spades was led to dummy's entry, the Queen of Spades. There was no difficulty from here on, since three spade tricks, one heart trick, and six diamond tricks were assured. The deal was:

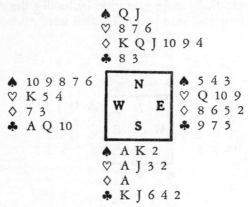

♠ Q J
♡ 8 7 6
◊ K Q J 10 9 4
♣ 8 3

♠ 10 9 8 7 6   ♠ 5 4 3
♡ K 5 4   ♡ Q 10 9
◊ 7 3   ◊ 8 6 5 2
♣ A Q 10   ♣ 9 7 5

♠ A K 2
♡ A J 3 2
◊ A
♣ K J 6 4 2

3. The following deal presents a situation which has become a standard one amongst the better players, but it is not completely familiar to most bridge players. When it arose in actual combat, the South declarer was Jack Shore of New York City.

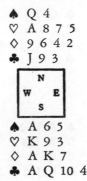

♠ Q 4
♡ A 8 7 5
◊ 9 6 4 2
♣ J 9 3

♠ A 6 5
♡ K 9 3
◊ A K 7
♣ A Q 10 4

On West's opening lead of the spade ten against South's *three notrump* contract, dummy's Queen was put up, and East covered with the King. This was permitted to hold the trick, after which the defenders also won the second round of the suit. When the third round was led, declarer captured it with his Ace.

Upon observation it became obvious that to make his contract declarer had to win four club tricks. There was no choice but to get to dummy via its sole entry — the Ace of Hearts — and hopefully to lead a club playing East for the King. Which club should he lead?

He led the nine-spot, and took the finesse, which worked. Now the Jack of Clubs was led, and East's King was again successfully finessed. Then came a third club from dummy, declarer's Queen winning. And that was that. The deal was:

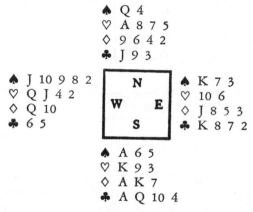

```
              ♠ Q 4
              ♡ A 8 7 5
              ◊ 9 6 4 2
              ♣ J 9 3
♠ J 10 9 8 2      N        ♠ K 7 3
♡ Q J 4 2    W       E     ♡ 10 6
◊ Q 10                     ◊ J 8 5 3
♣ 6 5             S        ♣ K 8 7 2
              ♠ A 6 5
              ♡ K 9 3
              ◊ A K 7
              ♣ A Q 10 4
```

It may appear, on casual observation, that declarer did nothing which the less-skilled player would not have done. *But if the first club lead from dummy had been the Jack, declarer would not have been able to make four club tricks.* With the Jack winning, the nine would then have been led — and declarer would have been forced to capture it in his own hand with the ten-spot. There would now have been no way to enter dummy to take the finesse for the third time.

The reader might say, "Well, on the lead of the Jack, why does not declarer 'get out of his own way' by playing the ten-spot?" If he does that, then on the second lead of the nine, East will cover with the King, forcing declarer to capture the trick with the Ace. Now East's eight-spot will have been promoted into a winner.

The reader will do well to study this particular situation, for it arises frequently enough to warrant remembering.

4. Every bridge player, at one time or another, finds himself in an over-ambitious contract. The test of a good bridge player is his ability to extricate himself from these occasional apparently hopeless positions. The South declarer on the deal which follows was Oswald Jacoby, of Dallas, Texas.

♠ 9 6 4
♡ 8 7 3
◇ A K J 4
♣ 6 5 2

♠ A Q 3
♡ A K
◇ Q 9 8 3
♣ A Q J 10

The contract was *six notrump,* against which West opened the Queen of Hearts, taken by declarer's King.

Ossie perceived that to make his contract, dummy had to be entered four times, three times to take club finesses, and once to take a spade finesse. On the face of it, there appeared to be only three entries — but Ossie created the vitally-needed fourth entry.

On winning the opening heart lead, the eight of diamonds was led to dummy's Jack, and a club finesse was taken — with success. Dummy was then re-entered by leading the nine of diamonds, taken by the board's King, after which another club finesse was taken. Since both opponents had followed to two rounds of diamonds, there was just one diamond outstanding. Now declarer could afford to lead his Queen of Diamonds and overtake it with dummy's Ace, to successfully finesse clubs again. Then came the fourth entry to dummy: declarer's *three-spot of diamonds was led, and overtaken by dummy's four.* The spade finesse was now tried, and when it worked, declarer's slam contract was fulfilled.

Admittedly declarer was lucky in finding both the King of Clubs and King of Spades favorably located — if either one of these "key" cards had been in the West hand, the contract would automatically have been defeated. But it took more than luck to fulfill the contract: that fourth entry had to be created. If the three of diamonds had been led to dummy's Jack at trick two, the fourth entry would have disappeared forever. The deal was:

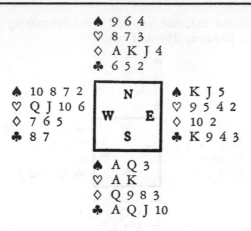

5. In the two deals which follow, the only entry to dummy is in the suit which you are trying to establish. The better players have learned how to maintain communication within that suit while establishing it; the less-skilled players sever their own lines of communication.

♠ 6 2
♡ 7 5
◊ K 8 7 5 4 2
♣ 10 7 3

♠ A K 5 3
♡ A Q 9
◊ A J 6
♣ A J 4

West opened the four of hearts against South's *three notrump contract,* East's Jack being captured by declarer's Queen. The Ace of Diamonds was then cashed, both opponents following suit, after which the Jack of Diamonds was led, West putting up the Queen. The natural impulse now would be to reach for dummy's King — and if you do, you go down!

Should you win the trick with the King of Diamonds, East will fail to follow suit. Now there will be no entry to both establish and cash dummy's diamonds.

But if you permit West's Queen to win the second diamond lead, your baby six of diamonds will serve as an entry to dummy's now-established diamond suit, and you will wind up making five diamond tricks instead of just two. The deal was:

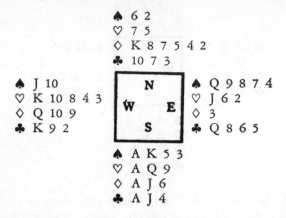

```
              ♠ 6 2
              ♡ 7 5
              ◇ K 8 7 5 4 2
              ♣ 10 7 3
♠ J 10              N              ♠ Q 9 8 7 4
♡ K 10 8 4 3   W       E          ♡ J 6 2
◇ Q 10 9           S              ◇ 3
♣ K 9 2                           ♣ Q 8 6 5
              ♠ A K 5 3
              ♡ A Q 9
              ◇ A J 6
              ♣ A J 4
```

6. In this deal, as on the preceding one, the safety of the contract demands that a trick be conceded to the opponents in order to maintain communication with dummy.

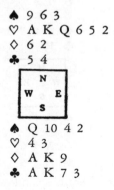

```
              ♠ 9 6 3
              ♡ A K Q 6 5 2
              ◇ 6 2
              ♣ 5 4
                  N
              W       E
                  S
              ♠ Q 10 4 2
              ♡ 4 3
              ◇ A K 9
              ♣ A K 7 3
```

The opening lead against South's *three notrump* is the Queen of Clubs, which is captured by declarer's King.

Normal play would be to cash the Ace of Hearts, then the King of Hearts — and then it is too late, for you are down!

Recognizing that dummy is devoid of any outside entry, and perceiving that just *five* heart tricks are needed to fulfill the contract, an expert player would lead a low heart at trick two and allow the opponents to win it. Declarer's remaining heart would then serve as an entry to dummy's heart suit. The deal was:

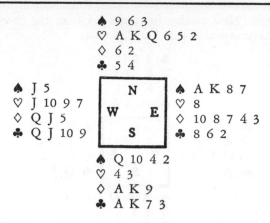

♠ 9 6 3
♡ A K Q 6 5 2
◊ 6 2
♣ 5 4

♠ J 5
♡ J 10 9 7
◊ Q J 5
♣ Q J 10 9

♠ A K 8 7
♡ 8
◊ 10 8 7 4 3
♣ 8 6 2

♠ Q 10 4 2
♡ 4 3
◊ A K 9
♣ A K 7 3

7.   The slightly complex deal which follows was played by Donald
Oakie, of San Francisco. Before presenting the way Mr. Oakie played it,
let us assume that you are the South declarer at a *four spade contract*.

♠ 8 5
♡ K Q 9 2
◊ K 6 4
♣ 10 8 6 4

♠ A K Q J 10 4
♡ 8 5
◊ A 8 3
♣ K 5

West opens the Queen of Diamonds which is taken by your Ace.
How do you play the hand? Probably you lead three rounds of trumps,
exhausting the opponents of trumps. Then you lead a heart, West
plays low, and you put up dummy's Queen, which holds the trick.
Now how do you get off dummy to enter your own hand in order to
lead another heart towards dummy's King? You cannot — and you
ultimately lose two clubs, one heart and one diamond.

Donald foresaw this "entry" problem: that if dummy's Queen of
Hearts won the first heart trick, he would be unable to get off dummy —
if he drew trumps immediately.

So, after winning the opening diamond lead, declarer drew one round
of trumps, then led a heart, dummy's Queen winning. The board's last
trump was then led to re-enter the South hand, and declarer drew the

adverse trumps. Now another heart was led from the closed hand and the contract became guaranteed. The deal was:

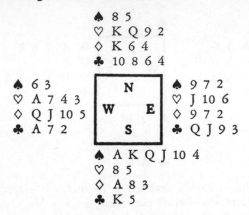

As the reader can see, on dummy's established King of Hearts declarer was able to discard his losing diamond.

8. It is the recognition of the necessity of getting to dummy which frequently compels one to get rid of a high-card, to get out of his own way, as it were. Let us assume that it is imperative to have a future entry to the North hand in the following situation:

◇ Q J 10

5 of Diamonds led

◇ K 3 2

West opens the five of diamonds, dummy's ten-spot is played, and East follows with a small diamond. To be certain of getting to dummy later, you capture dummy's ten with your own King — and the Q J in the North hand will automatically create a future entry for you. If you permit dummy's ten-spot to win, the opponents can effectively prevent you from getting to dummy in diamonds by declining to take your King when it is led.

An extension of this "unblocking" is evidenced on the following deal, in which declarer actually sacrificed a winner to make sure that she would be able to gain access to dummy. The South declarer was Doris Fuller of New York City.

♠ J 10 9
♡ A K 5
◇ 6 4 3
♣ 7 5 3 2

♠ K 6 4
♡ Q J 9
◇ A K 7
♣ A Q J 10

It is preferable — from the viewpoint of teaching — if the bidding is not presented, for an enthusiastic North pushed the contract to *four notrump*.

West opened the three of spades, which East captured with the Ace — and Doris discarded the King of Spades! East returned a low spade, West's Queen winning. A third spade then put dummy's Jack into the lead.

The club finesse was now successfully taken, after which dummy was re-entered via the Heart Ace, to take another club finesse. On this latter trick West showed out. The Jack of Hearts was led next, to be overtaken by dummy's King. The third club finesse now gave declarer four club tricks, and her contract. The deal was:

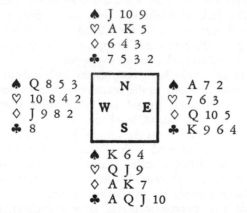

♠ J 10 9
♡ A K 5
◇ 6 4 3
♣ 7 5 3 2

♠ Q 8 5 3
♡ 10 8 4 2
◇ J 9 8 2
♣ 8

♠ A 7 2
♡ 7 6 3
◇ Q 10 5
♣ K 9 6 4

♠ K 6 4
♡ Q J 9
◇ A K 7
♣ A Q J 10

Had declarer not thrown her King of Spades on East's Ace at trick one, she would have been unable to get to dummy three times to take the three needed finesses in the club suit.

9.   The following deal illustrates how the entry problem was handled at an overbid grand slam contract in hearts. It also presents the way in which it *should have been handled*. Since there is no sense in creating an enemy for me, let us say that I "forgot" the name of the South declarer.

♠ 6 3
♡ A 9
◇ A Q 10 5 3 2
♣ A Q 5

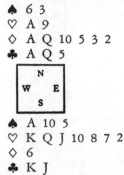

♠ A 10 5
♡ K Q J 10 8 7 2
◇ 6
♣ K J

West opened the King of Spades against South's *seven heart contract,* declarer's Ace winning. It was readily apparent that South had to somehow dispose of a losing spade to fulfill the contract. This could be done by either taking a diamond finesse or by establishing a long card winner in the diamond suit. Declarer correctly elected to establish the diamond suit.

After winning the opening spade lead, declarer removed the adverse trumps in two rounds. He then led a diamond to the Ace and trumped a diamond. The Jack of Clubs was next led to dummy's Queen, and another diamond was ruffed in the closed hand, West showing out. With the King of Diamonds not dropping, declarer was doomed. He actually went down two tricks, losing two spades.

The diamond suit could have been established without difficulty had declarer given more thought to the matter of dummy's entries. At trick two the Ace of Diamonds should be cashed, after which a diamond is ruffed *high* in the closed hand, to eliminate the danger of an over-ruff. The board is then re-entered via the nine of hearts, and a third round of diamonds is led and trumped high. Then comes a heart to dummy's Ace, and a fourth diamond ruffed, East's King dropping. Dummy is now re-entered via the Queen of Clubs, and on the two established diamonds declarer discards his two losing spades.

As the hand was incorrectly played by our declarer, the success of his contract depended on the six adverse diamonds being divided 3-3, or on one of the opponents holding a doubleton King of Diamonds. As we played it — by not removing the trump entries to dummy —

the contract was assured whether the diamonds broke 3-3 or 4-2.
The deal was:

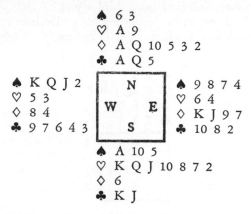

♠ 6 3
♥ A 9
♦ A Q 10 5 3 2
♣ A Q 5

♠ K Q J 2   ♠ 9 8 7 4
♥ 5 3   ♥ 6 4
♦ 8 4   ♦ K J 9 7
♣ 9 7 6 4 3   ♣ 10 8 2

♠ A 10 5
♥ K Q J 10 8 7 2
♦ 6
♣ K J

10. On the deal which follows, our declarer perceived that he
needed two entries to dummy — which he did not have — to establish
and cash dummy's heart suit, and he recognized that the opponents were
too good to give him a "present" of the suit. So he utilized his one
entry to dummy in order to attack another suit. Our South declarer was
Dave Clarren, of Minneapolis, Minn.

♠ 9 3
♥ K Q J 8 7
♦ 8 6 2
♣ 7 5 4

♠ A K Q 4
♥ 10 9
♦ A Q 3
♣ A Q 6 2

South arrived at a normal *three notrump contract*, West opening a
low diamond, and declarer capturing East's ten-spot with the Queen.

It was quite obvious to Dave that if he played the ten of hearts and
let it ride, whichever opponent had the Ace would decline to take it,
thereby rendering dummy's heart suit "hors de combat." So instead,
he led the ten of hearts, and overtook it with dummy's Jack (hoping,
of course, that maybe the opponents' Ace would capture the trick).

However, dummy's Jack was permitted to win the trick. A club was then led, and South's Queen successfully finessed, after which the Ace of Clubs was cashed, followed by a third round of clubs, East's King winning, with both opponents following suit. Declarer's fourth club was now promoted into a winner, and it became his ninth trick. The actual deal was:

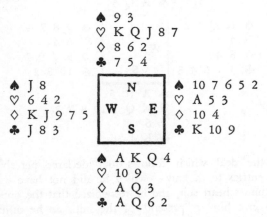

```
              ♠ 9 3
              ♡ K Q J 8 7
              ◇ 8 6 2
              ♣ 7 5 4

♠ J 8            N            ♠ 10 7 6 5 2
♡ 6 4 2                       ♡ A 5 3
◇ K J 9 7 5   W     E         ◇ 10 4
♣ J 8 3                       ♣ K 10 9
                 S
              ♠ A K Q 4
              ♡ 10 9
              ◇ A Q 3
              ♣ A Q 6 2
```

The reader may raise the question, "But what if West had not opened a diamond, thereby giving declarer a trick?" Actually the question is out of order. We are not concerned with what might have been, or what was not. We are concerned only with the facts as they are. With the diamond opening, declarer had seven sure tricks, and he had to find the best way of getting two more. In answer to the question, however, let me say that without the diamond opening, declarer would have gone down.

All of which reminds me of an anecdote which has to do with the subject of "*if*."

An explorer was relating how one day he was climbing along a narrow mountain path, when behind him he espied a lion. The explorer started running up the path with the lion in hot pursuit. Suddenly the explorer came to a dead end — and he did not care for the situation. He hurriedly looked around and he saw a small hole into which he quickly crawled. When the lion arrived on the scene a split-second later, our explorer was safe, and out of reach of the overly-fat lion who could not squeeze into the hole.

When our explorer was asked what would have happened *if* he had not found the hole he replied simply "I would not ever again be asked to answer any hypothetical questions."

11. The following deal presents a type of situation which is frequently encountered, and which the expert has learned to handle mechanically. Most players, however, tend to get a bit careless on it — and it sometimes proves costly.

♠ 7 5 4 2
♡ 9 5
◇ K Q J 7 3
♣ J 3

♠ A K
♡ A K 6 3
◇ 9 8 2
♣ A Q 6 5

South is playing *three notrump* and West opens the Queen of Spades, taken by declarer's King. Let us suppose that declarer then leads the deuce of diamonds, puts up dummy's King, and East's Ace wins the trick. A spade is returned, South's Ace winning. The eight of diamonds is led next, dummy's Queen is played — and East shows out. Declarer then returns to his own hand, and here is the diamond situation:

◇ K 7 3

◇ 10 6   N W E S

◇ 9

Declarer plays his remaining diamond, *the nine-spot, West plays low* — and declarer cannot ever get to cash dummy's diamonds.

But suppose that, on the first diamond lead, declarer had led the *nine* of diamonds, and on the second diamond lead he played the *eight-spot*. On the third diamond lead this would be the situation:

◇ K 7 3

◇ 10 6   N W E S

◇ 2

On the lead of the *deuce*, West's ten-spot could now successfully be finessed, and the entire diamond suit be brought home. The deal was:

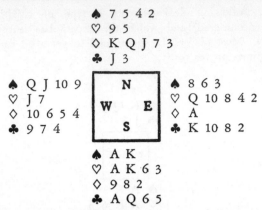

♠ 7 5 4 2
♡ 9 5
◊ K Q J 7 3
♣ J 3

♠ Q J 10 9   ♠ 8 6 3
♡ J 7   ♡ Q 10 8 4 2
◊ 10 6 5 4   ◊ A
♣ 9 7 4   ♣ K 10 8 2

♠ A K
♡ A K 6 3
◊ 9 8 2
♣ A Q 6 5

12. This final entry deal was played by David Carter of St. Louis, Missouri. I would be willing to wager that at least 99 out of 100 non-expert players would have failed to fulfill the grand slam contract:

♠ 8 3
♡ A K 9 7 5
◊ J 9 3
♣ 9 7 2

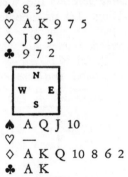

♠ A Q J 10
♡ —
◊ A K Q 10 8 6 2
♣ A K

Against South's *seven diamond contract* West opened the Queen of Clubs, which was captured by declarer's King.

On superficial examination it would appear that the contract depended on a successful spade finesse. Actually, however, the chances of making the grand slam were much better than 50-50.

At trick two the *ten of diamonds* was led to dummy's Jack, and a low heart returned, which declarer trumped with his Queen. Then came the eight of diamonds, overtaken by dummy's nine, and another heart led, declarer again trumping high. Next came the *deuce of diamonds* to dummy's three-spot.

Now the Ace and King of Hearts were cashed, both opponents having followed suit to the four rounds of hearts which had been played. On the Ace and King of Hearts declarer discarded the Jack and ten of Spades. Since dummy's fifth heart was the sole surviving heart, declarer led it next, and discarded his Queen of Spades. A grand slam bid and made — without taking a finesse. The deal was:

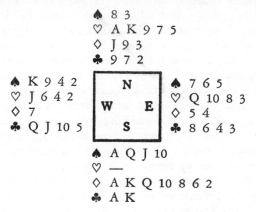

```
              ♠ 8 3
              ♡ A K 9 7 5
              ◇ J 9 3
              ♣ 9 7 2
♠ K 9 4 2       N       ♠ 7 6 5
♡ J 6 4 2    W     E    ♡ Q 10 8 3
◇ 7                     ◇ 5 4
♣ Q J 10 5      S       ♣ 8 6 4 3
              ♠ A Q J 10
              ♡ —
              ◇ A K Q 10 8 6 2
              ♣ A K
```

Had the declarer, upon winning the opening lead, started to draw trumps by playing either the Ace of Trumps, or the trump deuce to dummy's nine or Jack, it would have become impossible to ever establish and cash dummy's fifth heart. For the establishment and cashing of the fifth heart, three entries to dummy were needed — two entries to trump out two hearts, and one entry to cash the fifth heart. Only by preserving the deuce of diamonds, thereby creating an entry out of the *three of diamonds,* could this be done.

Admittedly declarer was lucky to find the eight adverse hearts divided 4-4. But I think you will agree that to fulfill his contract Dave Carter had to take full advantage of his luck.

THE DRAWING OF TRUMPS AND ITS POSTPONEMENT

Fᴙᴏᴍ birth, through infancy, through adolescence, and, finally, through maturity, there is indelibly ingrained in the mind of the potential bridge-player the concept that whenever he obtains the lead in a suit contract, the first thing he should always do is to take away the opponents' trumps. This is sound *general* advice. In every suit contract, declarer's *first thought* should be concerned with the taking away of the opponents' trumps, for when he declines to remove them, it is tantamount to leaving the enemy a weapon that he had the opportunity of destroying. But to "always take the opponents' trumps away" is a dangerous outlook to possess, for in dogmatically applying it declarer can cause his own self-destruction. After all, there are numerous situations where the drawing of trumps should be postponed; for instance, where it is imperative for declarer to trump away a loser or two with dummy's trumps; or, where a trump entry in dummy is required after one of dummy's suits has become established; or where declarer must discard one or more losers before the opponents have a chance to regain the lead to capture your losers. To use one's trumps merely as extractors without bothering to analyze the specific situation at hand, must inevitably lead to losing many a contract which should not have been lost.

There are no hard-and-fast rules or principles which determine when the adverse trumps should be picked up immediately. Probably the nearest thing to a principle with respect to the drawing of trumps is this: *unless a more important use exists for declarer's own or dummy's trumps, the opponents' trumps should be drawn as quickly as possible.*

Let us now look at three simple examples which illustrate this question of when the drawing of the adverse trumps should be postponed.

1.

      ♠ J 10 4
      ♡ 3
      ◇ K 7 2
      ♣ 10 8 7 4 3 2

```
        N
     W     E
        S
```

      ♠ K Q 9 8 6 5 2
      ♡ A 9 4
      ◇ A Q 8
      ♣ —

South is playing a *six spade contract* against which West opens the King of Clubs, declarer ruffing. If South now leads a trump, he will go down, for East, upon taking the Ace will return a trump. It will then become impossible for declarer to ruff out both of his losing hearts, and he will ultimately lose another trick.

As is obvious, after ruffing the opening club lead, declarer should lead the Ace of Hearts, and then ruff a heart in dummy. He then returns to his own hand via either a diamond or a club, to trump out his remaining heart. Trumps are now led, and all the defenders can ever make will be the Ace of trumps.

2.

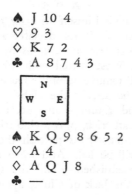

♠ J 10 4
♡ 9 3
◇ K 7 2
♣ A 8 7 4 3

♠ K Q 9 8 6 5 2
♡ A 4
◇ A Q J 8
♣ —

Again South finds himself in a *six spade contract,* and this time West opens the King of Hearts, declarer's Ace winning. To lead trumps now would be downright foolish, for the defenders, upon winning with the Ace, will cash a heart trick to defeat declarer.

So, naturally, declarer defers the drawing of trumps for a brief moment. At trick two he leads a diamond to dummy's King, and cashes the Ace of Clubs, upon which he discards his losing heart. Now trumps are drawn, and all is well.

The reader might raise the question: suppose the King of Diamonds is trumped? While this may happen, it is a most unlikely possibility. But even if there were a greater risk of the diamond King being trumped, declarer would still have to take that risk, for if he led a trump instead, *he would go down to defeat 100% of the time.* From a theoretical point of view, it boils down to taking a line of play which involves a very slight risk, as opposed to taking a line of play which will result in inevitable defeat.

3.

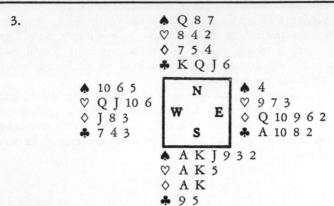

```
              ♠ Q 8 7
              ♡ 8 4 2
              ◇ 7 5 4
              ♣ K Q J 6
♠ 10 6 5         N        ♠ 4
♡ Q J 10 6              ♡ 9 7 3
◇ J 8 3     W       E   ◇ Q 10 9 6 2
♣ 7 4 3         S        ♣ A 10 8 2
              ♠ A K J 9 3 2
              ♡ A K 5
              ◇ A K
              ♣ 9 5
```

Once again South finds himself in a *six spade contract,* against which West opens the Queen of Hearts, declarer winning with the King.

When declarer starts drawing trumps by playing the Ace and King, he will discover that West started with three trumps. If he now leads a third trump, he will remove dummy's Queen of Spades, a vitally-needed entry. Then, when he attacks the clubs, East can decline to take his Ace until the second round — and declarer will now be unable to avoid the loss of a heart trick, plus a club trick, resulting in his defeat.

Proper play, consequently, is to cash the Ace and King of trumps, after which a club will be led. And when East takes his Ace, dummy's club Jack will be established — and the Queen of Spades will then serve as an entry to the Jack of Clubs, upon which declarer will discard his losing heart.

The following illustration is virtually the same as in the preceding, with just one significant card being changed.

```
              ♠ Q 8 7
              ♡ 8 4 2
              ◇ K 7 4
              ♣ K Q J 6
                  N
              W       E
                  S
              ♠ A K J 9 3 2
              ♡ A K 5
              ◇ A 5
              ♣ 9 5
```

West again opens the Queen of Hearts against South's *six spade contract.* With the King of Diamonds in dummy as a sure entry, it is no longer necessary to delay the drawing of all the trumps. In this situation, declarer pulls all of West's trumps and then leads a club, which East can take whenever he chooses. When declarer next obtains the lead, he simply plays a low diamond to dummy's King, and on the Jack of Clubs he discards his losing heart.

The preceding examples have been simple ones, illustrating the three major situations in which the drawing of trumps must be either postponed altogether, or the total drawing of them deferred. The three major situations, to repeat, are:

1. Where it is imperative for declarer to use his or dummy's trumps to ruff out one or more inevitable losers.
2. Where it is imperative for declarer to discard one or more of his own losers before the opponents are able to regain the lead (via a trump) to capture those losers.
3. Where a trump entry is required in dummy in order to be able to cash the high cards in one of dummy's to-be-established suits, so that declarer can discard one or more of his losers.

Let us now turn our attention to some actual deals where the problem of drawing trumps versus not drawing trumps confronted declarer, and see how these problems were resolved.

1.

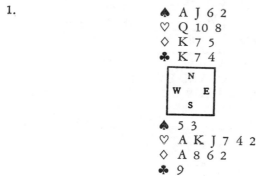

```
        ♠  A J 6 2
        ♡  Q 10 8
        ◊  K 7 5
        ♣  K 7 4
          ┌─────────┐
          │    N    │
          │ W     E │
          │    S    │
          └─────────┘
        ♠  5 3
        ♡  A K J 7 4 2
        ◊  A 8 6 2
        ♣  9
```

South arrives at a *four heart* contract, against which West opens the club Queen, dummy plays low, as does East, after which West follows with another club, which declarer ruffs. Potentially, South has four losers: one which he has lost in clubs, one in spades, and two in diamonds. Of course, if the six missing diamonds are divided 3-3, then South will lose but one diamond trick. And, on this reasoning, most bridge players would draw trumps, and then play for the adverse diamonds to be divided 3-3. When the diamonds would fail to divide as hoped for, declarer would now go down.

The correct play of the above hand is relatively simple. At trick three, the King of Diamonds is cashed, followed by a diamond to the Ace, and then a third diamond is conceded to the opponents. Now nothing can prevent declarer from ruffing his fourth diamond with dummy's ten of hearts, for the game-going trick. Played in this fashion, declarer will make his contract whether diamonds are divided 3-3 or 4-2.

From the viewpoint of minimum risk, one round of trumps should be cashed prior to playing the King of Diamonds. This play will take care of the situation where one of the opponents might have just a singleton diamond and a singleton trump. For those who might be inclined to draw two rounds of trumps, let me point out that if this is done, then when an opponent wins the third round of diamonds, he might now play a third trump, removing dummy's last trump, thereby preventing declarer from ruffing his fourth diamond.

The deal was:

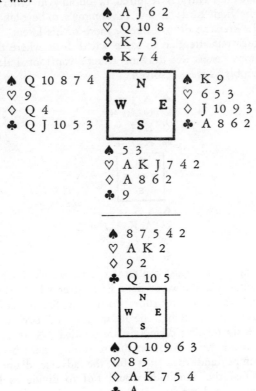

```
                ♠ A J 6 2
                ♡ Q 10 8
                ◇ K 7 5
                ♣ K 7 4
  ♠ Q 10 8 7 4   ┌─────────┐   ♠ K 9
  ♡ 9            │    N    │   ♡ 6 5 3
  ◇ Q 4          │ W     E │   ◇ J 10 9 3
  ♣ Q J 10 5 3   │    S    │   ♣ A 8 6 2
                └─────────┘
                ♠ 5 3
                ♡ A K J 7 4 2
                ◇ A 8 6 2
                ♣ 9
```

2.

```
                ♠ 8 7 5 4 2
                ♡ A K 2
                ◇ 9 2
                ♣ Q 10 5
                ┌─────────┐
                │    N    │
                │ W     E │
                │    S    │
                └─────────┘
                ♠ Q 10 9 6 3
                ♡ 8 5
                ◇ A K 7 5 4
                ♣ A
```

South is playing *four spades*. West opens the Queen of Hearts which dummy's King captures. The normal impulse now is to lead a trump, figuring that the three missing trumps will be divided 2-1. *If trumps are touched, declarer will go down!*

Correct play at trick two is to promptly start cross-trumping the hand: diamonds are ruffed in dummy, and hearts and clubs are ruffed in the closed hand. Let the opponents make their three trumps by ruffing wherever they wish.

If trumps are attacked immediately, declarer will run into the A K J in the West hand — and West will now continue trumps. The result will be that *six of dummy's and declarer's trumps will be picked up by West's A K J*, thereby effectively preventing declarer from making more than nine tricks. And, as the reader can realize, these six trumps could be used separately and independently for cross-trumping purposes. The complete deal was:

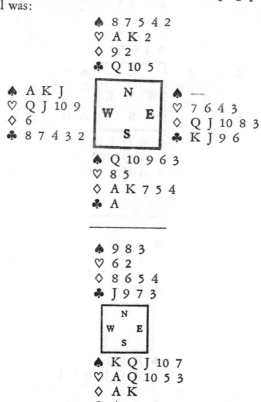

3.

South arrives at a *four spade contract* against which West opens the Queen of Diamonds, declarer's Ace winning. Once again, if declarer touches trumps, *he will go down*, for the defenders will then continue trumps, and it will be impossible for declarer to ruff out any of his hearts.

From declarer's point of view, he has losing hearts to dispose of — and they can be disposed of only by ruffing them in dummy. Therefore, at trick two, declarer should promptly play the Ace and another heart, the defenders winning the latter trick. Even if they now shift to a trump, playing the Ace followed by another trump, declarer will still have one trump left in dummy to ruff the third round of hearts — and his contract will now be fulfilled.

The actual deal was:

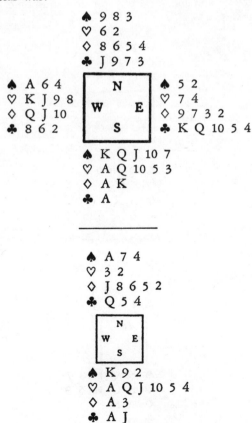

    ♠ 9 8 3
    ♡ 6 2
    ◊ 8 6 5 4
    ♣ J 9 7 3

♠ A 6 4   ♠ 5 2
♡ K J 9 8   ♡ 7 4
◊ Q J 10   ◊ 9 7 3 2
♣ 8 6 2   ♣ K Q 10 5 4

    ♠ K Q J 10 7
    ♡ A Q 10 5 3
    ◊ A K
    ♣ A

4.

    ♠ A 7 4
    ♡ 3 2
    ◊ J 8 6 5 2
    ♣ Q 5 4

    ♠ K 9 2
    ♡ A Q J 10 5 4
    ◊ A 3
    ♣ A J

West opens the Queen of Spades against South's four heart contract. How would you play the hand?

On the face of it, it appears as though declarer should win the trick with dummy's Ace, and then take either the heart finesse (trump) or the club finesse. Most players would probably take the trump finesse, having been taught to draw trumps as quickly as possible. A small minority would lean towards the club finesse instead, for even if the heart finesse worked, there would be no assurance of avoiding the loss of a heart trick; whereas if the club finesse worked, a sure trick would thereby be gained.

Actually, neither of the above plays is the correct one. Proper play is to win the opening spade lead with declarer's King, after which the Ace of Clubs is cashed, followed by the Jack of Clubs. Now dummy's Queen has become established as a winner, upon which declarer can discard either his losing spade or his losing diamond. Of course, the Ace of Spades is still in dummy, as an entry.

The above deal, in my opinion, serves as an excellent example of why it is impossible to present any over-all principle to govern the question of when to draw trumps at once and when not to. It is recognized, of course, that whenever trumps are not drawn, declarer is always running the theoretical or practical risk that something "unforseen" might happen — specifically that he may find a sure winner being trumped. But it is never a matter of a risk in the abstract; it is usually a matter of one risk pitted against another — the matter of taking a lesser risk as opposed to taking a greater risk. The club finesse on the above deal was approximately a 50-50 proposition; the trump finesse much less than 50%, since to avoid the loss of a trump trick necessitated East's holding to be specifically the K x doubleton. The odds in favor of the establishment of dummy's club Queen, and its cashing before trumps were drawn, was much greater than 50%, since the risk in the club Queen being trumped on the third round of the suit was relatively slight: the eight missing clubs had to be divided either 8-0; 7-1; or 6-2. And the probability of them being so divided was much less than the probability that they were divided normally, either 5-3 or 4-4. [1]

As can be seen then, the "riskiest" way of playing this hand was to take immediately the trump finesse; the second riskiest way was to take the club finesse; and the "safest" way was to postpone the drawing of trumps, and to play for either of the opponents to hold no fewer than three clubs so that a loser could be discarded on the Queen of Clubs.

---

[1] See Chapter III, "The Percentage Play," page 83.

The complete deal was:

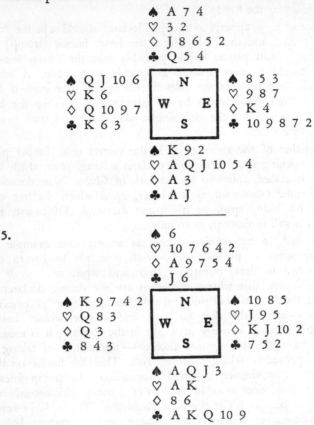

```
                    ♠ A 7 4
                    ♡ 3 2
                    ◇ J 8 6 5 2
                    ♣ Q 5 4
  ♠ Q J 10 6                      ♠ 8 5 3
  ♡ K 6            N              ♡ 9 8 7
  ◇ Q 10 9 7    W     E           ◇ K 4
  ♣ K 6 3          S              ♣ 10 9 8 7 2
                    ♠ K 9 2
                    ♡ A Q J 10 5 4
                    ◇ A 3
                    ♣ A J
```

5.
```
                    ♠ 6
                    ♡ 10 7 6 4 2
                    ◇ A 9 7 5 4
                    ♣ J 6
  ♠ K 9 7 4 2                     ♠ 10 8 5
  ♡ Q 8 3          N              ♡ J 9 5
  ◇ Q 3         W     E           ◇ K J 10 2
  ♣ 8 4 3          S              ♣ 7 5 2
                    ♠ A Q J 3
                    ♡ A K
                    ◇ 8 6
                    ♣ A K Q 10 9
```

South arrives at a *six club contract,* against which West opens a trump. For declarer to draw the opponents' trumps would be to concede defeat — declarer has a more important use for his trumps than to use them as "extractors."

The opening trump lead is won by declarer's Queen, after which the Ace and King of Hearts are cashed. Then the nine of trumps is led to dummy's Jack, after which a heart is ruffed in the closed hand. Trumps are now drawn, and declarer then re-enters dummy via the diamond Ace, to discard his losing diamond and a losing spade on the board's two established hearts. A spade will then be his only loser.

Was there a risk involved in cashing the Ace and King of Hearts prior to picking up the opponents' trumps? Of course there was. It was

quite possible that one or the other of the opponents was either void
of hearts or had a singleton. But how else was it possible to make
the hand except to first cash the Ace and King of Hearts, and then use
dummy's Jack of trumps as an entry to trump a third round of hearts?

6. This question of conserving a vitally-needed trump entry (as
opposed to drawing trumps at once) can be evidenced in the deal
which follows:

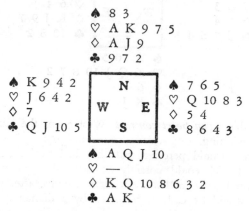

♠ 8 3
♡ A K 9 7 5
♢ A J 9
♣ 9 7 2

♠ K 9 4 2
♡ J 6 4 2
♢ 7
♣ Q J 10 5

N W E S

♠ 7 6 5
♡ Q 10 8 3
♢ 5 4
♣ 8 6 4 3

♠ A Q J 10
♡ —
♢ K Q 10 8 6 3 2
♣ A K

South has landed in a *seven diamond contract,* against which West
opens the Queen of Clubs, declarer's King winning. If two rounds of
trumps are taken immediately, to pick up the opponents' trumps, a spade
finesse will ultimately have to be taken — and as the reader can see,
it will lose.

But if at trick two declarer leads a trump to dummy's nine, and
then trumps a low heart (with a high trump), followed by another
trump to dummy's Jack after which a second heart is ruffed high, the
contract will be made without the necessity of resorting to a spade finesse.
For now dummy's Ace of trumps can be used as an entry for declarer to
cash the Ace, King, and the fifth heart which has become established.
On them declarer discards the Queen, Jack and ten of spades.

On this deal there was absolutely no danger in not drawing the
opponents' trumps, since declarer, in ruffing a heart, trumped high to
avoid the danger of an overruff. But the fact remains that perhaps not
too many bridge players would have played it correctly, for they would
have played two rounds of trumps as quickly as possible.

7.   An "entry" situation almost identical to the one on the preceding hand is the theme of the following deal, which was presented in the preceding chapter:

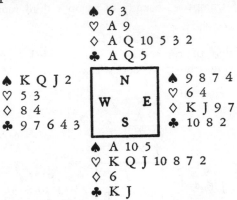

♠ 6 3
♥ A 9
♦ A Q 10 5 3 2
♣ A Q 5

♠ K Q J 2   N   ♠ 9 8 7 4
♥ 5 3   W   E   ♥ 6 4
♦ 8 4   S   ♦ K J 9 7
♣ 9 7 6 4 3   ♣ 10 8 2

♠ A 10 5
♥ K Q J 10 8 7 2
♦ 6
♣ K J

Against South's *seven heart contract,* West opens the King of Spades, declarer's Ace winning.

Most declarers would perceive that they had twelve sure tricks, and that a diamond trick could possibly be established for the thirteenth. The normal impulse would then be to draw trumps, after which the Ace of Diamonds would be cashed, followed by a diamond ruff. Dummy would then be re-entered via a club, and another diamond ruffed. When it would then be revealed that the adverse diamonds broke badly, the entire hand would collapse.

Proper play of this hand is to lead a diamond to the Ace at trick two, and then ruff a diamond high. Then would follow a trump to dummy's nine-spot, and another diamond ruffed high. Now another trump is led to dummy's Ace, and a fourth round of diamonds ruffed. From here in the play would be routine, since there would be two established diamonds in dummy, with a club to serve as an entry to them.

Again, was there a risk in not drawing trumps? A slight risk, yes — that one of the opponents had *no* diamonds, and would ruff the Ace. After that, no risk whatsoever exists. And the alternative? To draw trumps, and then to play for diamonds to be divided 3-3. So far as the fulfillment of the contract was concerned, was not the immediate drawing of trumps the greater risk?

8.   The two deals which follow present situations where trumps *should be drawn as quickly as possible.* Paradoxically, those bridge

players who normally draw trumps at once would probably not do so on
these two deals.

♠ 8 4 3
♡ Q 9 6 2
♢ 10 7 5
♣ A K 8

♠ A K 2
♡ A J 10 7 4
♢ A K
♣ 7 4 2

Against South's *four heart contract* West opens the Jack of Clubs,
dummy's King winning. "Normal" play would now be to lead the
Queen of Hearts, and finesse East for the King — and the contract
would then be defeated!

Why take the trump finesse? Why run the risk of relinquishing the
lead to the opponents while they still have trumps? *Do you not have ten
sure tricks?* Two spades, four hearts, two diamonds, and two clubs are
there for the taking. Why not play the Ace of Hearts, followed by
another heart, making haste to draw trumps as quickly as possible?
To defer the drawing of trumps on this hand is to defy the opponents
to hurt you — and they might do it. The deal was:

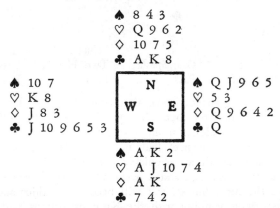

♠ 8 4 3
♡ Q 9 6 2
♢ 10 7 5
♣ A K 8

♠ 10 7
♡ K 8
♢ J 8 3
♣ J 10 9 6 5 3

♠ Q J 9 6 5
♡ 5 3
♢ Q 9 6 4 2
♣ Q

♠ A K 2
♡ A J 10 7 4
♢ A K
♣ 7 4 2

On looking at all four hands, some readers may disapprove of my
"deceit!" They may claim that I misled them by not telling them that

East dropped the *Queen of Clubs* on the opening club lead. And, that, if they had known the true state of affairs, then certainly they would have forsaken the heart finesse, realizing that if West had the King, he would then (not being blind) play another club for East to trump. I accept the responsibility for this concealment — but if I had not concealed the Queen of Clubs, the reader would probably have come up wih the right solution based on a "little" reason as opposed to a "big" reason.

Admittedly the dropping of the Queen of Clubs should serve to forewarn the observant declarer against taking the heart finesse. But even if the Queen of Clubs had not dropped, why run the risk of "delaying" the drawing of trumps? Why take the chance of permitting the opponents to obtain the lead *while they still have trumps?* *Why jeopardize your contract?*

9.

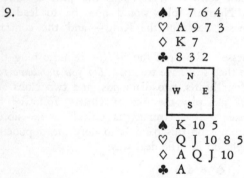

♠ J 7 6 4
♡ A 9 7 3
◇ K 7
♣ 8 3 2

♠ K 10 5
♡ Q J 10 8 5
◇ A Q J 10
♣ A

The bidding:

SOUTH	WEST	NORTH	EAST
One Heart	One Spade	Two Hearts	Pass
Four Hearts	Pass	Pass	Pass

West, after bidding spades, opens the King of Clubs, declarer's Ace winning. Again, if declarer counts his winning tricks, he will perceive ten of them: one in spades, four in hearts, four in diamonds, and one in clubs — provided of course, that none of his sure winners gets trumped. So trumps are drawn as quickly as possible: the Ace of Hearts, followed by another heart . . . and it is smooth sailing from here in.

If you take the heart finesse, you will become a sadder and a wiser man, for East, upon winning with the King of trumps will return a spade, and you will wind up getting your King of Spades trumped on you. The complete deal was:

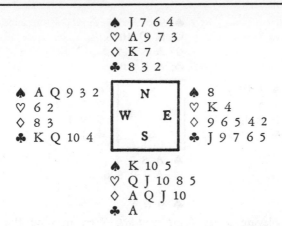

♠ J 7 6 4
♡ A 9 7 3
◇ K 7
♣ 8 3 2

♠ A Q 9 3 2
♡ 6 2
◇ 8 3
♣ K Q 10 4

♠ 8
♡ K 4
◇ 9 6 5 4 2
♣ J 9 7 6 5

♠ K 10 5
♡ Q J 10 8 5
◇ A Q J 10
♣ A

As in the preceding, you were "tipped" off as to how to play the hand correctly: West had overcalled in spades, and you, looking at your own hand and the dummy, knew that East had one or two spades at most. And, if he also happened to have the King of Hearts, a spade return would doom you.

But even if spades had not been bid, why run the risk of a trump finesse when ten tricks are yours? Is not the trump finesse a luxury which you can ill-afford? If you do not think so, just ask your partner.

10.   Probably the most obvious type of hand on which trumps should not be drawn is the one where declarer has either a void or a singleton in a suit, and dummy has a void or a singleton in some other suit. In these situations, logic, reason, and the naked eye rebel at drawing trumps; and both instinct and judgment tell you to start trumping first in one hand, then in the other, then the first, then the second, etc., until all your trumps have been utilized to the maximum. This type of play is known as "the cross-ruff."

It is a basic principle of the cross-ruffing type of hand, that prior to embarking on the cross-ruff, *the sure winners in the fourth suit should be cashed.* [2] If you do not cash them, an opponent who has run out of a suit which you are in the process of trumping will be able to discard his cards in the fourth suit, and will ultimately be able to trump your winners in that suit.

The following deal presents all the "angles" of the cross-ruffing type of hand:

[2] By the "fourth suit" is meant the suit remaining after excluding the trump suit, and the two suits which are going to be ruffed in dummy's and declarer's hands.

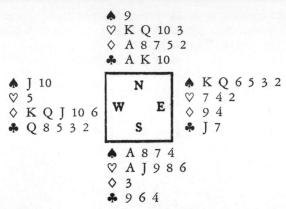

```
              ♠ 9
              ♡ K Q 10 3
              ◇ A 8 7 5 2
              ♣ A K 10
♠ J 10          ┌───────┐         ♠ K Q 6 5 3 2
♡ 5             │   N   │         ♡ 7 4 2
◇ K Q J 10 6    │ W   E │         ◇ 9 4
♣ Q 8 5 3 2     │   S   │         ♣ J 7
              └───────┘
              ♠ A 8 7 4
              ♡ A J 9 8 6
              ◇ 3
              ♣ 9 6 4
```

South is playing a *six heart contract,* West opening the King of Diamonds, and declarer capturing the trick with his Ace. By observation, declarer perceives that his three losing spades can be ruffed in dummy, and that his only loser on the hand will be a club trick. But since declarer cannot return to his own hand except via the trump suit to keep ruffing spades in dummy, the only entries to his hand can be obtained by trumping diamonds. So it is his intention to keep trumping spades in dummy, and returning to his own hand by trumping diamonds. There is no danger of the opponents overtrumping either dummy or declarer after the first round of each suit has been trumped, since declarer will then have every high trump.

As per principle, before initiating the "cross-ruff" declarer cashes his high cards in the fourth suit, clubs, specifically the Ace and King of Clubs. Then comes a low diamond (the Ace having won the opening lead) which is ruffed in the closed hand, followed by the Ace of Spades and the ruff of a spade in dummy. By continuing this process until all the spades have been trumped, declarer will have twelve tricks: the Ace of Spades, the Ace of Diamonds, the Ace and King of Clubs, three trump tricks from dummy by ruffing three spades, four trump tricks in declarer's hand by having ruffed four diamonds, and the Ace of trumps remaining in declarer's hand.

Had declarer not cashed the Ace and King of Clubs before embarking on the cross-ruff, he would have gone down. In this situation, East, not being able to follow suit to the third and fourth rounds of diamonds, would have discarded his two clubs. And later, when declarer attempted to cash the high clubs, East would have trumped them.

11.   Speaking generally on the subject of trumping out losers, the purpose in life is to get *dummy* to make use of his trumps for trumping

purposes, as opposed to declarer using his trumps to trump out losers. The theory behind this is thereby to enable dummy to win a trick with a trump which would otherwise be wasted. For example:

♡ 9 6 4

```
      N
  W       E
      S
```

♡ A K Q J 10

With *hearts* as trumps, if South were to use any of his own five trumps to ruff out one or more of North's losers, he would be gaining nothing, since he could always make his five trumps outright by merely cashing them. Nothing would be gained if South trumped one or two losers that dummy might possess, since the total number of trump tricks won in the South hand would still be five, whether the five were obtained by adding four and one, or three and two, etc.

But if South can trump one, two, or three tricks in the North hand, before trumps are drawn, he will be winning tricks which he otherwise could not make. If one loser can be trumped in dummy, South will make six trump tricks; if two losers can be ruffed in dummy, South will make seven trump tricks; and if three losers can be ruffed with dummy's three trumps, South will have eight trump winners, since he can always win his own five tricks outright.

Stating this as a general approach, the proper technique to obtain the maximum utilization of trumps is to try to get the "weak" (short) trump hand to do the ruffing, as opposed to getting the "strong" (long) trump hand to ruff. In so doing, extra trump tricks will be won, tricks which otherwise could not be obtained. Thus, adhering to this approach, the declarer usually fixes his eye on dummy's trumps to see whether they might be profitably employed for ruffing.

One of the major exceptions to this rule is, of course, the cross-ruff, which has just been presented, wherein declarer uses not only dummy's trumps, but equally his own, for trumping purposes.

Another major exception to this rule is the type of play known as "dummy reversal." Before getting to this play, permit me to briefly summarize the gist of what has just been presented, and to use it as a sort of prologue to the dummy-reversal play.

Normally, declarer's attitude is to view his own hand as the supreme one, and the dummy's hand as a secondary, or supplementary one. When he looks over his losing tricks, he usually does so from the viewpoint of his own hand. And, in virtually all deals, this approach is the correct one. But there are certain types of situations in which the declarer's hand should be looked upon as the secondary holding of the partnership. After all, since it makes no difference which hand wins the majority of the tricks as long as the partnership gathers them in, the rational approach is to view your prospects from the standpoint of the combined hands. If it seems advisable to make dummy the declarer, to transpose yourself to thinking in terms of the open hand being the declarer, then you must do so. The essence of the "dummy-reversal" play is the thinking in terms of dummy being the declarer, and the basic feature of this play is *to do the ruffing in the closed hand.*

Here are the characteristic features of the "dummy-reversal" play:

1. *Declarer* will always have a singleton or a void in his own hand.

2. *Declarer's hand* will always possess a loser which cannot be gotten rid of by normal means; that is, by either trumping it in dummy, or by discarding it on some established card in dummy.

3. *Dummy's trumps* must be high enough and long enough to pick up the adverse trumps without loss of a trick.

Let us look at a "dummy reversal" hand:

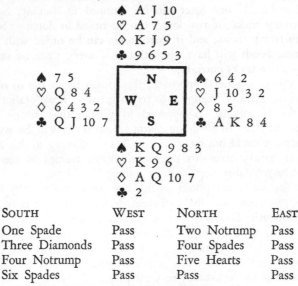

SOUTH	WEST	NORTH	EAST
One Spade	Pass	Two Notrump	Pass
Three Diamonds	Pass	Four Spades	Pass
Four Notrump	Pass	Five Hearts	Pass
Six Spades	Pass	Pass	Pass

West opens the Queen of Clubs against South's six spade contract, and continues with a club, South ruffing. On counting his sure winners, South can count only 11: five in spades, two in hearts, and four in diamonds. With the "dummy-reversal" play, however, twelve tricks can be made.

After ruffing the second club lead, a trump is then led to dummy's Jack, after which another club is ruffed. The Queen of Spades is then led, and overtaken by dummy's Ace, and dummy's remaining club is ruffed with South's last trump, the King. A heart is now led to the board's Ace, and the ten of spades is laid down, picking up East's last trump. On this trick, South discards his losing heart. It is now a routine matter to cash the King of Hearts, and the four top diamonds.

Played in this fashion, South ruffed three clubs in his own hand, and made three trump tricks in the North hand! This totalled six winners, added to which were the Ace and King of Hearts and four diamonds, adding up to twelve tricks.

Let us now summarize this deal with respect to the characteristic features of the dummy's reversal play:

1. Declarer had a singleton (club) in his own hand.

2. Declarer's hand possessed a loser (a heart, in this case) which could not be disposed of by either trumping it in dummy, or discarding it on some established card in dummy (actually, declarer discarded his heart on one of dummy's trumps).

3. Dummy's trumps were high enough and long enough to pick up the adverse trumps without loss of a trick. (This presumes a normal division of the adverse trumps, in this case, a 3-2 division). In actual play, the opponents' trumps were all picked up by dummy's A J 10.

As the reader can perceive, what actually happened was that declarer's hand was treated as the dummy; he did all the ruffing with the South hand, while the North hand was viewed as the "master" hand to pick up the opponents' trumps (normally a function of the declarer's hand).

The following deal is another illustration of the dummy-reversal play:

```
                    ♠ Q 9 8 4
                    ♡ A K 3
                    ◊ J 9 8
                    ♣ Q 7 5
    ♠ A K J 10      ┌─────────┐      ♠ 7 6 5 3 2
    ♡ J 10 6 4      │    N    │      ♡ Q 8 7
    ◊ 7 6 2         │ W     E │      ◊ 5
    ♣ 10 8          │    S    │      ♣ J 9 4 3
                    └─────────┘
                    ♠ —
                    ♡ 9 5 2
                    ◊ A K Q 10 4 3
                    ♣ A K 6 2
```

The bidding:

SOUTH	WEST	NORTH	EAST
One Diamond	Pass	Two Notrump	Pass
Six Diamonds	Pass	Pass	Pass

West opens the King of Spades, declarer ruffing. Again, declarer has eleven sure tricks, and the twelfth can be made if the adverse clubs break 3-3, or if the four missing trumps are divided 2-2, in which case declarer's fourth club can be ruffed in dummy for declarer's twelfth trick.

Upon ruffing the opening spade lead, declarer leads the Ace of trumps, and then a trump to dummy's eight-spot. When the 3-1 division in trumps is divulged, the hope of ruffing the fourth club vanishes. The success of the contract now hinges on a 3-3 break in clubs — or the "dummy-reversal" play.

At trick four declarer leads a spade from dummy, and ruffs it in his own hand. Dummy is then re-entered via the heart Ace, and a third spade is ruffed in the closed hand. Once again declarer returns to dummy (via the Heart King), and dummy's fourth spade is trumped with declarer's remaining trump. The club Queen is then employed to re-enter dummy once again and dummy's Jack of trumps is cashed, picking up West's last piece of trump, declarer discarding a low heart on this trick. Declarer now has twelve tricks: four of his trumps were used to ruff dummy's four spades, three trumps were used to pick up the adverse trumps (one of his trumps, and two of dummy's), for three more tricks, two top hearts and three top clubs — for a total of twelve tricks.

Again, conditions were ripe for a dummy-reversal play: (1) declarer had a void; (2) declarer had a loser (in hearts) which could not be disposed of; and (3) dummy's trumps were high enough and long enough to pick up the adverse trumps if the latter were normally distributed (no worse than 3-1).

Incidentally, if the adverse trumps were divided, 4-0, then dummy's three trumps would not have been long enough to pick up the adverse trumps. Had this been the case, declarer would have discovered it when he led the first round of trumps at trick two. Trumps would then have been drawn, and declarer would have pinned his hopes on a 3-3 break of the six missing clubs.

So much then for the "dummy-reversal" play — a mighty handy tool to have around when the occasion for its use presents itself.

COUNTING THE DISTRIBUTION OF THE OPPONENTS' CARDS

Iₙ bridge, "counting" is always with you: you count your points or honor-tricks in bidding; you count your winning and losing tricks; you count trumps when you are declarer, so that you can draw the opponents' trumps; you count your score, etc. But there is another type of counting in bridge, which is generally known as "counting a hand." By "counting a hand" is meant trying to reconstruct the original suit distribution of the opponents' cards, the purpose being either to locate a key card, or to enable you to determine more precisely which of two or three optional lines of play is the proper percentage play.

Years ago, "counting a hand" was assumed by the average bridge player to be too difficult to absorb, and it was a subject that was considered to be "for experts only." But, in the words of Tennyson, just as "the old order changeth, yielding place to new," so "counting a hand" has now become public property, and is not nearly so difficult as the reader might have been led to believe. If you do not think you will ever be able to count out the opponents' cards, let me assure you that you are wrong. After you get through reading the next four pages and applying what will be recommended, I can virtually guarantee that in a short time you will have no difficulty in counting out the opponents' cards. Let us examine the following "counting" hand:

1.

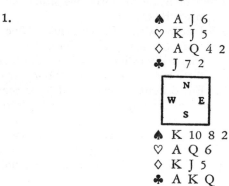

     ♠ A J 6
     ♡ K J 5
     ◊ A Q 4 2
     ♣ J 7 2

     ♠ K 10 8 2
     ♡ A Q 6
     ◊ K J 5
     ♣ A K Q

You are sitting South, playing a *seven notrump* contract, against which West opens the ten of hearts, dummy's Jack winning. How do you play the hand?

Your sure winning tricks are now counted: two in spades, three in hearts, four in diamonds, and three in clubs, for a total of twelve.

Further examination reveals that hearts, diamonds and clubs are eliminated as a source of the thirteenth trick — no more than ten tricks can ever be obtained from these three suits. So your eye naturally turns to — and remains with — *the spade suit, for within that suit lies your sole hope of fulfilling the grand slam contract.*

Getting more specific, the success of your contract depends on locating the Queen of Spades. If you can locate that card, a finesse for it will be routine, and a grand slam will be chalked up. Who has that card, East or West?

Let me point out that any player in the world — no matter how poorly he plays — can fulfill the grand slam contract 50% of the time. All he has to do is to point his finger at one of the opponents and say: "You, my friend, have the Queen of Spades!" And half the time he will be right, and half the time wrong. But I think you will agree with me that this would be a heck of a way to play the hand.

Now let us get to the expert way of playing it. You win the opening heart lead with dummy's Jack, and you are now going to try to locate the Queen of Spades. You cash the King of Hearts — *and East fails to follow suit!*

You have just come into possession of a tremendous amount of significant information concerning the distribution of the opponents' cards. East started with just one heart, which means that West's original heart holding consisted of six hearts. At this moment you know almost half of West's thirteen cards, and you are going to figure out his other seven cards, the aim of this endeavor being to isolate the spade suit so that you can determine the location of the Queen.

Three rounds of clubs are led next, West following suit. Nine of West's cards are now accounted for: 6 hearts and 3 clubs. The four top diamonds are then played (declarer discarding a spade on the fourth one), and West again follows to three rounds of this suit. Your "count" is now virtually complete: West had 6 hearts, 3 clubs, and 3 diamonds. So he had just one spade *at most.* [1] Dummy's Ace of Spades is then laid down, everybody following suit.

Has the light dawned? All of West's cards are now known to declarer: 6 hearts, 3 diamonds, 3 clubs and 1 spade (which was not the Queen). Must not the Queen of Spades be in the East hand, unless West started with 14 cards?

The Jack of Spades is next led off dummy and East's known Queen is finessed with the utmost assurance — the finesse has to win. The complete deal was:

---

[1] He might have had the 13th club, in which case he would have started with no spades.

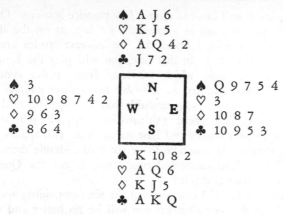

♠ A J 6
♡ K J 5
◇ A Q 4 2
♣ J 7 2

♠ 3
♡ 10 9 8 7 4 2
◇ 9 6 3
♣ 8 6 4

♠ Q 9 7 5 4
♡ 3
◇ 10 8 7
♣ 10 9 5 3

♠ K 10 8 2
♡ A Q 6
◇ K J 5
♣ A K Q

Let us briefly recheck the approach to "counting" as embodied in the play of the above hand. Observation of the combined hands revealed that there were no optional ways of playing this hand: you either "guessed" where the Queen of Spades was (victory) or you misguessed (total defeat).

The spade suit was left until the very end. The three other suits were played first, and West's hand counted, resulting in the discovery that West possessed a maximum of one spade. When it turned out that West's singleton spade was not the Queen, East *had to* have that card. And so East was successfully finessed for the Queen of Spades.

Why did we pick on West, to count *his hand* instead of East's? It is a general principle of counting that when somebody fails to follow suit, you count *his partner's hand*. On the given deal, when East showed up with but one heart, why should we have gone through the trouble of counting East's twelve remaining cards when it was so much easier, knowing that West had started with six hearts, to count his remaining seven cards? After all, as any school child knows, it is easier to count to seven than it is to twelve. So we count the hand of the one about whom we know the most at the outset.

Now let me teach you how to count the opponents' distribution. The next time you play bridge with your foursome, take a few minutes off for practice before engaging in serious competition. Keep the North-South cards on the above deal as they are. Shuffle up the other 26 cards. You sit South holding the given South cards, and play the grand slam contract. Let two of your friends sit East and West respectively. Tell them not to open a spade (otherwise you will win 13 tricks on the opening lead). Now play the hand to locate the Queen of Spades, using the identical approach as on the actual hand just presented. You will see how easy it will become after a few practice sessions. Of course, it will not always come out as a guaranteed thing, as on the illustrated deal. Sometimes you will discover that the adverse spades are divided 4-2, instead of 5-1, or 6-0. In that case, you will play the hand on the assumption that the hand which possesses four spades contains the Queen, for it is axiomatic that *he who has the greater number of cards in a given suit is the one* who probably has any specific card you are looking for. Forgetting about mathematics, suppose you learn that West started with four spades and East started with two spades. One of them has the Queen. If you take those six cards, shuffle them up, and make two piles of four cards and two cards, is not the Queen more likely to be in the four-card pile?

You may ask, "What if I discover that the six outstanding spades were divided 3-3?" In this one situation you will be no better and no worse off than you were before, because it will now be strictly a 50-50 proposition. In this latter instance, you will lift your eyes skyward, entreatingly, and finesse one way or another. But whenever you learn that spades were divided either 4-2, or 5-1, or 6-0, you have just become a player who has secured a tremendous edge over those who either forget, or were too lazy to count. Surely the attempt to gain distributional information is worth the extra expenditure of "counting," as opposed to finessing just one way or another, in haphazard fashion.

2. Let us look at another "counting" hand:

♠ A K 8 3
♡ A 5 4
◇ 9 5
♣ J 10 9 8

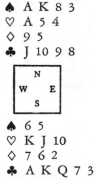

♠ 6 5
♡ K J 10
◇ 7 6 2
♣ A K Q 7 3

After East had opened the bidding with *one diamond,* South arrived at a *five club contract.* West opened the Queen of Diamonds, which was overtaken by East's King, and the Diamond Ace was then laid down. East then shifted to the Spade Queen, dummy's King winning.

Two rounds of trumps were then cashed, both opponents following suit, after which South ruffed his remaining diamond, *West discarding a heart.* The "counting" process now begins, with the success of the contract depending on locating the Queen of Hearts. East is known to have started with six diamonds (West had just two), and two trumps (he had followed suit twice). East also had the Queen of Spades. South now led the Ace of Spades, and then trumped a spade in the closed hand, East following suit both times. East had started, then, with 6 diamonds, 2 clubs, and 3 spades. A trump was led next to dummy, and the fourth spade ruffed, East again following suit. The "count" was now complete. East originally held 4 spades, 6 diamonds and 2 clubs. Therefore, he had but *one heart!*

Declarer's King of Hearts was then cashed, East following suit — and all of East's cards were accounted for. The Queen of Hearts had to be in the West hand. So declarer led the Jack of Hearts, successfully finessing West for the Queen. The deal was:

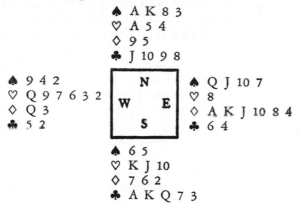

```
              ♠ A K 8 3
              ♡ A 5 4
              ◊ 9 5
              ♣ J 10 9 8

♠ 9 4 2          N          ♠ Q J 10 7
♡ Q 9 7 6 3 2              ♡ 8
◊ Q 3        W     E        ◊ A K J 10 8 4
♣ 5 2             S         ♣ 6 4

              ♠ 6 5
              ♡ K J 10
              ◊ 7 6 2
              ♣ A K Q 7 3
```

3. Here is another deal where "counting" located a sought-for Queen. The occasions for this type of counting occur quite frequently.

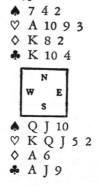

```
              ♠ 7 4 2
              ♡ A 10 9 3
              ◊ K 8 2
              ♣ K 10 4

                 N
              W     E
                 S

              ♠ Q J 10
              ♡ K Q J 5 2
              ◊ A 6
              ♣ A J 9
```

The bidding:

SOUTH	WEST	NORTH	EAST
One Heart	One Spade	Two Hearts	Pass
Four Hearts	Pass	Pass	Pass

West opened the King of Spades, continued with the Ace, East discarding a club, and then played a third spade, East ruffing. East now shifted to a diamond, declarer's Ace winning.

It was apparent that the fulfillment of the contract depended on guessing the location of the Club Queen, and that declarer either had to toss a coin to determine where that card was, or he had to do it in bridge-wise fashion, that is, by "counting." He correctly elected to count, saving the toss of a coin for his weekly poker game.

West was known to have held *six spades* originally, East having failed to follow to the second round. Three rounds of trumps were now led, West following suit to all three rounds. So West also had *three hearts,* in addition to his *six spades.* Then followed a diamond to dummy's King, and a third round of diamonds was trumped by declarer. West, who had followed suit to East's diamond lead at trick four, followed suit again to the last two diamond tricks.

West, therefore, had started with 3 spades, 6 hearts, and 3 diamonds. He had, then, one club at most (he could have had another diamond). Declarer's next play was to lead a club to dummy's King, West following with a low club. And that was that — East had to have the Queen of Clubs, which declarer then successfully finessed. The complete deal was:

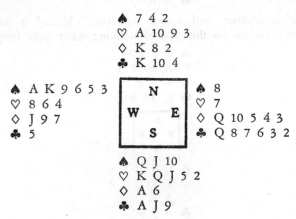

```
                    ♠ 7 4 2
                    ♡ A 10 9 3
                    ◇ K 8 2
                    ♣ K 10 4

♠ A K 9 6 5 3    ┌─────────┐    ♠ 8
♡ 8 6 4          │    N    │    ♡ 7
◇ J 9 7          │ W     E │    ◇ Q 10 5 4 3
♣ 5              │    S    │    ♣ Q 8 7 6 3 2
                 └─────────┘
                    ♠ Q J 10
                    ♡ K Q J 5 2
                    ◇ A 6
                    ♣ A J 9
```

4.

    ♠ 6 4 2
    ♡ 10 8 7 3
    ◇ A 9 5
    ♣ J 10 4

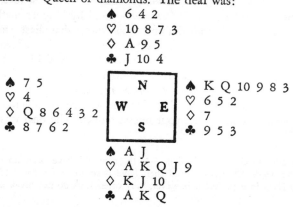

    ♠ A J
    ♡ A K Q J 9
    ◇ K J 10
    ♣ A K Q

Against South's *six heart contract* West opened the seven of spades, East's Queen falling to declarer's Ace. Three rounds of trumps were then drawn, East following suit three times. Then came three rounds of clubs, everybody following suit. Where was the Queen of Diamonds? No hurry to find out — possibly the opponents might even help you.

So South now led his losing Jack of Spades, East winning with the King (and there are those days when East returns a diamond, giving you a "free" finesse). East then exited with the ten of spades, South trumping. On this third round of spades, West failed to follow suit. Now came the "reconstruction" of *East's* hand.

East had started with *six spades,* (West having had but two); he had *three hearts* (by observation) ; and *three clubs* (by observation). So he had, at most, *one diamond* (he could have had the 13th club). The King of Diamonds was cashed next, East following with a low one — and all of East's original 13 cards were now accounted for: 6 spades, 3 hearts, 3 clubs, and 1 diamond. Declarer now finessed West for the "marked" Queen of diamonds. The deal was:

    ♠ 6 4 2
    ♡ 10 8 7 3
    ◇ A 9 5
    ♣ J 10 4

    ♠ 7 5   ♠ K Q 10 9 8 3
    ♡ 4   N   ♡ 6 5 2
    ◇ Q 8 6 4 3 2 W E ◇ 7
    ♣ 8 7 6 2   S   ♣ 9 5 3

    ♠ A J
    ♡ A K Q J 9
    ◇ K J 10
    ♣ A K Q

5. As was mentioned, when you are counting out the distribution of an opponent's hand, you will not always get a perfect count. But almost always you will get sufficient information to avail yourself of a "percentage play" as opposed to taking a straight 50% finesse. Witness the following deal as an illustration of this point:

♠ K Q
♥ 7 5 2
♦ K 10 3
♣ Q J 8 6 4

♠ A J 9 5 2
♥ A K Q
♦ A J 5
♣ K 3

You are South, playing a *six notrump contract*, against which West opens a low spade, dummy's Queen winning. A club is then led to the King, which is taken by West's Ace, and West returns a spade to dummy's King, East discarding a heart. You now know that West started with five spades, and one club. To complete the count on West's clubs, you then cash the Queen and Jack, discarding a spade from your own hand, West showing out on the third round of the suit. [2]

West therefore started with five spades and two clubs. Now the Ace, King and Queen of hearts are cashed, everybody following suit. So you know then that West originally started with 5 spades, 3 hearts, and 2 clubs. So he had just *3 diamonds* — and by "higher mathematics," looking at your hand and dummy, you know that East started with *4 diamonds*. The odds here do not warrant the staking of your life on locating the Queen of Diamonds, but you have available a play which is superior to a 50% chance of a random finesse. *He who has more cards of a suit always figures to have any one specific card that you seek.* You therefore finesse East for the Queen of Diamonds — and breathe a sigh of relief when your finesse works. The deal was:

---

[2] If the adverse clubs had broken 3-3, there would have been no necessity for counting, since 12 tricks would then have been there for the taking. As the reader will learn in experience, however, very often suits do not break as one might desire.

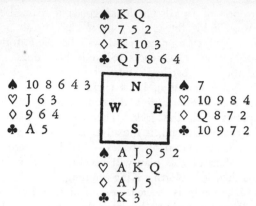

```
                    ♠ K Q
                    ♡ 7 5 2
                    ◊ K 10 3
                    ♣ Q J 8 6 4
    ♠ 10 8 6 4 3        N          ♠ 7
    ♡ J 6 3                        ♡ 10 9 8 4
    ◊ 9 6 4         W     E        ◊ Q 8 7 2
    ♣ A 5              S           ♣ 10 9 7 2
                    ♠ A J 9 5 2
                    ♡ A K Q
                    ◊ A J 5
                    ♣ K 3
```

6. If the reader will glance back at Deal 4 (P. 209), he will notice something which was not presented at that time. Namely, that one often deliberately gives away a trick (which would have been lost anyway) in order to obtain a more complete "count" of the opponents' distribution. On Deal 4, the Jack of Spades was given away, with the result that declarer eventually did obtain a thorough picture of East's original thirteen cards.

On the deal which follows, the theme is the giving away of a trick in order to obtain a complete count. This deliberate conceding of a sure loser is a necessity on a large proportion of the deals in which "counting" is essential for determining the proper line of play.

```
                    ♠ K 7 4
                    ♡ 7 6 3
                    ◊ A 10 5
                    ♣ A K 10 4
                       N
                    W     E
                       S
                    ♠ A 8 3
                    ♡ A 8 4
                    ◊ K 8 6 3
                    ♣ Q 7 5
```

Against South's *three notrump* contract West opens a low heart, East plays the Queen and South permits the Queen to win. The ten of hearts is then continued, declarer again "holding up," West overtakes with the Jack, and returns a third round of the suit, declarer's Ace winning. On this trick East discards a low spade — and West is known to have started with five hearts.

Declarer's prospect of fulfillment looks good: if diamonds break 3-3, (except when West holds the Q J x) or if clubs break 3-3, or if the Jack of Clubs is doubleton, nine tricks will be there for the taking. But declarer, having past experiences to guide him, does not count his chickens before they are hatched. Furthermore, if West ever obtains the lead, he will cash a couple of heart tricks.

At trick four South leads a low diamond putting in dummy's ten, which East captures with the Jack. This diamond play is made to establish the thirteenth diamond, if the adverse diamonds are divided 3-3. East now plays back the Queen of Spades — and he is permitted to hold the trick. The wisdom of this play will become apparent in a moment. Another spade is then led, North's King winning.

The Ace of Diamonds is cashed next, followed by a diamond to declarer's King, West discarding a heart on the latter trick. The diamond suit has now been eliminated as a source of an additional winning trick.

The Ace of Spades is cashed next, West discarding another heart — and the "truth" is known: West started with *five hearts* (East failed to follow to the third round), *two spades* and *two diamonds* (West failed to follow the third round of either of these suits). Therefore, West had exactly four clubs originally, and East had precisely two clubs.

Declarer now cashes dummy's Ace of Clubs, and then leads a club to his Queen, both opponents following suit. Since West is known to have the two remaining clubs, declarer leads his last club and finesses dummy's ten-spot, resulting in a glorious ending to a well-played hand. The actual deal was:

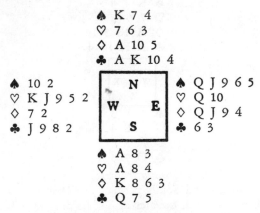

```
                    ♠ K 7 4
                    ♡ 7 6 3
                    ◇ A 10 5
                    ♣ A K 10 4
    ♠ 10 2              N        ♠ Q J 9 6 5
    ♡ K J 9 5 2    W       E     ♡ Q 10
    ◇ 7 2                        ◇ Q J 9 4
    ♣ J 9 8 2           S        ♣ 6 3
                    ♠ A 8 3
                    ♡ A 8 4
                    ◇ K 8 6 3
                    ♣ Q 7 5
```

7. On many "counting" hands the inexperienced player, after progressing part of the way, too often jumps to a conclusion based on

feeling, rather than following through to the end. He thus becomes "unscientific" where he just as easily could have been "scientific." And, as a consequence, he adopts an incorrect line of play. Let me illustrate this by presenting two deals, both of which contain the identical North-South hands. The East-West hands, however, are quite different.

(a)

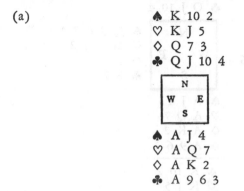

♠ K 10 2
♡ K J 5
♢ Q 7 3
♣ Q J 10 4

♠ A J 4
♡ A Q 7
♢ A K 2
♣ A 9 6 3

The contract is *six notrump,* West opening the Jack of Diamonds, dummy's Queen winning. Declarer now takes the club finesse. If the finesse wins, declarer will be able to take four club tricks by repeated finesses, three diamonds, three hearts, and two spades, for a total of 12.

But when the club finesse loses — as it does — declarer has but 11 tricks, and it becomes obvious that the twelfth can be made only by locating the Queen of Spades, which necessitates "counting."

When West wins the club finesse with his King, he returns a diamond, East fails to follow suit, and declarer takes the trick with his King. The inexperienced "counter" now says: "Well! West started with six diamonds, so East probably has the other suits. I guess I will finesse East for the Spade Queen." Sometimes he is right, and sometimes he is wrong.

It would have been so easy to obtain a complete count of West's hand. West had started with 6 *diamonds.* If two more rounds of clubs had then been played, declarer would have learned that West also had 3 *clubs.* And by cashing his three top hearts, declarer would have discovered that West also possessed *three hearts.* By subtraction South would then have known that West had at most one spade. Dummy's King of Spades would then have been cashed, West following suit — and the Queen of Spades would *have had to have been* in East's hand, and declarer would have successfully finessed for it.

On the above deal, then, whether declarer proceeded by "feeling" or "fact," he would have made his contract. But there are those other days when feeling runs a poor second to fact, as will be illustrated in a moment. The actual deal was:

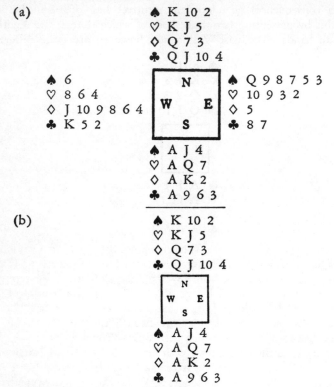

(a)

♠ K 10 2
♥ K J 5
♦ Q 7 3
♣ Q J 10 4

♠ 6
♥ 8 6 4
♦ J 10 9 8 6 4
♣ K 5 2

♠ Q 9 8 7 5 3
♥ 10 9 3 2
♦ 5
♣ 8 7

♠ A J 4
♥ A Q 7
♦ A K 2
♣ A 9 6 3

(b)

♠ K 10 2
♥ K J 5
♦ Q 7 3
♣ Q J 10 4

♠ A J 4
♥ A Q 7
♦ A K 2
♣ A 9 6 3

The same *six notrump contract*. The same Jack of Diamonds lead, taken by North's Queen. And the same unsuccessful club finesse, West's King winning, West then returning a diamond, East showing out, and declarer capturing the trick with the King.

The "count" is now at this stage identical to that on the preceding deal: West started with 6 diamonds and the King of Clubs. Upon playing two more rounds of clubs, declarer discovers that West started with just two of them, since he fails to follow to the third round of the suit. Declarer now plays the hearts — and West shows out on the first round of the suit!

Again, the "count" of West's hand is 100% correct: West had exactly *6 diamonds,* exactly *2 clubs,* exactly *zero hearts* — and therefore he had to have exactly *five spades.* This means, by looking at your hand and dummy, that East started with precisely *two* spades.

Take those seven spades, including the Queen, shuffle them up, give West his five and East his two. Who figures to have been given the Queen? West, of course. So you now take the "percentage play" (no guarantees) of finessing West for the Spade Queen. There are days, of course, when East's two spades happen to be the Q x. But there will be many more days when East's two spades are x x.

As I stated, there is no guarantee of the Queen being in the hand of five spades. But what we are pitting our percentage play against is the alternative play of taking a 50-50 finesse. If spades were somehow divided 3½ and 3½ in the hands of the opponents, then it would be a 50-50 proposition as to the location of the Queen. But with a 5-2 division, five out of seven times the Queen will be in the hand of five. With a 3½-3½ division, only 3½ times out of seven will you be able to guess who holds the Queen. Would you not rather avail yourself of a line of play which offers success five times out of seven, as opposed to one which offers success 3½ times out of seven?

8.   This final hand cannot be strictly classified as a "counting" hand. Nevertheless, it is illustrative of the application of "counting" to other fields of bridge play: [3]

```
            ♠ 9 8 2
            ♡ J 10
            ◇ 7 5 4
            ♣ Q J 8 6 3
                ┌─────┐
                │  N  │
                │W   E│
                │  S  │
                └─────┘
            ♠ A Q
            ♡ A Q 9
            ◇ A 8 3 2
            ♣ A K 7 5
```

Against South's *three notrump contract* West opens the King of Diamonds and continues with the Queen when the King is permitted to win the trick. On the lead of the Queen, East fails to follow suit, declarer winning with the Ace (since East is known to have no more diamonds, the hold-up play has accomplished its purpose: to break the communication between the defenders' hands).

Declarer sees that he has eight sure winners. The ninth trick is obtainable (in theory) by taking either a spade finesse or a heart finesse. But if whichever finesse declarer takes loses, then he will be down,

---

[3] Specifically, the "throw-in" play, which is discussed in Chapter X.

since West will cash his remaining diamonds. Which finesse should you take?

I would venture to say that probably 99% of all bridge players would play this hand incorrectly. They would first run all their clubs, and then relying on either intuition, or an interpretation of the opponents' discards, would take one finesse or the other. Half the time they would make their contract, and half the time they would not.

Yet the right play, which is admittedly difficult, will guarantee their contract, regardless as to where either the King of Spades or King of Hearts is located!

After winning the second diamond lead, declarer cashes the Ace and King of Clubs, both opponents following suit. By " counting," or by observing, declarer knows that the opponents had two clubs apiece — and now have *no more clubs.*

Declarer then leads a diamond, and West will cash his diamonds — four altogether, since it is known that East had but one diamond, and that therefore West started with five diamonds, declarer having captured one of them with his Ace. But what does West play back after he cashes his diamonds? He has no more clubs — and he must therefore lead a heart or a spade into declarer's A Q combination in one of those suits, thereby giving declarer a free finesse and his ninth trick.

If East had failed to follow to the first round of diamonds, then declarer, by counting, would have known that West had started with 6 diamonds.

Now, of course, he would not have thrown West into the lead via a diamond, since West would have cashed *five* diamonds. He would then have had to guess which King East possessed (if any). The actual deal was:

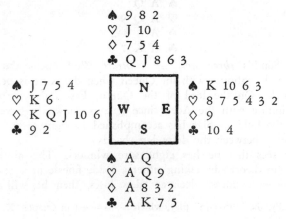

```
                    ♠ 9 8 2
                    ♡ J 10
                    ◇ 7 5 4
                    ♣ Q J 8 6 3

    ♠ J 7 5 4           N           ♠ K 10 6 3
    ♡ K 6                           ♡ 8 7 5 4 3 2
    ◇ K Q J 10 6   W       E        ◇ 9
    ♣ 9 2               S           ♣ 10 4

                    ♠ A Q
                    ♡ A Q 9
                    ◇ A 8 3 2
                    ♣ A K 7 5
```

In conclusion, on this deal, if you "guess" to take the spade finesse, you will make three notrump; but if you elect to take the heart finesse instead, you will go down. As you can see, by "counting" and then throwing West into the lead with a diamond, the guesswork is eliminated, and uncertainty is transformed into certainty.

Let me conclude with a brief, but most important reminder about counting the distribution of the opponents' cards. "Counting" begins *when one of the opponents fail to follow suit.* When this happens, you count the hand of *the partner* of the one who has failed to follow suit; in so doing, the counting is less arduous, since you have less counting to do. As you play then, and one of the opponents shows out, no matter what you are thinking about, drop that original line of reasoning and make a mental note of the failure of one of the opponents to follow suit. Once this habit of paying attention to the opponents' distribution is acquired, counting will become a natural, and henceforth habitual, consequence.

Chapter IX

PSYCHOLOGICAL STRATEGY

OR

THE ART OF DECEPTION

THERE is no doubt that the primary reason why the experts are such consistent winners is that they possess great technical skill in both bidding and play. But the fact remains that the possession and application of all the relevant technical knowledge is not sufficient automatically to make you a great bridge player. Even if you become thoroughly familiar with all the principles of sound play, and with all of the involved situations which require special treatment, you cannot attain the lofty heights of expertness until you have learned how to *deceive*. After all, there will arise numerous situations when skillful play, and even perfect intuition, are not enough to fulfill some given contract. Where all seems lost, and control of your destiny seems not to belong to you, the effective application of deception and camouflage can often alter your apparent predestination.

When observation reveals that you are doomed to defeat if the opponents play correctly, your only salvation lies in the hope that you can trick them into playing incorrectly. Such chicanery is available to both the declarer and the defenders. More often than not, however, this practice of deception brings better results when declarer applies it, since a defender, by a deceptive play, may easily mislead his partner as to the true state of affairs. The declarer, on the other hand, has no partner to fool.

These deceptive plays can take many varied forms: a "tricky" lead based on an interpretation of the bidding; or a false-card; or a high card unnecessarily thrown off; or a discard made at a time when it will greatly confuse an opponent; or the winning of a trick with a high-card when you could have won it with a low card; or a trick refused for a reason the opponent can only guess at, etc. The purpose of all these deceptive plays is, of course, *to create an incorrect impression in the mind of the opponent you are trying to deceive,* with the desired effect being that he will then think and plan as you want him to do.

In this chapter there will be presented various deceptive plays and maneuvers, all of which have arisen at one time or another in actual combat. To attempt to memorize these defensive plays, or to put them into a pattern of behavior, will serve only to make a stereotyped player of you, and the opponents will get to know your style, to profit thereby. For instance, a player who is known always to "false-card" is just as much of an open book to his opponents as is the player who never "false-cards." So, in studying the deceptive plays which will be presented, your purpose should be to analyze and understand the motivation which gave birth to them, rather than to memorize them in order to earmark them for future reference. In adopting this approach, the imagination within you will tend to rise to the fore when necessity so demands.

The subject of deceptive opening leads is not discussed in this chapter, since this topic is presented in Chapter XI, "Opening Leads."

A. DECEPTION IN ACTION

Let us start off by making you the "victim" of a deceptive play. You are sitting West, defending against a *three notrump contract* arrived at via the following bidding:

SOUTH	WEST	NORTH	EAST
One Notrump	Pass	Three Notrump	Pass
Pass	Pass		

```
                    ♠ 9 5
                    ♡ A Q 6
                    ◊ Q J 10 9 5
                    ♣ 8 7 4

    ♠ K 10 7 3 2    ┌─────────┐
    ♡ 7 5 2         │    N    │
    ◊ K 3           │  W   E  │
    ♣ 10 9 6        │    S    │
                    └─────────┘
```

You open the three of spades; the five-spot is played from dummy; your partner puts up the Jack; and declarer, after due deliberation, more or less reluctantly wins the trick with the Ace.

Dummy is then entered via the Queen of Hearts, and a diamond finesse is taken, losing to your King. What do you return?

If you are a "thinking" person, your thoughts will probably be along the following lines:

"My partner surely has the Queen of Spades, for if he didn't, declarer would have captured the opening lead with the Queen,

and not with the Ace. But why, since declarer had only the Ace of
Spades as a stopper, didn't he employ the 'hold-up' play on the
opening lead? . . . Undoubtedly because he saw that he would
have to take the diamond finesse in such a manner that if it lost,
it would lose only to me, the 'dangerous' hand with the established
spades. Therefore he probably figured that it would be just a waste
of time to hold-up, since to eliminate spades from my partner's
hand would have served no purpose. So, since my partner has the
Queen of Spades, here goes a low spade which my partner's Queen
will win, and he'll then return a spade and I'll run the rest of the
suit . . ."

On this reasoning, you now return a low spade — and declarer wins
the trick with the *Queen!* He then proceeds to fulfill his contract,
with an overtrick. Let us look at all four hands and you will see how
declarer tricked you — and why he did:

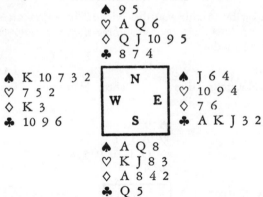

```
                    ♠ 9 5
                    ♡ A Q 6
                    ◊ Q J 10 9 5
                    ♣ 8 7 4
  ♠ K 10 7 3 2          N          ♠ J 6 4
  ♡ 7 5 2                           ♡ 10 9 4
  ◊ K 3          W         E        ◊ 7 6
  ♣ 10 9 6                          ♣ A K J 3 2
                       S
                    ♠ A Q 8
                    ♡ K J 8 3
                    ◊ A 8 4 2
                    ♣ Q 5
```

From declarer's point of view, it was apparent that *if East* had the
King of Diamonds, then declarer would have no problem, for he would
easily win five diamonds, four hearts, and a spade. But if he won the
opening lead with the Queen of Spades, and the diamond finesse lost
to West, the latter would perceive the futility of either continuing spades
(declarer would still have the known Ace), or leading either a heart
or a diamond. By elimination, West would realize that the only hope
of defeating declarer would be in the club suit — and West would in
all probability shift to a club as the sole hope of the defenders.

So, to take out "insurance" against the King of Diamonds being in the
West hand, and the subsequent shift to clubs which would then in all
probability be forthcoming, declarer won the opening lead with the
Ace of Spades, thereby misleading West into believing that East possessed

the Queen of Spades. And he succeeded in convincing West of that
"fact," with the desired effect — a spade was continued.

To repeat, if East had the diamond King, then the contract was
guaranteed whether declarer won the opening lead with the Ace or the
Queen of Spades. But if West had the vital King of Diamonds, then
deception was necessary in order to avoid the shift to clubs. If you,
sitting West, returned a spade at trick four, you certainly have nothing
to be ashamed of. I am sure that at least 99 out of 100 players would
have done the same thing. And I am certain that you will agree that
the success of declarer's false-carding strategy was well-deserved.

Here is another chance for you to avoid being the victim of declarer's
deceptive tactics. This deal occurred back in the 1930's — and the
victim was one of the nation's top-notch players.

You are sitting *East,* and the bidding has proceeded as indicated:

SOUTH	WEST	NORTH	EAST
One Club	Pass	One Diamond	Pass
Two Notrump	Pass	Three Notrump	Pass
Pass	Pass		

♠ Q 3 2
♡ J 6
◊ K Q J 9 5
♣ 9 6 5

```
        N
   W        E        ♠ A 10 9 7
                     ♡ Q 10 5 3
        S            ◊ 10 4 2
                     ♣ 10 2
```

Your partner, West, opens the four of clubs, and you put up the
ten which is captured by declarer's Jack. Declarer then lays down the
Ace of Diamonds, after which he plunks down the King of Spades.
Do you take the Ace of Spades — or do you not?

Well, let us think. When declarer lays down the Ace of Diamonds
and then shifts to the King of Spades, it certainly seems as though he
has no more diamonds, and is trying to create an entry to dummy's
diamonds via the spade Queen. As far as the club situation is concerned,
you are not sure, but it appears as though declarer still has a club stopper
left. So, to prevent declarer from getting to the board to cash dummy's
diamonds, you decline to capture his offering of the King of Spades.
And, when it is all over, you have become a sadder, but a wiser, man.
The actual deal was:

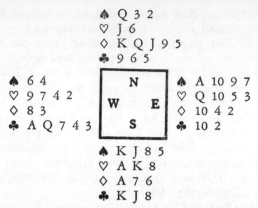

```
              ♠ Q 3 2
              ♡ J 6
              ◇ K Q J 9 5
              ♣ 9 6 5
♠ 6 4           N            ♠ A 10 9 7
♡ 9 7 4 2                    ♡ Q 10 5 3
◇ 8 3       W       E        ◇ 10 4 2
♣ A Q 7 4 3     S            ♣ 10 2
              ♠ K J 8 5
              ♡ A K 8
              ◇ A 7 6
              ♣ K J 8
```

From declarer's point of view, his "worry" was that East might have the Ace of Spades, and a club return by East would then mean declarer's defeat if West had five clubs originally. Declarer counted that he had eight sure winners, and if he could create the illusion that he had just the singleton Ace of Diamonds, then his chance of "stealing" the King of Spades for his ninth trick was virtually assured. And, as the reader can see, he did "steal" the trick.

Incidentally, if West had the Ace of Spades, then no matter what West did would have no effect on the final outcome, for declarer's King of Clubs was a stopper against West. And, in this case, declarer was certain to make an "honest" spade trick.

The deal which follows may seem like some sort of fantasy, but it actually arose in real life, and was played — trick for trick — as will be presented. The final contract by South was *two notrump*. Let us look at all four hands while the play progresses:

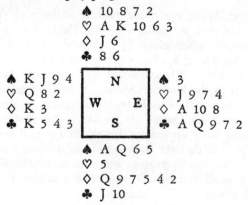

```
              ♠ 10 8 7 2
              ♡ A K 10 6 3
              ◇ J 6
              ♣ 8 6
♠ K J 9 4       N            ♠ 3
♡ Q 8 2                      ♡ J 9 7 4
◇ K 3       W       E        ◇ A 10 8
♣ K 5 4 3       S            ♣ A Q 9 7 2
              ♠ A Q 6 5
              ♡ 5
              ◇ Q 9 7 5 4 2
              ♣ J 10
```

Against South's two notrump contract West opened the four of spades, dummy's seven of spades capturing the trick. I am certain that no declarer ever found himself in a more hopeless position — and our declarer was fully aware of the "nightmarish" circumstances in which he was living. It was futile to try to establish either the diamond suit or the heart suit because of the lack of entries. Also, it seemed that the opponents would shift to clubs when they obtained the lead.

So declarer took the bull by the horns, and led a club off dummy, East played low, declarer put up his ten-spot — *and it won the trick!* Looking at all four hands, the reader may say that it was absurd for West not to have taken the King — and I am sure that in retrospect West will be the first to agree with you. But West had what he thought was a valid reason for his declination — he did not have a good return to make, and he felt sure that he would always make his King later, since it appeared that declarer would continue to attack clubs.

Declarer then led a low diamond, and West hopped right up with his King. Seeing the diamond eight fall from the East hand, West decided that it was a "come-on" signal, so he continued the suit, East's Ace capturing the trick. Convinced that declarer still had at least the K J of Clubs remaining, East now made a "safe" exit with his remaining diamond, declarer's Queen winning. Declarer now had nine tricks: two spades, two hearts, four diamonds, and one club. Unbelievable, perhaps, but "facts is facts."

On frequent occasions it will be readily apparent to declarer after the opening lead has been made, that his contract is an impossible one to fulfill if the opponents realize the full strength of their combined values. In such cases it is often possible for declarer to play in such a fashion that the opponents will fail to get together quickly enough; and, as a consequence, declarer is enabled to sneak through a trick or two. Of such a type is the following deal:

♠ A 3
♡ J 7 4
◇ A 9 6 3 2
♣ A J 8

```
┌─────────┐
│    N    │
│ W     E │
│    S    │
└─────────┘
```

♠ 10 9
♡ K 10 9 3
◇ K 5
♣ K Q 7 4 3

The (not recommended) bidding:

NORTH	EAST	SOUTH	WEST
One Diamond	Pass	Two Clubs	Pass
Three Clubs	Pass	Three Notrump	Pass
Pass	Pass		

West leads the five of spades, and declarer quickly recognizes the hopelessness of his position: he has eight tricks, and as soon as the opponents obtain the lead they will cash at least four spade tricks. What to do? Should declarer take his eight tricks and run? Or shall he devise some stratagem in an attempt to "steal" his ninth trick?

What our declarer actually did was to win the opening lead with dummy's Ace of Spades. He then led the Jack of Hearts, and when East followed with a low heart, declarer put up his King — and it won the trick! The contract was now there for the taking — and take it he did. The complete deal was:

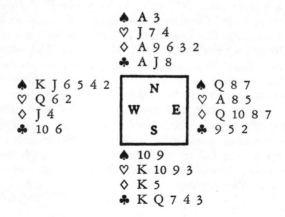

    ♠ A 3
    ♡ J 7 4
    ◇ A 9 6 3 2
    ♣ A J 8

♠ K J 6 5 4 2   ♠ Q 8 7
♡ Q 6 2   ♡ A 8 5
◇ J 4   ◇ Q 10 8 7
♣ 10 6   ♣ 9 5 2

    ♠ 10 9
    ♡ K 10 9 3
    ◇ K 5
    ♣ K Q 7 4 3

When declarer led the Jack of Hearts, should East have taken his Ace? Did East know who had the King of Spades? As a matter of fact, did not South figure to have that card for his three notrump bid?

As far as declarer was concerned, if West had the Ace of Hearts, then declarer would figure to lose two extra tricks. But he felt that the risk was warranted with the game at stake.

If deception is to accomplish its desired effect, it must be performed with spontaneity, and not with hesitation. This point is illustrated on the deal which follows:

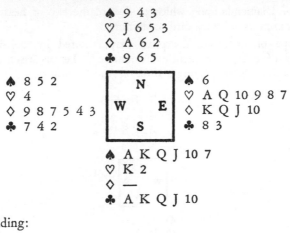

The bidding:

NORTH	EAST	SOUTH	WEST
Pass	One Heart	Six Spades	Pass
Pass	Pass		

West, on lead, opened his four of hearts, on which dummy played the three, East took his Ace — and South promptly dropped the King! After a few moments of deliberation, East returned the King of Diamonds — and declarer was home.

Whether East's return was the logical one or not does not concern us here. What is of import is the motivation responsible for South's discard of the *King of Hearts*.

From South's point of view, he *knew* that West had started with a singleton heart, for West, following accepted procedure, generally led the highest card in partner's suit. South observed the three-spot in dummy and the deuce in his own hand. The four-spot which was led had to be West's only heart since he had none higher, and there were none lower that West could have held. If, on the opening lead, South had dropped the deuce, then East, observing the two, three, and four being played to the first trick, would also have known that West had originally started with a singleton heart — and a heart return would then enable West to ruff declarer's King, for the setting trick.

So, declarer looking ahead, dropped the King on the opening lead — concealing the deuce — leading East to believe that declarer had started with the singleton King, and that West had started with the four and the deuce. And, once East returned anything but a heart, the contract became assured, since dummy had come up with two "accidental" cards:

the Ace of Diamonds upon which to discard the two of hearts; and the nine of trumps as an entry card to dummy.

The type of defensive deceptive play featured in the deal which follows is of a type frequently encountered. Let us assume that you are the South declarer, playing a *three notrump contract:*

♠ K 10 6 3
♡ 4 2
◊ A J 8 2
♣ K 7 3

♠ J 9 4
♡ K J 5
◊ K 6 5
♣ A Q 8 2

The bidding:

SOUTH	WEST	NORTH	EAST
One Club	Pass	One Diamond	One Heart
Pass	Pass	One Spade	Pass
One Notrump	Pass	Two Notrump	Pass
Three Notrump	Pass	Pass	Pass

West opens the seven of hearts, which East captures with the Ace, and returns the eight of hearts which you win with your Jack. You count seven sure winners: two in hearts, two in diamonds, and three in clubs. Your best hope of picking up the two additional tricks lies in West having the Queen of Spades. You therefore lead the nine of spades, play a low spade from dummy, and East captures the trick with the Ace, after which he returns a heart which you win with the King.

You then cash the Ace, King, and Queen of Clubs, for if the adverse clubs break 3-3, your fourth club will become the ninth trick, and the necessity of again finessing for the "marked" Queen of Spades will no longer exist. But the clubs fail to break, West showing up with four of them. So what choice do you have but to lead a low spade, finessing dummy's ten-spot, and when East wins this trick with the Queen, you are a bit surprised; and when he cashes his established hearts to inflict a one trick set on you, the value of "deception" becomes self-evident. The complete deal was:

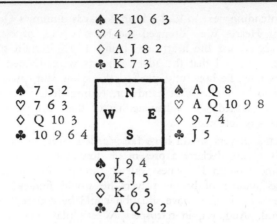

As the reader can appreciate, had East captured the first spade trick with the Queen instead of with the Ace, declarer would have abandoned the spade suit, to attack the diamond suit instead, making four tricks therein. But East's timely false-card lured declarer into remaining with the spade suit.

If the reader will look at all four hands on the deal which follows, he will truly wonder how South managed to go down at his *three notrump contract,* especially when I point out that he promptly attacked the heart suit. But he did go down — because of a magnificent deceptive play made by West.

```
                 ♠ A K J
                 ♡ Q 9 5 3 2
                 ◊ 9 6 2
                 ♣ A 3
  ♠ 9 6            ┌─────────┐        ♠ Q 10 8 5
  ♡ K J 10         │   N     │        ♡ 8 7 4
  ◊ J 4            │ W     E │        ◊ Q 10 7 5
  ♣ Q 10 9 8 6 2   │   S     │        ♣ J 7
                   └─────────┘
                 ♠ 7 4 3 2
                 ♡ A 6
                 ◊ A K 8 3
                 ♣ K 5 4
```

West opened the ten of clubs, declarer taking the trick with dummy's Ace. To develop the heart suit seemed proper, so declarer led a heart to his Ace, intending next to lead a heart towards dummy's Queen. But on the Ace of Hearts West dropped the King! And, of course, declarer promptly abandoned the heart suit, being 100% certain that the King was a singleton, and that the adverse hearts were divided 5-1. Having eight tricks now, he hopefully attacked the spade suit, playing either for the Queen to be in the West hand; or, failing that, for the six adverse spades to be divided 3-3. When neither of these prospects materialized, his contract was defeated.

How many players would have false-carded with the King of Hearts, deliberately giving declarer a present of dummy's Queen? I am certain that if some modern Diogenes walked through all the streets of this nation, the number of bridge players he would find who would have played the King in the above situation could be counted on the fingers of one hand. And, yet, in retrospect, West's play was the only correct one.

From West's point of view, did he not know that declarer, after taking the Ace of Hearts, was going to play another heart, thereby establishing all of dummy's hearts except the one trick that West could take with his King? Surely the play of the King on the Ace figured to get declarer to abandon the establishment of the heart suit. And although West could not be sure that declarer would not be able to make his contract by attacking some other suit, *he was sure that the heart suit, if developed by declarer, would give him four heart tricks.* Hence the "sacrifice" of the King.

On this matter of the "sacrifice," the reader will note that the play of the King would not have resulted in the loss of a trick even if declarer had properly diagnosed the falsecard! Is it not true that if declarer had the Ace and another heart, then all West could ever make would be one heart trick? Even with the King being tossed on the pyre, did not West still have the J 10 against dummy's Queen, a sure winner if hearts were continued? At worse, West's falsecard of the King merely postponed the development of a heart trick for him. At best, exactly what did happen: defeat for declarer.

In this day and age, in all fields of competitive endeavor, there are selected the "best — of the year": best actor, best dressed woman, best football team, etc., etc. The following deal, featuring a play by declarer, was acclaimed by Albert H. Morehead, Bridge Editor of the *New York Times,* as the "best play by declarer for the year 1949." The hero of the deal was Howard Schenken.

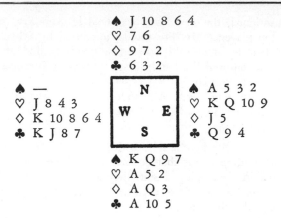

The bidding:

EAST	SOUTH	WEST	NORTH
One Spade	One Notrump	Two Diamonds	Pass
Pass	Two Notrump	Pass	Pass
Pass			

West opened the six of diamonds, East played the Jack, and Mr. Schenken captured the trick with his Queen. It was obvious to South that it would be impossible for him to make the four spade tricks needed to fulfill his contract. East had opened the auction with a one spade bid, and since there were but four spades outstanding, East had all of them. Therefore, since West would show out on the first round of spades, East would certainly "hold-up" his spade Ace until the fourth round, thereby effectively preventing Mr. Schenken from cashing dummy's fifth spade (East, by the way, was Sam Fry, Jr.).

Mr. Schenken, without any hesitation, found the winning play. At trick two he returned a low diamond, which West captured, after which another diamond was led by West, clearing the suit. On this trick East discarded the *deuce of spades,* telling his partner not to lead that suit. It now became a cinch for declarer, for there was no way that the defenders could prevent Howard from cashing four spades, two diamonds, the Ace of Clubs, and the Ace of Hearts.

Of course, it is quite apparent that if East had not discarded the two of spades, then the contract could not have been fulfilled. But Mr. Schenken had foreseen that East would discard what definitely appeared to be the most worthless card in his hand — the deuce of spades. In playing the hand as he did, Mr. Schenken stamped himself as not only an expert bridge player and technician, but as a first-class psychologist.

As was mentioned, the East hand was held by Sam Fry, Jr., one of the nation's top players. Mr. Fry was so impressed by Schenken's play of the hand that he stated: "I was 6,500 points behind at the time, and yet I actually enjoyed the hand. It's a pleasure to be fooled by such a magnificent deceptive play."

What more can one say? Although the hand was played at an uninspiring two notrump part-score, it certainly rates being called "one of the best-played hands of this — or any other — year."

It is an accepted psychological fact that the defenders will tend to shy away from leading a suit that declarer has attacked, figuring that if he is interested in developing a suit, they are not going to help him. By capitalizing on this principle, declarer fulfilled an "impossible" slam contract on the following deal:

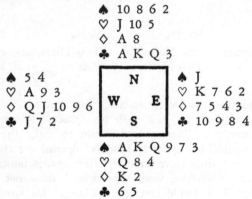

```
              ♠ 10 8 6 2
              ♡ J 10 5
              ◇ A 8
              ♣ A K Q 3
  ♠ 5 4                      ♠ J
  ♡ A 9 3          N         ♡ K 7 6 2
  ◇ Q J 10 9 6   W   E       ◇ 7 5 4 3
  ♣ J 7 2          S         ♣ 10 9 8 4
              ♠ A K Q 9 7 3
              ♡ Q 8 4
              ◇ K 2
              ♣ 6 5
```

The bidding:

SOUTH	WEST	NORTH	EAST
One Spade	Pass	Two Clubs	Pass
Three Spades	Pass	Five Spades	Pass
Six Spades	Pass	Pass	Pass

South's acceptance of North's invitation to a slam was an overbid, to put it mildly. But his play of the hand was superb.

West opened the Queen of Diamonds, dummy's Ace winning. The Ace of Trumps was then cashed, after which a trump was led to dummy's ten-spot. Now came the "deception": the Jack of Hearts was led, and passed around to West, who captured the trick with the Ace. West then made the "safe" return of the Jack of Diamonds, declarer's King taking the trick. South now played all his trumps but one, arriving at this position:

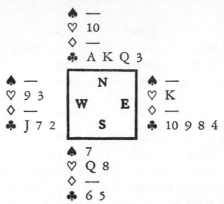

Declarer now led his last trump, discarding the ten of hearts from dummy — and East was squeezed. If he discarded the King of Hearts, then declarer's Queen would be promoted into a winner; if, instead, East threw away a low club, then dummy's three of clubs would become established as a winning trick.

For those readers who feel that West should have returned a heart, let me point out that if declarer had held the K 8 4 of hearts instead of the Q 8 4, then the heart return would have given declarer two heart tricks, had he guessed the location of the heart nine. Please do not misinterpret my position, however — I am not justifying West's neutral return of a diamond. I am merely trying to register my disapproval of East when he called West's return "an imbecilic return."

There are many situations that arise in which you would like to have the opponents lead a certain suit, but you simply cannot force them to do so. An expert player, in these situations, has learned how to coax or entice them into leading that suit, by making them believe that he is either weak in that suit, or has no interest in it. A play of this type is the theme of the following deal. Let us look at it first from the viewpoint of the West defender:

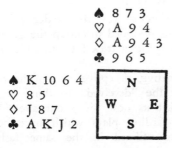

The bidding:

SOUTH	WEST	NORTH	EAST
One Heart	Pass	Two Hearts	Pass
Four Hearts	Pass	Pass	Pass

You open the King of Clubs, South dropping the ten-spot, and then continue with the Ace, upon which South plays the Queen. Your next lead is the Jack of Clubs, and on it declarer tosses the deuce of spades. What do you lead to trick four?

Certainly not a club, for that would give declarer a ruff in one hand, and a discard from the other. A diamond looks unattractive — and would turn out badly if declarer had, for example, the K 10 x. A heart lead might trap your partner's hypothetical Queen. A spade — well, you do not care about leading away from the King, but why did declarer toss away the deuce of spades? Perhaps a spade lead then . . .

Whatever you ultimately elect to do is, in a certain sense, immaterial. The important thing is the dangerous trend of thought into which declarer's discard has led you — and sometimes you cannot shake it off, as though you were under a hypnotic spell doing as you are being commanded to do. The complete deal was:

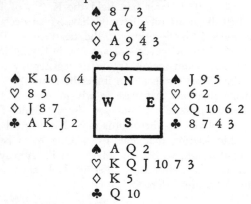

                 ♠ 8 7 3
                 ♡ A 9 4
                 ◊ A 9 4 3
                 ♣ 9 6 5

    ♠ K 10 6 4   N   ♠ J 9 5
    ♡ 8 5   ♡ 6 2
    ◊ J 8 7   W   E   ◊ Q 10 6 2
    ♣ A K J 2   S   ♣ 8 7 4 3

                 ♠ A Q 2
                 ♡ K Q J 10 7 3
                 ◊ K 5
                 ♣ Q 10

Looking at it through declarer's eyes, the reader will see that his discard of the spade deuce was designed to entrap the gullible. If West could be lured into leading a spade at trick four, then declarer's contract would be guaranteed.

So much, then, for imaginative, deceptive, spur-of-the moment plays which are calculated to get the "deceived" to think as the deceiver would like him to think. Let us now direct our attention to certain specific deceptive and false-carding plays which have become pretty much standardized, and are utilized in the same fashion as any technically-correct play would be utilized when the occasion for its employment arises.

B. DECEPTIVE PLAYS BY THE DEFENDERS

It has been stated and illustrated that deceptive tactics by the defenders must be "handled with care." The reason for this, of course, is that in most cases the defenders must cooperate to the maximum extent in order to defeat declarer. And, where a deceptive play is apt either to confuse or to mislead partner as to the nature of the deceiver's holding, the defense figures to collapse. But there are definite situations where a defender can deceive declarer without deceiving or misleading partner.

Probably the oldest "chestnut" is the following:

♠ K 10 9 2

♠ Q J   N
        W   E   ♠ 6 5
         S

♠ A 8 7 4 3

Declarer is in a *spade contract,* and he leads the three of spades. It is accepted psychological strategy for you, sitting West, to put up the Queen, thereby hoping to induce declarer into believing that your Queen is a singleton. The desired effect of the play is to get declarer to now finesse your partner for the Jack. Of course this play will not work all the time, especially since it is a standard play known to all players. The expert player, in this situation, has learned to "mix them up"; sometimes he plays the Jack, and sometimes the Queen. In the long run, by playing the Queen, you will win a trick with the Jack more often than you would have won a trick with the Queen had you put up the Jack on the first spade lead. From declarer's point of view, when he sees the Queen put up, he knows that about half the time you were dealt a blank Queen, and that you had no choice when you played the Queen. And in the remaining fifty percent of the situations — when you were dealt the Q J doubleton — half of the time you play the Queen, and half the time, the Jack. So, when the Queen comes up, it figures to be a singleton more often than not.

The same situation is also applicable — and to the same extent — when you are on lead. Suppose in the above situation South had opened the bidding with one spade, and upon being raised to two spades by North, South contracted for game at four spades. In this case, holding the Q J of Spades, you would be reasonably sure that the declarer and dummy had the outstanding high spades — and the opening lead of the *Jack* might well lead declarer into thinking that your partner possessed the Queen, since if you had the Q J, your "normal" lead would have been the Queen. But, again, if you have required a reputation for always leading the J from a Q J doubleton, declarer will correctly diagnose the situation, and catch your Queen. If, however, you are known to "mix them up," declarer may well accept the lead at face value, and be fatally misled.

If the reader does not want any part of this psychological warfare, permit me to point out that if West avoids leading spades altogether, declarer, left to his own resources will probably cash the Ace and King playing for the four adverse spades to be divided 2-2. If the reader does not agree, surely he will concur in the following: if a spade *is not led originally,* then declarer, as soon as he leads trumps, *50%* of the time he will lay down the Ace first, thereby automatically avoiding the loss of a spade trick since your other honor must drop on his next lead. And, even had he led the King from dummy on his first spade lead, dropping your Queen or Jack, he would still have a 50-50 chance of guessing whether your honor was a singleton or part of the Q J doubleton. By leading the Jack (or Queen) yourself, you deprive declarer of the opportunity of laying down his Ace first — and in so doing you create for yourself the possibility of winning a trick.

A most interesting deal with respect to this Q J doubleton situation occurred some years ago. Permit me to present it verbatim from a newspaper column that I once wrote:

```
                    ♠ A 7 5 2
                    ♡ Q J 9
                    ◊ 10 8 3
                    ♣ A Q 4

   ♠ Q J          ┌─────────┐          ♠ 9 8
   ♡ 8 4 2        │    N    │          ♡ 7 5 3
   ◊ J 6 5 2      │ W     E │          ◊ K 9 7 4
   ♣ J 9 8 6      │    S    │          ♣ K 10 5 3
                  └─────────┘
                    ♠ K 10 6 4 3
                    ♡ A K 10 6
                    ◊ A Q
                    ♣ 7 2
```

SOUTH	WEST	NORTH	EAST
One Spade	Pass	Three Spades	Pass
Four Notrump	Pass	Five Hearts	Pass
Six Spades	Pass	Pass	Pass

Opening lead — Two of Diamonds.

"It is all well and good to try to outsmart the defenders when you, as declarer, can see that it is impossible to bring home your contract by straightforward, technically-correct play. But too many players, unfortunately, resort to guile when there is no necessity to do so.

"The above deal serves as an example of a declarer who elected to try to outguess the opponents instead of spending his time looking for a superior line of play. And, despite a favorable opening lead by West, declarer lost his contract.

"West opened the deuce of diamonds, East's King falling to declarer's Ace. A low trump was now led towards the board, (i.e., dummy) and West played the Jack which dummy's Ace captured. Since West had the reputation of being a crafty and tricky player, who had a definite tendency towards falsecarding, declarer now went into a huddle with himself before making his next play. His trend of thought proceeded along the following lines:

" 'I'm certain that West, being a 'cute' guy, would not have played the Jack of trumps if he had held both the Queen and the Jack. Had he held both of these cards, he would have tried to fool me by falsecarding with the Queen. Therefore it seems to be a cinch that West's Jack of Spades was a singleton . . . I'm going to finesse East for the Queen of Spades.'

"So, on the basis of this reasoning, declarer's next play was a low trump off the board, and when East followed low, declarer put up his ten-spot. West, as is evident, won this trick with his Queen, and declarer ultimately went down a trick, since it was impossible to avoid the loss of a club trick to East.

"Proper play of this hand should have been as follows: After winning the opening diamond lead, a trump is led towards the board, dummy's Ace taking West's Jack. Declarer then returns a trump, putting up his King. With West's Queen falling on this trick, the contract, of course, becomes guaranteed. But suppose West's Jack had been a singleton, meaning that East had originally started with the Q x x, the contract would nevertheless have been guaranteed at this point!

"Let us assume that when the second round of trumps is played — declarer putting up his King — West shows out, leaving East with the high Queen of trumps. Declarer would now lay down his Queen of Diamonds, after which he would re-enter dummy via the Queen of Hearts, and ruff dummy's last diamond in his own hand, eliminating diamonds from both hands. This would now be the North-South position, East possessing the Queen of trumps:

♠ 7 5
♡ J 9
◊ —
♣ A Q 4

♠ 10 6
♡ A K 10
◊ —
♣ 7 2

"South's hearts would now be cashed, and if East chose to ruff a heart, he would be confronted with the option of either returning a club into dummy's A Q, or else returning a diamond which would enable declarer to discard a club from his own hand while simultaneously trumping the trick in dummy. Or, if East refused to ruff a heart while declarer was cashing them, declarer would then throw East into the lead with the spade Queen, and the same 'end-play' position would be reached: East would be forced either to play back a diamond, which would give declarer a ruff in one hand and a discard from the other, or else to return a club into dummy's A Q.

"By refusing to 'guess' the trump situation, the slam contract was there for the taking. The only way it could be defeated if played in the above manner, was for East to have started with a singleton diamond (just about impossible in view of West's opening lead of the diamond deuce) ; or, if East started with a void in hearts, a most extremely unlikely possibility. But even if the 'impossible' did develop — that East ruffed the second lead of diamonds or the first lead of hearts — there would still be available the 50-50 chance that West held the King of Clubs, in which case the spade Queen would be declarer's only loser."

Another standard, and frequently occurring, deceptive play available to the defenders is the following:

♣ K J 9 5 3

♣ Q 8 6   ♣ 10 2

♣ A 7 4

Declarer is obviously trying to establish the club suit, and he lays down the Ace from his own hand, West playing the six, while dummy follows with the three. You are sitting East. Your correct play is the *ten-spot,* and not the deuce. The ten is bound to start a train of thought in declarer's mind. Undoubtedly declarer had started out by deciding to finesse West for the Queen of Clubs at trick two. But with the ten being dropped by you, he may now feel that perhaps you had started with the Q 10 doubleton — and if he then cashes the King to drop your hoped-for Queen, your partner's Queen will now be created into a winner. Of course, if declarer also has the Queen (in addition to the Ace), then the play of the ten-spot costs nothing. It is obvious, however, that if you always play the ten-spot in the above, or similar situations, the opponents will fail to take you seriously.

A variation of the above is the following:

◊ A K J 9 8

◊ 7 6 4 3 | N | ◊ Q 10
              W   E
               | S |

◊ 5 2

Let us assume that the contract is *notrump,* and the declarer is attacking the diamond suit. He leads the Ace from dummy — and on it you drop the Queen. Will not declarer be led to believe that the ten-spot is in the West hand — and will he then not enter the South hand in order to lead a low diamond and finesse your partner for the ten-spot? Of course it is true that, in the example given, the declarer might have finessed for the Queen if East had played the ten-spot first — but the initial play of the Queen makes it almost an absolute certainty that he will finesse for the ten, enabling you to make a trick which you might or might not have otherwise made.

Of course, this play might turn out to be disastrous, as is frequently the end-result of a deceptive play that boomeranged. For instance, suppose that this had been the situation:

◊ A K J 9 8

◊ 7 6 4 | N | ◊ Q 10
            W   E
             | S |

◊ 5 3 2

On the play of the Ace, if you drop your Queen, declarer will then cash the King prior to finessing for the ten-spot. And, with your ten-spot falling, declarer will now have five diamond tricks. If, in this illustration, you had played "normally" by dropping the ten-spot first, then you would have stood a chance of winning a trick with your Queen via declarer's subsequent unsuccessful diamond finesse.

But, if you had diagnosed the situation, and had guessed that declarer had started with only two diamonds (instead of three), then your play of the Queen on the first lead of the suit would have gained you a trick.

Another variation of this play was created in actual competition by Mike Michaels, one of Washington's life masters:

♣ K J 9 8 6

♣ Q 10   N / W E / S   ♣ 7 4 2

♣ A 5 3

The remainder of the cards are unimportant. At one stage of the bidding, however, South had raised North's club bid, pretty much marking the Ace of Clubs as being in the South hand. The final contract was six notrump. At trick two, South led the three of clubs — and Mike played the Queen into the jaws of dummy's King-Jack. Can you blame declarer for subsequently leading the nine-spot off dummy, and finessing East for the ten-spot? Wouldn't you, as declarer, have concluded that West's Queen had been a singleton?

A standard false-card that can never cost anything is the following.

♠ A J 9 5 4

♠ 10 6 2   N / W E / S

♠ K 8 7

Declarer leads the King of Spades, you play the deuce, the four-spot is played from dummy, and your partner, East, follows with the three-spot. The seven of spades is then led out of the South hand — and the only proper card for you to play is *the ten-spot*. In so doing, declarer will realize that if your ten-spot is the normal play, then either you have the sole Queen left, or that East started with the Q x x originally. If the latter situation exists, then the Queen will become a winner no matter what declarer plays. In playing the ten-spot, then, declarer might be enticed into taking a finesse where otherwise, if left to his own resources, he might have decided to cash dummy's Ace in the hope of dropping East's Queen. No matter what the result, your play of the ten-spot can never become a losing play — and it might well be the winning play, as it would be if this were the set-up:

```
              ♠ A J 9 5 4
                  ┌───────┐
                  │   N   │
  ♠ 10 6 2        │ W   E │        ♠ Q 3
                  │   S   │
                  └───────┘
              ♠ K 8 7
```

At this point, I think it would not be amiss to interject two standard, but highly dangerous, false-carding situations which are often employed by a defender, and result in an unhappy ending.

The first of these is the opening lead against a notrump contract of the *fifth-highest* of a suit instead of the conventional fourth-highest (for instance, leading the deuce of spades from K 10 7 3 2, instead of the proper three-spot). The purpose of this deceptive lead, of course, is to mislead declarer into believing that you hold but four cards of that suit (when you lead the deuce as the fourth-highest, you are known to have three cards higher and none lower). In so misleading him, your hope is that he will then incorrectly diagnose the distribution of the defenders' cards, and as a result will play improperly. Sometimes the desired effect is achieved. But much more often you succeed in convincing your partner that you have but four cards in that suit, causing him to defend incorrectly in the subsequent play; that is, if partner has a respectable five-or-six card suit of his own, he will tend to try to develop his own suit, instead of trying to help you develop your "four-card" suit. But if you had told him the truth, he would not go changing horses in midstream. To deliberately mislead your partner as to the length of your suit borders on the ridiculous.

The second standard and highly-dangerous false-carding situation is the following:

```
              ♡ A J 10 9
                  ┌───────┐
                  │   N   │
  ♡ 8 7 5         │ W   E │        ♡ K Q 2
                  │   S   │
                  └───────┘
              ♡ 6 4 3
```

Declarer leads the three of hearts, putting in the nine-spot from dummy — and the "wise-guy" East wins it with *the King*, his purpose being to trick declarer into believing that the Queen is in the West hand. Who cares what declarer thinks? No matter how declarer subsequently plays the heart suit, *won't East always win another heart trick?* Why, then, mislead partner into believing that declarer possesses the Queen of Hearts? If East does deceive partner, then in the later play partner will refuse to lead a heart and East might desperately be wanting a heart lead to obtain a second trick in that suit. Why deceive partner as to the true state of affairs? The deceit stands only to lose, and never to gain.

An apparently analogous situation, and yet completely different, is the following:

♡ A J 10 8 3

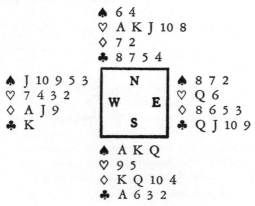

♡ K Q

Let us say *hearts are the trump suit,* although the same would apply if it were a side suit. Declarer leads the deuce of hearts, puting up the ten-spot from dummy. The normal false-card is to take the trick with the King, in the hope that by so doing declarer will be led to believe that West possesses the Queen. The fear here is that declarer, left to his own resources, may next play the Ace, catching your remaining honor. The capturing of the initial heart lead with the King may convince declarer that he should finesse West for the Queen on the next lead of the suit — which would be proper if East's King were the normal play. Bear in mind, however, that in the above situation you should not always win the trick with the King, for if you do you will mark yourself as a consistent false-carder — and if you then ever win the trick with the Queen declarer will know that you do not possess the King.

There is a type of deceptive play which, on superficial examination, appears to be of the dangerous variety. In the hands of the novice it is, admittedly, a dangerous play to make. In the hands of the expert, however, it has been rendered non-dangerous, for he has learned to apply it with *no visible hesitation:*

```
              ♠ 6 4
              ♡ A K J 10 8
              ◊ 7 2
              ♣ 8 7 5 4
♠ J 10 9 5 3      N        ♠ 8 7 2
♡ 7 4 3 2                  ♡ Q 6
◊ A J 9      W      E      ◊ 8 6 5 3
♣ K              S         ♣ Q J 10 9
              ♠ A K Q
              ♡ 9 5
              ◊ K Q 10 4
              ♣ A 6 3 2
```

West led the Jack of Spades against South's *three notrump* contract, declarer's Queen winning. Declarer then played the nine of hearts, letting it ride. East nonchalantly followed with the six-spot!

Honestly, now, would not you finesse again for the Queen, being certain that West held it? Our declarer did, and went down two tricks.

From East's point of view, he might well have been sacrificing the Queen. But he properly felt that it was a worthwhile risk, for if he won the trick with the Queen, all of dummy's hearts would be good. So he took his calculated risk — and it paid off.

As a final word on East's "abnormal" hold-up play, let me state that if you have the urge to live dangerously — as East did — make your play without hesitation. If, on declarer's lead of the nine of hearts, East had deliberated for a while prior to declining to take his Queen, declarer would not have taken the second finesse in hearts.

A deal almost identical to the preceding one is the following, the defenders being Waldemar von Zedtwitz sitting East, and Harry Harkavy, sitting West. Both are from Miami Beach, Florida.

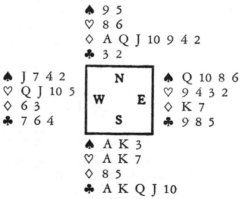

Although six diamonds was a guaranteed contract, North-South arrived at *six notrump*, against which West opened the Queen of Hearts. This was taken by declarer's King, after which declarer led the eight of diamonds, and took the finesse. The eight-spot won the trick when von Zedtwitz followed with the seven-spot!

South then cashed five club tricks, West discarding two spades, while East discarded two hearts. West, incidentally, was very careful to hold on to the "insignificant" six of diamonds, since he knew that his partner must have the diamond King left (if declarer had it, declarer could take at least seven diamond tricks, five club tricks, and the King of Hearts which had already been taken).

If you were declarer, and had not seen all four hands, would you take the diamond finesse again? If you would, then you, too, would go down two tricks.

The opportunity to avail oneself of the standard deceptive play which follows, arises very often:

♠ K Q 10 2

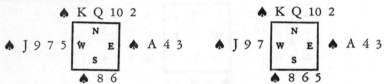

W E ♠ A 4 3

Let us say South is playing a notrump contract and he leads a low spade, putting in the King from dummy. Your only correct play is to let him win the trick, *without any hesitation on your part.* If you capture the King with the Ace, then on the next lead of the suit by declarer he is a cinch to finesse successfully your partner for the Jack. But if you decline to take your Ace on the first lead of the suit, then declarer may well be led to believe that West possesses the spade Ace. And, if he needs just two spade tricks, then on the second lead of the suit from the South hand, he will probably put up dummy's Queen — and when you win the trick with your Ace (to declarer's surprise), you will have established partner's Jack. Either of the following might have been the situation:

♠ K Q 10 2   ♠ K Q 10 2

♠ J 9 7 5 W E ♠ A 4 3   ♠ J 9 7 W E ♠ A 4 3

♠ 8 6   ♠ 8 6 5

On the question of playing low "without any hesitation" on the first spade lead: when the King is played from dummy, do not go into a profound study as to whether to take your Ace or not. If you do, you might just as well show declarer your Ace, for he will know you have it. Make up your mind not to take the King with the Ace as soon as you see the dummy. Then declarer will have a pure guess as to the location of the Ace.

The deceptive play made by the East defender in the deal which follows is neither a "set" situation nor a spur-of-the-moment one. But the deceiver had waited for two years for the opportunity to employ it, and it finally arose in the 1954 National Championships held in Washington, D. C. The East defender was Dick Freeman, one of the original "Quiz Kids," who, at the age of 18, in 1952, was the nation's youngest life master. How would you have played the following combination of cards, as declarer, if you had found yourself in a *six club* contract:

♣ A Q 6

♣ J 9 7 3 2

You lead the deuce of clubs, West puts up the four-spot, dummy's Queen is played, and it wins, East dropping the *eight-spot*. Would you not assume that East had either the singleton eight — in which case you would have to lose one club trick — or that he had the doubleton 10 8, in which case if you now get back to the South hand and lead the Jack of Clubs, you will avoid the loss of any club tricks, for the Jack will catch East's now-singleton ten while simultaneously smothering West's King? So you return to the South hand via some other suit, lead the Jack of Clubs — and *West* fails to follow suit! You now must lose two club tricks. Here is the actual situation:

♣ A Q 6

♣ 4   ♣ K 10 8 5

♣ J 9 7 3 2

There are two angles involved in Dick's refusal to take his King on the first lead of the suit, and his simultaneous false-card of the eight-spot. First, if he had taken the King, then declarer's next lead would automatically have been a club to the Ace, revealing the fact that West was now void — and East's ten-spot would then be finessed, resulting in East making just one club trick. Second, if in refusing to take the King on the first lead, he had played the five-spot, then declarer might well have decided to play West for the K x originally, and he would next have led a low one to the Ace (instead of the Jack). And, again, when West would show out, East's ten-spot would be successfully finessed. But the play of the eight-spot on the first club lead led declarer to realize that if the eight-spot were East's normal play, then the King was possessed by West, and that East might well have held the 10 8 doubleton originally. Of course, this was precisely the impression and the trend of thought that East hoped to create in declarer's mind by his deceptive play — and his triumph was a well-deserved one.

The deal which follows is the final one in "deception by the defenders," and it contains a type of play which, while not a standard deceptive play, is one which would be made into a"pat" situation if the opportunity for its use arose more frequently. On this deal, which arose in a local tournament, only the matter of an overtrick was involved, but our West defender did not know this when he made his play:

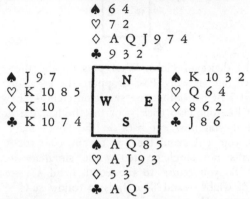

```
                          ♠ 6 4
                          ♡ 7 2
                          ◇ A Q J 9 7 4
                          ♣ 9 3 2
    ♠ J 9 7                              ♠ K 10 3 2
    ♡ K 10 8 5          N                ♡ Q 6 4
    ◇ K 10          W       E            ◇ 8 6 2
    ♣ K 10 7 4          S                ♣ J 8 6
                          ♠ A Q 8 5
                          ♡ A J 9 3
                          ◇ 5 3
                          ♣ A Q 5
```

Against South's *three notrump contract,* West opened his four of clubs, East's Jack being captured by declarer's Queen. The three of diamonds was then led — and West put up the King! Looking at all four hands, you would, of course, take the King with the Ace, and bring in the entire diamond suit. But what if East's King were a singleton, as it certainly appeared to be? In this case, East would have started with the 10 x x x of diamonds — and to take the King with the Ace would prevent declarer from cashing more than three diamond tricks. So, to guarantee taking five diamond tricks — and his contract — declarer permitted West's King to win the trick . . . I wonder how many defenders would have "earned" the King of Diamonds had they been in the West seat?

C. DECEPTIVE PLAYS BY DECLARER

The situations to be presented here, as in the preceding section on "Deception by the Defenders," are situations which have become pretty much standardized, and are an integral part of the declarer's arsenal of psychological weapons. Let us assume you are sitting South, playing a *spade contract,* and West opens the *King of Hearts:*

```
                  ♡ 7 5 3
                      N
    ♡ A K 9 6    W       E    ♡ J 10 4
                      S
                  ♡ Q 8 2
```

On the lead of the King of Hearts, the three is played from dummy, East plays the four — *and you should play the eight-spot, not the deuce.* You know, since you hold the deuce, and the three and four are in evidence, that if you play the deuce then West will know that his partner's four-spot was the lowest that he had, and therefore will interpret it as a signal not to continue the suit. [1] And, if hearts are not continued, you will never make your Queen of Hearts. But if on the opening lead of the King of Hearts, you play the eight-spot, then West might well assume that East has the deuce — and that therefore East's play of the four-spot was the beginning of a high-low signal to get West to continue the heart suit. And, if that is done, then you have just tricked West into giving you a heart trick. By playing the eight-spot, you stand to gain a trick — and can never lose anything thereby.

In many situations which "appear" to be comparable to the above, declarer often makes an untimely and incorrect false card, thereby encouraging the leader to continue a suit which declarer was hoping that the leader would discontinue. Such a type situation is the following:

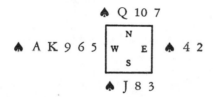

♠ Q 10 7

♠ A K 9 6 5   N W E S   ♠ 4 2

♠ J 8 3

Against South's *four heart contract,* West opens the King of Spades, East following with the four-spot (which as *we* can see but West cannot, is the beginning of a high-low signal to get West to continue the suit so that he can trump the third round). If declarer now falsecards with the eight-spot (as is often done), West will undoubtedly notice the absence of *both the two and three of spades* — and will then assume that his partner probably has one of these cards, in which case the four-spot must have been the beginning of a high-low signal to get the spade suit continued. And, if it is continued, then declarer will lose three spade tricks, East trumping the third round.

But if on the lead of the King of Spades, declarer plays normally, dropping the three, West will not know for sure where the deuce is: after all, South might easily have held just the 3 2 doubleton, with East holding the J 8 4. And if West does not continue spades, then declarer

---

[1] The subject of defensive signals is presented at length in Chapter XII.

can always develop a sure trick after trumps are drawn. To falsecard with the eight-spot is to invite disaster — and disaster will usually accept your invitation.

Probably the most frequently successful ruse that is perpetrated by declarer is presented in the situation which follows. The reason for its success is that the duped are victims of a slogan which once was a national shibboleth: "Always cover an honor with an honor."

♡ K 7 3 2

♡ A J 10 9 5

You are in a *heart contract,* and your West opponent has, for the last 15 years, been known always to "cover an honor with an honor." So you lead the Jack of Hearts — and if West has the Queen, he will automatically play it on your Jack. If, when you lead the Jack, West does not cover, you will *know* that he does not have the Queen. You will now overtake the Jack with dummy's King, and promptly finesse East for the Queen, which he will have, since West, if he held the Queen, would have covered your Jack with it.

Even if you do not know West's habits, the play of the Jack is still the proper play, its purpose being to entice West into covering. If, however, West follows with a low heart, you are no better and no worse off than you were when you started. You will probably play the King and then the Ace, in the hope of dropping the Queen. By leading the Jack first, you may eliminate the necessity of guessing the whereabouts of the Queen. It certainly costs you nothing to try it.

Another "pat" situation that actually works much more frequently than it logically should, is the following:

♠ 8 6 5 3 2

♠ Q J 10 7 4

Spades are the trump suit, and it is perfectly apparent that you must lose two spade tricks unless the opponents blunder, and their Ace and King fall on the same trick. If you lead a low spade from the North hand, East, holding either the A x or K x will automatically play low, and two tricks will inevitably be lost. Of course, if East has the blank Ace or singleton King, he will have to play his singleton; and, again, two tricks will have to be lost, since in this case West will have either the K x or A x.

But if you lead the Queen from your own hand, you will be amazed at how often West, holding the K x, will go up with the King, fearing that if he does not, your Ace will catch his King on the next round. And, if he goes up with the King, he will catch his partner's singleton Ace, (he will also catch H—— from his partner).

Please do not try to convince me that it would be foolish for West, holding the K x, to play the King on your Queen. I do not need to be convinced — of course it is foolish: surely if declarer held the Ace, he would not be playing the Queen first. Either he would have gotten to the board to take a finesse with his A Q; or else he would have cashed the Ace before playing the Queen, in the hope of catching a singleton King. Certainly it is foolish and illogical to go up with the King holding the K x — but I am dealing with a fact which has been confirmed by experience: West will, on occasion, play the King from K x — and you will have just found an ally.

A type situation which the expert always looks for is the following:

♡ J 10 3 2

```
    N
 W     E
    S
```

♡ K

Declarer is playing a *club contract,* and he would not be adverse to avoiding the loss of a heart trick. His best play, from a psychological point of view, is to lead *the Jack of Hearts* from the North hand, in the hope that if East has the Ace he will play low, believing that declarer might be trying to finesse for the Queen. What would you do, sitting East, if declarer led the Jack of Hearts and this were the situation:

♡ J 10 3 2

```
    N
 W     E    ♡ A 8 5
    S
```

If you put up the Ace, you would be all right if declarer had the singleton King. But suppose this were the situation:

♡ J 10 3 2

♡ Q 9 6 4   [N W E S]   ♡ A 8 5

♡ K 7

In the above situation your play of the Ace would give declarer his King of Hearts, whereas if you had played low, declarer, too, might have played low, hoping you had the Queen.

Certainly, in the given deceptive situation, it costs declarer nothing to lead the Jack from dummy, rather than the deuce, for in so doing, the chance of stealing a trick with the singleton King is increased. Again, this "fact" is based on experience: if the deuce is led, East is more apt to play his Ace than if the Jack is led. And, in passing, if West has the Ace, it makes no difference what card declarer leads off dummy — his King will be taken by West's Ace.

Now for the final deal in this chapter on the art and technique of camouflage. To me, the deceptive play made by declarer is the simplest, and yet the finest example that I have seen in many years of convincing the opponents to believe beyond a shadow of a doubt that a certain situation existed — and too late they discovered that what had appeared to be a reality had been a mirage.

You are sitting West, defending against South's *six club* contract. South has bid both Hearts and Clubs.

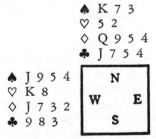

♠ K 7 3
♡ 5 2
◇ Q 9 5 4
♣ J 7 5 4

♠ J 9 5 4
♡ K 8
◇ J 7 3 2
♣ 9 8 3

You elect to open the deuce of diamonds, and declarer, with no deliberation, plays the Queen from dummy, which your partner covers with the King, and South captures the trick with the Ace. South then leads the ten of trumps, and overtakes it with dummy's Jack, after which he leads a low heart, putting up his Queen. You, of course, capture the trick with your King, and triumphantly lay down your high Jack of Diamonds. Declarer trumps your Jack, and then proceeds to waltz in with his slam contract. Here is the complete deal:

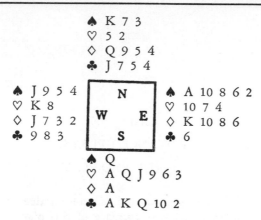

Our South declarer was Sam Fry, Jr., of New York City. It was readily apparent to him that if the heart finesse lost he was doomed to defeat — unless the opponents failed to return a spade. So, to take out insurance against West holding the King of Hearts, Sam put up the Diamond Queen from dummy, thereby creating the indelible impression that he held at least two diamonds. After all, who but an idiot (or an expert) would play the Queen from dummy when he himself had only the singleton Ace?

After capturing East's King of Diamonds with his Ace, declarer then led the ten of clubs, and overtook it with dummy's Jack. A low heart was now led, South's Queen being captured by West's King.

Can you blame West for returning the Jack of Diamonds? Did not declarer figure to have started with the A x of Diamonds? Frankly, would he not have made the identical play if he had held the A x of Diamonds? As a matter of fact, if West had returned a spade instead of the Jack of Diamonds, it would have been an irrational play.

With the diamond return which South trumped, it then became routine to draw trumps, and to discard the dummy's spades on South's established hearts. He then ruffed his Queen of Spades in dummy, for the slam-going trick.

CHAPTER X

ADVANCED PLAYS:

I. THE END-PLAY

O NE of the most interesting plays in contract bridge is the "end-play." Despite the high frequency of occurrence of this play, the fact remains that only the experts seem to be familiar with its application. Somehow or other, the misconception has arisen that the "end-play" is most difficult to master, and as a result of this attitude it has been shrouded with an unjustified air of complexity by most bridge writers.

In essence, the end-play is but another application and extension of an elementary principle which was presented and illustrated earlier: that it is more advantageous to force an opponent to lead up to your tenace holdings than it is to lead up to them yourself. For instance:

♠ 3 2

♠ A Q

If you are compelled to lead the deuce of spades from the North hand, your finesse of the Queen will succeed 50% of the time. But if you can get *West* to lead a spade you will make two spade tricks 100% of the time. Basically the above illustration depicts the "longing" that underlies the successful execution of the end-play; *to force* an opponent to make a lead which will present you with a trick that you otherwise could not, or might not, have obtained.

Technically, the term "end-play" applies to a type of declarer's action which occurs in the later stages of the play of the hand. The principle involved is deliberately to put one of the opponents into the lead, in order to force him to make a lead favorable to declarer. The end-play is also known as the "throw-in play," the "strip-and-end-play," and the "elimination play."

250

Let us revert back to the illustration just presented, where it was pointed out that if you could get West to lead a spade, you would have won a trick which you might not have won had you been compelled to lead the suit yourself:

♠ 3 2

Suppose that you knew that West had the Ace of Hearts. Could you not be assured of winning two spade tricks with the following combination of cards by means of the end-play:

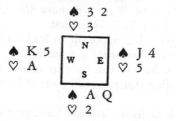

♠ 3 2
♡ 3

♠ K 5　　　　　♠ J 4
♡ A　　　　　　♡ 5

♠ A Q
♡ 2

Let us assume that North has the lead. Most bridge players, being unfamiliar with the end-play, would now lead the deuce of spades and hopefully finesse South's Queen. And, as is evident, North-South would then win but one of the final three tricks.

But familiarity with end-plays would net North-South two tricks instead of just one. A heart would be led from the North hand, West being compelled to capture the trick with the Ace. He would then have no choice but to lead a spade, giving South two spade tricks.

Another illustration:

◇ 6
♣ 8 2

◇ A　　　　　◇ 10
♣ A Q　　　　♣ 6 3

◇ 9
♣ K 7

North is on lead. The "end-play-conscious" declarer, if he had the "feeling" that West possessed the Ace of Diamonds, would now lead the six of diamonds from the North hand, West's Ace winning. No matter which club West then led, South would win a trick with his King. In no other way could South win a club trick except by throwing West into the lead via the Diamond Ace.

Another simple illustration:

```
                    ♣ A J 3
                   ┌───────┐
                   │   N   │
      ♣ Q 8 6 5    │ W   E │    ♣ 9 7 4
                   │   S   │
                   └───────┘
                    ♣ K 10 2
```

As the reader can see, if South guesses that West possesses the Queen of Clubs, then the making of three club tricks becomes routine via a successful finesse. In actual play, however, South sees only two hands — and half the time West will have the Queen of Clubs, and half the time that card will be held by East.

But if South can get either opponent to lead a club, then the making of three tricks becomes automatic, for South will then be obtaining a "free finesse"; that is, he will not have to finesse for the Queen, since the opponents, in leading that suit, will succeed in presenting South with a third club trick.

Obviously, then, it is to declarer's advantage to give the opponents the lead in some other suit, in order to force them to lead a club. Suppose this is the situation at trick ten, with either East or West possessing the Ace of Spades, the remainder of the adverse cards being clubs:

```
                    ♠ 6
                    ♣ A J 3
                   ┌───────┐
      ♠ A          │   N   │    ♠ —
      ♣ Q 8 6      │ W   E │    ♣ 9 7 5 4
                   │   S   │
                   └───────┘
                    ♠ 4
                    ♣ K 10 2
```

If South now leads a spade from either hand, West will be compelled to capture the trick, after which he will have no choice but to lead a club, enabling South's ten-spot (or North's Jack) to win the trick. Had East held the spade Ace, the same result would have been achieved: East's compulsory club lead would have trapped partner's Queen, thereby promoting dummy's Jack of Clubs into a winner.

All of the simple examples above have illustrated the end-play at the exact moment when it takes place, by throwing one opponent into the lead via some other suit. There has been no distortion in the above presentation of the definition of the end-play. However, no mention has been made of the preliminary steps essential to attaining this end position, which, of course, must be developed before the end-play can be brought to a successful conclusion.

As the reader will learn through studying the contents of this chapter, one can plan from the outset — or fairly early in the play — for the end-play position to develop. This planning is not at all difficult once the approach to the end-play is understood.

Let me introduce an illustration of the preparation or planning for an end-play by presenting a deal from actual combat. In this deal the necessity for developing an end-play situation arises from the fact that if declarer leads a certain suit himself, *he figures to lose three tricks;* whereas, if he can get the opponents to lead that suit, he will lose *only two tricks.* The particular combination of which declarer is so apprehensive is one which was presented in Chapter II, namely the Q x x facing the J x x.

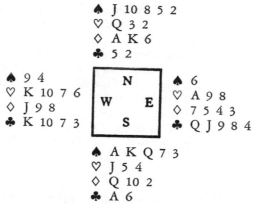

Against South's *four spade contract* West opened a trump, declarer winning, after which West's remaining trump was picked up.

It was apparent to declarer that there were four potential losers: three in hearts and one in clubs. But if declarer could get the opponents to lead a heart, then the heart losses would be restricted to just two tricks. So preparations were made to force the opponents to lead hearts.

Declarer now cashed the Ace, King, and Queen of Diamonds. Next came the Ace of Clubs, followed by declarer's remaining club, leaving this position:

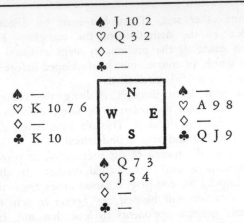

It was immaterial as to which of the opponents elected to win the preceding club trick. Whoever won the trick could not lead a club or a diamond, for to do so would enable declarer to trump that lead in dummy while simultaneously discarding a heart from his own hand. Therefore, a heart lead had to be made — and declarer lost only two heart tricks.

One of the fundamental characteristics of the end-play is the elimination of side suits before throwing an opponent into the lead. On the above deal, for example, if diamonds had not been eliminated from both declarer's and dummy's hands, prior to leading the club, the opponents, upon obtaining the lead, would have been able to return a diamond at no cost to them. Declarer would then have been compelled to lead a heart himself — and he would have lost three heart tricks.

On the deals which follow, illustrating the different types of end-plays, the identical fundamental characteristic is apparent in all of them: *reaching a situation in which an opponent is thrown into the lead at the precise moment when he is forced to lead back only the suit that declarer desires to be led back.*

1.   The theme of this end-play is exactly the same as on the preceding deal: the avoidance of the lead from a suit containing Q x x x opposite J x x. On this deal, however, an additional factor is added: the declining of a 50-50 chance of a finesse in order to force the opponents to make a lead which would be favorable to you.

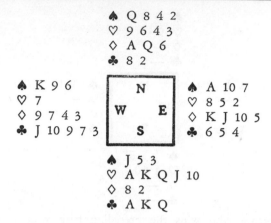

♠ Q 8 4 2
♡ 9 6 4 3
◇ A Q 6
♣ 8 2

♠ K 9 6   ♠ A 10 7
♡ 7   ♡ 8 5 2
◇ 9 7 4 3   ◇ K J 10 5
♣ J 10 9 7 3   ♣ 6 5 4

♠ J 5 3
♡ A K Q J 10
◇ 8 2
♣ A K Q

South arrived at a *four heart* contract against which West opened the club Jack, declarer's Queen winning. Trumps were then drawn, after which the Ace and King of Clubs were cashed, the diamond six being discarded from dummy on the latter trick. Here was the North-South situation at this point:

♠ Q 8 4 2
♡ 9
◇ A Q
♣ —

♠ J 5 3
♡ J 10
◇ 8 2
♣ —

If declarer now took the diamond finesse, it would have lost. A diamond would then have been returned, dummy's Ace winning — and declarer would then have been forced to lose three spade tricks.

But if, instead of taking the diamond finesse, declarer cashes the Ace of Diamonds, and then plays the Queen, he will be throwing one of the opponents (whoever has the King) into the lead while simultaneously eliminating diamonds from both hands. This would then be the position:

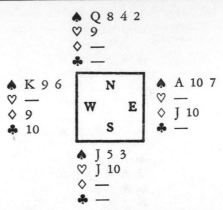

♠ Q 8 4 2
♡ 9
◇ —
♣ —

♠ K 9 6
♡ —
◇ 9
♣ 10

♠ A 10 7
♡ —
◇ J 10
♣ —

♠ J 5 3
♡ J 10
◇ —
♣ —

What difference who wins the preceding trick with the King of Diamonds? Any lead that the opposition now makes will give declarer a trick he could not have made on his own. A diamond or a club lead will permit declarer to ruff the trick in dummy while discarding a spade from his own hand. And a spade lead will establish a spade trick for declarer.

2. On this deal North-South arrived at an optimistic *six spade contract*, which was fulfilled through an end-play.

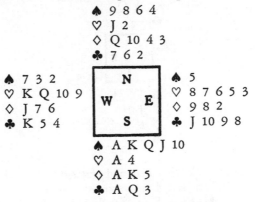

♠ 9 8 6 4
♡ J 2
◇ Q 10 4 3
♣ 7 6 2

♠ 7 3 2
♡ K Q 10 9
◇ J 7 6
♣ K 5 4

♠ 5
♡ 8 7 6 5 3
◇ 9 8 2
♣ J 10 9 8

♠ A K Q J 10
♡ A 4
◇ A K 5
♣ A Q 3

The bidding:

SOUTH	WEST	NORTH	EAST
Two Spades	Pass	Two Notrump	Pass
Three Notrump	Pass	Four Spades	Pass
Six Spades	Pass	Pass	Pass

West, on lead, opened the King of Hearts, declarer's Ace winning. Three rounds of trumps were then drawn, exhausting the opponents of trumps. Then came the Ace, King, and Queen of Diamonds, both opponents following suit to all three rounds. On dummy's ten of diamonds declarer then discarded his three of clubs, after which he played the Jack of Hearts, throwing West into the lead with his "marked" Queen of Hearts. Here was the position at trick ten, with West having the lead:

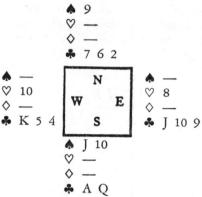

```
              ♠ 9
              ♡ —
              ◇ —
              ♣ 7 6 2
♠ —                        ♠ —
♡ 10      ┌─────────┐      ♡ 8
◇ —       │ N       │      ◇ —
♣ K 5 4   │ W     E │      ♣ J 10 9
          │    S    │
          └─────────┘
              ♠ J 10
              ♡ —
              ◇ —
              ♣ A Q
```

If West led a club, declarer would win two club tricks; if, instead, West led a heart, dummy would trump it while declarer simultaneously discarded his Queen of Clubs. Declarer's only loser would be the heart trick which he "conceded" to West.

3. This deal illustrates an end-play situation which was created when declarer, after eliminating two side suits, took a "deep" finesse which, even if it lost, guaranteed the fulfillment of his contract.

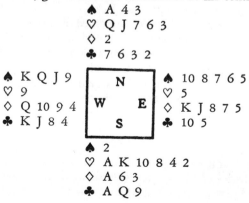

```
                  ♠ A 4 3
                  ♡ Q J 7 6 3
                  ◇ 2
                  ♣ 7 6 3 2
♠ K Q J 9     ┌─────────┐     ♠ 10 8 7 6 5
♡ 9           │ N       │     ♡ 5
◇ Q 10 9 4    │ W     E │     ◇ K J 8 7 5
♣ K J 8 4     │    S    │     ♣ 10 5
              └─────────┘
                  ♠ 2
                  ♡ A K 10 8 4 2
                  ◇ A 6 3
                  ♣ A Q 9
```

The bidding:

SOUTH	WEST	NORTH	EAST
One Heart	Pass	Four Hearts	Pass
Six Hearts	Pass	Pass	Pass

West's opening spade lead was captured by dummy's Ace, and a spade was then ruffed in the closed hand. The Ace of trumps was cashed next, followed by the Diamond Ace, and a ruff of a diamond in dummy. The board's remaining spade was now trumped by declarer, after which declarer's last diamond was ruffed in dummy, leaving this situation:

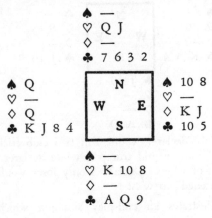

The deuce of clubs was then led, declarer's nine-spot was put up, West captured the trick with his Jack — and West had become the victim of an end-play! If West returned a spade or a diamond, it would be trumped in dummy while declarer discarded his Queen of Clubs. Or, if West elected to return a club, South would be "forced" to win two tricks with his A Q. Had South finessed his Queen of Clubs instead of the nine-spot he would have lost his contract, for West, upon capturing the trick with the King, would merely have returned a low club.

4.   On this deal it became obvious at trick three that West had a sure trump trick — and declarer gave it to him at the precise moment when the end-play position had been attained:

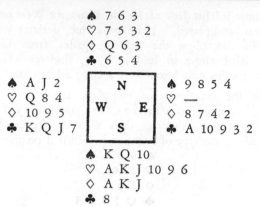

The bidding:

SOUTH	WEST	NORTH	EAST
Two Hearts	Pass	Two Notrump	Pass
Three Hearts	Pass	Four Hearts	Pass
Pass	Pass		

The King of Clubs was opened, followed by the Queen of Clubs, declarer ruffing. When East showed out on declarer's next lead of the trump Ace, it became apparent that West's Queen of Hearts was a sure winner. The King of Trumps was then cashed, leaving the Queen outstanding. Declarer next led his Jack of Diamonds, overtaking it with dummy's Queen, after which the board's last club was ruffed by the South hand. Thus clubs were eliminated from both the North and South hands. Now the Ace and King of Diamonds were taken, leaving this situation:

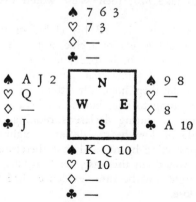

Declarer now led his Jack of Hearts, throwing West into the lead — and West was "end-played." If he led a club, declarer would ruff it in dummy while discarding the ten of spades from his own hand. If, instead, West chose to lead a spade, declarer would make two spade tricks. South's only losers were a club, a heart, and a spade.

5. While the occasions for end-plays arise more often in suit contracts (as opposed to notrump), the opportunity to employ the end-play in notrump contracts does develop frequently enough to warrant a study of the type of situation in which it occurs:

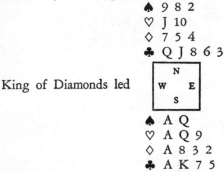

King of Diamonds led

♠ 9 8 2
♡ J 10
◇ 7 5 4
♣ Q J 8 6 3

♠ A Q
♡ A Q 9
◇ A 8 3 2
♣ A K 7 5

Against South's *three notrump* contract West opened the King of Diamonds which held the trick. Then came the Queen of Diamonds, East showing out, and declarer captured the trick with his Ace.

The "better-than-average" player would now count his tricks: one in spades, one in hearts, one in diamonds, and five in clubs. He would then perceive that the ninth trick could be made by a successful finesse in either spades or hearts — and he would recognize that if whichever finesse he elected to take *lost*, then West would cash his established diamonds.

He would now probably play all his clubs, in the hope that the opponents' discards would give him a clue as to which finesse to take. That is, if West discarded a high spade, telling *his* partner to lead a spade, then declarer would know that the spade King was adversely located. Declarer would then hopefully attempt the heart finesse, not because it was a sure thing to win, but rather because the spade finesse was sure to lose. Or, if during declarer's running of the clubs, East threw away a couple of low hearts, declarer might deduce that East had no interest in protecting hearts, and that therefore he did not have the King. Declarer would, in this case, tend to take the spade finesse, not because it was right, but because "evidence" had indicated that the heart finesse would lose.

What it would boil down to would be this: if declarer "guessed" which King was favorably located, he would make his contract; if he misguessed — took the "wrong" finesse — he would go down.

But an "end-play conscious" declarer would make his contract 100% of the time! After winning the second trick with his diamond Ace, the expert declarer would cash his Ace and King of Clubs, *both opponents following suit.* Clubs would then have been eliminated from the enemies' hands. Declarer would also know that West had started with five diamonds, East having failed to follow suit to the second round. Declarer would then lead a diamond, and West would cash all his cards in that suit (four diamonds in toto), leaving this situation with West on lead:

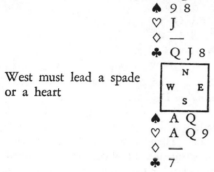

♠ 9 8
♡ J
◊ —
♣ Q J 8

West must lead a spade
or a heart

♠ A Q
♡ A Q 9
◊ —
♣ 7

As the reader can see, West would now be compelled to lead either a spade or a heart, giving declarer his ninth trick via a free finesse. No matter where the major suit Kings were located, declarer would obtain his ninth trick. The actual deal was:

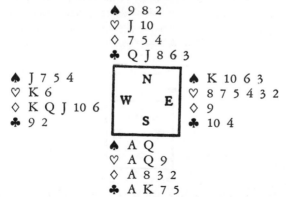

♠ 9 8 2
♡ J 10
◊ 7 5 4
♣ Q J 8 6 3

♠ J 7 5 4
♡ K 6
◊ K Q J 10 6
♣ 9 2

♠ K 10 6 3
♡ 8 7 5 4 3 2
◊ 9
♣ 10 4

♠ A Q
♡ A Q 9
◊ A 8 3 2
♣ A K 7 5

6. This deal presents a notrump hand where the contract could be made only by "counting out" an opponent's hand, and then, instead of

taking a finesse, throwing that opponent into the lead to set up an "end-play."

```
              ♠ K Q 5
              ♡ 8 7 4
              ◇ K Q 7
              ♣ K Q 7 2
♠ 8 7                        ♠ 10 9 3 2
♡ K J 3         N            ♡ 10 9 6 2
◇ 5 4 3      W     E         ◇ 9 8 6 2
♣ J 10 9 8 4    S            ♣ 5
              ♠ A J 6 4
              ♡ A Q 5
              ◇ A J 10
              ♣ A 6 3
```

Against South's *six notrump contract* West opened the Jack of Clubs, North's King winning. A club was then returned to South's Ace, East discarding *the deuce of diamonds*. Declarer then cashed four spade tricks, discarding a low heart from dummy on the fourth spade. West followed to two rounds of spades, and on the third and fourth spade he discarded a heart and a club. Then came the King, Queen, and Ace of Diamonds, everybody following suit. Now declarer took inventory.

West was known to have started with five clubs, East having shown out on the second club lead, and West still had two clubs left, having discarded a club on a spade lead. By observation West was known to have started with three diamonds and two spades. Therefore, he originally had held three hearts, of which one had been discarded. Here was the situation then, at trick ten, the whereabouts of the heart King being unknown:

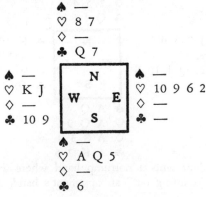

```
              ♠ —
              ♡ 8 7
              ◇ —
              ♣ Q 7
♠ —                        ♠ —
♡ K J          N           ♡ 10 9 6 2
◇ —         W     E        ◇ —
♣ 10 9         S           ♣ —
              ♠ —
              ♡ A Q 5
              ◇ —
              ♣ 6
```

Since West was known to have two clubs and two hearts at this point, declarer then cashed dummy's Queen of Clubs, and led another club throwing West into the lead, *to play a heart.* No matter which of the opponents held the King of Hearts, declarer was assured of winning the last two tricks with his A Q of hearts.

7. Very often, when the success of a contract seems to depend on a finesse, the possibility of an end-play should be considered. Such is the theme of the deal which follows, where declarer refused to take either of two available finesses, and, instead, played for a guaranteed end-play to assure his contract.

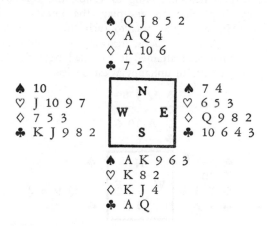

The bidding:

SOUTH	WEST	NORTH	EAST
One Spade	Pass	Three Spades	Pass
Four Notrump	Pass	Five Hearts	Pass
Five Notrump	Pass	Six Clubs	Pass
Six Spades	Pass	Pass	Pass

West opened the Jack of Hearts, dummy's Queen winning, after which the opponents' trumps were picked up in two rounds. Then came the Ace and King of Hearts, thereby eliminating that suit from both the North and South hands, and leaving this situation:

♠ Q J 8
♡ —
◇ A 10 6
♣ 7 5

```
        N
    W       E
        S
```

♠ 9 6 3
♡ —
◇ K J 4
♣ A Q

At this point, if declarer guessed the location of the Diamond Queen, or failing that, if East held the King of Clubs, the contract would be fulfilled. But, by employing an end-play, the guesswork became an unnecessary risk. His next play was to cash the Ace of Clubs, after which he played the Queen of Clubs, throwing West into the lead (the same result would have been attained if East had held the Club King). Here was the position with an unhappy West on lead:

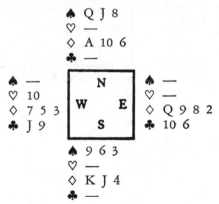

♠ Q J 8
♡ —
◇ A 10 6
♣ —

♠ —   ♠ —
♡ 10   ♡ —
◇ 7 5 3   ◇ Q 9 8 2
♣ J 9   ♣ 10 6

♠ 9 6 3
♡ —
◇ K J 4
♣ —

If West now led either a heart or a club, declarer would trump the trick in dummy while discarding a diamond from his own hand. If, instead, West elected to lead a diamond, declarer would make three diamond tricks regardless of the location of the Queen of Diamonds.

On this deal anybody who is a good guesser can fulfill the contract by guessing that East possesses the Queen of Diamonds. But, just in case one is not a good guesser, the end-play will guarantee the fulfillment of the small slam.

8. On this deal declarer fulfills his contract by avoiding a guess as to the location of either of two adverse key cards, and instead, employing an end-play to achieve his goal. The deal also serves to illustrate why it is more advantageous generally to play a hand in a good trump suit, as opposed to notrump.

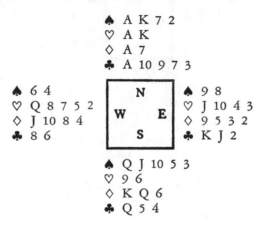

```
                    ♠ A K 7 2
                    ♡ A K
                    ◊ A 7
                    ♣ A 10 9 7 3
    ♠ 6 4                              ♠ 9 8
    ♡ Q 8 7 5 2        N              ♡ J 10 4 3
    ◊ J 10 8 4    W         E         ◊ 9 5 3 2
    ♣ 8 6              S              ♣ K J 2
                    ♠ Q J 10 5 3
                    ♡ 9 6
                    ◊ K Q 6
                    ♣ Q 5 4
```

The bidding:

North	East	South	West
Two Notrump	Pass	Three Spades	Pass
Four Spades	Pass	Six Spades	Pass
Pass	Pass		

Looking at all four hands, the reader can see that the slam can be made by leading a low club from dummy towards declarer's Queen, taking an indirect finesse. But if the location of the King and Jack of Clubs were changed, this indirect finesse might well result in declarer losing two club tricks. By employing an end-play the slam contract becomes guaranteed, irrespective as to where the adverse club honors are located.

Against the *six spade* contract West opened the Jack of Diamonds, dummy's Ace winning, after which two rounds of trumps were drawn. The Ace and King of Hearts were now cashed. Then came the King and Queen of Diamonds, a club being discarded from dummy on the latter trick. Here was the situation after the first seven tricks, the lead being in the South hand:

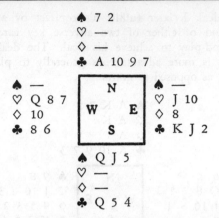

♠ 7 2
♡ —
◇ —
♣ A 10 9 7

♠ —
♡ Q 8 7
◇ 10
♣ 8 6

♠ —
♡ J 10
◇ 8
♣ K J 2

♠ Q J 5
♡ —
◇ —
♣ Q 5 4

South then led the four of clubs, putting up dummy's ten-spot, East's Jack winning. No matter what East played back, the contract was now guaranteed. If he played back a club, declarer would make two club tricks. If instead, he chose to return either a heart or a diamond, declarer would discard his losing club from the South hand while trumping the trick in dummy.

9.   Just how imperative the "elimination" of suits is to the successful execution of an end-play, can be observed from the following deal:

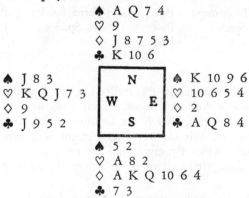

♠ A Q 7 4
♡ 9
◇ J 8 7 5 3
♣ K 10 6

♠ J 8 3
♡ K Q J 7 3
◇ 9
♣ J 9 5 2

♠ K 10 9 6
♡ 10 6 5 4
◇ 2
♣ A Q 8 4

♠ 5 2
♡ A 8 2
◇ A K Q 10 6 4
♣ 7 3

West opened the King of Hearts against South's *five diamond contract,* declarer's Ace winning. A heart was promptly returned and ruffed in dummy, after which a trump was led to declarer's Ace. South's remaining heart was then ruffed by North, and a trump led to declarer's King, leaving this position:

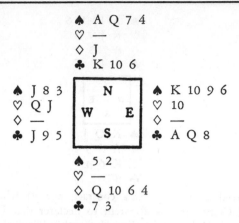

♠ A Q 7 4
♡ —
◇ J
♣ K 10 6

♠ J 8 3
♡ Q J
◇ —
♣ J 9 5

N
W   E
S

♠ K 10 9 6
♡ 10
◇ —
♣ A Q 8

♠ 5 2
♡ —
◇ Q 10 6 4
♣ 7 3

As hearts had been eliminated from both hands, the stage was now set for an end-play. The three of clubs was led from the South hand, and when West followed with the nine-spot, dummy's ten was played, East winning the trick with the Queen.

If East returned a heart, declarer would of course trump it in dummy while discarding a club (or spade) from his own hand; if, instead, East returned a spade, declarer would make two spade tricks; or, if East chose to play back a club, dummy's King would be promoted into a winner, upon which declarer would later discard his losing spade.

On the lead of the low club by South, had West put up his Jack, the identical end-play would have developed. In this case, the Jack would have been covered by dummy's King, East taking the trick with his Ace. Dummy's ten of clubs would then have become promoted into a winner if East elected to return a club.

As is apparent, had hearts not been eliminated from both the North and South hands, East, upon winning the club lead, would simply have returned a heart, and declarer would then have been compelled to lose another club trick, in addition to a spade trick.

At this point, there can be no doubt that a knowledge of the end-play is definitely mandatory if the reader is to get the most out of his cards. Otherwise, easily makable contracts will needlessly be lost.

10. As has been observed in previous illustrations, the known location of an adversely-held "key" card tends to orient declarer towards thinking in terms of an end-play — that is, by "throwing" the possessor into the lead at any precise moment. The following deal concerns itself with this exact situation:

♠ A 10 8 6
♡ K J 7 5
◊ 8 7 3
♣ A J

♠ K Q J 9 7 2
♡ A 6 3
◊ K 6 4
♣ 8

South arrived at a *four spade* contract, against which West opened the King of Clubs. It was apparent to declarer that East must be kept out of the lead, since a lead through South's King of Diamonds could spell defeat. It was equally apparent to declarer that West possessed the Queen of Clubs.

Upon winning the opening lead of the club King, two rounds of trumps were drawn, picking up the adverse pieces. Then came the Ace and King of Hearts. Now the Jack of Clubs was played throwing West into the lead. *On this trick declarer discarded his remaining heart.* Here was the position, at this point, with West being in the lead:

♠ 10 8
♡ J 7
◊ 8 7 3
♣ —

♠ Q J 9 7
♡ —
◊ K 6 4
♣ —

If West led a club, declarer would trump it in dummy while discarding a diamond from his own hand. If, instead, West led a diamond, then declarer would make his King, regardless of the location of the Ace. And, if West led the Queen of Hearts (in theory) declarer would trump it, enter dummy via a trump, and on the then-established Jack of Hearts he would discard a losing diamond. Or if West led a low heart, dummy's Jack would be put up — and it would either win (if West were leading away from the Queen) or it would be covered by East's hypothetical Queen, declarer ruffing. In this latter case, the board's remaining heart would then become established as a winner. The actual deal was:

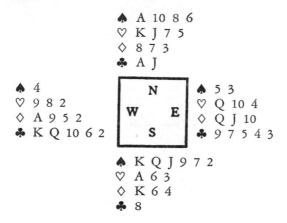

♠ A 10 8 6
♥ K J 7 5
♦ 8 7 3
♣ A J

♠ 4
♥ 9 8 2
♦ A 9 5 2
♣ K Q 10 6 2

♠ 5 3
♥ Q 10 4
♦ Q J 10
♣ 9 7 5 4 3

♠ K Q J 9 7 2
♥ A 6 3
♦ K 6 4
♣ 8

11. The following deal is a most interesting one, in which declarer had the option of end-playing *either* of the opponents:

♠ K 10 8 7 6 4 2
♥ Q 4
♦ 5
♣ A 6 2

♠ A Q J 5 3
♥ A 9
♦ A J 4
♣ K 8 3

The bidding:

SOUTH	WEST	NORTH	EAST
One Spade	Pass	Three Spades	Pass
Six Spades	Pass	Pass	Pass

West opened the Jack of Clubs, dummy's Ace winning, East dropping *the Queen*. The Ace of trumps was then cashed, East following suit. Now came the Ace of Diamonds, followed by another diamond which was trumped in dummy. The closed hand was then re-entered via the King of Clubs, East discarding a heart, after which declarer's remaining diamond was ruffed in dummy, leaving this situation:

♠ K 10 8 4
♡ Q 4
♢ —
♣ 6

♠ Q J 5 3
♡ A 9
♢ —
♣ 8

At this point declarer knew that West had started with six clubs (East having failed to follow to the second round of clubs); West was also known to have started with three diamonds, since he had followed suit to three rounds; and he had no spades originally. Therefore he had *at most* four hearts (he might have had another diamond). And, since West had a *maximum* of four hearts, East had started with a *minimum* of five hearts.

How declarer played the hand from here depended on whom he thought held the King of Hearts. If he thought that West held this vital card, then the proper play would be to throw West into the lead via a club, to force West to lead away from the King of Hearts (if West led either a diamond or a club, declarer would ruff it in dummy while simultaneously discarding his losing heart). If declarer thought that East held the King of Hearts, then the correct play would be to play the Ace of Hearts and another heart, forcing East to capture dummy's Queen. East would then be end-played, for he had no clubs to return, and if he returned either a heart or a diamond, declarer would discard his losing club while trumping the trick in dummy.

On "percentage," declarer concluded that East figured to have the King of Hearts, since East was known to have at least five hearts, while West had a maximum of four hearts (it is an accepted fact that the hand which is known to have more of a suit than does the partner, figures to have any specific card in that suit). So declarer played the Ace and another heart, throwing East into the lead. And East was end-played. The complete deal was:

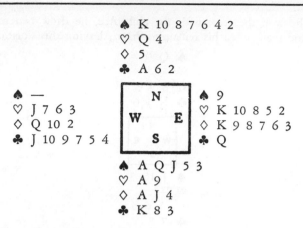

♠ K 10 8 7 6 4 2
♡ Q 4
◇ 5
♣ A 6 2

♠ —
♡ J 7 6 3
◇ Q 10 2
♣ J 10 9 7 5 4

♠ 9
♡ K 10 8 5 2
◇ K 9 8 7 6 3
♣ Q

♠ A Q J 5 3
♡ A 9
◇ A J 4
♣ K 8 3

12. How the postponement of a finesse resulted in a fulfilled contract via an end-play is the theme of this deal. As it turned out, the finesse which would have lost became unnecessary, and by not taking it immediately, declarer never had to take it, thereby gaining a trick:

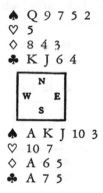

♠ Q 9 7 5 2
♡ 5
◇ 8 4 3
♣ K J 6 4

♠ A K J 10 3
♡ 10 7
◇ A 6 5
♣ A 7 5

The bidding:

SOUTH	WEST	NORTH	EAST
One Spade	Two Hearts	Two Spades	Three Hearts
Four Spades	Pass	Pass	Pass

West, on lead against South's four spade contract, opened the King of Hearts, after which he shifted to the three of clubs. Had declarer put up dummy's Jack, he would have lost his contract. But he played low from dummy, realizing that he could later finesse for the Queen of Clubs.

After he won the trick with the club Ace, he drew two rounds of trumps, and then ruffed his remaining heart, leaving this situation:

♠ Q 9
♡ —
◇ 8 4 3
♣ K J 6

♠ J 10 3
♡ —
◇ A 6 5
♣ 7 5

As is apparent, there are three potential losers, and declarer has already lost a heart trick. Declarer now played a diamond to his Ace, and then led another diamond for the defenders to win. East captured the latter trick with his Jack, after which he cashed the King of Diamonds, leaving this position:

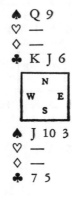

♠ Q 9
♡ —
◇ —
♣ K J 6

♠ J 10 3
♡ —
◇ —
♣ 7 5

Whatever East now led, declarer had no more losers; if he played a heart or a diamond, declarer would get rid of his losing club while trumping the trick in dummy; and, of course, if East chose to lead a club, dummy's King and Jack would capture two club tricks.

The reader may raise the question: "But why didn't *West* win one of the diamond tricks and lead another club through dummy's K J"? If he had done so, declarer would have finessed dummy's Jack. The reason why he didn't do so can be evidenced from the complete deal:

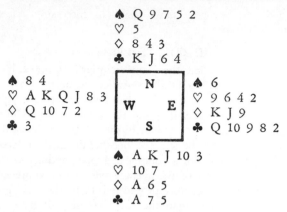

♠ Q 9 7 5 2
♡ 5
◇ 8 4 3
♣ K J 6 4

♠ 8 4
♡ A K Q J 8 3
◇ Q 10 7 2
♣ 3

♠ 6
♡ 9 6 4 2
◇ K J 9
♣ Q 10 9 8 2

♠ A K J 10 3
♡ 10 7
◇ A 6 5
♣ A 7 5

The answer as can be seen, was that West had *no more clubs!* As was mentioned, if declarer were ever forced to take the club finesse, he would have done so. But he was never forced to take it.

Also, if the Jack of Clubs had been played to the first trick, covered by East's Queen, and taken by declarer's Ace, the contract would have been defeated. For, in this situation, East, upon obtaining the lead via a diamond, would have cashed another diamond, and then exited with the ten of clubs, forcing dummy's King. But with the K J of Clubs retained in dummy, East was unable to lead a club without giving declarer a present of a trick.

In summation, all end-plays have one major characteristic in common: they almost always occur toward the end of the play, at trick eight or later, although on rare occasions they will arise earlier. The end-play occurs at the precise moment when an opponent is put in the lead at a time when the only lead he can make must be to declarer's advantage. The "declarer's advantage" may be any one of a number of situations: the opponent who has been "thrown into the lead" may be forced to lead into declarer's tenace position, thereby giving declarer a trick via a free finesse. Or he may be forced to lead a suit of which neither declarer nor dummy has any, thereby enabling one hand to trump the trick, with the other hand simultaneously discarding a loser.

A certain amount of preparation is required before the end-play can be accomplished. This preparation consists of eliminating from both hands that suit or suits which it is not desirable for the opponent to return when he is thrown into the lead.

The practicability and beauty of the end-play is that it frequently offers a line of play which is superior to the taking of a doubtful finesse, or, at best, a finesse which offers a 50-50 chance. Viewed in this light, familiarity with the end-play must result in increasing one's chances of making any given contract.

II. THE "SQUEEZE"

It is an accepted fact that the "squeeze play" is probably the most exciting and most fascinating of the so-called advanced plays. To most players, the squeeze seems so complex that they will frequently make no attempt to understand the meaning and the inner workings of the play; and, as a consequence, contracts which should be made easily if only declarer were familiar with the squeeze, become doomed to defeat.

Actually, the squeeze is not a complicated play, and its mechanics are not at all beyond the ability of the average person to comprehend. I can assure the reader that if he has progressed from the first page up to this chapter, and has understood the contents, he will have no trouble in assimilating and applying this play when the occasion presents itself.

THE SIMPLE SQUEEZE

The "squeeze play" is a play utilized by declarer in which he *forces* an opponent either to discard a potentially-winning trick, or to discard a guard to a potentially-winning trick. And, in so doing, declarer is able to create a trick for himself. The squeeze, as the end-play, almost always develops near the end of a hand. As an illustration of the basic form of the squeeze, look at the following situation:

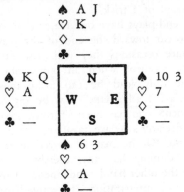

♠ A J
♡ K
◇ —
♣ —

♠ K Q   ♠ 10 3
♡ A   ♡ 7
◇ —   ◇ —
♣ —   ♣ —

♠ 6 3
♡ —
◇ A
♣ —

If South now leads the Ace of Diamonds, West has become the victim of a squeeze. If West discards the Ace of Hearts, then dummy's King of Hearts will be promoted into a winner. If, instead, West discards his Queen of Spades, then dummy's Ace and Jack of Spades will both be winners, since dummy's Ace of Spades will capture West's now-singleton King of Spades.

From the above illustration, the reader can actually see the completion of the squeeze at the precise moment when West *is forced* either to discard the Ace of Hearts, or to discard the Queen of Spades, thereby unguarding the King and promoting dummy's Jack of Spades into a winner. The completion of the squeeze is simple enough to understand. But the attainment of this end requires two preliminary steps, namely *card placing* and *preparation*.

By "card placing" is meant two things: (1) counting the opponents' hands as the play progresses, so that declarer can determine whether a "squeeze" can be created, and (2) locating certain "key" cards which the opponents possess. The features of counting out an opponent's hand have been presented in Chapter VIII. The knowledge of where the missing "key" cards are located can be had from the clues which might be divulged in the opponents' bidding, from their opening (and subsequent) leads, from their discards and signals, and by the actual cards which they are forced to play from trick to trick.

By "hand preparation" is meant the building up to, and the ultimate attainment of, the precise proper moment when the squeeze becomes operative. How this develops will be observed from the deals which follow. But before coming to this, let us see what conditions are required before the squeeze can become operative.

It was mentioned earlier that in a squeeze, declarer forces an opponent to discard either a potentially-winning trick or a guard to a potentially-winning trick. How can he "force" an opponent to do this? It is really a simple matter, a law of nature, a principle of physics, or call it what you will: if an adversary holds four important cards, and is compelled to reduce his hand to three cards, he *must* let one go; or, if the opponent holds three important cards, and is compelled to reduce his hand to two cards, he *must* part with one of his important cards; or, if the opponent possesses two important cards and is compelled to reduce his hand to one card, he *must* relinquish one of the cards. And, as the reader has observed from the preceding illustration, when an opponent discards one of his important cards, declarer is able to create a winning trick for himself.

Now to the all-important question: *why* is an opponent forced to discard a vital card? The reason lies in the presence of a *threat card* (or cards) in either declarer's hand or in dummy. A *threat card* is a losing card that can be promoted into a winning card when an opponent is forced to make a discard of a higher card in that suit, thereby establishing your threat card as a winner. Let us revert to the illustration previously presented:

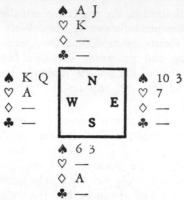

As the reader can see, North's King of Hearts is a "threat" card against West's Ace, and the Jack of Spades is a "threat" card against West's Queen of Spades. When South leads the Ace of Diamonds, West must release either his Ace of Hearts, or his Queen of Spades — and whichever he elects to do, one of North's threat cards will be promoted into a winner.

It should be apparent that the only way in which a threat card can become a winner is if the threatened hand is compelled to play *before* the possessor of the threat card. That is, the "threatened" must be in the position of being ambushed. A few illustrations of these "threat" card positions should firmly establish this situation in the reader's mind.

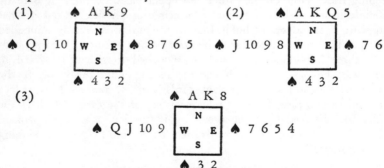

In (1), the nine of spades is a threat card against West's potentially-winning spade trick. And, if at any time during the play West releases the ten of spades, dummy's nine-spot will be promoted into a winner.

In (2), the five of spades is a threat card against West. If West is forced to discard a spade, dummy's five-spot will become promoted into a winner.

In (3), the presence of the eight of spades in dummy constitutes a
threat card against West. Should West be forced to discard
both the nine and ten of spades, dummy's eight-spot will
become established as a winning trick.

It is a fundamental principle of the squeeze that in order for it to
work *two threat cards must exist* so that an oppponent will be forced
to take a choice of discarding one or the other of his potentially-winning
tricks before you take the option of your discard. If only one threat
card exists, the opponent will always have an unnecessary surplus card
to throw off, and no squeeze can be developed. For instance, in the
earlier example:

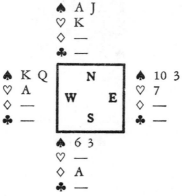

North's two threat cards are the Jack of Spades and the King of
Hearts. But if the Jack of Spades and the ten of spades were
interchanged, then no squeeze could be developed. To illustrate:

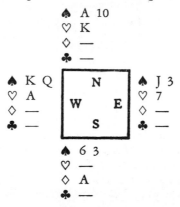

In the above case, on the lead of the Ace of Diamonds, West could safely discard the Queen of Spades, since North's ten of spades is not a threat card, East being able to protect that suit.

To conclude this basic presentation of the rudiments of the squeeze, it should be readily apparent that no squeeze can become operative unless there exists a line of communication between dummy's and declarer's hand; that is, no card in dummy can act as a threat card unless there is a way to get to dummy after the threat card becomes established. There must be present, therefore, an entry to the hand which contains the threat card.

The following deal illustrates the squeeze in its simplest form:

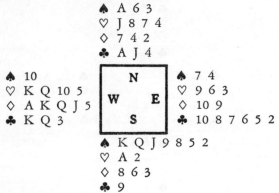

♠ A 6 3
♡ J 8 7 4
◊ 7 4 2
♣ A J 4

♠ 10
♡ K Q 10 5
◊ A K Q J 5
♣ K Q 3

♠ 7 4
♡ 9 6 3
◊ 10 9
♣ 10 8 7 6 5 2

♠ K Q J 9 8 5 2
♡ A 2
◊ 8 6 3
♣ 9

The bidding:

WEST	NORTH	EAST	SOUTH
One Diamond	Pass	Pass	Two Spades
Double	Three Spades	Pass	Four Spades
Double	Pass	Pass	Pass

West opened the King of Diamonds, and then followed up by playing the Ace and Queen. Then came the King of Hearts, declarer's Ace winning.

Dummy now had one sure threat card against West in the Jack of Hearts (West was known to possess the Queen of Hearts); and if West also had the King and Queen of Clubs, then dummy's Jack of Clubs constituted a second threat card against West. *Since there was no way to avoid the loss of a heart trick unless either the Jack of Hearts or the Jack of Clubs were promoted into a winner, then a squeeze on West became the only hope for declarer.*

Six rounds of trumps were then played, leaving this position:

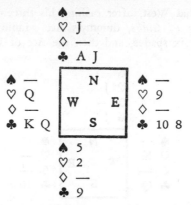

South now led the five of spades — and West *had to* discard one of his potential winners. If he discarded the Queen of Hearts, dummy's Jack would become a winner (dummy discarding the Jack of Clubs if West discarded the Queen of Hearts). If West elected to discard the Queen of Clubs, then dummy's Jack of Clubs would become established as a winning trick (the heart Jack being thrown from dummy if West discarded the club Queen). In this situation, West was unable to preserve both of his vital cards, which dummy threatened, and he became the victim of a squeeze.

As the reader can see, the "squeeze" was possible because dummy, with its threat cards, also had an entry in the Ace of Clubs. Without this entry, no squeeze would have been possible and declarer would have been compelled to lose a heart trick. Reverting to this deal again, let us see what might have been if West had elected to play the *Club* King at trick four instead of the Heart King.

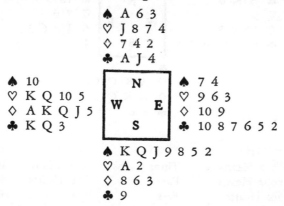

Suppose then, that West, after cashing his three top diamonds, had next led the *King of Clubs,* dummy's Ace winning. Declarer would again have played six spades, and then the Ace of Hearts, leaving this position:

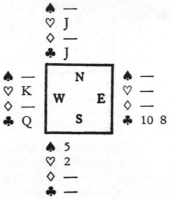

Now no squeeze could be developed, since there was no entry to dummy. If declarer led his remaining trump, West could afford to discard his Queen of Clubs. Dummy's Jack of Clubs would now be established — but it would be uncashable.

Another example of the squeeze is the following:

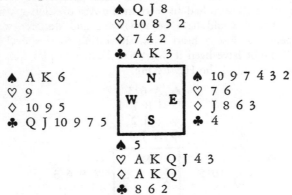

The bidding:

SOUTH	WEST	NORTH	EAST
Two Hearts	Three Clubs	Four Clubs	Pass
Four Hearts	Pass	Five Hearts	Pass
Six Hearts	Pass	Pass	Pass

West's opening lead is the King of Spades, after which he shifts to the Queen of Clubs, dummy's Ace winning. South can now count eleven sure winners: 6 hearts, 3 diamonds, and 2 clubs. There is no simple way to avoid the loss of a club trick, for nothing can be developed in either the North or South hands. Two hopes exist: (1) either to throw the losing club on the floor (which, in addition to being illegal, unsportsmanlike, and in bad taste, will probably be detected, or (2) to "squeeze" West. And, if South knows the mechanics of the squeeze, he will see that a squeeze on West can be developed.

First, declarer knows that West's opening lead of the spade King denotes possession of the Ace; and, second, West surely started with at least five clubs (probably six) judging from his three club overcall. So, at this moment, South knows five of West's remaining cards: the spade Ace, and four clubs. When South cashes his eleven tricks, prior to playing on the eleventh trick, West will be reduced to three cards, the spade Ace and two clubs. What will West play to the eleventh trick? Will he not either have to relinquish the Ace of Spades, or discard one of his two remaining clubs? If he discards the Ace, then dummy's Queen of spades will become a winner; or, if he elects to discard the ten of clubs, then dummy's low club will be promoted into a sure trick.

Declarer, upon winning the second trick with dummy's Ace of Clubs, then proceeds to take five rounds of trumps, after which the Ace, King, and Queen of Diamonds are cashed. It does not matter how West's diamonds and hearts are divided; at trick eleven this *must be* the position:

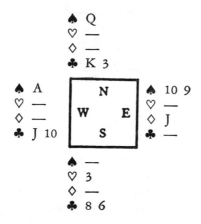

South now leads the three of trumps — and West has just become the victim of a squeeze. No matter what he discards, declarer must win all the rest of the tricks. If West discards the Ace of Spades, dummy will throw away the three of clubs; if West discards the ten of clubs, the Queen of Spades will be discarded from dummy.

The above deal presents all the features of the squeeze:

1. The counting of West's hand at trick two, resulting in the conclusion that West started with a minimum of five clubs, and that he still possesses the Ace of Spades.

2. The preparation for the squeeze by cashing the trumps and the side tricks.

3. The completion of the squeeze by leading declarer's last trump, *forcing* West to make a discard that results in the creation of an additional trick in dummy.

Let us look at another "squeeze" deal, in which the bidding clearly indicated that a certain finesse would lose. And, rather than take that finesse, declarer decided to play for a squeeze instead:

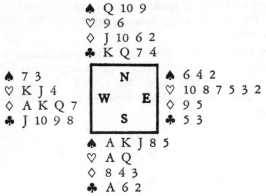

```
              ♠ Q 10 9
              ♡ 9 6
              ◊ J 10 6 2
              ♣ K Q 7 4
  ♠ 7 3           N          ♠ 6 4 2
  ♡ K J 4                     ♡ 10 8 7 5 3 2
  ◊ A K Q 7    W     E        ◊ 9 5
  ♣ J 10 9 8       S          ♣ 5 3
              ♠ A K J 8 5
              ♡ A Q
              ◊ 8 4 3
              ♣ A 6 2
```

The bidding:

SOUTH	WEST	NORTH	EAST
One Spade	Double	Two Spades	Pass
Four Spades	Pass	Pass	Pass

West opened the King of Diamonds, upon which East played the nine. The Ace of Diamonds then followed, after which the Queen was played, East discarding a low heart. West's remaining diamond was then led, East ruffing, and declarer overruffing.

South now picked up the adverse trumps, leaving this situation at trick seven:

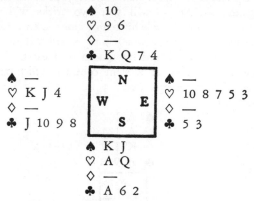

South, of course, is fully aware of the fact that in order to fulfill his contract, he must win all the remaining tricks. As it stands, the Queen of Hearts is a potential loser. The avoidance of the loss of a heart trick can be accomplished in one of two ways, theoretically: (1) by taking a successful heart finesse, or (2) by playing for the six adverse clubs to be divided 3-3 in which case the Queen of Hearts can be discarded on dummy's fourth club.

Remembering the bidding, South correctly feels that the heart finesse will be a losing play, for the King of Hearts figures to be in the West hand.

South now leads the King of Clubs, after which he plays a club to his Ace. He then plays his King of trumps. Here is the situation with four cards remaining in each hand:

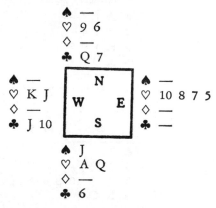

Now comes the "squeeze" card: declarer plays the Jack of trumps and West is squeezed. If West discards the Jack of Hearts, then South — diagnosing the situation — will win two tricks with the Ace and Queen. If, instead, West discards his ten of clubs, then a lead to dummy's Queen of Clubs will drop West's Jack, and establish dummy's seven-spot, upon which declarer will discard his Queen of Hearts.

Let us now take a look at a slam contract which appeared to be hopeless unless the opponents made a mistake — or unless a squeeze could be developed.

♠ A J
♡ A J 4
◇ K J 9 3
♣ A 9 8 4

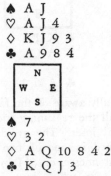

♠ 7
♡ 3 2
◇ A Q 10 8 4 2
♣ K Q J 3

Let us suppose that you are sitting South, and your partner has bid rather ambitiously, putting you into a *seven diamond contract*. West opens the King of Hearts, which you capture with dummy's Ace.

On taking inventory you can count only twelve tricks: one in spades, one in hearts, six in diamonds, and four in clubs. Unless West voluntarily throws away the Queen of Hearts, thirteen tricks cannot be made unless a squeeze can be developed. Let us view all four hands as South is playing his grand slam contract:

♠ A J
♡ A J 4
◇ K J 9 3
♣ A 9 8 4

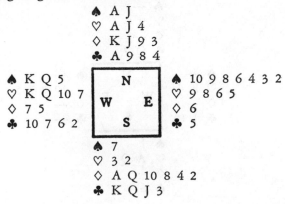

♠ K Q 5
♡ K Q 10 7
◇ 7 5
♣ 10 7 6 2

♠ 10 9 8 6 4 3 2
♡ 9 8 6 5
◇ 6
♣ 5

♠ 7
♡ 3 2
◇ A Q 10 8 4 2
♣ K Q J 3

After winning the King of Hearts with dummy's Ace, you cash five rounds of trumps, discarding a heart from dummy on the fifth trump. Then come four rounds of clubs, ending up in the South hand, with this being the position as trick eleven is about to be played:

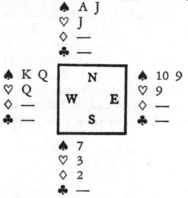

You now lead the deuce of diamonds — and West is a "dead duck," for if he discards the Queen of Hearts, then dummy's Jack will become a winner; if he discards the Queen of Spades instead, then dummy's Jack of Spades will be promoted into a winning trick.

In all of the "squeeze" situations thus far presented, it has been West who has been the victim, caught between declarer who led the squeeze card, and dummy who had a card promoted into a winner because of a forced discard which West was compelled to make. The following deal illustrates the preparation and execution of what is known as a "backward" squeeze. In this case it is East who is squeezed when South leads the squeeze card, and dummy discards an insignificant card:

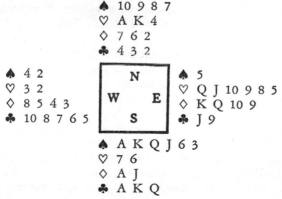

The bidding:

EAST	SOUTH	WEST	NORTH
Four Hearts	Five Spades	Pass	Seven Spades
Pass	Pass	Pass	

As is apparent, North-South found themselves in an over-ambitious *seven spade contract*. To the average player, the situation would have been a completely hopeless one, since there appeared to be no way of disposing of the diamond loser. To the expert player, a "hopeless" situation such as this can mean just one thing: the hope for a squeeze.

West's opening lead was the three of hearts, dummy's Ace winning. Five rounds of trumps then followed, a diamond being discarded from dummy on the latter trick. Then came three rounds of clubs, leaving this situation:

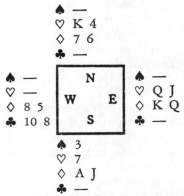

South next led his three of trumps, discarding a diamond from dummy — and East was squeezed. If he discarded the Jack of Hearts, then dummy's four-spot would become a winner; if instead, he let go of the Queen of Diamonds, then declarer's Jack would be promoted into a winner.

There is one most vital point concerning the application of the squeeze which has not as yet been presented: *no squeeze can be developed until declarer's sure winners come to exactly one trick short of his contract, and his losers have been yielded first to the opponents.* That is, if your contract is six notrump, and you have 11 sure winners, one losing trick must be conceded to the opponents before the squeeze can be developed. If your contract is three notrump, before you can effect a squeeze you must lose four tricks, leaving yourself with *eight* sure winners. Similarly, if your contract is four spades, you must have lost three tricks first, leaving yourself with *nine* sure winners, before you can effect a squeeze play on one of the opponents. Summing this up, in the form of a principle, *in order to develop the squeeze position, declarer must have precisely one loser in his hand, and he must be exactly one trick short of his contract,* with no way of disposing of his one loser except by squeezing an opponent out of a potential winner, thereby creating a winner upon which he can dispose of his loser.

To illustrate this point of being *exactly one trick* removed from your contract before an opponent can be squeezed out of his important cards, the following deal serves as a good example. In this deal, declarer *did not* develop a squeeze, and lost his contract.

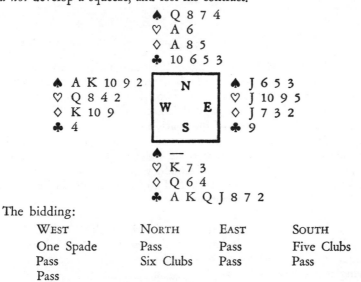

```
                    ♠ Q 8 7 4
                    ♡ A 6
                    ◇ A 8 5
                    ♣ 10 6 5 3

   ♠ A K 10 9 2   ┌─────────┐   ♠ J 6 5 3
   ♡ Q 8 4 2      │    N    │   ♡ J 10 9 5
   ◇ K 10 9       │ W     E │   ◇ J 7 3 2
   ♣ 4           │    S    │   ♣ 9
                  └─────────┘
                    ♠ —
                    ♡ K 7 3
                    ◇ Q 6 4
                    ♣ A K Q J 8 7 2
```

The bidding:

WEST	NORTH	EAST	SOUTH
One Spade	Pass	Pass	Five Clubs
Pass	Six Clubs	Pass	Pass
Pass			

Against the slam contract West opened the King of Spades, declarer ruffing. One round of trumps then followed after which declarer cashed the Ace of Hearts, the King of Hearts, and then ruffed his remaining heart in dummy. At this moment, declarer took inventory, and counted eleven tricks: seven clubs, one diamond, the Ace of Hearts, King of Hearts, and a heart ruff in dummy. His hope of fulfilling the contract, he perceived, was in squeezing West, who was known to possess the Ace of Spades (from West's lead) and probably the King of Diamonds (since East had failed to respond). The two "threat" cards were, of course, dummy's Queen of Spades and declarer's own Queen of Diamonds.

So declarer now proceeded to run all his trumps except one, arriving at this position:

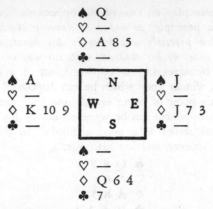

When declarer led his last trump, West had no problem: he simply discarded his "useless" nine of diamonds, and there was now no way for declarer to avoid the loss of two tricks and his contract.

Where did declarer go wrong? Well, one of the conditions essential to the successful completion of the squeeze is that declarer have *precisely one loser* in his hand. Our declarer had two losers in his hand — two diamonds — and West therefore could not be squeezed, since he could not be forced to discard a potentially-winning trick. Therefore, to have effected a squeeze, one trick had to be given up earlier, so that declarer would remain with but *one* loser.

What declarer should have done was *to concede the opening spade trick* to West, discarding a diamond on the trick. No matter what West led to trick two, declarer would win and play the hand as he did before, ruffing his losing heart and playing all his trumps but one, arriving at this position:

Now when declarer leads his last trump, West has no "useless" card to discard — and he is squeezed. If he discards the diamond ten, declarer's Queen will become a winner; if he discards the Spade Ace, then dummy's Queen will be promoted into a winning trick.

The time has now arrived for the "examination" on the squeeze, its recognition, and its execution. The deal which follows arose in a National Championship event in 1946.

♠ 6 4 3
♡ Q 9 7 3
◇ A K Q 7
♣ 10 8

♠ A K 8 5
♡ 2
◇ 9 3
♣ A K Q J 9 5

The bidding:

SOUTH	WEST	NORTH	EAST
One Club	Pass	One Diamond	Pass
Two Spades	Pass	Three Notrump	Pass
Four Clubs	Pass	Five Clubs	Pass
Six Clubs	Pass	Pass	Pass

West, on lead, opened a low heart, East's Ace winning. East then returned a heart, declarer ruffing.

On taking inventory, declarer perceived that he had eleven tricks: six in clubs, three in diamonds, and two in spades. And there was no possibility of either ruffing out a loser, or of creating a winner by establishing some side suit. So the only hope was that either dummy's fourth diamond could win a trick, or somehow declarer might win another trick in spades. Therefore, the slam could be made only by a "squeeze", to get an opponent to discard a diamond or some spades. Let us follow the play by looking at all four hands:

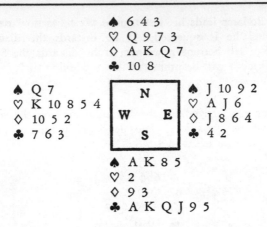

After trumping the second heart lead, declarer then played four trumps, discarding a heart and a spade from dummy, and leaving this position:

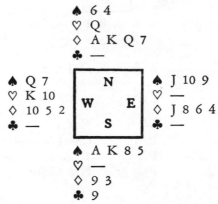

Now came declarer's last trump, a spade being discarded from dummy — and poor East, who had already discarded one spade in order to protect his Jack of Diamonds, was forced to discard either another spade (establishing declarer's low spades) or to discard a diamond (which would promote dummy's seven-spot into a winner).

From an expert point of view, the success of the squeeze depended on either of the opponents holding four or more spades, and four or more diamonds originally. If this distribution existed, then when declarer played his remaining trump, that opponent would be unable to protect both his diamonds and his spades — which was exactly what happened.

On this question of "threat" cards, it might be well to point out to the reader that when both threat cards are in the same hand, only the opponent who plays directly *before* the hand with the threat cards can be squeezed. To illustrate:

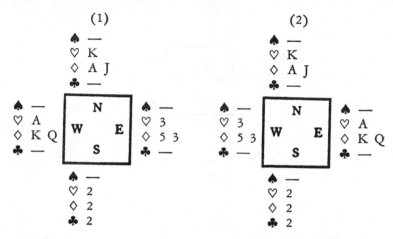

(1)   (2)

Clubs are trumps, and in (1), South leads the two of clubs. As is apparent, West is squeezed by North's "threat" cards. If West discards the Heart Ace, dummy's King becomes a winner; if he discards the Queen of Diamonds, unguarding the King, then dummy's Jack of Diamonds becomes a winner.

In (2) when the deuce of clubs is led, North must discard before East, and the squeeze will not work, for East simply waits to see what North discards, and then discards accordingly.

To repeat: when both threat cards are in the same hand, the squeeze will work only on the adversary who plays *before* the hand containing the threat cards.

THE DOUBLE SQUEEZE

There is actually very little difference between the simple squeeze (which has just been covered) and the double squeeze. The double squeeze is nothing more than a combination of a direct squeeze and a backward squeeze in the same deal. In the direct squeeze, the opponent who plays *before* dummy is squeezed; and in the backward squeeze, the opponent who plays *after* dummy is squeezed. In the double squeeze, both of these opponents are squeezed simultaneously. Here is the double squeeze in its basic form:

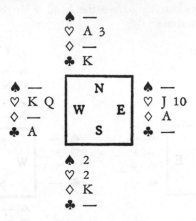

♠ —
♥ A 3
♦ —
♣ K

♠ —   ♠ —
♥ K Q   ♥ J 10
♦ —   ♦ A
♣ A   ♣ —

♠ 2
♥ 2
♦ K
♣ —

Spades are trumps, and South now leads his last trump. West, in order to prevent dummy's club King from being promoted into a winner, cannot discard his Ace of Clubs, and is therefore compelled to play his Queen of Hearts. From dummy, declarer now discards his now useless "threat" card against West, the King of Clubs. If East then discards his Ace of Diamonds, he will establish declarer's "threat" card, the King of Diamonds, into a winner. So East, also, is compelled to discard a heart. As the reader can see, with both opponents having been forced to discard hearts, dummy's three of hearts has now become a winner.

Summarizing the above briefly, the double squeeze works like this: The declarer leads a card to which neither opponent can follow suit, and it immediately squeezes the left-hand opponent. This opponent elects to discard protection in a suit rather than a high card which is threatened by a high card in dummy. Now dummy discards his high-card threat card against that opponent. On the same trick the right-hand opponent now finds himself in the identical position, of being forced either to relinquish a high card threatened by declarer's high card, or else to part with his protection in a suit. And whichever discard he chooses to make, declarer has gained a trick.

Let us take another look at the double squeeze at the precise moment when it becomes effective, and then we shall proceed to an actual hand where it has arisen:

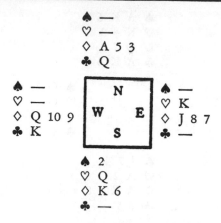

Again *spades* are trumps, and declarer leads the deuce of spades. West must hang on to the King of Clubs, or else dummy's Queen will be promoted into a winner. So he discards the nine of diamonds, and dummy discards the now-useless threat card of the Queen of Clubs. It is now East's turn to be squeezed. If he discards the Heart King, declarer's Queen will become a winner. Or, if he discards the seven of diamonds instead, then declarer will be able to win three diamond tricks by cashing the King, Ace, and the five-spot.

The preparation for a double-squeeze is just about the same as that required for a simple squeeze. The declarer, by observing, counting, or by "feeling", perceives that a direct squeeze on his left-hand opponent may be possible, and also that a backward squeeze on his right-hand opponent may be possible at the same time. Although the double-squeeze requires paying closer attention to the discards of the opponents than does the simple squeeze, there is really nothing mysterious about its preparation and its completion. With a bit of study, and experience, it can be mastered.

The double-squeeze becomes operative when the declarer can eliminate one or two suits from both of the opponents' hands, and can then continue to lead cards to which the squeezed players are unable to follow suit, thereby forcing each of them to make a fatal discard.

The deal which follows was played by one of the nation's top-ranking players, Edward Hymes, Jr.

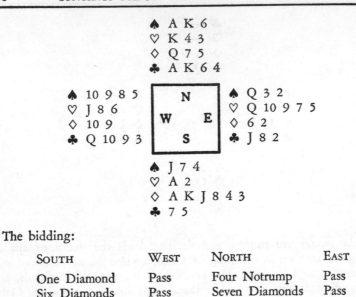

♠ A K 6
♡ K 4 3
◇ Q 7 5
♣ A K 6 4

♠ 10 9 8 5
♡ J 8 6
◇ 10 9
♣ Q 10 9 3

♠ Q 3 2
♡ Q 10 9 7 5
◇ 6 2
♣ J 8 2

♠ J 7 4
♡ A 2
◇ A K J 8 4 3
♣ 7 5

The bidding:

SOUTH	WEST	NORTH	EAST
One Diamond	Pass	Four Notrump	Pass
Six Diamonds	Pass	Seven Diamonds	Pass
Pass	Pass		

If the reader does not approve of the bidding, he should bear in mind that it occurred in the early thirties, when contract bridge was still in its infancy.

West opened the ten of spades, dummy's King winning. An examination of the North-South hands revealed twelve sure winners, with no possibility of creating the thirteenth trick except by some sort of squeeze. Based on the opening lead, Mr. Hymes felt that East was the possessor of the Queen of Spades, since West was not the type of person to lead away from a Queen against a grand slam contract.

South then played two rounds of trumps, picking up the adverse pieces, after which he cashed the Spade Ace, in the hope that he might catch the Queen. Then came the Ace of Clubs, King of Clubs, and a third club which declarer ruffed. All the clubs were now gone except the Queen, the whereabouts of which was unknown — and dummy's six of clubs constituted a threat card against it. Mr. Hymes then played two more rounds of trumps; leaving this position:

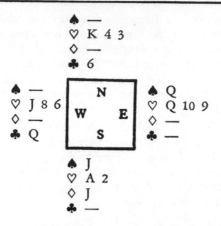

Declarer now led his last diamond, and West was forced to throw a heart in order to protect the Queen of Clubs. The six of Clubs was then discarded from dummy. Now the vise tightened on East — and closed — for in order to protect his Queen of Spades against South's Jack (West's opening lead of the ten-spot had denied possession of the Jack), East also had to discard a heart. The last three tricks were taken by the Ace of Hearts, King of Hearts, and four of hearts, to fulfill the seven diamond contract.

In order to recognize a double-squeeze situation, the reader must become aware of the following: when the squeeze is in three suits (the double squeeze), it is absolutely essential that the commanding card of one suit be held by one opponent, and the commanding card of the other suit be held by the other opponent (in the above deal, the Queen of Clubs was held by West and the Queen of Spades by East). The third suit will be the one in which declarer holds the commanding cards and a low one, so that both opponents will be compelled to keep protection (stoppers) in that suit as long as possible (hearts, in the above deal). When the squeeze becomes effective, each opponent will have to hold on to his own commanding card in one of the three suits, but in order to do it he will have to relinquish his protection in declarer's commanding suit (the heart suit in the above deal) — always hoping that partner can hold on to *his* protection in that suit. When the double-squeeze is operative, however, (as on Mr. Hymes' deal), the partner cannot keep his protection either.

A second requirement for the successful execution of the double squeeze is that both declarer's hand and dummy's must contain an entry. This enables declarer to lead from one hand to the other, as the squeeze reaches its culmination, so that if either opponent elects to keep his stopper in a suit and throw off the commanding card in one of the other suits, declarer can get to the hand which now contains the newly-acquired commanding card. In the actual deal, Mr. Hymes had the Ace of Hearts as an entry to his own hand, and the King of Hearts as an entry to dummy.

Now to the final point, which is as equally applicable to the double squeeze as it is to the single squeeze: no double squeeze can be executed unless the number of sure winning tricks is within one trick of the number required to fulfill the contract. That is, the double squeeze provides just one additional trick. On the immediately-preceding deal, Mr. Hymes had 12 sure winners.

Let us look at one more illustration of the double squeeze, as it was developed in actual combat:

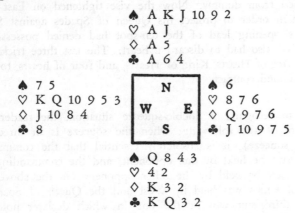

♠ A K J 10 9 2
♡ A J
◊ A 5
♣ A 6 4

♠ 7 5
♡ K Q 10 9 5 3
◊ J 10 8 4
♣ 8

♠ 6
♡ 8 7 6
◊ Q 9 7 6
♣ J 10 9 7 5

♠ Q 8 4 3
♡ 4 2
◊ K 3 2
♣ K Q 3 2

South is playing a *seven notrump contract*, against which West opens the King of Hearts, dummy's Ace winning. Twelve sure tricks are in evidence, and the thirteenth can be made if the six adverse clubs are divided 3-3. But when declarer cashes the Ace, King, and Queen of Clubs, the bad club distribution is revealed. Five spades are then taken, South discarding a heart from his own hand on the fifth spade. The Jack of Hearts is, of course, a threat card against West, who is known to have the Queen of Hearts, and the three of clubs is a threat card against East, who is known to possess the high club. This is the position, prior to the lead of dummy's sixth spade:

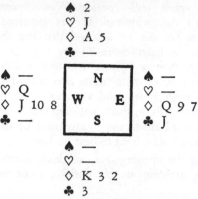

♠ 2
♡ J
◇ A 5
♣ —

♠ —
♡ Q
◇ J 10 8
♣ —

♠ —
♡ —
◇ Q 9 7
♣ J

♠ —
♡ —
◇ K 3 2
♣ 3

When the deuce of spades is now led from dummy, East is forced
to discard a diamond in order to protect the club Jack. South then
discards the three of clubs, the threat card against East. On this trick,
West, to preserve his Queen of Hearts, must also part with a diamond —
and declarer now makes three diamond tricks, having effectively squeezed
each of the opponents.

THE VIENNA COUP

The Vienna Coup is an expert play which is made in preparation for
a squeeze play. The play consists of deliberately cashing a high card,
thereby promoting into supremacy a card of that suit in an opponent's
hand — and then proceeding to squeeze him out of that card by forcing
him either to discard it, or to unguard another suit. The following
deal illustrates the Vienna Coup position — which our declarer *failed*
to recognize:

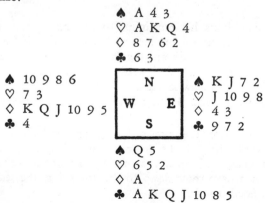

♠ A 4 3
♡ A K Q 4
◇ 8 7 6 2
♣ 6 3

♠ 10 9 8 6
♡ 7 3
◇ K Q J 10 9 5
♣ 4

♠ K J 7 2
♡ J 10 9 8
◇ 4 3
♣ 9 7 2

♠ Q 5
♡ 6 5 2
◇ A
♣ A K Q J 10 8 5

Against South's *seven club contract* West opened the King of Diamonds, declarer's Ace winning. It was apparent to declarer that 12 tricks were there for the taking, and that the thirteenth could be made if the six adverse hearts were divided 3-3. But if the hearts do not break favorably, then a squeeze situation will exist if the same opponent who holds four or more hearts also holds the King of Spades, since the board's fourth heart, and declarer's own Queen of Spades will constitute threat cards against that opponent; and that opponent will be forced to discard either the fourth heart or the King of Spades when proper "pressure" is brought to bear on him.

So, upon winning the opening diamond lead, South then proceeds to run six club tricks, arriving at this position prior to playing his last trump:

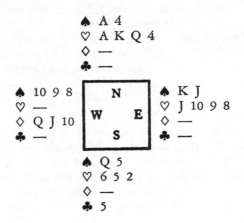

♠ A 4
♡ A K Q 4
◇ —
♣ —

♠ 10 9 8
♡ —
◇ Q J 10
♣ —

♠ K J
♡ J 10 9 8
◇ —
♣ —

♠ Q 5
♡ 6 5 2
◇ —
♣ 5

When South now leads his remaining trump, no squeeze develops for *he* has to discard from dummy before East discards. If he discards the four of spades, East will discard the Jack of Spades, and East will ultimately win a heart trick. If, instead, the low heart is discarded from dummy, East will likewise discard a heart, and East's King of Spades will then win a trick. Putting it succinctly, the squeeze fails to materialize.

But note the difference if dummy's Ace of Spades had been cashed earlier, thereby establishing East's King as the highest-ranking spade (with declarer's Queen of Spades becoming the threat card). The situation would then have come down to the following, the lead being, as before, in the South hand:

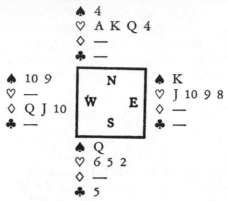

```
              ♠ 4
              ♡ A K Q 4
              ◇ —
              ♣ —
♠ 10 9      ┌─────────┐      ♠ K
♡ —         │    N    │      ♡ J 10 9 8
◇ Q J 10    │ W     E │      ◇ —
♣ —         │    S    │      ♣ —
            └─────────┘
              ♠ Q
              ♡ 6 5 2
              ◇ —
              ♣ 5
```

South would now lead the five of clubs, discarding the spade four from dummy — and East would be truly squeezed, as the reader can see. If East discards the King of Spades, then declarer's Queen is a winner; if East elects to discard a heart instead, then dummy's four of hearts would become a winning trick.

THE PROGRESSIVE SQUEEZE

The progressive squeeze occurs when *one* opponent is squeezed in *three* suits, and he is forced to unguard first one suit, then the second suit, and finally, the third suit, until he is reduced to nothingness. The play is somewhat analogous, as far as the end result is concerned, to the victim of a boa constrictor being inexorably squeezed until eventually the end comes. Or, for those of you who cannot stand such a realistic analogy, the progressive squeeze might be compared to a chain reaction.

The following deal illustrates the "progressive" squeeze:

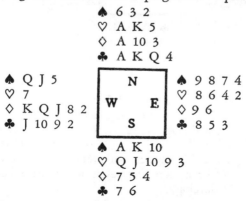

```
                ♠ 6 3 2
                ♡ A K 5
                ◇ A 10 3
                ♣ A K Q 4
♠ Q J 5       ┌─────────┐      ♠ 9 8 7 4
♡ 7           │    N    │      ♡ 8 6 4 2
◇ K Q J 8 2   │ W     E │      ◇ 9 6
♣ J 10 9 2    │    S    │      ♣ 8 5 3
              └─────────┘
                ♠ A K 10
                ♡ Q J 10 9 3
                ◇ 7 5 4
                ♣ 7 6
```

The bidding:

SOUTH	WEST	NORTH	EAST
One Heart*	Pass	Three Clubs	Pass
Three Hearts	Pass	Four Diamonds	Pass
Four Hearts	Pass	Seven Hearts	Pass
Pass	Pass		

* Not a recommended opening bid — except when it turns out well.

As is apparent, South is in as seemingly hopeless a contract as one could be in: he has 11 tricks, with no hope of creating the two additional winners needed to fulfill his contract. In these hopeless situations, there are just two things that can be done: either concede defeat and save time, or play out your high cards in the hope that some sort of squeeze can be developed.

West opened the King of Diamonds, dummy's Ace winning. Declarer then cashed four heart tricks, and West had no trouble finding three discards: he threw away the deuce, eight and Jack of Diamonds. But when declarer led his fifth heart, West could feel the vise tightening, for here was the position as declarer led his fifth heart:

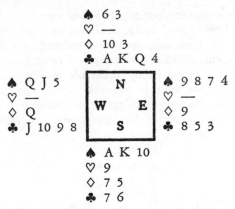

When South now leads the nine of hearts, West cannot discard the diamond Queen, for to do so would establish dummy's ten-spot; nor can he discard a club, for in so doing all of dummy's clubs would be promoted into winners. So, having no choice, he discards the five of spades in the hope that his partner can protect the spade suit (had he discarded a diamond or a club, the result would have been the same as what actually did develop).

Declarer now cashes the Ace and King of Spades, felling West's Q J, after which he leads the ten of spades. And again West finds himself in an impossible position, for he cannot discard either a club or the diamond without giving dummy the remainder of the tricks. West has just become a doomed man. So, by the use of this progressive squeeze, declarer was able to make thirteen tricks on a hand which contained only eleven sure winners. As soon as West was squeezed into unguarding one suit, this latter suit was played at him, forcing him to unguard another suit.

THE PSEUDO-SQUEEZE

No discussion of the squeeze could be complete without an explanation and illustration of its step-brother, the "pseudo-squeeze." The pseudo-squeeze — or "false" squeeze, translating from the Greek — is not a squeeze at all! It is an attempt by declarer to make the opponents *think that they are being squeezed,* with the hoped-for result being that the opponents will guess incorrectly as to what to discard, and will thereby create a trick for declarer. As the reader knows, when an opponent is forced to guess, he can (and does) quite often make a mistake.

The pseudo-squeeze, then, is not a true squeeze, and it very seldom works against an expert player who is on the alert, and who watches the discards made by his expert partner. But against the non-expert, the pseudo-squeeze frequently works, especially as the hour grows late and the non-expert starts yawning occasionally.

As in the true squeeze, declarer plays his last trump, or some other high card, and an opponent is forced to guess what card to hold. If he guesses correctly, or if his partner was able to convey the proper information by his discards, then declarer's ruse, or attempt at deception, is of no avail. But as was stated, the opponents will often guess wrong, and declarer's attempt at chicanery will have been successful. Furthermore, whatever the result, it costs declarer nothing to try, for the extra trick cannot otherwise be procured.

Look at the deal which follows, as an example of the "pseudo-squeeze." And, after it is over, I am sure that had you been sitting West, receiving no assistance whatsoever from your partner, you will admit that you would have been confronted with a pure guess as to what to discard — and that as often as not you would have guessed incorrectly, through no fault of yours.

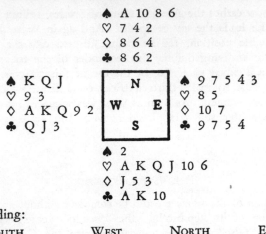

The bidding:

SOUTH	WEST	NORTH	EAST
One Heart	Double	One Spade	Pass
Four Hearts	Double	Pass	Pass
Pass			

West, on lead, cashed his three top diamonds, *East discarding a low club* on the latter trick, and then shifted to the King of Spades, dummy's Ace winning. Declarer then played all his trumps but one, *East discarding three low spades,* leaving this position prior to declarer's playing of the last trump.

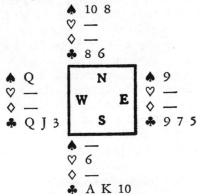

Declarer now led the six of hearts, and poor West had a problem which he could not intelligently solve. Were declarer's last three cards the A K x of clubs, or were they the A K doubleton of clubs and the nine of spades? It was six of one and half a dozen of the other, and he guessed incorrectly by discarding the three of clubs, thereby enabling declarer to take the last three tricks.

West could have had his dilemma solved by East. What East should have done was to discard *all* of his spades. Then West, by counting East's five spade plays would have known that declarer had no more spades (one of East's spades would have been discarded on the third round of diamonds; another would have been played on West's lead of the spade King; and three spades would have been discarded on declarer's first five trump leads, East following suit to two rounds).

Incidentally, if West, at trick four, shifts to the Queen of Clubs instead of the spade King, then a true and "legitimate" squeeze will be developed. Declarer will win the Queen of Clubs with the King, and he will then play all his trumps except the last, arriving at this position:

```
              ♠ A 10
              ♡ —
              ◇ —
              ♣ 8 6

  ♠ K Q         N          ♠ 9 7
  ♡ —                      ♡ —
  ◇ —       W       E      ◇ —
  ♣ J 3         S          ♣ 9 7

              ♠ 2
              ♡ 6
              ◇ —
              ♣ A 10
```

Now on the lead of declarer's six of hearts, West would have to either unguard the King of Spades, establishing dummy's ten-spot, or discard the club three, thereby promoting declarer's ten of clubs into a winner.

But, as it was actually played, West's shift to the King of Spades removed dummy's entry card — the spade Ace — and the squeeze was destroyed. However, with an assist from East, declarer's "pseudo-squeeze" procured its hoped-for-effect.

In this concluding section on squeezes, I should like to state (and illustrate) that very often declarer will be confronted with the option of taking a finesse for a vitally-needed trick or of trying for a squeeze instead. And quite frequently, when he elects to attempt the squeeze, declarer will have to guess whether the invisible and speculative squeeze has worked or it has not. Because of the uncertainty, or the inability to diagnose accurately as to whether or not a squeeze has worked, most players prefer to take the simple 50-50 finesse, for then at least they can see immediately whether success has crowned their efforts.

Permit me to "challenge" you with this "guessing" situation by presenting the following North-South cards, and at the same time conducting the defense:

♠ 10 8 5 4
♡ A K Q 7
◇ 8 7
♣ J 7 6

♠ A K Q J 2
♡ 6 5
◇ A Q 3
♠ Q 8 4

North-South vulnerable.

The bidding:

South	West	North	East
One Spade	Pass	Two Hearts	Pass
Three Spades	Pass	Four Spades	Pass
Pass	Pass		

West opens the deuce of clubs against your *four spade contract,* and East captures the trick with the King, after which he plays the Club Ace, West discarding a low heart. Another club is then led, West, trumping your Queen. West then leads a trump which you capture with dummy's ten of spades. You need all of the remaining tricks to fulfill your contract.

As is apparent, your low diamond can be discarded later on dummy's Queen of Hearts. Do you then eventually take a diamond finesse for your game-going trick? Or do you play for a squeeze, hoping that the hand that has four or more hearts also has the King of Diamonds, in which case he will be squeezed?

Well, the better player would probably say to himself: "East has shown up with six clubs headed by the A K. In all probability he does not also have the King of Diamonds, for if he did he would have made a three club overcall, especially since he was not vulnerable." On this reasoning, declarer would either have a feeling that West had the King of Diamonds, or he would have convinced himself that

West held that card, and that therefore the diamond finesse would be a losing play.

After winning the spade return at trick four, declarer would then play three more rounds of trumps, East discarding three clubs. The known position at this point would be:

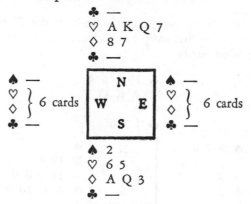

When declarer would then lead his last trump, West would discard the Jack of Diamonds, declarer discarding a diamond from dummy. Now a heart would be led, and the Ace, King, and Queen cashed, declarer discarding his three of diamonds on the Queen of Hearts. On this latter trick, East would fail to follow suit, discarding a diamond. This would now be the position:

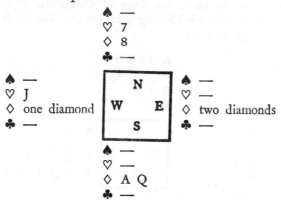

Now what is declarer to do: to finesse or not? On the last spade that South led, West had (reluctantly?) parted with the Jack of Diamonds. Does he have just the singleton King left at this point, having been forced to discard the Jack of Diamonds in order to protect the Jack of Hearts against the dummy's threat card, the seven of Hearts? Or was West being real smart, discarding the Jack of Diamonds from a Jack-Ten combination, which would then mean that he had the blank ten of diamonds left instead of the blank King? What is the diagnosis? What do you do?

Well, it is like "Who came out, the Lady or the Tiger?" for those of you who remember that story by Stockton. Take your choice of the two following West hands:

(1)

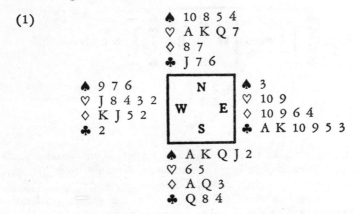

If the above is West's hand, then the squeeze has worked, for you have forced West to blank his King of Diamonds, which your Ace can now catch, thereby establishing your Queen. But if the following had been the original hand:

(2)

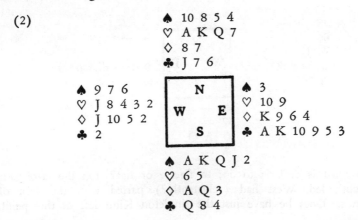

Now you will look downright silly if you play the Ace to catch West's hoped-for blank King — and your partner will tell you about it too — for in this situation the simple finesse of East's diamond King would have been the winning play.

So, having seen both sides, I leave you with — to finesse or squeeze? And your guess is as good as mine.

III. Coups

The word "coup" is a French word meaning "a master stroke." As far as its application to bridge is concerned, the coup is a brilliant, specialized, type of play which is truly a master stroke. These specialized plays all have definite names appended to them. As the reader will soon perceive, some of the coups are plays made by the declarer, while others are defenders' plays. Virtually all of these coups have been handed down from the distant past, when Whist was the card game of the day, and bridge had not yet been invented.

Although the diverse coups presented here differ quite widely in their structure, and have very little — if anything — in common with one another, they are grouped together in this chapter because they are all known as "coups." While the occasions for the utilization of these coups are not too frequent, the reader who is deeply concerned with improving his game will do well to study them, and earmark them for future reference.

A. The Bath Coup

This is a most elementary play, involving nothing more than a hold-up play with an A J x combination. The play is quite undeserving of the grand-sounding name it bears.

```
              ♠ 6 3
            ┌─────────┐
            │    N    │
♠ K Q 10 5  │ W     E │  ♠ 9 8 7 2
            │    S    │
            └─────────┘
              ♠ A J 4
```

West opens the King of Spades, and declarer plays the four-spot from his own hand, hoping thereby to get West to continue the suit. If he does, declarer will win two tricks with his A J. If West does not continue, then declarer can make but one spade trick. This particular play was first observed in Bath, England, hence the title, "Bath Coup."

B. THE DESCHAPELLES COUP

In marked contrast to the Bath Coup, the Deschapelles Coup is a brilliant play employed by a defender. The play is so named in honor of a French Whist player of days gone by, who is reported to have first discovered it.

Actually, there are two variations of the play, each involving the deliberate sacrifice of a trick in order to (1) prevent the establishment of a suit in dummy, or (2) hope to create an entry in partner's hand.

(1) The deliberate sacrifice of a sure trick in order to prevent the establishment and cashing of a suit held by dummy.

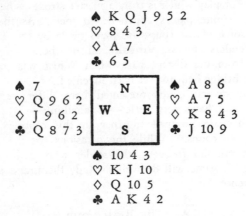

```
                    ♠ K Q J 9 5 2
                    ♡ 8 4 3
                    ◇ A 7
                    ♣ 6 5
  ♠ 7                  N          ♠ A 8 6
  ♡ Q 9 6 2                       ♡ A 7 5
  ◇ J 9 6 2       W       E       ◇ K 8 4 3
  ♣ Q 8 7 3          S          ♣ J 10 9
                    ♠ 10 4 3
                    ♡ K J 10
                    ◇ Q 10 5
                    ♣ A K 4 2
```

Against South's *three notrump contract* West opens the deuce of hearts, East winning the trick with his Ace. If East automatically returns a heart, declarer can make his contract by taking his King (correctly interpreting West's lead of the deuce as showing a four-card suit). He then attacks the spade suit, and makes five spades, one heart, one diamond, and two clubs.

But East, perceiving that if dummy's Ace of Diamonds is knocked out immediately it will effectively prevent the cashing of the to-be-established spade suit, promptly bangs down the King of Diamonds at trick two. If dummy wins the trick with the Ace, declarer can win but two spade tricks since East will not take the Ace of Spades until the third round. And, if declarer declines to take the "sacrificial" King of Diamonds, the automatic diamond continuation will remove dummy's Ace of Diamonds.

In sacrificing the King of Diamonds, East gave declarer a present of the Queen of Diamonds — but he robbed declarer of three spade tricks.

(2) The deliberate sacrifice of a potential trick in an attempt to create an entry in partner's hand.

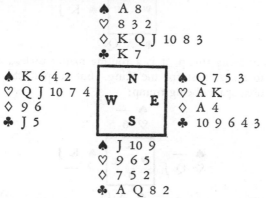

♠ A 8
♡ 8 3 2
◇ K Q J 10 8 3
♣ K 7

♠ K 6 4 2
♡ Q J 10 7 4
◇ 9 6
♣ J 5

♠ Q 7 5 3
♡ A K
◇ A 4
♣ 10 9 6 4 3

♠ J 10 9
♡ 9 6 5
◇ 7 5 2
♣ A Q 8 2

How South contrived to arrive at a three notrump contract is immaterial. The fact is that the contract would have been fulfilled if it were not for a brilliant defensive play — in the form of the Deschapelles Coup — by East.

West opened the Queen of Hearts, which East took with the Ace, and then cashed the King of Hearts. Of the 11 cards remaining in his hand, there was just one card that he could have played to defeat three notrump — and he played it: *the Queen of Spades!*

The reader can see the effect of this play. If the declarer won the trick with dummy's Ace, then when East subsequently obtained the lead with the Ace of Diamonds, a spade lead to West's King would enable West to cash his hearts, to inflict a three-trick set on declarer; and if declarer declined to take the Spade Queen, then a spade continuation would knock out dummy's Ace while simultaneously establishing West's King as an entry.

To repeat, if at trick three East had played any card other than the Queen of Spades, declarer would have fulfilled his contract.

C. THE TRUMP COUP

This is a play where declarer holds a finessing position in the trump suit over his right-hand opponent — but he has no trump to lead from dummy. Nevertheless, he is able to finesse successfully his right-hand opponent by leading some other suit from dummy at a precise moment, thereby *forcing* his right-hand opponent to trump the trick. Declarer then overtrumps, and the result comes out exactly the same as a finesse that worked. Let me illustrate this:

♠ 3 2

♠ A Q

With *spades* being trump, it is a routine matter to lead the deuce of spades and to finesse East for the King. But suppose the following is the end position, spades being trump:

♠ —
♡ 6 5

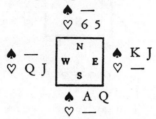
♠ —
♡ Q J

♠ K J
♡ —

♠ A Q
♡ —

If, at trick twelve, the six of hearts is led from the North hand, East is *forced* to trump, and declarer overtrumps, thereby avoiding the loss of a trump trick. This latter position, at trick twelve, has developed ino *the trump coup.*

As contrasted to the Deschapelles Coup, which requires no long-range planning, the Trump Coup requires preparation before it can be achieved. *The trump coup invariably occurs at trick 9, 10, 11, or 12, never sooner,* and the prerequisite for its successful execution is that the right-hand opponent has nothing remaining in his hand except a guarded high trump. If the opponent has other suits in his hand, then when some side suit is led from dummy, the opponent will *not be forced to trump,* and can discard from his side suit instead. To illustrate:

♠ —.
♡ —
◇ 9 4
♣ 7

♠ —
♡ —
◇ J 10
♣ J

♠ K J
♡ J
◇ —
♣ —

♠ A Q
♡ 2
◇ —
♣ —

If *spades* are trump, and the nine of diamonds (or seven of clubs) is led from the North hand, East will simply discard the Jack of Hearts — and he will ultimately make a trump trick, or West will capture trick 11. But if the following had been the situation, East would have been "couped":

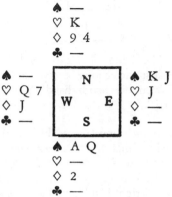

The King of Hearts is led from dummy, East follows suit with the Jack, and declarer discards his deuce of diamonds. Now both East and declarer have two trumps apiece — and when a diamond is led from dummy at trick twelve East *is compelled* to trump. Declarer, of course, overtrumps, and his Ace of trumps wins the thirteenth trick.

The trump coup is not restricted to trapping a King. It is just as frequently employed to trap a Queen or a Jack (sometimes even a ten or nine-spot:

With *hearts* as trump, the nine of spades is led from dummy in each of the above illustrations — and East has become the victim of a coup, for no matter which trump he plays (and he is *forced* to play a trump), South will overtrump and take the last trick.

Before presenting the requirements which must exist before a coup can become operative, permit me to introduce a final illustration:

```
              ♠ —
              ♡ K Q J
         ┌─────────────┐
♠ —      │      N      │  ♠ Q 7
♡ 9 6 5  │  W       E  │  ♡ 10
         │      S      │
         └─────────────┘
              ♠ K J 3
              ♡ —
```

Spades are trump. The King of Hearts is led from dummy, East following suit. South has no choice except to ruff — and since the next lead must come from the South hand, East cannot be prevented from making a trump trick.

The basic condition which must exist before the trump coup can be successfully executed is that *the declarer must possess exactly the same number of trumps as his right-hand opponent.* The second condition is that the lead must come *from dummy* at the precise moment when declarer's right-hand opponent has *nothing left but trumps* (with declarer having the same number as his opponent).

In the immediately-preceding illustration, if earlier in the play declarer had been able to have trumped a heart with the three of spades, the trump coup would have been effective:

```
              ♠ —
              ♡ K Q
         ┌─────────────┐
♠ —      │      N      │  ♠ Q 7
♡ 9 6    │  W       E  │  ♡ —
         │      S      │
         └─────────────┘
              ♠ K J
              ♡ —
```

Now the position for the trump coup would be perfect: (1) declarer would have exactly the same number of trumps as his right-hand opponent; (2) the lead would be in dummy, compelling East to play before declarer; and (3), East would have nothing but trumps left, so he could not discard from some side suit.

As the reader can appreciate from all the preceding illustrations, planning and preparation are essential to the attainment of the trump coup position. Actually, the mechanics of it are reasonably simple, for basically it is a matter of declarer reducing his trumps to the same number as those held by his right-hand opponent. This is accomplished by ruffing one or two (or as many as are required) of dummy's cards.

Then with the lead being in dummy at precisely the right moment, declarer's right-hand opponent will be "couped."

Let us take a look at the trump coup in action:

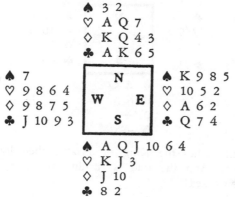

♠ 3 2
♡ A Q 7
◇ K Q 4 3
♣ A K 6 5

♠ 7
♡ 9 8 6 4
◇ 9 8 7 5
♣ J 10 9 3

♠ K 9 8 5
♡ 10 5 2
◇ A 6 2
♣ Q 7 4

♠ A Q J 10 6 4
♡ K J 3
◇ J 10
♣ 8 2

The bidding:

SOUTH	WEST	NORTH	EAST
One Spade	Pass	Three Notrump	Pass
Four Spades	Pass	Six Spades	Pass
Pass	Pass		

West opened the Jack of Clubs, dummy's King winning, after which a trump finesse was successfully taken. The board was then re-entered via the club Ace, and another finesse taken against East's King, West discarding a diamond.

At this point declarer knows that East still possesses the guarded King of trumps. Since dummy has no more trumps to lead, the only way declarer can hope to avoid the loss of a trump trick is by a coup. What declarer must attempt to do then, is to first reduce his trumps to two, so he can have the same number as East. And, secondly, he must end up in dummy at trick twelve, so that he can lead from there and force East to trump, thereby compelling East to unguard his King.

At trick five declarer leads a heart to dummy's Ace, after which he trumps a club. He then leads a diamond, East taking dummy's Queen with his Ace, and returns a diamond, dummy's King winning. A third round of diamonds is then led, declarer ruffing. Declarer has now reduced his trump holding to the exact number that East possesses: two. Here is the position at this point, with trick ten about to be led to from the South hand:

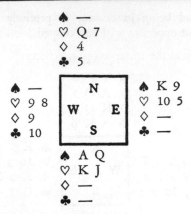

Declarer next cashes the King of Hearts, then leads a heart to dummy's Queen. And the lead is in dummy at trick twelve. The trump coup has worked!

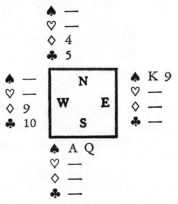

On the lead of either a diamond or club from dummy, East's King of Spades is trapped.

One of the most important things necessary for the accomplishment of the trump coup has not as yet been presented: a good sense of timing is most essential. For example, on the preceding deal, at trick seven, East won the trick with his Ace of Diamonds, and returned a diamond to trick eight, dummy's King winning. If declarer had then led a fourth club to trump, East would have discarded a heart — and declarer would have been unable to cash three heart tricks. But, since

clubs had already been played three times, declarer properly assumed
that East might discard a heart on the fourth club. So, instead, declarer
trumped a diamond, which suit had been played only twice before, on
the reasonable assumption that East was more likely to hold another
diamond, as opposed to his possessing the last club.

The trump coup, then, necessitates not only the knowledge of its
mechanics, but a certain amount of imagination and foresight in
visualizing the probable distribution of the "to-be-couped" opponent's
cards. A single error in timing — trumping the wrong suit, thereby
enabling the opponent to discard — may mean the loss of the whole
hand. All in all, it is impossible to execute a coup successfully without
looking ahead and planning what is going to happen at each trick.
If you do not plan to look ahead and prepare for the position you
must attain at trick twelve, you will be defeated unless you possess the
fortunate faculty of stumbling into the right position.

D. The Grand Coup

Probably the most famous trump coup is The Grand Coup.
While this sounds super-complex, it is precisely the same play as the
trump coup just illustrated. The only difference is that the trump-
shortening play is accomplished by ruffing one or two of dummy's
winning tricks (instead of low, losing cards). The sole reason that I
can think of for introducing the "Grand Coup" is that it is occasionally
a topic of conversation amongst bridge players — and I certainly do not
want my readers to appear to be ignorant.

Let us look at the Grand Coup in the deal which follows. The cards
here are virtually the same as in the preceding deal:

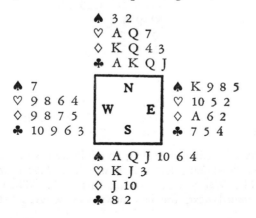

```
              ♠ 3 2
              ♡ A Q 7
              ◇ K Q 4 3
              ♣ A K Q J
   ♠ 7            N         ♠ K 9 8 5
   ♡ 9 8 6 4                ♡ 10 5 2
   ◇ 9 8 7 5    W   E       ◇ A 6 2
   ♣ 10 9 6 3               ♣ 7 5 4
                  S
              ♠ A Q J 10 6 4
              ♡ K J 3
              ◇ J 10
              ♣ 8 2
```

The difference between this deal and the preceding one is that dummy has the A K Q J of clubs instead of the A K 6 5.

The contract is again *six spades,* against which West opens the ten of clubs. Exactly the same play takes place as in the preceding deal, trick for trick. Declarer, in shortening his trumps to get to the same number as East possesses, ruffs the Queen of Clubs, a winner, instead of ruffing a low club as he did on the previous deal. This, then, is the Grand Coup — the ruffing of a winning trick, or tricks, in order that declarer might reduce his trump holding to the same length as that possessed by his right-hand opponent.

On certain occasions, in order to obtain the necessary entries to dummy for declarer's trump-reducing process, and to put the lead in dummy at the precise moment essential for "couping" his right-hand opponent, an entry has to be created. Such is the theme of the following grand coup deal, where an apparently-unnecessary finesse had to be taken in order to obtain a vitally-needed entry. The deal was played in a tournament a long time ago — 1930 — and the successful declarer was Louis H. Watson, one of the top-ranking players of the 1930's.

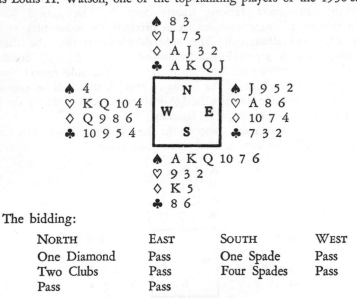

The bidding:

NORTH	EAST	SOUTH	WEST
One Diamond	Pass	One Spade	Pass
Two Clubs	Pass	Four Spades	Pass
Pass	Pass		

West opened the King of Hearts, and followed with the Queen, after which came a low heart, East's Ace winning. East now shifted to a low spade, Mr. Watson's Ace taking this trick. When the King of Spades was cashed next, the bad news was received — that East still had the protected Jack of Spades. Since dummy had no spades, it became obvious that the contract could be fulfilled only if a trump coup were successful. To accomplish this, three entries to dummy were essential: two entries in order for declarer to reduce his trump holding to the same as that possessed by East; and a third entry so that at trick twelve the lead would be in dummy to trap East's J 9.

At trick six declarer led a club to dummy's Ace, and then cashed the King of Clubs. Now the Jack of Clubs was led, and declarer trumped his sure winner. Two more entries were needed to dummy — and declarer had but one, the Ace of Diamonds.

At trick nine declarer led the five of diamonds — and finessed dummy's Jack! The Queen of Clubs was led next, and declarer again trumped a sure winner, reducing his trumps to the Q 10 doubleton. On this trick East discarded a diamond. The King of Diamonds was then led, overtaken by dummy's Ace, and the coup position had been attained:

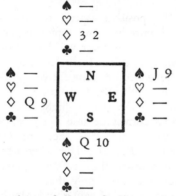

On the lead of the three of diamonds, East was ambushed.

Actually, had West been either clairvoyant or had accidentally pulled the wrong card, he could have thwarted Mr. Watson's "best-laid plans." On the lead of the low diamond from the South hand, had West put up the Queen of Diamonds, South would not have been able to obtain his extra entry. For, in this case, he would have been compelled to capture it with the Ace, and the King of Diamonds remaining in his hand would effectively have prevented his reaching dummy a second time via the diamond suit.

E. The Vienna Coup

This coup has already been presented and illustrated in the section on "The Squeeze" (p. 297). The play consists of deliberately establishing a high-card for an opponent — and then proceeding to squeeze him out of it.

CHAPTER XI

DEFENDERS' PLAY: OPENING LEADS

In the opinion of our expert players, about 40% of all game contracts are either *fulfilled* or *defeated* by the defenders' opening lead! This figure, of course, can never be established scientifically, but it is nevertheless an obvious fact that a proper or improper opening lead will very frequently spell the difference between victory and defeat. Since the initial lead is of such paramount importance in the defenders' opening campaign to defeat declarer, the understanding of the basic principles involved in making the opening lead becomes absolutely essential.

Before presenting the positive aspects of this subject of opening leads, I should like to introduce the topic on a note of pessimism. There has never been, and there never will be, a bridge-player who will always make the winning opening lead. In bridge, as in other games of chance, or as in the world of competitive sports, losing plays will be made at one time or another by the most gifted and skilled players in their respective sports. Even the top-flight bridge experts will never be anywhere near 100% correct because "percentage" is against them. But these top-flight players are what they are (winning tournament after tournament) because they are right a greater percentage of the time than are their competitors, the "average" players. In brief, to be an expert bridge-player does not imply that you will always be right, but rather that your percentage of winning leads, bids, and plays will be higher than those of your competitors.

Bearing in mind then that the subject of the selection of the opening lead is not an exact science, the reader should realize that the principles which are about to be presented are not given with an unconditional guarantee. Nevertheless, he should diligently apply himself to learning them, for the occasions for their use will be arising continually during any session of play.

On the opening leads which follow, only general advice will be given in many of the situations — that is, you will not be told to "always lead this" or "never lead that." But there are certain definite principles which are fundamental and correct, and which should not be deviated from if the best results are to be obtained. These fundamental principles will be strongly emphasized when they are illustrated.

THE VARIOUS TYPES OF OPENING LEADS

The leads which follow are *not* "classified" — that is (1) is not better than (2), or (3), etc. The six types of opening leads which will now be presented, illustrated, and discussed, cover all the leads which experience has demonstrated as being efficient and potentially-winning leads.

1. Lead the suit which your partner has bid.

2. Lead from a sequence of three touching high-cards (A $\underline{K}$ Q x; $\underline{K}$ Q J; $\underline{Q}$ J 10 x x; $\underline{J}$ 10 9; etc.).

3. Lead from a sequence of two touching high-cards (A $\underline{K}$ x; K $\underline{Q}$ x x; $\underline{Q}$ J x; $\underline{J}$ 10 x x: etc.).

4. Lead the fourth-best of a suit.

5. Lead a singleton, a doubleton, a tripleton.

6. Lead a trump.

---

1. Lead The Suit Which Your Partner Has Bid.

This is what is known as a *directed lead,* and it is one of the best leads that you can make. The reason why it is a good lead should be apparent: when your partner bids a suit, either as an overcaller or as the opening bidder, he is doing so because he has a suit which figures to win tricks. So, if the opponents purchase the contract, and you are on lead, your instinctive reaction will be to lead his suit, whether the final contract is in a suit or in notrump.

The only time that you will not lead his suit will be on those comparatively rare occasions when you will have a better lead of your own. That is, if you have, let us say, the A K Q of some other suit, a lead of *your* suit must be the more desirable lead, for your suit is certain to win immediate tricks. Another situation where partner's suit should not be led would be where *your* best suit is headed by the K Q J. In this case, by leading the King of your suit (which will be captured by the Ace), you will be promoting the Queen and Jack of that suit into two potentially-winning tricks. These latter leads — "sequence leads," as they are called — will be the topic of discussion in the next section.

Bear in mind, then, that you will lead your partner's suit unless you have a really good lead of your own — and most of the time you will not have a good lead of your own. Let us see *which card* of partner's suit you will lead if you have two or more cards of his suit.

Suppose your right-hand opponent has become the declarer. During the auction, your partner has bid *hearts*. You have no good lead of your own, and therefore you are going to lead hearts. *Which* heart should you lead?

(1).   ♡ — 6 3; Q 2

(2).   ♡ — 9 7 3; 7 5 2

(3).   ♡ — 10 6 3; J 5 2; Q 8 4; K 8 2

(4).   ♡ — A 8 3; A 8 7 5

(5).   ♡ — 10 7 5 4; J 9 6 2; Q 8 5 4; K 10 7 3; K 9 8 6 2; J 8 7 5 3

(6).   ♡ — A K 5; K Q 4 2; Q J 7 6; J 10 3; 10 9 5 2

In each illustration above, the underlined is the proper card to lead. In (4), where two cards are underlined, the explanation will be given.

(1). When you are leading your partner's suit, and you have just two cards of that suit, you will lead the *higher* card: the six from 6 3; the Queen from Q 2.

(2). When you possess three cards in your partner's suit, and the highest card is *lower than a ten-spot*, you will lead the *highest* card of that suit.

(3). When you have three cards in your partner's suit, headed by either the ten, Jack, Queen or King, you will lead the *lowest* card in that suit. There is just one standard exception to this, which will be discussed in (6).

(4). Whenever you possess the Ace of your partner's suit (without the King), whether it be the A x, A x x, A x x x, etc., you will *always lead the Ace against a suit contract*. But *against a notrump contract*, whether it be 1 NT, 2 NT, or 3 NT, if you have *three or more* of your partner's suit, headed by the Ace, you will lead the following:

The three-spot from A 8 3.

The five-spot from A 8 7 5.

The four-spot from A 10 6 4 3, etc.

That is, from three cards headed by the Ace, you will lead your third-highest card; from four or more headed by the Ace, you will lead your fourth-highest card; from five or more headed by the Ace, you will lead your fourth-highest card.

The reason for the lead away from an Ace against a notrump contract is this: when your partner has bid a suit, and the opponent sitting directly over him has bid notrump, the latter has a "stopper" in your partner's suit. So, by not leading your Ace, you will be retaining a stopper over declarer, and your Ace will subsequently capture one of his stoppers. If instead, you improperly choose to lead your Ace, all you will get for your efforts will be a low card of declarer's.

(5). When you have four or more cards in the suit which your partner has bid, headed by either the ten, Jack, Queen or King, your lead will be your fourth-highest card in that suit. From the 10 7 5 4, the four-spot; from K 10 7 3, the three-spot; from J 8 7 5 3, the five-spot; etc. There is one standard exception to this, the explanation of which is presented below.

(6). Whenever you have the following *touching* (adjacent in rank) high cards of your partner's suit, no matter how many cards you have of his suit, you will lead the underlined against *either a suit contract or a notrump contract:*

A _K_ x; _K_ Q x; _Q_ J x; _J_ 10 x;

A _K_ x x; _K_ Q x x; _Q_ J x x; _J_ 10 x x;

A _K_ x x x; _K_ Q x x x; _Q_ J x x x; _J_ 10 x x x, etc.

When you have the 10 9 _x_, 10 9 x _x_, 10 9 x _x_ x of your partner's suit, against either a suit or a notrump contract, you will lead the third-highest if you have three of his suit, and the fourth-highest if you have four or more of his suit. For purposes of making the opening lead, the ten and nine in combination are not considered to be touching.

All of the above has been illustrated with reference to *hearts,* the suit which your partner bid. Of course you realize that it applies equally to any suit which your partner bids, whether it be hearts, spades, diamonds or clubs.

So, when your partner has bid a suit, and you are going to lead his suit because you do not have a better lead of your own, it is a relatively simple matter to make the right lead: you have been *directed* to the correct lead.

But when your partner has not bid, and you are on lead against the opponents' contract, your choice as to what to lead is not so easy to make, for you have nothing definite to guide you. In these situations you will be making what is commonly termed "a lead in the blind." The sections which follow will illustrate the various types of "blind" leads.

In making these "blind" opening leads, it is of paramount significance as to whether the final contract has ended up in a suit or in notrump; that is, your selection of the correct lead will vary, depending on whether the final contract is in a suit or in notrump. Therefore, in the remainder of this chapter, each section will be broken down into (a) opening leads against a suit contract and (b) opening leads against a notrump contract.

2.   Lead From A Sequence of Three Touching High Cards
      (A _K_ Q x; _K_ Q J; _Q_ J 10 x; _J_ 10 9)

a. *Against a Suit Contract*

When you are fortunate enough to have been dealt any of the above combinations (three or more cards of a suit, headed by three touching high cards), the lead of the underlined card is one of the most effective leads which you can make. When you lead the King from a K Q J x combination, for example, if the King is captured by the opponents' Ace, your Queen and Jack will have been promoted into the two highest-ranking cards in that suit, and they figure to win two tricks.

Stated as a principle, whenever you have a sequence of three touching high cards, you will lead the top card of that sequence. The only exception to this is when you specifically possess a suit headed by an A K Q or an A K combination with low cards. Conventionally, the standard lead is the *King,* not the Ace. When you lead the King, it will win the trick. Your partner will then know that you have the Ace, for if declarer had held the Ace, he probably would have captured your King with it. (Of course, if you should ever lead a King, which declarer does capture with the Ace, your partner will know that you have the Queen of that suit, for a King is not led in the blind except when it is part of a sequence).

b. *Against a Notrump Contract.*

Against notrump contracts, it is essential to try to develop winning tricks out of low cards, to establish your suit before declarer establishes his suit. A "blind" opening lead should always be made *from your longest suit against a notrump contract,* in order to establish winners out of the low cards in that suit. For example, you hold:

♠ 5 4
♡ Q J 10
♦ A 7 3
♣ Q 10 6 4 2

If your right-hand opponent has become the declarer at a *three notrump* contract, your correct opening lead would be the *four of clubs,* for you are interested in establishing as many winners as possible in the club suit. Against a suit contract, your proper opening lead would be the *Queen of Hearts.* Against a suit contract, it is losing policy to try to develop winners out of the low cards of a suit, for by the time you have developed them the opponents will capture them by trumping.

Let us look at an illustration to clarify this latter point. Suppose you held:

> ♠ A K 4 3 2
> ♡ x x x
> ◇ x x x
> ♣ x x

If the final contract were, let us say, *four clubs,* you would lead the King of Spades, fully aware of the fact that you will not be able to win more than two spade tricks (with the Ace and King). For, when you got around to playing the third spade, even if your partner still held the Queen, one of the opponents would win the trick by trumping the Queen.

At a notrump contract, you know that you can always win two tricks with your Ace and King of Spades. But in addition, at the same notrump contract, there is a very good chance that you can also win tricks with a few low cards of your spade suit. Therefore, against a notrump contract, your opening lead should be your fourth-best spade, the *three-spot.* On the following hand, South is the declarer at a *three notrump* contract:

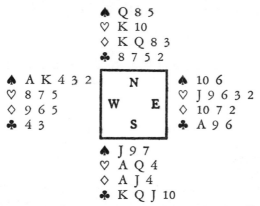

Against South's three notrump contract, West leads the three of spades, dummy plays low, and East's ten-spot is captured by declarer's

Jack. Declarer now counts his tricks — and he counts eight winners: one in spades, three in hearts, and four in diamonds. In order to get his ninth trick, he now leads the King of Clubs, to promote his Queen into a winner.

East takes the King with the Ace, and promptly returns the six of spades, the suit which his partner has opened. West wins this trick with the King of Spades, and another trick with the Ace of Spades. Now the only remaining spades in play are West's four and two — and each of them wins a trick, thereby defeating declarer's three notrump contract.

Looking at the above hand again, you can perceive that if West had originally led his King and Ace of Spades, and then followed up by playing a low spade, his two remaining spades would have been promoted into winners. But, when East subsequently obtained the lead, he would have had no spade to return, and West would have been unable to cash his established spades. By opening a low spade, not only did West concede a spade trick early in the play, but he left his partner with a low spade, which card served as an "entry" to the West hand — that is, the communication between the defending hands was maintained, with East being able to reach West via the six of spades.

It was mentioned previously that if the final contract had been in a suit (clubs), you would then have led the King of Spades. When the King had won the trick, you would then have played your Ace of Spades, after which you would have led a third spade. On this trick dummy's Queen would have been played — and your partner would win the trick by trumping. He would have then cashed his Ace of Clubs, for the setting trick.

3. Lead From a Sequence of Two Touching High Cards
    (A _K_ x; _K_ Q x x; _Q_ J x; _J_ 10 x x)

a. *Against A Suit Contract*

As with a sequence of three touching high cards, when you have two touching high cards, you may lead the higher card of that sequence (except where you have the A K x; A K x x; etc., in which case you will make the conventional lead of the King). The lead from a two-card sequence consisting of the K Q, the Q J, or the J 10 is nowhere near as good as the lead from a three-card sequence, but in the absence of a better lead, the two-card sequence lead figures to win more often than not. (From an A K doubleton, the Ace is the conventional lead).

b. *Against a Notrump Contract*

As with three-card sequences, two-card sequences are ignored when it comes to leading against notrump contracts. At notrump contracts, your eyes will search for your longest suit, regardless as to whether it contains a sequence or not. For example, if you are on lead against your right-hand opponent's three notrump contract and you hold:

(1)	(2)
♠ Q 8 7 5 3	♠ 10 8 5 3 2
♡ J 10 4 2	♡ Q J 10
◇ 8 3	◇ 7 2
♣ 9 5	♣ K 4 3

On Hand (1), the five of spades will be led.

On Hand (2), the three of spades will be led. With this hand, were the final contract in a suit, the opening lead of the Queen of Hearts would figure to be the best lead.

You should now be familiar with the fact that "sequence" leads, when made in the blind, are utilized against suit contracts. Against notrump contracts, the sequence lead is replaced by the lead from the longest suit. In one type of situation, against notrump contracts, there is a happy combination of both the "sequence lead" and the "longest suit lead." If you hold:

♠ 9 4
♡ Q J 10 7 3
◇ A J 4
♣ 8 6 2

Against a notrump contract, your correct opening lead is the *Queen of Hearts*. This lead, from a *three-card sequence,* is made against a *notrump contract only when that sequence happens to be within your longest suit.* At all other times you lead the fourth-highest of your longest suit (why the "fourth-highest" is led will be the theme of the following section on leads). If you happen to have a two-card sequence within your longest suit, you make the normal lead of your fourth-highest card. That is, with:

♠ 9 3
♡ 8 5 2
◇ Q J 6 5 3
♣ K 10 7

Against a notrump contract you lead the five of diamonds. [1] (If the opponents are in a spade, heart, or club contract, the lead of the Queen of Diamonds is an acceptable one).

A simple exception to the top of sequence leads against notrump contracts arises when the leader possesses an A K or A K Q combination in his longest suit.

There has already been presented (p. 323) the situation where the leader against a notrump contract held the A K x x x, and the correct lead was his fourth-best. The fourth-best lead would also be proper holding the A K x x x x. If the leader holds the A K x x, it is highly debatable as to whether this suit should be led at all against notrump since but one trick can be developed, and declarer might well be given a trick which he otherwise might never obtain. In this latter case it is suggested that if a second four-card suit is possessed, that suit should be led as opposed to leading from the A K x x suit.

But consider the following A K combinations:

(a)   A K Q 3   (b)   A K J 3   (c)   A K 10 9

With the above combination the King (as opposed to fourth-best) is generally considered to be the preferable opening lead. In (a), the advantage is apparent, for the Queen can be led to the second round and control of the suit retained. In (b), the King is led, and if partner subsequently obtains the lead, he can return the suit through declarer's hypothetical Queen. In (c), the King is led to explore the suit, but the suit is to be discontinued if declarer seems to hold the Queen. The hope here is that partner has the Jack and that he will ultimately obtain the lead to play his Jack through declarer's Queen. That is:

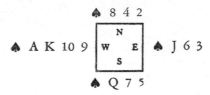

♠ 8 4 2

♠ A K 10 9   ♠ J 6 3

♠ Q 7 5

4.   Lead the Fourth-Best of a Suit.

In different sections of this chapter, you have been told to lead the "fourth-best" or "fourth-highest" of a suit. Why, you may be asking yourself, "fourth-best"? Why not third-best? Or fifth-best?

---

[1] Where you hold the Q J 9 x x, the lead of the Queen is considered to be a justifiable deviation.

You lead the fourth-best (fourth-highest) because that lead will allow your partner to apply the famous Rule of Eleven, thereby enabling your partnership to properly defend against declarer's contract.

This Rule of Eleven, is a precise mathematical rule, which will always work when the fourth-best of a suit is led. As the partner of the leader, you *will always know the exact number of cards which declarer holds in his hand which are higher than the card led by the opener.*

When the fourth-highest card of a suit is led, the partner of the leader will subtract the number (spots) of the card led from the number 11. For example, should your partner's fourth-best lead be the six of spades, you will subtract 6 from 11. *The remainder* (5, in this case), *will always be the number of cards held by the three other players* — dummy, you, and the declarer — *which are higher than the card led.* Putting this rule in diagram form:

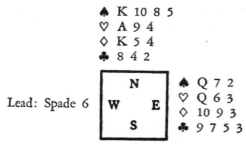

♠ K 10 8 5
♡ A 9 4
◇ K 5 4
♣ 8 4 2

Lead: Spade 6

♠ Q 7 2
♡ Q 6 3
◇ 10 9 3
♣ 9 7 5 3

South is the declarer at a three notrump contract, and West, your partner, opens the six of spades. After this lead, the dummy is put face up on the table, for all to see. Declarer plays the five of spades from dummy. What do you, as the East defender, play?

If you apply the Rule of Eleven, you will play the deuce of spades — and your partner's six-spot will win the trick!

When West led the six of spades against declarer's three notrump contract, he was leading his fourth-best (the longest suit is usually led against a notrump contract). East therefore subtracts 6 from 11. That leaves exactly five cards in the North, East and South hands which are higher than the six-spot. Three of these high-cards (the King, 10, and 8) are visible in dummy's hand. Two of those higher cards — the Queen and 7 — are in the East hand. Therefore, since all five of the missing higher cards are accounted for, *South can have no spade higher than the six-spot!* So, West's six of spades must win the trick if East plays the two of spades.

Examining this situation a little closer, West's original spade holding must have been at least the A J 9 6, with or without the 3 and/or 4 of spades. That West had the A J 9 of spades *must be,* for unless he did he could not be leading the six-spot as his fourth-best.

Against a *suit contract,* when no better lead is available, the lead of the fourth-best of a suit serves as a "decent" lead (that is, when your partner has not bid, and you do not have a sequence of top cards from which to lead).

(1)	(2)	(3)
♠ K 8 4 3 2	♠ K 8 4 3	♠ A Q 4 3 2
♡ 9 5 2	♡ 9 5 2	♡ 9 5
◇ Q 7 2	◇ Q 7 3 2	◇ Q 7 3 2
♣ Q 6	♣ Q 5	♣ 9 5

You hold each of the above three hands, and South arrives at a *four heart* contract, your partner not having done any bidding. You are sitting West, and you have to make the opening lead.

(1). Lead the three of spades, your fourth-best.

(2). Lead the three of spades, your fourth-best, from your *longest* and *strongest* suit.

(3). Lead the two of diamonds, your fourth-best in diamonds. Do not lead the three of spades, for against a suit contract, you *never lead away from an Ace,* for Aces were born to capture Kings and Queens. Therefore, since the lead of a spade is not recommended, you make the "second-choice" lead of the fourth-best diamond.

Against a *notrump* contract, the lead of the fourth-highest is the preferred lead, assuming your partner has not bid. In (1) the three of spades is led; in (2) the three of spades; and in (3), the three of spades, from your longest suit.

5. *Lead a Singleton, a Doubleton, or a Tripleton*

On many occasions you will have a "problem" as to what to lead, for your partner will not have bid, you will not have been dealt a sequence in any suit, and the only four-card suit (or suits) which you possess will have been bid by the opponents, making the lead of the fourth-highest an undesirable one.

Concerning this latter point, when an opponent has bid a suit, he has forewarned you that he has strength in that suit. Consequently, you will tend to shy away from leading that suit — even if it is your best suit — for to do so can only help your opponents, since it will be a lead into their strength. In these situations, you may elect to lead from a short suit: either a doubleton, a tripleton, or a singleton.

Let us now examine the pros and cons with respect to leading a "worthless" tripleton, doubleton or singleton:

a. *Against a Suit Contract*

(1) The Lead From a Doubleton or Tripleton.

When you do not have a positive lead to make, a lead from a doubleton or a tripleton is a "lesser of evils" lead. On the hand which follows, the opponents having bid both spades and hearts, with the contract having been purchased by them for *four spades,* it is up to you to make the opening lead:

$$\spadesuit \; Q \; 7 \; 6 \; 2$$
$$\heartsuit \; Q \; J \; 5 \; 4$$
$$\diamondsuit \; 9 \; 6 \; 3$$
$$\clubsuit \; 7 \; 2$$

With spades and hearts being eliminated as worthwhile leads, you are now confronted with the choice of leading from either your "worthless" (no high cards, nothing to develop) tripleton diamond, or from your worthless doubleton club. Which of the two suits to lead is an out-and-out guess, even to the best players in the world. Whichever suit you elect to lead, your lead will be the *highest card in that suit.* That is, if you decide to lead diamonds, you will lead the *nine-spot;* if you elect to lead clubs, you will lead the *seven-spot.* Actually, in the above situation, your preferable lead is from the doubleton club, for that offers a better hope of being able eventually to win a trick in that suit by trumping.

Stated as a principle, when you elect to lead from a worthless doubleton or a worthless tripleton, you will lead *the top card of that suit.* This lead is commonly referred to as a "top of nothing" lead, and when you make it, partner will recognize it as such, as opposed to it being your "fourth-highest." He will then come to the proper conclusion that you have no high-card strength in that suit, which will serve as an invaluable guide to him in making future leads.

(2) The Lead of a Singleton.

The lead of a singleton against a suit contract has much to recommend it. This lead is based on "wishful thinking." Your hope, when you lead the singleton, is that your partner has the Ace of that suit, and upon winning your lead with his Ace, he will return that suit — and you will be able to capture the second trick *by trumping.* Even if your partner does not have the Ace of your singleton suit, the possibility still exists that you may subsequently be able to win a trick by trumping that suit, which will be the case if your partner is able to obtain the lead before all your trumps are drawn.

On the following hand, the lead of the singleton club against the opponents' *four spade* contract figures to be the winning lead:

♠ x x x
♡ A Q x x
◇ x x x x
♣ x

Even though you have a four-card suit to lead from, the lead of the singleton club offers much more hope of creating a winning trick.

b. *Against a Notrump Contract*

(1)   The Lead From a Doubleton or Tripleton.

As you now know, against notrump contracts your lead will be the fourth-highest of your longest and strongest suit. But, again, you will shy away from leading in a suit which an opponent has bid, for the latter has displayed strength in that suit. If you do not have any other four-card or longer suit — other than the one which the opponent has bid — and your partner has made no bid, you will then be confronted with the option of making a second-choice, "wishful-thinking," lead from a tripleton or doubleton in the hope that your partner has length and strength in the suit which you are leading. Sometimes it will turn out as you hoped; sometimes it will not.

A "worthless" tripleton, incidentally, is a three-card suit headed by the nine or lower; a "worthless" doubleton is a two-card suit headed by the nine-spot or lower.

On occasion, you will be compelled to make a lead from a three-card suit which is not "worthless"; that is, A x *x*, K x *x*, Q x *x*, J x *x*, or 10 x *x*. This will happen when your longest suit is the one which an opponent has bid, and your partner has not bid any suit. In these situations, you will lead the *third-highest,* the underlined card. Your partner will be slightly misled by this lead, since he will assume that you are leading your fourth-highest. But this "misinformation" to partner will be compensated for by your partner realizing that you have at least one high card in the suit which you are leading. He will then be enabled intelligently to determine whether to return your suit when he obtains the lead.

A doubleton lead — either "worthless" or not — is very seldom made against a notrump contract, for, on probability, you do not figure to find your partner with a sufficient number of that suit to render it a profitable lead.

AGAINST ANY NOTRUMP CONTRACT, *A SINGLETON IS NEVER LED,* (unless your partner has bid that suit).

6. The Opening Lead of a Trump.

The lead of a trump against a suit contract is recommended in two situations: (1) where you are afraid to make a lead in any other suit, lest that lead be beneficial to declarer; (2) where the bidding has indicated that dummy will be able to trump some of declarer's losing tricks, and you therefore want to get rid of dummy's trumps. For example, if your right-hand opponent has arrived at a *four spade* contract, and you hold:

(1)	(2)
♠ 8 6 3	♠ 7 5 3
♡ Q 6 4 2	♡ A J 6 2
◇ Q 8 5	◇ K 8 4
♣ Q 7 6	♣ K 10 6

The lead of a heart, diamond, or club is unattractive on either of the above hands, and it might well lose a trick for the defenders. So, as the least dangerous lead, a trump is led.

Another illustration. If you are sitting West, and the bidding has proceeded:

WEST	NORTH	EAST	SOUTH
Pass	Pass	Pass	One Spade
Pass	Two Clubs	Pass	Two Hearts
Pass	Two Notrump	Pass	Three Hearts
Pass	Three Spades	Pass	Four Spades
Pass	Pass	Pass	

and your hand is:

♠ 8 7 4
♡ K J 9 2
◇ 10 6 4
♣ Q 8 3

you should lead a trump, a spade.

From the bidding on the above hand, you know that South has at least five spades and five hearts (South has opened the bidding with *one spade,* and has rebid *hearts,* showing five of the latter. Since he bid spades first, he must, therefore, have no fewer than five spades, for otherwise he would have opened the bidding with one heart). Also, since North prefers spades to hearts, he must have either more spades than hearts, or the same number. From your position — you have winning heart tricks in back of declarer — if you can remove dummy's trumps, you will make some heart tricks. The complete deal:

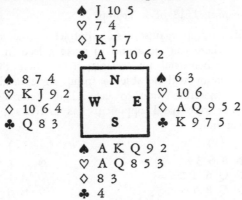

```
                    ♠ J 10 5
                    ♡ 7 4
                    ◇ K J 7
                    ♣ A J 10 6 2
   ♠ 8 7 4            N          ♠ 6 3
   ♡ K J 9 2                     ♡ 10 6
   ◇ 10 6 4      W      E        ◇ A Q 9 5 2
   ♣ Q 8 3            S          ♣ K 9 7 5
                    ♠ A K Q 9 2
                    ♡ A Q 8 5 3
                    ◇ 8 3
                    ♣ 4
```

If you do not lead trumps, declarer will be able to trump two of his hearts in dummy, and thereby fulfill his contract. With a trump opening, and a trump continuation when you again obtain the lead, declarer will be compelled to lose two heart tricks, and two diamond tricks.

WHEN TO LEAD THE OPPONENTS' SUIT

As far as knowing when you should steer away from making an opening lead in the suit which an opponent has bid, no hard and fast rule can be given. Some illustrations, however, may serve to clarify the situation:

Where your best suit is a fairly solid one, it should be led despite the fact that an opponent has bid it:

(1)	(2)	(3)
♠ K Q J 8 3	♠ Q J 10 8 5	♠ Q 10 7 4 2
♡ 9 2	♡ 8 4	♡ 8 4
◇ K J 7 2	◇ K J 7 2	◇ K J 7 2
♣ 8 4	♣ 3 2	♣ 3 2

Let us assume that the final contract is in *hearts*. In (1), you will lead the King of Spades, despite the fact that one of the opponents has bid spades; in (2), you will also lead the Queen of Spades, even if spades were bid by an opponent. In (3), you will not lead a spade in the face of a spade bid by the opponents. As to what you should lead, no recommended answer can be given. Sometimes the three of clubs will be the winning lead; at other times the fourth-best diamond will turn out to be the most effective lead.

In each of the above situations, had the final contract been *notrump*, with one of the opponents having bid spades, what to lead would be highly problematical. In (1) and (2), a spade lead might prove to be the winning lead; in (3), a diamond would be the suggested lead.

When your *only* decent suit has been bid by the opponents, what to lead becomes a matter of guesswork and wishful thinking. For instance, you hold the following hand and the opponents have arrived at a *four spade contract*, with one of them having bid hearts:

♠ 9 7 2
♡ Q 10 7 3 2
♢ 6 5 2
♣ 8 3

There are days when your partner has good diamonds, and there are days when he has good clubs. Not knowing which day it is, probably the preferable lead is to play a club, because of the hope that (1) either you will help establish partner's suit or, (2), that you may get to ruff a third round of clubs.

Suppose, however, that you hold the same hand, and the opponents arrive at a *three notrump* contract after having bid *hearts*. What do you lead?

Hearts having been eliminated as a lead, you are confronted with the option of leading one of three ragged suits. Whatever you lead in this case would be classified as a "desperation" lead; you have nothing which might be developed and cashed, for you have no entry. Your only chance then is to try to find your partner's good suit.

What is done in these situations is to lead from your best three-card suit, no matter how barren it is. Now and then you will "hit" partner's suit and establish it. Which suit do you lead? According to the experts, a spade lead is called for because the spade suit is just a mite stronger than the diamond suit; that is, the nine-spot is more likely to aid in developing partner's suit than the six-spot. As the reader can well appreciate, there is no guarantee given with the above suggestion.

These "desperation" short-suit leads should not be confused with the short-suit leads which are very often made against *suit contracts*. In the latter situations, short suit leads are often made because the leader is reluctant to make a dangerous lead away from strength, lest he thereby give declarer a trick. Suppose the contract is *four spades*, with declarer also having bid clubs. You hold:

      ♠ Q 7 4
      ♡ 8 3
      ◊ A Q 6 2
      ♣ K J 7 5

To lead a spade, club, or diamond is quite likely to give declarer a present of a trick. By elimination then, a heart lead (the eight-spot) becomes proper, not because it is right as such, but rather because any other lead may result in your partnership losing a trick.

A more positive short-suit lead, against either a suit or a notrump contract is what is called a "short-suit sequence" lead. These leads are made — as in the previous situation — when the leader is afraid of making a dangerous lead. Suppose you hold the following hand:

      ♠ Q 8 7
      ♡ J 10 4
      ◊ A J 3 2
      ♣ A J 7

Against either a suit or no trump contract, no lead is attractive, and either a spade, diamond or club lead might well give declarer a trick which he otherwise could not get. The Heart Jack is therefore selected as the opening lead, primarily because it is safe.

In the absence of an attractive lead against a notrump contract, the short-suit sequence lead is also properly made from the following holdings, the top card being led: Q̲ J x; J̲ 10 x; 1̲0 9 x; or even Q̲ J; J̲ 10; 1̲0 9. The lead from K Q x or K Q doubleton is not recommended, since it will lose a trick more often than it will gain. The contract is three notrump and you hold:

♠ 8 6 4 3	♠ A Q 4	♠ K Q 6
♡ 8 5 2	♡ 7 5 3 2	♡ 9 6 5 3
◊ Q̲ J 2	◊ J̲ 10	◊ 1̲0 9
♣ 9 4 3	♣ 8 5 4 2	♣ 8 5 4 3

In each of the above, the top diamond is the recommended lead.

THE OPENING LEAD AFTER PARTNER HAS DOUBLED THE FINAL CONTRACT IN NOTRUMP OR IN A SLAM

Whenever your partner has doubled a final contract in either notrump or a slam, and you are on lead, his double commands you to make a specifically-prescribed, conventional, lead. In these situations, your judgment concerning what you would normally have led is superseded by what partner has *commanded* you to lead. Let us examine the various types of leads which partner has called for when he made a penalty double of the final contract.

A. When Your Partner Has Doubled a Final Contract in *Notrump*.

1. If your partner has bid a suit, his double is an inviolable command to you to lead *his suit*.

♠ Q J 10 9 2
♡ 2
◇ J 10 9
♣ 8 6 5 3

Your partner has overcalled in Hearts, and has doubled the final contract of three notrump. You are on lead — and you will open your singleton deuce of hearts. Bear in mind that this is strictly a "no choice" situation. When your partner doubles after he has bid, he is in effect saying that he can defeat declarer's contract if you lead his suit. An example from "real life":

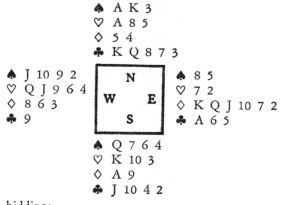

♠ A K 3
♡ A 8 5
◇ 5 4
♣ K Q 8 7 3

♠ J 10 9 2   ♠ 8 5
♡ Q J 9 6 4   N   ♡ 7 2
◇ 8 6 3   W   E   ◇ K Q J 10 7 2
♣ 9   S   ♣ A 6 5

♠ Q 7 6 4
♡ K 10 3
◇ A 9
♣ J 10 4 2

The bidding:

NORTH	EAST	SOUTH	WEST
One Club	One Diamond	One Notrump	Pass
Two Notrump	Pass	Three Notrump	Pass
Pass	Double	Pass	Pass
Pass			

If West does not open a diamond, South will have no difficulty in making at least 10 tricks. With the directed (commanded) diamond lead, declarer will suffer a two-trick set.

2. If *you* have bid a suit, your partner's double of an eventual *notrump* contract by the opponents demands that you lead *your* suit. To illustrate:

♠ A J 9 5 2
♥ A
♦ 7 4 2
♣ Q J 10 9

With the above hand you open the auction with *one spade,* after which the opponents arrive at a *three notrump* contract, which your partner doubles. If you had changed your mind about leading spades when the opposition arrived at three notrump, re-change it, for your partner's double demands that you lead spades. Here is the actual deal, which arose in a recent tournament:

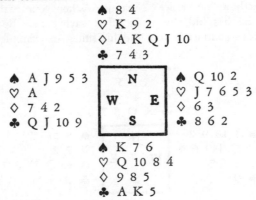

♠ 8 4
♥ K 9 2
♦ A K Q J 10
♣ 7 4 3

♠ A J 9 5 3   ♠ Q 10 2
♥ A   ♥ J 7 6 5 3
♦ 7 4 2   ♦ 6 3
♣ Q J 10 9   ♣ 8 6 2

♠ K 7 6
♥ Q 10 8 4
♦ 9 8 5
♣ A K 5

The bidding:

WEST	NORTH	EAST	SOUTH
One Spade	Two Diamonds	Pass	Three Notrump
Pass	Pass	Double	Pass
Pass	Pass		

The reader's opinion of East's double probably coincides with mine: it was a pure gambling bid, and a very risky gamble at best. But our opinion has nothing to do with the conventional significance of East's double. The bid said: "Partner, lead a spade."

With the low spade lead South could make only eight tricks. Had a club been led, South would have taken a minimum of 10 tricks.

3. If both partners have bid, and the opponents arrive at a *notrump* contract which your partner doubles, your opening lead is a matter of judgment. There is no accepted convention to cover this specific situation. A bit of advice, however, might be in order.

Generally speaking, when you cannot come to any intelligent conclusion as to whether to lead your own suit or partner's, lean towards leading his suit. From the viewpoint of future partnership morale, if it turns out that your failure to lead his suit enabled the opponents to make their contract, your partner will probably give you a lecture on why he bid his suit, etc., etc. On the other hand, if you lead his suit, and it subsequently develops that this lead was an "unfortunate" one, your partner will have no complaints.

4. When neither partner has bid, a double of a final notrump contract by leader's partner demands that the opening lead be *the first suit bid by dummy* (lead the *highest* card in that suit). To illustrate:

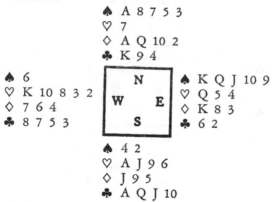

♠ A 8 7 5 3
♡ 7
◇ A Q 10 2
♣ K 9 4

♠ 6
♡ K 10 8 3 2
◇ 7 6 4
♣ 8 7 5 3

♠ K Q J 10 9
♡ Q 5 4
◇ K 8 3
♣ 6 2

♠ 4 2
♡ A J 9 6
◇ J 9 5
♣ A Q J 10

The bidding:

NORTH	EAST	SOUTH	WEST
One Spade	Pass	Two Clubs	Pass
Two Diamonds	Pass	Three Notrump	Pass
Pass	Double	Pass	Pass
Pass			

If West makes his "normal" lead of the fourth-best heart, declarer will easily establish the diamond suit to fulfill his

contract. With West leading spades — the commanded lead
of the first suit bid by dummy — declarer is automatically
defeated.

Years ago, in the above situation, a double of the final
notrump contract was only a *suggestion* to doubler's partner
to lead dummy's first-bid suit. If, in the leader's judgment, he
had what he felt was a more desirable lead, he had the right
to ignore the suggested lead, and, instead, to make any other
lead. As it is currently used by the great majority of the better
players, the double of a final notrump contract (in the absence
of a bid by either partner) is *a command to lead dummy's first
bid suit.*

It was my good fortune, a few years ago, to be on the right
end of a hand on which, due to a misunderstanding by the
defenders concerning this question of "suggestion" versus
"command," my contract was fulfilled. Permit me to introduce
it:

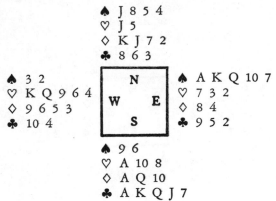

```
              ♠ J 8 5 4
              ♡ J 5
              ◇ K J 7 2
              ♣ 8 6 3
♠ 3 2                          ♠ A K Q 10 7
♡ K Q 9 6 4     N             ♡ 7 3 2
◇ 9 6 5 3    W     E          ◇ 8 4
♣ 10 4          S             ♣ 9 5 2
              ♠ 9 6
              ♡ A 10 8
              ◇ A Q 10
              ♣ A K Q J 7
```

The bidding:

SOUTH	WEST	NORTH	EAST
One Club	Pass	One Spade	Pass
Three Notrump	Pass	Pass	Double
Pass	Pass	Pass	

Despite East's "suggestion" of a spade lead, West chose to
lead a heart. Had he led a spade, East would have rattled off
five spade tricks.

B. Leading Against a Slam When Your Partner Has Doubled The Slam Contract.

1. When your partner has doubled a slam contract, whether you or he (or both) have or have not bid, it is an accepted convention that his double commands the lead of *the first suit by dummy* (exclusive of trumps). To illustrate:

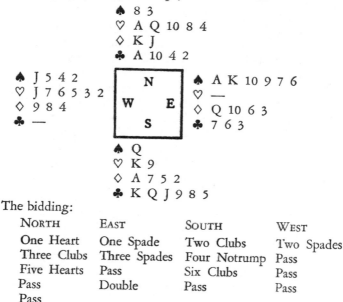

♠ 8 3
♡ A Q 10 8 4
◇ K J
♣ A 10 4 2

♠ J 5 4 2
♡ J 7 6 5 3 2
◇ 9 8 4
♣ —

N
W   E
S

♠ A K 10 9 7 6
♡ —
◇ Q 10 6 3
♣ 7 6 3

♠ Q
♡ K 9
◇ A 7 5 2
♣ K Q J 9 8 5

The bidding:

NORTH	EAST	SOUTH	WEST
One Heart	One Spade	Two Clubs	Two Spades
Three Clubs	Three Spades	Four Notrump	Pass
Five Hearts	Pass	Six Clubs	Pass
Pass	Double	Pass	Pass
Pass			

Without East's double, West would undoubtedly have made the "safe" and normal lead of a spade. With the double, West made the conventional, directed lead of dummy's first-bid suit, *hearts,* which East trumped, after which the Ace of Spades was cashed for the setting trick.

In the reader's mind, some speculation might arise as to what West would have led if South had "run" to six notrump after East's double (this, of course, is academic speculation). Had this happened, the ensuing proper bidding would have been: Pass, Pass, Pass. West's opening lead now (in the absence of East's double) would have been the normal spade lead, and South would have been set five tricks undoubled. Had East doubled six notrump, West would dutifully have led a heart — and the slam contract would have been fulfilled.

On this question of doubling slams, I should like to introduce briefly an attitude which is universally accepted. In theory, the double of a slam contract calls for the lead of the first suit bid by dummy not for the purpose of scoring an additional 50 or 100 points, but strictly for the purpose of commanding your partner to make an abnormal lead. After all, when the opposition arrives at a slam contract, they will very rarely go down more than one trick. To double the slam bidders merely to pick up a pittance of extra points is bound to be losing policy, for a double based on hope (a smattering of Kings and Queens) is usually nothing more than the enticing delusion of a thoughtless optimism. A double on "hope" is bound to give declarer an extra insight into how properly to play the hand, for the double will have tipped him off as to where the missing high-cards are. So, a word to the wise being sufficient, when you double a slam contract, be sure that your double will command the lead which will immediately deal declarer his death-blow, and will not boomerang.

2. If the dummy-to-be has bid no side suit (it might have raised trumps) but the declarer has bid some side suit or suits, the double of a slam contract commands that the doubler's partner lead *the first side suit* bid by declarer. While the occasions for the application of this specific convention do not arise too frequently, it is nevertheless a worthwhile proposition for the reader to familiarize himself with this convention, and earmark it for future reference.

"Unorthodox" Leads Made in Actual Competition

Any reader who has played more than one session of bridge is fully cognizant of the fact that on many deals there is simply no logical opening lead to make; that is, your partner has not bid, you do not have any sequence of high cards from which to lead, you have no singletons or doubletons, your best suit (and maybe also your second-best) has been bid by the opponents. What do you lead?

Let us see what our top-flight experts have done when they were confronted with some of the above-mentioned situations. In the selected deals which will be presented, these experts guessed right. But — and accept my word for this — if I were writing a book to illustrate how often the experts have guessed wrong on their opening lead, I doubt whether I could raise all the money necessary to buy sufficient paper to do a complete job.

1. The Lead "By Ear."

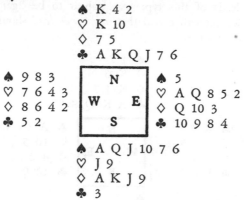

```
              ♠ K 4 2
              ♡ K 10
              ◊ 7 5
              ♣ A K Q J 7 6
  ♠ 9 8 3        N        ♠ 5
  ♡ 7 6 4 3               ♡ A Q 8 5 2
  ◊ 8 6 4 2    W     E    ◊ Q 10 3
  ♣ 5 2           S       ♣ 10 9 8 4
              ♠ A Q J 10 7 6
              ♡ J 9
              ◊ A K J 9
              ♣ 3
```

The bidding:

NORTH	EAST	SOUTH	WEST
One Club	Pass	One Spade	Pass
Three Clubs	Pass	Three Spades	Pass
Four Spades	Pass	Six Spades	Pass
Pass	Pass		

Based on the bidding, West, Helen Sobel, realized that to lead a club or a spade would be to concede victory to declarer. "By ear," therefore, the correct lead had to be a heart or a diamond. Which to lead? She led a heart, and declarer was down one. When a kibitzer commented on Helen's "excellent" lead, Helen, quite naturally, refused to take any credit for it. I wonder what the kibitzer's comment would have been if the North-South heart and diamond holdings had been interchanged?

```
              ♠ K x x
              ♡ x x
              ◊ K x
              ♣ A K Q J x x
                  N
                W     E
                  S
              ♠ A Q J 10 x x
              ♡ A K J x
              ◊ J x
              ♣ x
```

2. The Lead By A Process of Elimination.

Although leads of this type may appear to be "gambling" leads, a moment's reflection will reveal that *any other lead* should be considered the "gambling" lead.

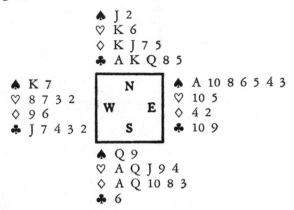

```
                    ♠ J 2
                    ♡ K 6
                    ◊ K J 7 5
                    ♣ A K Q 8 5
    ♠ K 7              N          ♠ A 10 8 6 5 4 3
    ♡ 8 7 3 2                     ♡ 10 5
    ◊ 9 6          W      E       ◊ 4 2
    ♣ J 7 4 3 2        S          ♣ 10 9
                    ♠ Q 9
                    ♡ A Q J 9 4
                    ◊ A Q 10 8 3
                    ♣ 6
```

The bidding:

SOUTH	WEST	NORTH	EAST
One Heart	Pass	Two Clubs	Pass
Two Diamonds	Pass	Four Notrump	Pass
Five Hearts	Pass	Six Diamonds	Pass
Pass	Pass		

What would you have led? Well, the opponents had bid clubs, diamonds, and hearts. Spades were the only unbid suit. West, who happened to be William Root, of Miami Beach, Florida, led spades by the above process of elimination. And the lead of the King of Spades, followed by a spade continuation, defeated the slam contract.

3. The Deceptive Lead.

(a) There is one great danger in making a "deceptive" lead: it is apt to mislead partner more often than it misleads declarer. And, when it misleads partner, not only is the one specific hand lost, but partner will thereafter tend to view your future leads with suspicion and distrust. Nevertheless, the deceptive lead has its little niche in the world of bridge. To illustrate:

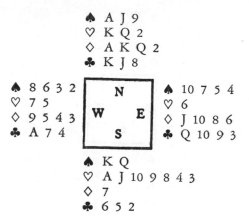

The bidding:

NORTH	EAST	SOUTH	WEST
Two Notrump	Pass	Three Hearts	Pass
Four Hearts	Pass	Six Hearts	Pass
Pass	Pass		

The fact that six notrump is unbeatable does not concern us. What is of import is that West — George Rapee, of New York City — opened the four of clubs. What would you have played from dummy if you had been sitting in the South seat? The actual South player chose to play dummy's Jack, and he went down a trick.

From George's point of view, he had no attractive lead to make. He did feel that North, for the two notrump bid, figured to have the King of Clubs. It was his hope that East had the Queen of Clubs. On this reasoning — including the embodiment of wishful thinking — West opened the four of clubs.

From declarer's point of view, he never gave even a passing thought to the possibility that West was underleading an Ace against a slam contract, for such leads are "never" made. But a lead away from a Queen was normal. Hence his play of the Jack from dummy.

(b)   Another illustration of the deceptive lead:

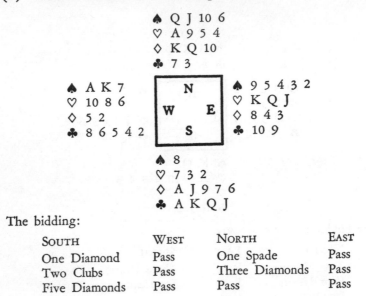

```
                    ♠ Q J 10 6
                    ♡ A 9 5 4
                    ◇ K Q 10
                    ♣ 7 3

    ♠ A K 7           N           ♠ 9 5 4 3 2
    ♡ 10 8 6                      ♡ K Q J
    ◇ 5 2          W     E        ◇ 8 4 3
    ♣ 8 6 5 4 2       S           ♣ 10 9

                    ♠ 8
                    ♡ 7 3 2
                    ◇ A J 9 7 6
                    ♣ A K Q J
```

The bidding:

SOUTH	WEST	NORTH	EAST
One Diamond	Pass	One Spade	Pass
Two Clubs	Pass	Three Diamonds	Pass
Five Diamonds	Pass	Pass	Pass

That three notrump was an ironclad contract is immaterial. Against South's five diamond contract, West, Gloria Turner of Chicago, deceptively opened the Ace of Spades (the King is the normal lead from A K x) because she did not wish declarer to know that she held the Ace and King of Spades in front of the spade bidder. She then shifted to a low heart, which was captured by dummy's Ace.

If you were declarer, would you not assume that East held the spade King? Our declarer did. After cashing the King and Queen of trumps, he then laid down dummy's Queen of Spades, discarding a heart when East followed with a low spade. West, of course, won this trick with the King of Spades, and led a heart which East won for the setting trick. Had the King of Spades been opened, declarer would undoubtedly have established one of dummy's high spades by ruffing out the Ace for a heart discard.

(c)   The deceptive lead which is presented in the deal that follows is not recommended, since in the long run it figures to deceive your partner and ruin the defense more often than it will gain by deceiving declarer. But when the lead has the hoped-for effect — of misleading declarer — the defenders rejoice while the declarer gnashes his teeth.

♠ A 9 5
♡ 7 6
◊ K 10 8 3
♣ A 10 5 2

♠ K Q J 7
♡ Q 10 4
◊ A J 9
♣ K J 9

You are sitting South, having arrived at a *four notrump* contract, on bidding which was "out of this world." West opens the *two* of hearts, and East's Jack is captured by your Queen. Since you are accustomed to playing with "honest" players, West's deuce of hearts lead was his fourth-best, so he started with exactly four hearts (and East, therefore, also had just four hearts originally).

You count nine sure winners: four in spades, one in hearts, two in diamonds, and two in clubs. If you can guess the location of either minor-suit Queen, you will have your game-going tenth trick. But the thought suddenly occurs: why guess? Can you not cash four spade tricks, eliminating spades from the opponents' hands, and then lead a heart? The opposition will now cash three heart tricks, after which *they* will be compelled to lead either a club or a diamond, giving you a "free" finesse for the Queen in whichever suit they elect to lead.

On this reasoning, derived from the observation of the deuce of hearts opening lead, declarer cashed four spade tricks and then led a heart. What happened next still seems like a nightmare to our declarer, for West's two of hearts lead had been his *sixth-best!*

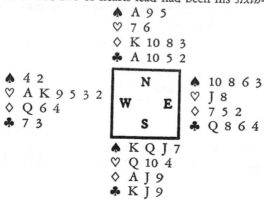

♠ A 9 5
♡ 7 6
◊ K 10 8 3
♣ A 10 5 2

♠ 4 2
♡ A K 9 5 3 2
◊ Q 6 4
♣ 7 3

♠ 10 8 6 3
♡ J 8
◊ 7 5 2
♣ Q 8 6 4

♠ K Q J 7
♡ Q 10 4
◊ A J 9
♣ K J 9

(d) One final illustration of the deceptive lead, the hero of this deal being your author:

Thursday, April 22, 1948. The San Francisco Chronicle
Contract Contacts: Brilliant
Opening Lead by Karpin
by Maureen Bailey

"Charles Solomon, one of the top-ranking life masters of the country and a widely read bridge author and columnist, told us about the following hand which stars a brilliant opening lead by Fred Karpin, another luminary of the contract world. It is based on a theory which we first heard expounded by the late Charles Schwartz, a wizard on defense. The bidding went:

NORTH	EAST	SOUTH	WEST
One Heart	Pass	Three Clubs	Pass
Three Diamonds	Pass	Four Notrump	Pass
Five Hearts	Pass	Seven Notrump	Pass
Pass	Pass		

The five heart call was the Blackwood response to show two Aces. Now you are West on opening lead with the following:

♠ J 10 9 7
♡ 6 2
◊ K 9 8
♣ J 7 5 3

What do you lead?

Well, here was Mr. Karpin's reasoning before he made that choice, as Mr. Solomon related it to us:

"South's three club bid, followed by his subsequent jump to 7 NT seems to indicate that he holds a very good club suit. The fact that South, after finding that North held two aces, plunged right into the 7 NT contract without inquiring about Kings, seems to substantiate my suspicion that South's club suit is pretty solid. In fact I'm just about sure that South expects to make that grand slam on the basis of bringing home his clubs. But . . . South doesn't know, as I do, that the club suit is not going to break. I could, of course, make the perfectly safe opening lead of the spade Jack. However, if I do that, declarer may be forced to take the diamond finesse after finding out about the club situation and that diamond finesse may be all he needs to make his contract. So . . .

"I'll lead a diamond on the reasonably sound assumption that declarer will surely not risk a finesse on the very first trick unless no better line of play is available. Here goes with the nine of diamonds."

"And as you will see by looking the entire hand over, this is the only opening which will defeat the contract.

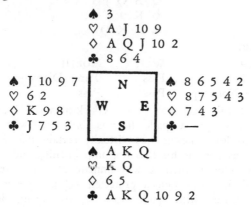

"No declarer in his right mind will take that diamond finesse on the opening lead with what looks like six sure club tricks, four sure heart tricks, three sure spade tricks, and the Ace of Diamonds for frosting. Whereas, if West makes any other opening, declarer will try out his club suit, find it doesn't break and be forced to finesse the diamonds whether he likes to or not."

4. Spectacular Opening Leads.

The leads on the two following deals were made by a couple of our experts in actual competition, and are included here merely to stress the element of imaginative defense which has become second nature to the expert. The reader will do well to examine these two deals even if the occasions for the proper use of these specific imaginative leads very seldom occur.

(a)

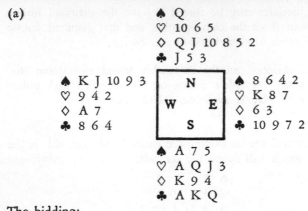

♠ Q
♡ 10 6 5
♢ Q J 10 8 5 2
♣ J 5 3

♠ K J 10 9 3
♡ 9 4 2
♢ A 7
♣ 8 6 4

♠ 8 6 4 2
♡ K 8 7
♢ 6 3
♣ 10 9 7 2

♠ A 7 5
♡ A Q J 3
♢ K 9 4
♣ A K Q

The bidding:

SOUTH	WEST	NORTH	EAST
Two Notrump	Pass	Three Diamonds	Pass
Three Notrump	Pass	Pass	Pass

The hero of this deal was Lester Glucksman, of New York City. Having decided to open a spade, he was confronted with the choice of which spade to lead. Lester was virtually certain that South had the Ace of Spades as part of his two notrump opening bid. If South also had the spade Queen, then it was immaterial which spade was led. If dummy had the spade Queen protected (Q x; Q x x) then it also made no difference which spade was led, for again, declarer would win two spade tricks. But if dummy happened to have a blank Queen of Spades, then a low spade lead (or the Jack) would be giving declarer a present of the spade Queen. On this reasoning, West laid down the King of Spades — and declarer still has not quite recovered.

(b)

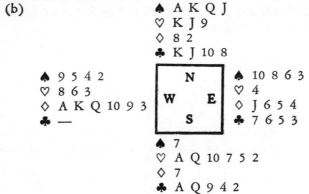

♠ A K Q J
♡ K J 9
♢ 8 2
♣ K J 10 8

♠ 9 5 4 2
♡ 8 6 3
♢ A K Q 10 9 3
♣ —

♠ 10 8 6 3
♡ 4
♢ J 6 5 4
♣ 7 6 5 3

♠ 7
♡ A Q 10 7 5 2
♢ 7
♣ A Q 9 4 2

The bidding:

WEST	NORTH	EAST	SOUTH
Three Diamonds	Double	Pass	Four Notrump*
Pass	Five Diamonds	Pass	Six Hearts
Pass	Pass	Pass	

* The Blackwood Slam Convention.

Rightly or wrongly, West decided that the only way in which the slam could be defeated would be if he could get to ruff a club. So, with the fervent hope that East held the Jack of Diamonds, West opened the *three of diamonds!* East captured this trick with his Jack. Fully realizing that West had made the very risky underlead of the A K Q of Diamonds *only for a purpose,* East soon came upon the reason: West had a void in some side suit — either clubs or spades — and wanted a ruff. Reverting back to the bidding, East found the proper answer. South had bid the small slam virtually all by himself, holding no high cards in either spades or diamonds, and no more than the A Q of hearts. So East deduced that South had to have quality in clubs, and probably also length. East therefore returned a club, West ruffing it for the setting trick. The East and West players, by the way, were Edgar Kaplan and Alfred Sheinwold, respectively, both of New York City.

This chapter has been devoted exclusively to the subject of *opening* leads. After the opening ("blind") lead, when dummy has become exposed, what you should lead will depend on three factors: (1) what your partner *signals* you to lead, which will be the theme of the next chapter, (2) what you see in dummy to guide you, and (3) *imagination,* should no direct assistance be available from (1) and (2). Illustrations of each of these points will be presented as we go along.

CHAPTER XII

DEFENDERS' PLAY: SIGNALS

W HEN the declarer is playing a hand, he sees all of the 26 cards which he is playing (his hand and dummy's), and is thereby enabled to plan out his campaign intelligently. The defenders' task is not so simple, for each must try to figure out what his partner is holding. From the defenders' point of view, in order to successfully attack and counterattack, they must rely on a system of "signals" to convey to each other what line the defense should follow. In defensive play it is of vital importance that each partner be on the alert to receive whatever information his partner is trying to transmit.

There are five major types of signals which the defenders employ in their "business." They are:

1. The Positive Signal ("come-on" in this suit).

2. The Negative Signal ("no interest" in this suit).

3. The Temporizing Signal ("undecided" about this suit).

4. Signalling with The Picture Cards.

5. The Suit-Preference Signal.

The Positive and Negative Signals (numbers 1 and 2) are discussed together.

1. The "Come-On" Signal and (2) The "No Interest" Signal.

The "come-on" signal is probably the most important single weapon that the defenders possess in their arsenal of aggressive warfare. When your partner opens a suit, and you want him to continue playing that suit, *you play an unnecessarily-high card on his lead.* He will then know that you desire the continuation of his suit. For example:

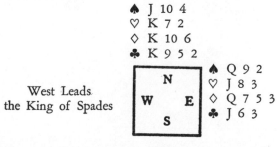

```
              ♠ J 10 4
              ♡ K 7 2
              ◇ K 10 6
              ♣ K 9 5 2
                              ♠ Q 9 2
                    N         ♡ J 8 3
  West Leads                  ◇ Q 7 5 3
the King of Spades  W    E    ♣ J 6 3
                    S
```

Suppose that South has purchased the contract at *four hearts,* and your partner, West, opens the King of Spades, upon which the four-spot is played from dummy. You know that an opening lead of a King is made from either an A K combination or from a K Q combination. Since you yourself hold the Queen, you therefore know that your partner has led from an A K combination. Your proper play on his King, to encourage the continuation of the spade suit, *is to play the nine-spot.* West will then lead the Ace, upon which you will play the deuce. West will now realize that your "abnormal" play in spades — putting up the nine first, and then playing the two on the next trick — indicates your desire to have that suit played again. He will then lead a third spade, which you will win with your Queen. Your come-on signal will have accomplished its purpose: to get partner to continue the suit which he started originally. This come-on signal is also known as a "high-low" signal [1] — playing a higher-than-necessary card first, and then playing a lower one on the next round of that suit.

Another illustration:

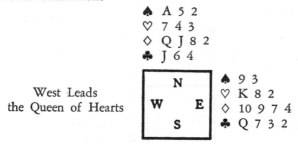

```
                  ♠ A 5 2
                  ♡ 7 4 3
                  ◊ Q J 8 2
                  ♣ J 6 4
                 ┌─────────┐   ♠ 9 3
   West Leads    │    N    │   ♡ K 8 2
the Queen of Hearts │ W   E │   ◊ 10 9 7 4
                 │    S    │   ♣ Q 7 3 2
                 └─────────┘
```

South has become the declarer at *three notrump,* and West, your partner, opens the Queen of Hearts. When it comes your turn to play, you will put up the *eight-spot,* an unnecessarily high-card, to urge your partner to continue that suit when he again obtains the lead (declarer, of course, has the Ace).

Had you played the two of hearts, that two-spot would properly have been interpreted by partner as a most discouraging card, for there is nothing lower than a deuce. *Just as an unnecessarily high-card is an encouraging "come-on" signal, so, in diametrically opposite fashion, the playing of the two, or any low card, is a negative signal, telling your partner that you have no "interest" in the suit led, and would he please discontinue leading it.*

---

[1] This "come-on", "high-low" signal is also known as "The Echo."

One more example of a "come-on" signal:

```
            ♠ 9 3
            ♡ Q 7 5
            ◇ A 6 5 4
            ♣ K 6 4 3
```

West Leads
the King of Diamonds

```
                    ♠ 10 8 6 4
                    ♡ A 8 4 3
                    ◇ J 7 2
                    ♣ J 5
```

South's contract is *four spades,* and West leads the King of Diamonds, which dummy captures with the Ace. Since your partner, West, is known to have started with the K Q of Diamonds, you play the *seven-spot,* so that when he next obtains the lead, he will continue playing the diamond suit. Had you held, let us say, the 7 3 2 of diamonds, you would have played the discouraging two-spot, as a negative signal.

This "come-on" signal is extended to another very frequent situation. You are sitting East.

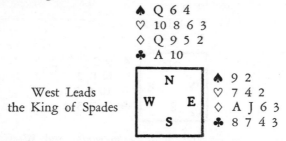

```
            ♠ Q 6 4
            ♡ 10 8 6 3
            ◇ Q 9 5 2
            ♣ A 10
```

West Leads
the King of Spades

```
                    ♠ 9 2
                    ♡ 7 4 2
                    ◇ A J 6 3
                    ♣ 8 7 4 3
```

Against South's *four heart* contract, your partner, West, opens the King of Spades, upon which you play the *nine-spot,* a come-on signal. His King wins, and he then continues with the Ace, upon which you play the deuce. He then leads a third spade, *and you win the trick by trumping it.* Playing the nine-spot first, and then following with the deuce on the next heart lead, is a "high-low," "come-on" signal. This signal is a command to partner to continue the suit which he has originally led.

A few paragraphs back, an illustration was presented of a "discouraging" signal, when your partner opened the Queen of Hearts, upon which you had the choice of playing an "encouraging" eight-spot, or a "discouraging" deuce of hearts. Always remember that when your partner opens a suit, he will carefully observe what card you play, so that he can be guided in continuing or discontinuing that suit. Therefore, as you observe his lead, scan the dummy, and decide whether you want to signal him that you like his suit, or that you have no interest in his suit.

Let us now look at these "signals" from the leader's position.

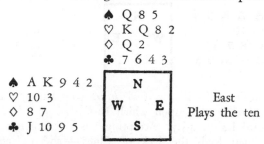

Against South's *four heart contract,* West opens the King of Spades, dummy plays the five-spot, and East puts up *the ten,* South dropping the six. Since the ten is an unusually high-card (an encouraging one), West then continues with the Ace, upon which East drops the three-spot. Observing that East has played "high-low," urging the continuation of the spade suit, West plays a third round of spades — and East trumps.

The actual deal was:

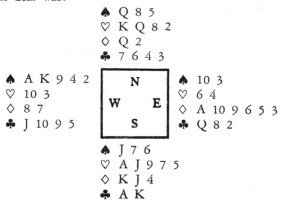

After winning the third spade lead by trumping, East now lays down his Ace of Diamonds, and thereby defeats South's four heart contract. Had East not signalled West to continue spades, and had East not trumped the third round of that suit, South would have fulfilled his contract.

Another hand:

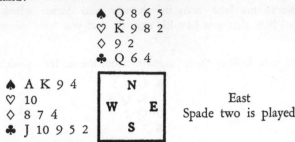

♠ Q 8 6 5
♡ K 9 8 2
◇ 9 2
♣ Q 6 4

♠ A K 9 4
♡ 10
◇ 8 7 4
♣ J 10 9 5 2

East
Spade two is played

South has again arrived at a *four heart* contract, and again West opens the King of Spades, upon which East *plays the deuce,* the most discouraging card he can play. Accepting this warning not to continue spades, West then leads the Jack of Clubs — and defeats declarer's contract. Had West continued playing the spade suit, declarer would have fulfilled his contract.

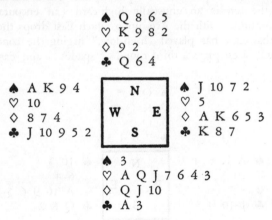

♠ Q 8 6 5
♡ K 9 8 2
◇ 9 2
♣ Q 6 4

♠ A K 9 4
♡ 10
◇ 8 7 4
♣ J 10 9 5 2

♠ J 10 7 2
♡ 5
◇ A K 6 5 3
♣ K 8 7

♠ 3
♡ A Q J 7 6 4 3
◇ Q J 10
♣ A 3

At trick two, West leads the Jack of Clubs, dummy puts up the Queen, East covers with the King, and South captures the trick with his Ace. It now becomes impossible for declarer to avoid the loss of one club trick (to West's ten-spot), two diamond tricks (to East's Ace and King), and the spade trick which he has already lost. But look at what happens if West continued with the Ace of Spades at trick two.

South would trump the Ace of Spades, after which he would play the King of trumps, picking up the two adverse trumps. Now, on the established Queen of Spades, South would discard his losing club.

From here in the play would be routine, and South would lose only two more tricks to East's Ace and King of Diamonds. So, as you can see, the observance of signals can well spell the difference between victory and defeat.

Quite often, the defenders give signals by their *discards*. That is, when a suit is played of which you have none, if you discard an unnecessarily high-card in another suit, you are telling your partner that you desire that latter suit to be led. For example:

♠ J 10 8 2
♡ J 9 3
◇ K 8 4 3
♣ K 7 6

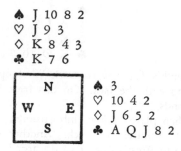

♠ 3
♡ 10 4 2
◇ J 6 5 2
♣ A Q J 8 2

South is the declarer at *four spades*, and your partner, West, opens a spade (trump) which declarer captures with his nine-spot. Declarer then lays down his Ace of Spades, upon which your partner follows suit. You have to make a discard — and it should be the *eight of clubs*, an unusually high card, telling your partner that when he obtains the lead, he should play a club. Otherwise, if you do not make this discard, your partner will have to guess which suit to lead. Since you are vitally interested in clubs being played, you must encourage your partner to lead that suit. This is accomplished by discarding the eight-spot of clubs, an unusually high card. Partner will then know that he has been directed to lead a club at his first opportunity.

Similarly, a discard of a very low card in another suit (not the one being played) is a signal to partner that you have no interest in that suit.

As you play more and more, you will discover that there will be frequent situations when you want to encourage your partner to lead a certain suit, but that you do not possess an unusually high card which you can discard to let him know about it. In these cases, you have at your disposal a "negative" signal which you can employ, and partner, by inference, will understand it. The deal which follows illustrates this "negative" signal.

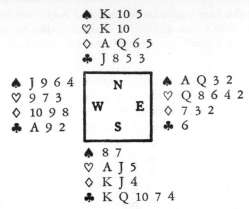

♠ K 10 5
♡ K 10
◇ A Q 6 5
♣ J 8 5 3

♠ J 9 6 4   ♠ A Q 3 2
♡ 9 7 3   ♡ Q 8 6 4 2
◇ 10 9 8   ◇ 7 3 2
♣ A 9 2   ♣ 6

♠ 8 7
♡ A J 5
◇ K J 4
♣ K Q 10 7 4

Against South's *five club* contract, West opened the ten of diamonds, South winning with the Jack. On this trick East followed suit with the two of diamonds.

Declarer then played a low club (trump), West also played low, and dummy's Jack captured the trick. Another club was then led, South's Queen falling to West's Ace. East discarded the *two of hearts*.

West now had to lead. From East's plays to the first three tricks, a few things were apparent to West: East did not want diamonds led, and he did not want hearts led (on the original diamond lead, East had followed suit with the deuce; on the second club lead, East had discarded the discouraging two of hearts, stating that he did not want hearts led).

By elimination, therefore, West led a spade, since that was the sole hope of defeating the contract — and East cashed two spade tricks! Had West led any other suit, declarer would have fulfilled his contract, for after drawing West's last trump, he would have played his King of Diamonds, and then his last diamond to dummy's Ace. On the Queen of Diamonds in dummy, declarer would then have discarded one of his two losing spades. But West's timely spade lead prevented declarer from getting rid of one of his losing spades.

From a "signalling" point of view, East would have liked to have given West a more positive signal to lead spades. That is, East would have enjoyed possessing the A Q 9 2 of Spades (rather than the A Q 3 2), for in this case he would have signalled by playing the nine-spot as his discard, an unusually high-card. But, unfortunately East had been dealt the A Q 3 2, and he correctly felt that if he played the three-spot, a very low card, West would construe it as a discouraging card.

So East was forced to make a negative signal, trusting that his partner would be able to interpret the "negative" signal in a positive fashion —

to lead the spade suit. By discouraging the heart lead, and discouraging the diamond lead, East suggested, inferentially, that he wanted a spade to be led.

3. The Temporizing Signal.

Thus far there have been presented the "positive" and "negative" signals, or, as they are sometimes called, the "encouraging" and "discouraging" signals. There is also another type of signal known as a "temporizing" signal. The occasions to use this latter type of signal probably occur just as frequently as do the opportunities to use either the positive or negative signal.

Let us look at the different types of signals as utilized by East in the three following illustrations:

1.

$$\spadesuit \; A \; 4 \; 2$$

$$\spadesuit \; K \; Q \; 10 \; 3 \quad \boxed{\begin{array}{c} N \\ W \quad E \\ S \end{array}} \quad \spadesuit \; J \; 9 \; 7 \; 5$$

$$\spadesuit \; 8 \; 6$$

Your partner, West, opens the King of Spades against South's notrump contract, and declarer plays low from dummy. You are East, and, of course, are anxious to have the suit continued since you know that your partner has at least the K Q 10 x. You therefore employ the encouraging "come-on" signal by playing the nine-spot.

2.

$$\spadesuit \; A \; 4 \; 2$$

$$\spadesuit \; K \; Q \; 10 \; 3 \quad \boxed{\begin{array}{c} N \\ W \quad E \\ S \end{array}} \quad \spadesuit \; 7 \; 6 \; 5$$

$$\spadesuit \; J \; 9 \; 8$$

Again, against South's *notrump* contract, your partner opens the Spade King, the deuce being played from dummy. You have no interest in spades being continued, so you play your lowest card, the five-spot, to discourage partner (should he continue spades, declarer would be able to win two spade tricks). Of course, if partner does continue spades in light of your signal, he is assuming complete responsibility.

3. But suppose that this is the situation against a notrump contract:

```
              ♠ A 4 2
                 N
♠ K Q 10 3  W  │   │  E   ♠ 9 8 7 5
                 S
              ♠ J 6
```

West again leads the Spade King, and dummy plays the deuce. Now which card do you play? You have four cards in partner's suit, and you know that he is leading from length in a suit headed by K Q J or K Q 10 — and yet you do not desire to encourage him too strongly (by playing the nine) for fear that he may not have the Jack. Nor do you want to discourage him lest the actual situation that I have presented exists (where by next playing his Queen he will be able to drop declarer's Jack).

Actually you should not want to either encourage or discourage him in positive fashion. The decision should be left to him. Therefore your proper play is the *seven* — a temporizing play. And how will your partner interpret this seven-spot? The answer is that in a certain percentage of the time he will have to guess as to the significance of that card. The remaining time — as will be illustrated in a moment — he will know with reasonable certainty that you gave him a temporizing signal. If, on the other hand, you play your lowest card, the *five-spot,* partner will assume that you have no interest in the suit, and will tend to abandon it (unless he has the K Q J x, in which case he will require no assistance or guidance from you).

When you play your seven-spot, partner, by observation, may feel that the seven-spot was not your lowest (the five would still be missing, declarer having followed with the six). If partner has no better lead, then the seven-spot will at least offer some mild encouragement.

Consider partner's reasoning a bit further. If he concludes that the seven-spot is not a completely discouraging signal, he will then speculate on what caused you to play it instead of a more discouraging card. He will realize that you cannot hold four or more to the Jack, for if you did you would have given a more vigorous signal like the eight or nine. He will then properly conclude that you hold something less than four to the Jack. He will also know that if you held just three low cards in the suit, you would have played your lowest (the five) and not the intermediate seven. By elimination, West would probably correctly determine that the reason for your play of the seven was that you held four low ones in the suit. His play of the Queen would then catch declarer's Jack.

Of course, the loophole in the above reasoning is the question of what East would have played holding the J 7 5 of Spades, in which case he would most ardently desire a spade continuation, and yet could do no better than to play the seven-spot to express this desire (it is not ethical to bang the seven on the table, bruising your knuckles, as if to say: "Partner, I'm not bruising my knuckles for exercise. I love your lead. Pray continue playing the suit"). Actually, in this one specific case, the play of the Jack would bring about the desired result. However, in probably 9 out of ten superficially similar cases, to signal with a Jack would be equivalent to throwing a trick out of the window. For instance:

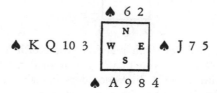

For East to play the Jack in this situation would result in establishing two spade tricks for declarer upon the called-for spade continuation.

In reading this section on the temporizing signal, the reader should not forget that the occasions for the proper employment of a temporizing signal arise just as often as do the opportunities for either an encouraging or discouraging signal. After all, contract bridge is not the sort of game in which the proper line of play becomes obvious from the start. Even after a few tricks have been played, it may not be easily discernible as to which line of defense is the winning one. Therefore one has to make allowance — via temporizing signals — to leave some leeway for a change of plans should it become necessary later on. Sometimes, for instance, you begin a high-low signal early in the play, and you may not get a chance to complete it until possibly seven or eight tricks later — at which time things might have changed, and you no longer want to complete it for the suit no longer offers hope; or, seven or eight tricks later, you may have the opportunity and the desire to complete your high-low signal. So, do not play mechanically when your partner opens a suit. Give him the proper signal, and the defense will proceed smoothly.

As the reader will quickly perceive if he thinks about it, signals by the defenders are not given only when they are on lead. That is, the defenders do not sit back to await their obtaining the lead before they begin to flash the "go," "stop," and "I'm not certain" signals. [2] These signals are also given while declarer is attacking.

---

[2] "Positive", "Negative", and "Temporizing" signals, respectively.

The reader is familiar with the fact that positive and negative signals are given in side suits while declarer is playing a suit of his own (p. 355); that is, the discard of a high-card in some side suit is a signal to partner that you want that side suit led; while a discard of a low card in a side suit disclaims any interest in that suit. A temporizing signal (for future utilization), can also be given within a suit while declarer is tackling *that suit*. To illustrate:

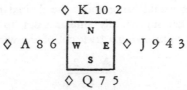

$\diamond$ K 10 2

$\diamond$ A 8 6 $\diamond$ J 9 4 3

$\diamond$ Q 7 5

Declarer leads the deuce of diamonds from the North hand, intending to play his Queen. What do you play? The normal reaction would be to play the three, with a "what difference does it make" attitude. Your proper play, however, is to play the *four-spot*, not the three. Declarer will then put up the Queen, which partner will capture with the Ace. At this point, of course, partner does not have the slightest idea as to whether you would like to have the suit led or not. However, in all probability, later on there will be presented you an opportunity to make a discard on the lead of a suit in which you have no cards. You will then discard the *three of diamonds,* and your partner will have observed that you went out of your way to give a "high-low" signal (the four-spot first, followed by the three-spot). He will then know with certainty that you hold the protected Jack over dummy, and he will lead the suit if he finds it necessary to the defensive campaign.

Let us look at the final illustration of the temporizing signal:

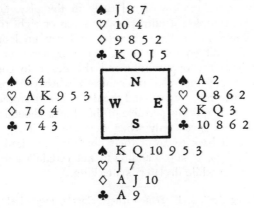

♠ J 8 7
♡ 10 4
$\diamond$ 9 8 5 2
♣ K Q J 5

♠ 6 4
♡ A K 9 5 3
$\diamond$ 7 6 4
♣ 7 4 3

♠ A 2
♡ Q 8 6 2
$\diamond$ K Q 3
♣ 10 8 6 2

♠ K Q 10 9 5 3
♡ J 7
$\diamond$ A J 10
♣ A 9

Partner opens the King of Hearts against South's *four spade* contract. Observing dummy's doubleton heart, you would like to cash two heart tricks, but you do not want your partner to lead a third round of hearts. If you play your deuce of hearts on his lead of the king, he might shift suits (and if he does declarer will fulfill his contract by getting rid of his remaining heart on dummy's high club).

On his opening lead of the King, you therefore play the six-spot, knowing that this will induce partner to cash his Ace. When he does cash the Ace, you follow with the *eight-spot,* thus failing to complete the high-low signal which your six-spot might have begun. If on the lead of the Ace you had followed with the deuce, partner might assume that you held just two, and he would then play a third round of hearts, thereby presenting declarer with his contract.

On your play of the eight-spot, partner will now unquestionably shift suits, and in all probability he will choose diamonds, since dummy's clubs will offer no inducement to the defenders. Declarer will then be doomed to defeat.

4. Signalling With The Picture Cards (Honors)

(a) The Play of the Queen on the King against a Suit Contract.

It is an established convention that when your partner opens a King against a suit contract, and you play the Queen on his King, the play of the Queen *demands* that he underlead his Ace (i.e., to lead low from) at trick two. Hence it is obvious that whenever you give this most drastic signal, you will have the *Queen and Jack* in your possession.

```
                ♠ 9 7 5
                ┌───────┐
                │   N   │
♠ A K 8 4       │ W   E │       ♠ Q J 2
                │   S   │
                └───────┘
                ♠ 10 6 3
```

Your partner opens the King upon which you play your Queen. Partner then leads a low spade which you capture with the Jack, after which a third round in the suit is taken by West's Ace.

Do not, therefore, go playing the Queen in the following situation:

```
                ♠ 9 7 5
                ┌───────┐
                │   N   │
♠ A K 8 4       │ W   E │       ♠ Q 2
                │   S   │
                └───────┘
                ♠ J 10 6 3
```

The contract is *four hearts,* and your partner opens the King of Spades. Should you play the Queen on the King, your partner will then underlead his Ace — and you will be sorry.

Relating this convention of the Queen on the King calling for the underlead of the Ace to the deal previously presented showing the complete four hands, had you held the Q J 6 2 of Hearts instead of the Q 8 6 2, there would have been no necessity of employing the temporizing signal of the six-spot. On the opening lead of the King of Hearts you would have played the Queen, as a direct, positive, signal for him to underlead the Ace. Then, upon capturing his low heart continuation with your Jack, you would have laid down the Diamond King.

On this play of the Queen on the King to show the Jack, here is a deal where, without the use of this convention, declarer would probably have fulfilled his contract:

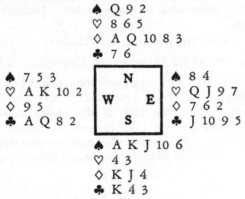

The final contract was *four spades* by South, arrived at after an opening bid of one club by West. The opening lead was the King of Hearts, upon which East played the Queen. A low heart was then led to East's known Jack, after which East shifted to the Jack of Clubs, defeating the contract. If, on the lead of the King of Hearts, East had mechanically played his nine-spot as a "come-on" signal, West might have then cashed his Ace — and declarer would then have fulfilled his contract.

In summary, then, the play of the Queen on partner's opening lead of the King demands the underlead of the Ace.

    (b)   When to Signal With an Honor — And When Not To.

          It is the relatively rare occasion when you should properly signal with an honor card, for in most cases you will be throwing away a potential trick in so doing. But there are those situations where it should be done, to guide more clearly your partner — without it costing anything — to the obviously-proper defense. Let us look at these two contrasting illustrations:

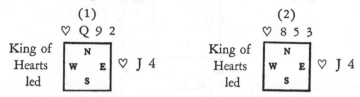

(1)   (2)

In each case South has arrived at a *spade* contract and your partner opens the King of Hearts. In (1) it is apparent that your partner is leading from an A K combination, since the Queen is in dummy, and you are desirous of trumping the third round of hearts. So, you play the Jack of Hearts on his King, initiating the high-low signal, and when partner then follows up by leading the Ace, you complete your signal by dropping the four-spot. Partner will then lead a third heart for you to trump. In (2), when partner opens the Heart King, you do not know whether he is leading from A K or K Q. If it is the latter, then by dropping the Jack, you may be tossing a trick out of the window. So you play the four-spot. The heart holding might have been:

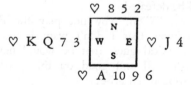

It has been illustrated that when your partner opens a King against a suit contract, and you have the Q J plus the desire to have the suit continued, you play the Queen, calling for the underlead of his Ace. Extending this, whenever your partner opens the Ace or King of a suit, and you have touching honors in his suit, play *the higher honor* to inform him that you also have the honor directly beneath the one which you have just played. That is, if your partner leads the King against a suit contract, and you hold the J 10 9, play the Jack not the ten or nine. The Jack play will not only inform him that you have the ten, but will also specifically deny possession of the Queen, since with the Q J you would have played the Queen. This information, thus conveyed to partner, is bound to serve as an invaluable aid to him in conducting the defense. Witness this hand:

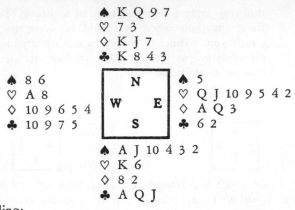

The bidding:

EAST	SOUTH	WEST	NORTH
Three Hearts	Three Spades	Pass	Four Notrump
Pass	Five Hearts*	Pass	Five Spades
Pass	Pass	Pass	

* The Blackwood Slam Convention.

West opens the Ace of Hearts, and you play the Queen, thereby denying possession of the King. Whatever your partner now plays, it will *not* be a heart. If he gets his finger on a diamond, then the five spade contract will be defeated.

The reader might say, "Well, why not play the deuce of hearts. Then my partner will know that I don't want hearts continued, and he will still have the identical guess that he would have had if I had played the Queen." All well and good on this particular hand, but situations like the following often arise:

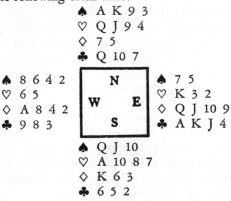

The bidding:

EAST	SOUTH	WEST	NORTH
One Diamond	Pass	Pass	Double
Pass	Two Hearts	Pass	Three Hearts
Pass	Four Hearts	Pass	Pass
Pass			

West dutifully opens the Ace of Diamonds, and if you play the nine, your partner may interpret it as a come-on signal. If he then continues diamonds, declarer will fulfill his contract. But if, on your partner's lead of the Ace you play the Queen of Diamonds, partner will know that you do not have the King. He will then most surely shift to clubs, since by looking at dummy he will realize that you must possess club strength for your opening bid.

5. The Suit-Preference signal.

This is a conventional signal which is put to excellent use by the better players, but which is misapplied by the majority of bridge players. Before introducing it, let us take another look at the "come-on" signal in its normal application:

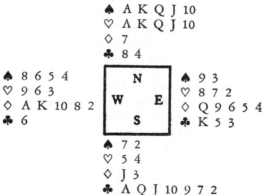

```
            ♠ A K Q J 10
            ♡ A K Q J 10
            ◇ 7
            ♣ 8 4

  ♠ 8 6 5 4        N        ♠ 9 3
  ♡ 9 6 3                   ♡ 8 7 2
  ◇ A K 10 8 2  W     E     ◇ Q 9 6 5 4
  ♣ 6              S        ♣ K 5 3

            ♠ 7 2
            ♡ 5 4
            ◇ J 3
            ♣ A Q J 10 9 7 2
```

Against South's *six club* contract your partner opens the King of Diamonds. Glancing at the dummy, you may feel quite pessimistic, for at the moment your King of trumps looks as if it will be trapped. But, on further examination, if you can get your partner to continue diamonds, dummy will be reduced to one trump, and your King of Clubs will then become "untrappable." So, on partner's lead of the Diamond King, you play the "unnecessarily-high" nine of diamonds, and when partner continues the suit, forcing dummy to ruff, declarer can no longer take two finesses through your King of Clubs.

We now come to the suit-preference signal, which, at superficial glance, may appear to be related to East's "come-on" signal of the nine-spot on the preceding deal. Actually, there is no relationship whatsoever:

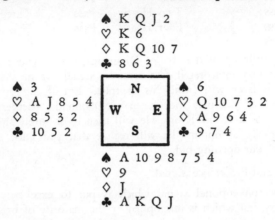

♠ K Q J 2
♡ K 6
♢ K Q 10 7
♣ 8 6 3

♠ 3
♡ A J 8 5 4
♢ 8 5 3 2
♣ 10 5 2

♠ 6
♡ Q 10 7 3 2
♢ A 9 6 4
♣ 9 7 4

♠ A 10 9 8 7 5 4
♡ 9
♢ J
♣ A K Q J

How North-South contrived to arrive at a *six spade* contract on the above North-South cards, missing two Aces, is irrelevant. Sufficient to say, it probably happens every day in every bridge club in the country. And I am certain that in a fair proportion of these situations the defense slips, and declarer "steals" his unmakable contract.

Against South's *six spade* contract West opened the Ace of Hearts, which won the trick. At a loss as to what to play next, West decided to shift to a club, and declarer waltzed home with his contract, discarding his diamond on dummy's heart King. Had West shifted to a diamond at trick two, East would have cashed his Ace. How could the defenders have gotten together to direct their defense? Answer: *the suit-preference signal.*

The purpose of this signal is to eliminate the guesswork as to which of *two suits* partner should play in situations analogous to the one just presented. The reference to "two suits" may appear to be a typographical error. Actually, it is not. Of the four suits, the trump suit is automatically eliminated, for when partner gives any signal whatsoever, it is never to direct a lead of the trump suit. Also, the suit which is being led, on which the suit-preference signal being given, is excluded. That leaves the leader with a choice of two "obvious" suits. In the hand just presented, after West cashed his Ace of Hearts, either a heart continuation or a trump lead were "impossible" plays. So it became a choice of diamonds or clubs.

On the lead of the Ace of Hearts, had East-West been employing this suit-preference signal, East would have played the *ten of hearts* which, upon examination of the dummy, could not have been construed as asking for a heart continuation. The ten-spot would have said to West: "Play the *higher ranking* of the two obvious suits!"

Stating this suit-preference signal as a principle, it comes to this:

Whenever partner plays an unnecessarily-high card which is *obviously* not a "come-on-in-this-suit" signal, it commands partner to lead the higher of the two self-evident suits; whenever partner plays a very low card which is obviously not a "no-interest-in-this-suit" signal, that low card asks partner to shift to the lower of the two obvious suits. If the partner of leader has no interest in either of the two obvious suits, he will play some intermediate card in the suit being led.

When correctly used, the play of either an unnecessarily-high card or an obviously low card will be unmistakable. Partner will invariably make the right shift when you properly direct him.

I mentioned some paragraphs back that this convention is "abused and misapplied" by the majority of bridge players. The reason behind this is that the offenders attempt to apply it where it should not be applied. For instance:

```
              ♠ A K 6
              ♡ K 7 5
              ◇ J 8 7 3
              ♣ 9 4 2

  ♠ 9 5 4 2     ┌─────────┐
  ♡ Q 6 3       │    N    │
  ◇ Q 9 6 2     │ W     E │
  ♣ A 6         │    S    │
                └─────────┘
```

Against South's *four spade* contract West elects to open the Ace of Clubs, East plays the ten, and South the three-spot. West, having recently discovered that there was a new toy called the "suit-preference" signal, now demonstrates his "learning" by banging down the Queen of Hearts, saying to himself, "My partner's ten of clubs was a signal to me to lead the higher of the two obvious suits." Utter nonsense! Partner wanted clubs continued, and so he, in conventional fashion, played the unnecessarily high ten-spot. The suit-preference signal is used only when it MUST be OBVIOUS another suit is wanted to be led. The actual deal was:

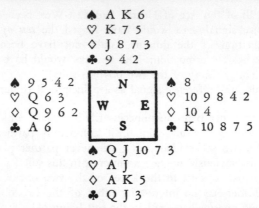

♠ A K 6
♡ K 7 5
◇ J 8 7 3
♣ 9 4 2

♠ 9 5 4 2
♡ Q 6 3
◇ Q 9 6 2
♣ A 6

♠ 8
♡ 10 9 8 4 2
◇ 10 4
♣ K 10 8 7 5

♠ Q J 10 7 3
♡ A J
◇ A K 5
♣ Q J 3

Probably the most frequent situation in which the suit preference signal is applied is when you are returning a suit which your partner is obviously going to trump, and you want to direct him to then play back a specific suit to you so that you can quickly re-obtain the lead and give him another ruff. The denomination of the card that you lead when you give him his first ruff becomes the clear-cut signal: if you play an unnecessarily high card, he is to return the *higher-ranking* of the two obvious suits (trumps and the suit being ruffed are eliminated); if you play an obviously low card, he is to return the lower-ranking of the two obvious suits: To illustrate:

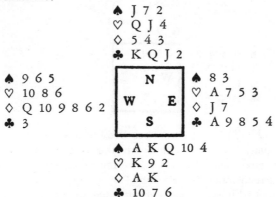

♠ J 7 2
♡ Q J 4
◇ 5 4 3
♣ K Q J 2

♠ 9 6 5
♡ 10 8 6
◇ Q 10 9 8 6 2
♣ 3

♠ 8 3
♡ A 7 5 3
◇ J 7
♣ A 9 8 5 4

♠ A K Q 10 4
♡ K 9 2
◇ A K
♣ 10 7 6

Against South's *four spade* contract, West opens the three of clubs, dummy plays low, and East's Ace captures the trick. It is, of course, perfectly apparent to East that the three-spot is a singleton, for it could not be fourth-best, nor could it be the top of a worthless doubleton or tripleton. So East is going to play a club for West to trump — and employing the suit-preference signal he returns the *nine-spot*. When West trumps the trick, he recognizes the nine-spot as being unnecessarily high, and he now plays back a heart (as opposed to a diamond), which East captures. East then returns another club for West to trump for the setting trick. It is apparent, of course, that if West had not played back a heart, declarer would have captured any other return, drawn trumps, and fulfilled his contract.

Suppose this had been the situation:

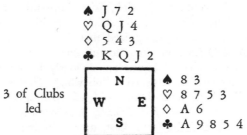

```
                    ♠ J 7 2
                    ♡ Q J 4
                    ◇ 5 4 3
                    ♣ K Q J 2
                                    ♠ 8 3
                            N       ♡ 8 7 5 3
   3 of Clubs       W       E       ◇ A 6
       led                          ♣ A 9 8 5 4
                            S
```

Upon winning the three of clubs opening lead, East would now lead back the *four* of clubs — an obviously low club directing West to return the lower of the two suits (*diamonds* versus hearts); and, upon it being done, he would then give West another ruff.

There is one final situation where the suit preference signal is normally utilized. This occurs when partner makes what is apparently an unnatural and abnormal lead, the only purpose of which could have been to get you into the lead. When this occurs, you will recognize that he is void of a suit and is trying to put you into the lead so that he can obtain a ruff. This form of suit-preference signal was employed on a hand which was introduced earlier (p. 348). Permit me to re-introduce it:

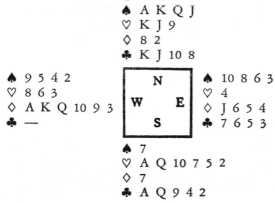

```
                    ♠ A K Q J
                    ♡ K J 9
                    ◇ 8 2
                    ♣ K J 10 8
   ♠ 9 5 4 2                         ♠ 10 8 6 3
   ♡ 8 6 3            N              ♡ 4
   ◇ A K Q 10 9 3   W       E        ◇ J 6 5 4
   ♣ —                               ♣ 7 6 5 3
                            S
                    ♠ 7
                    ♡ A Q 10 7 5 2
                    ◇ 7
                    ♣ A Q 9 4 2
```

The bidding

WEST	NORTH	EAST	SOUTH
Three Diamonds	Double	Pass	Four Notrump
Pass	Five Diamonds*	Pass	Six Hearts
Pass	Pass	Pass	

* The Blackwood   Slam Convention

Having made up his mind that the only way the slam could be defeated was if he could ruff a club, West hopefully opened the *three of diamonds*. When East won the trick with his Jack, after having regained his composure, he recognized that West had most dangerously underled his A K Q for a purpose: to ruff one of the two other suits.

Since the three of diamonds was an obviously low-card, applying the suit preference signal East returned a club which West ruffed.

Hypothetically, had West been void of spades, his opening lead would have been the *nine of diamonds,* an obviously high one, [3] with the hope that East held the Jack. East, upon winning, would then have returned a spade.

Some top-flight expert players have extended the use of this convention to situations where the signal is given on the play of some side suit (i.e. any suit except the trump suit). The signal is made by high-low discards. Here is a deal which arose a few years ago. George Rapee and B. J. Becker were sitting West and East, respectively.

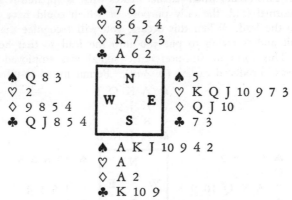

After East had opened with four hearts, North-South arrived at a *six spade contract.* West opened the two of hearts — which was quite

---

[3] The reader may wonder why West, in this case, would not have opened the ten-spot. The answer is that East, holding the Jack, might not overtake the ten. But with the nine being led, third hand would automatically play "high" holding the Jack.

obviously a singleton — dummy played the four-spot, East the seven, and South won with the Ace. The Ace, King, and Jack of trumps were then led, West winning with the Queen. On the last two spade plays, East discarded first the *King of Hearts,* then the three-spot.

It was obvious to West that East had gone out of his way first to discard the King, then the three. Why did he not play "normally?" He was employing the suit-preference signal, telling West that it was safe to play back the higher of the two remaining suits, *diamonds* as opposed to clubs (West was known to have no more hearts, and probably no more spades). The reader can see what would have happened had an "undirected" West laid down the Queen of Clubs after winning his Queen of trumps.

This signal, as it was used by Becker and Rapee, is dangerous to employ unless it is handled with care. That is, if East had discarded the *three of hearts* at his first opportunity, and then a higher heart, it would have been wrong for West to assume that East wanted the lower suit (clubs as opposed to diamonds) led. In this case the three-spot would have indicated merely that East had no positive interest in anything — and West would then have been left to his own resources.

On the actual deal, the fact that East was employing the suit-preference signal was *obvious* — because East had gone out of his way to play abnormally, by discarding the King first; whereas normally the three-spot would have been discarded first. It therefore became apparent to West that East was not discarding the King because of his animosity towards nobility, but because he was trying to convey a "high-low" message which the three-spot subsequently completed.

The following type of suit preference will occur infrequently. It is being introduced to illustrate the heights to which imagination can soar when exercised by the expert player.

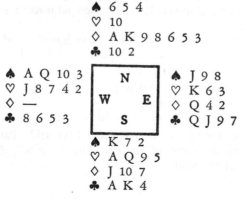

Against South's *three notrump* contract, West opened the heart four, East's King falling to South's Ace. South then laid down the Jack of Diamonds — and West had to discard.

There were three things West knew for sure (1) he did not want hearts led, since South was known to have the Queen (East had played the King at trick one); (2) he wanted spades led, but did not want to discard the unnecessarily high ten-spot as a signal, since it might cost him a trick; and (3), if the defense could not get five tricks in a hurry, they would never get them, in the face of dummy's to-be-established diamond suit. What should West discard then?

West also knew this: that partner dutifully was going to return a heart — and the problem was (1) how to stop him from returning a heart and, (2) how to get him to lead a spade without wasting the ten of spades. An unusual application of the suit-preference signal admirably handled the situation.

At trick two, on the lead of the diamond Jack, West discarded the *Jack of Hearts!* When declarer played low from dummy, East captured the trick with the Queen, and it was now his job to interpret the discard of the heart Jack.

It was perfectly obvious to East that West *did not* want a heart returned. Had West desired a heart play, all he had to do was to discard a spade or a club, and East would have been honor-bound to return a heart. Consequently, a return of a heart was eliminated.

Now why the Jack of Hearts instead of a low one? After all, if West, having opened a heart, had thrown away any heart, it would have said, "Partner, forget my suit. We can't do any business here."

And so East came to the logical conclusion that West was employing the suit-preference signal and that the discard of the Jack of Hearts was signalling: "Partner, return the higher of the two *obvious* suits." (hearts and diamonds being eliminated). East then returned a spade, and the defenders won a magnificent victory.

Had West's spade and club holding been interchanged, West would have discarded the *deuce* of hearts on the diamond lead:

♠ 8 6 5 3
♡ J 8 7 4 2
◇ —
♣ A Q 10 3

The discard of the two of hearts would have said "Partner, abandon hearts. Play back the *lower* of the two obvious suits." And so a club would then have been returned.

CHAPTER XIII

THIRD HAND PLAY: BASIC DEFENSE

(THE DEFENDERS ON THE ATTACK)

A̲LL bridge authorities, both past and present, have referred to *the partner* of the opening leader as "third hand," so we shall do likewise in this chapter. Actually, third hand is that *defender* who plays in third position to any given trick.

There have already been presented some of the reactions of third hand to the opening lead, to wit, the various signals which he gives the opening leader at tricks one and two; and the Rule of Eleven, [1] whereby third hand can often deduce declarer's holding in the suit led. As you are being introduced to this subject of basic elementary defense by third hand, the assumption is made that the only information third hand now possesses comes from the Rule of Eleven, the observation of his own hand and dummy, and the inferences drawn from partner's opening conventional or unconventional lead, which were presented in the chapters on "Opening Leads" and "Signals."

A.   Elementary Defense *Against Notrump* by Third Hand.

1.   The Lead of the Fourth-Highest

The reader at this point has a pretty good idea as to what to play third hand when partner opens a King, a Queen, or a Jack, for this lead is usually made from a sequence in the leader's longest suit. Depending on third hand's holding in the suit led, he will give either a positive, negative, or temporizing signal.

But the most frequent opening lead which third hand will have to consider in notrump will be a low card, the fourth-best from a long suit. In a few of these cases third hand will be able accurately to apply the Rule of Eleven, and come up with the correct answer as to what he should play. Where third hand is unable to apply the Rule to arrive at a "scientific" conclusion as to which card to play, he will almost invariably play *his highest card*. For example, against *three notrump* partner opens the five of clubs:

---

[1] See Chapter XI, page 327.

(1)   ♣ 8 2   (2)   ♣ 6 4 2

5 ♣ led   [N W E S]   ♣ K 7 4 3   5 ♣ led   [N W E S]   ♣ Q 10

In (1) East plays the King; in (2) East plays the Queen.

These two deals might have been:

(1)   ♣ 8 2   (2)   ♣ 6 4 2

♣ Q 10 6 5   [N W E S]   ♣ K 7 4 3   ♣ K 9 8 5 3   [N W E S]   ♣ Q 10

          ♣ A J 9   ♣ A J 7

The reader can see what would happen in each of the two above situations if third hand failed to play his highest card: South would make two club tricks where he was entitled to but one.

Let us see why third hand normally plays high on partner's lead of the fourth-highest. Put yourself in the position of third hand. Since partner has opened his longest suit, your first thought should always be to establish his suit — and to this end you sacrifice your high cards, thereby forcing declarer to win with his highest cards; and, as a consequence, you will be promoting your partner's high cards and tending to establish his low cards. The examples just given illustrate these points. This principle of third hand playing his highest card on partner's opening lead of a low card is familiar to most bridge players as the slogan of days gone by, "third hand high." The principle — as all principles — has its exceptions.

One of the exceptions to "third hand high" is when third hand's highest cards in the suit led are in sequence (A K, K Q, Q J, J 10, etc.). In these cases third hand will play *the lowest card in the sequence.* To illustrate:

(1)   ◇ 7 5 2   (2)   ◇ 8 6

4 ◇ led   [N W E S]   ◇ Q J 7   4 ◇ led   [N W E S]   ◇ J 10 9

In (1), the Jack of Diamonds is the correct play; in (2), the nine of diamonds.

This exception holds true, as a matter of fact, throughout third hand's play even after the first trick. It helps your partner read your hand throughout the entire play.

The reason for the play of the lowest card *of a sequence* by third hand is that in most situations this play will give the leader valuable information as to where the missing high cards in the suit are. Let us look at it from leader's point of view:

◊ 7 5 2

◊ K 10 6 4̲ | N W E S | ◊ J played

West opens the four of diamonds and East's Jack is captured by declarer's Ace. Does not West now know that East still possesses the Queen of Diamonds? If declarer had it, he would have captured the Jack with the Queen instead of wasting the Ace.

Another illustration:

◊ 8 6

◊ A Q 7 4̲ 2 | N W E S | ◊ 9 played

West opens the four of diamonds, and East's nine-spot is taken by declarer's King. Has not West just learned that East still possesses the Jack and ten? Had declarer possessed either of these two cards, he would have captured East's nine-spot as economically as he could, instead of capturing it with the King.

Another exception to "third" hand high arises when dummy comes down with certain combinations of cards including an honor — where, by applying the Rule of Eleven, third hand can come to a logical conclusion that it would be incorrect to play high. These situations will be presented in detail in the next chapter, but one illustration is in order: The contract is *three notrump,* and West opens the five of spades:

♠ Q 10 3

5 ♠ led | N W E S | ♠ K 9 6

On West's lead of the five of spades, dummy plays low. You are East, third hand. Applying the Rule of Eleven, you subtract 5 from 11, leaving 6. This informs you that North, East, and South have six cards higher than the five-spot. Since dummy has two cards higher, and you have three cards higher, you know that declarer has *but one card higher than the five-spot.* Therefore, in this case, you play *the nine-spot,* not the King. If you play the King, no matter what declarer has in spades, you have just established dummy's Queen as a potential winner. And it could be worse, for if declarer happens to have the Ace, you have just created three spade tricks for him by playing the King. The following illustrations present graphically why it is wrong to play the King, and why it is right to play the nine-spot:

(1)   ♠ Q 10 3   (2)   ♠ Q 10 3

♠ A J 8 5 [N/W E/S] ♠ K 9 6   ♠ J 8 7 5 [N/W E/S] ♠ K 9 6

                ♠ 7 4 2   ♠ A 4 2

In (1), the play of the King gives declarer a present of the Queen.

In (2), the play of the King gives declarer three spade tricks instead of two (he will later finesse your partner for the Jack, since he knows that you, with the K J over dummy's Queen, would have played the Jack and not the King).

As a principle, we might state third hand's position as this:

WHENEVER YOUR PARTNER OPENS WHAT IS OBVIOUSLY HIS FOURTH-BEST AGAINST A NOTRUMP CONTRACT, AND THIRD HAND'S TOP CARDS IN THE SUIT ARE NOT IN SEQUENCE, THIRD HAND SHOULD PLAY HIS HIGHEST CARD IF THE DUMMY HAS NO CARD HIGHER THAN THE TEN-SPOT. It is taken for granted, of course, that your highest card is higher than the ten-spot.

The above principle may appear to be complicated. Actually it is simple:

                ♠ 10 7 3

5 ♠ led [N/W E/S] ♠ Q 8 4

Your partner leads the five of spades, and no matter what is played from dummy, automatically you put up your Queen. The holding around the table might have been:

                ♠ 10 7 3

♠ A J 6 5 [N/W E/S] ♠ Q 8 4

                ♠ K 9 2

As was mentioned, in the next chapter there will be presented various specific situations where third hand should not automatically play high.

Let me now briefly mention the most obvious instances where third hand does not play high:

At the risk of being naive, the first situation would be where dummy plays a card higher than any that you possess, in which case it would be absurd for you to waste your highest card:

♠ A 7

3 ♠ led
```
      N
  W       E     ♠ J 5 2
      S
```

If dummy plays the Ace on your partner's lead of the three-spot, for you to put up the Jack would be ridiculous.

Another rather simple situation would be the following:

♢ Q 8 4

5 ♢ led
```
      N
  W       E     ♢ K J 3
      S
```

If the four is played from dummy on your partner's lead of the five-spot, you, of course, play the Jack, and not the King.

2. Returning Partner's Suit in Notrump Contracts.

It was pointed out earlier that when partner leads against a notrump contract, he is leading in his longest suit, and that *your first thought should always be to help establish his suit.* The first step in this direction was to play your highest card, as third hand, thereby forcing declarer to play a higher card to win the trick. In so doing, you tended to promote leader's high cards, and simultaneously to develop his low-cards in that suit into potential winners. The next step in helping to establish partner's suit is *to return his suit as soon as you obtain the lead.* There will be occasional situations where you will not return his suit — where, for instance, you have an excellent suit of your own and you feel that the probability of developing your own suit is greater than the probability of developing partner's suit. But in the great majority of cases, not having a superior suit of your own, you will promptly play back *his* suit. All of which brings us to the vital issue as far as the coordination of the defense is concerned: *which card of his suit do you return?* The answer can be stated as a two-part principle:

(1) Whenever you originally held *two or three* cards of partner's suit, you will always return the higher of the remaining cards.

(2) Whenever you originally held *four or more* of partner's suit, you will return what originally was your fourth-best.

Let's look at the why's and wherefore's of this principle:

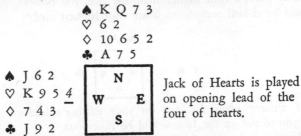

♠ K Q 7 3
♡ 6 2
◊ 10 6 5 2
♣ A 7 5

♠ J 6 2
♡ K 9 5 <u>4</u>
◊ 7 4 3
♣ J 9 2

Jack of Hearts is played on opening lead of the four of hearts.

Against South's *three notrump* contract you open the four of hearts, and your partner's Jack is captured by declarer's Queen. Declarer then plays the King of Diamonds, taken by your partner's Ace. Your partner now returns the *seven* of hearts, declarer puts up *the ten,* which you win with the King. What do you play back?

ANYTHING BUT A HEART WOULD BE AN ACCEPTED ANSWER. Your partner started with a maximum of three hearts — and declarer has at least the A 8 left. If you lead a heart, you are giving declarer a present of a trick.

How do you know that your partner had at most three hearts. Well, if he had held four or more originally, he would have returned his fourth-best, as per principle. *But the seven of hearts could not be his fourth-best, since declarer is known to have the Ace of Hearts* (if third hand held the heart Ace he would have played it at trick one). Therefore partner's seven of hearts is his highest remaining heart, and declarer still has the A 8 remaining. The actual hands might have been:

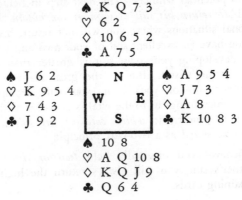

♠ K Q 7 3
♡ 6 2
◊ 10 6 5 2
♣ A 7 5

♠ J 6 2
♡ K 9 5 4
◊ 7 4 3
♣ J 9 2

♠ A 9 5 4
♡ J 7 3
◊ A 8
♣ K 10 8 3

♠ 10 8
♡ A Q 10 8
◊ K Q J 9
♣ Q 6 4

If West returns a third round of hearts declarer will fulfill his contract (three hearts, three diamonds, two clubs, and a spade).

Another illustration as to why "principle" should be followed in returning partner's suit against a notrump contract: (1) the fourth from the highest when holding four or more originally; (2) the higher remaining when holding two or three originally.

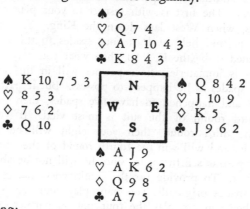

```
                    ♠ 6
                    ♡ Q 7 4
                    ◇ A J 10 4 3
                    ♣ K 8 4 3
 ♠ K 10 7 5 3                    ♠ Q 8 4 2
 ♡ 8 5 3          N              ♡ J 10 9
 ◇ 7 6 2       W     E           ◇ K 5
 ♣ Q 10          S              ♣ J 9 6 2
                    ♠ A J 9
                    ♡ A K 6 2
                    ◇ Q 9 8
                    ♣ A 7 5
```

The bidding:

SOUTH	WEST	NORTH	EAST
One Heart	Pass	Two Diamonds	Pass
Three Notrump	Pass	Pass	Pass

Against South's three notrump contract West opens the *five of spades,* East's Queen falling to declarer's Ace. South then takes a diamond finesse, losing to East's King. East is now going to return a spade. Which one?

If East returns the eight-spot, West will capture declarer's nine with the ten. West will then know that declarer still has the Jack (East would have put up the Jack at trick one if he had held the Q J). But West will not know whether the Jack is protected or not — that is, he will not know whether South started with the A J 9 or the A J 9 x — and if he assumes the Jack is guarded, he will not lay down the King.

From a positive point of view, if third hand returns the eight, West should *not* cash his spade King. Should East play back the eight-spot, West will know that East *did not have* four or more originally, since the eight could not have been the fourth-highest. West will therefore assume that South started with the A J 9 x, in which case to play the King would be to create a winner out of the Jack.

Third hand should return the deuce of spades, his fourth best. When declarer plays the nine, West will win with the ten — and he now can tell that declarer holds only one more spade, the Jack. He will then promptly lay down the King, and drop the Jack.

NOTE: If third hand holds five cards of suit led, he returns his *original* fourth best.

There are two additional, important, points concerning the defense on the above deal. The first is with respect to your play on the third round of spades, when West lays down the King. You, third hand, know that your partner held at least four spades to the King. If his top cards happened to be the K J 10, then what you play on the third round of spades is immaterial, since partner will in this case be able to cash as many spades as he happens to possess. But if partner did not have the Jack, [2] and happened to have five spades, then the card you play on the third round of the suit is most vital. If you play the four-spot on the third round, then your eight will be the highest outstanding spade, and will win the fourth round of the suit. This will "shut out" your partner's fifth spade, since he will not be able to obtain the lead to cash it. To provide for the contingency that partner might have held five spades originally, you must play your *eight-spot* on the third round. Then you can play the four-spot on partner's seven, after which he will have the lead to cash the three-spot. This is known as "unblocking," or getting out of partner's way, which will be discussed later on in "third hand" play.

As you can see, every spade that you played was most significant and meaningful. First, your highest, the Queen, to drive out declarer's stopper; second, the return of the deuce, to inform partner that you originally held four spades; and thirdly, the eight on the King, to "unblock" the suit. This was perfect defense — the maximum possible interchange of information, complete cooperation with partner, and, finally, getting out of his way.

The second major point with respect to the defense is how West knew that third hand's return of the deuce showed four spades as opposed to a doubleton Q 2. After all, in theory, the deuce might have been East's only remaining spade. The answer to this is found in the bidding: if East had held just the two spades (Q 2), declarer would have started with the A J 9 x x. Surely if declarer — no matter how bad a bidder he was — had held these five spades, he would not have opened with one heart, and then have jumped to three notrump over

---

[2] If partner had four spades, missing the Jack, then declarer would have started with the A J 9 x, in which case no matter what you played declarer would make his Jack of Spades.

North's two diamond response. Somewhere along the line he would have bid spades. So, since South could not have held five spades, then third hand's return of the deuce must have been his fourth-best — and West would then know that East had started with exactly four spades.

Almost always the defenders will have a clue analogous to the above, which will be derived from an interpretation of the opponents' bidding. So, if you play correctly as third hand, your partner will invariably arrive at the proper conclusion as to the precise situation that exists with respect to his suit.

There is just one type of exception to returning the fourth-best of partner's suit when you hold four cards in his suit. This exception occurs when you possess a sequence of three cards in his suit, including an honor. In these cases your correct return is to play back your highest card, to avoid blocking partner's suit. To illustrate:

(1)	(2)	(3)
♠ K Q J 5	♠ Q J 10 5	♠ J 10 9 3

In each of the above three situations, if partner opens his fourth-best spade against a notrump contract, you play the bottom card in your sequence as per principle — in (1) the Jack; in (2), the 10; in (3), the nine. Should you ultimately obtain the lead, *you will play back the top card in your sequence,* for if you play back the fourth-best, you are a cinch to block partner's suit if partner held five spades originally.

$$\text{♠ 8 3}$$

♠ A 7 6 _4_ 2 | N W E S | ♠ Q J _10_ 5

♠ K 9

The play to the first trick has gone: four of spades, three-spot from dummy, ten by East, and King by South. If when you obtain the lead (East), you return your fourth-best, the five-spot, partner's Ace will be compelled to capture declarer's nine. The suit will now be blocked, and West will be unable to cash his fifth spade. Your correct play then is to return the Queen.

To conclude the general point of returning partner's suit at notrump — unless you can *prove* that his suit cannot be established — let me present the following deal:

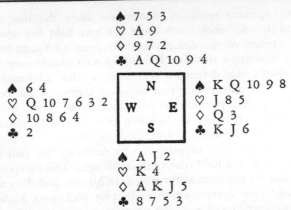

♠ 7 5 3
♡ A 9
◇ 9 7 2
♣ A Q 10 9 4

♠ 6 4
♡ Q 10 7 6 3 2
◇ 10 8 6 4
♣ 2

N
W   E
S

♠ K Q 10 9 8
♡ J 8 5
◇ Q 3
♣ K J 6

♠ A J 2
♡ K 4
◇ A K J 5
♣ 8 7 5 3

South became the declarer at *three notrump,* against which West opened the heart six, East's Jack being taken by declarer's King. Declarer then played the eight of clubs and let it ride, East's Jack winning.

When the deal was actually played, East, who evidently had fallen in love with his spade suit, shifted to the King of Spades which declarer captured with the Ace. It was now smooth sailing for declarer. He again led a club, losing to East's King. East then cashed his Queen of Spades, but the defenders were finished.

Had East applied the Rule of Eleven, he unhesitatingly would have returned the eight of hearts at trick two. West had opened the six of hearts, his fourth-best. Since the A 9 were in dummy, with East having the J 8, and declarer having won the opening lead with the King, East should have known that West had all the missing high-cards in hearts (11 minus 6 equals 5). By returning a heart, to be taken by dummy's Ace, all of West's hearts would then be established — and East had the five of hearts left, to return to West's hearts.

3. "Unblocking" By Third Hand Against Notrump Contracts.

By "unblocking" is meant getting out of partner's way so that he can cash all the established, or to-be-established cards in his suit. This was illustrated a few pages back when East "unblocked" with his eight of spades from Q 8 4 2. Let us look at a few standard unblocking situations:

◇ A K 5

◇ 10 8 7 4 2

N
W   E
S

◇ Q J 3

◇ 9 6

Partner opens the four of diamonds against South's *three notrump* contract, and dummy's King is put up. On the King you should play the Queen, accomplishing thereby a two-fold purpose: (1) to get your partner to continue the suit, and (2) getting out of his way by "unblocking." There is no doubt about the fact that partner is leading from a long suit. Therefore, declarer has very few diamonds. If you play your three-spot on the first trick, retaining your Q J, when you win the third round with the Queen you will be unable to get your partner into the lead for him to cash his diamonds (also, if you play your three on the first round, partner will probably never continue the suit, in the face of your discouraging signal). Consequently, to maintain communication between the defending hands, you should first play your Queen on the King and on the next lead of that suit, "sacrifice" your Jack on the Ace. This leaves you with the three-spot, and should either of you obtain the lead, partner's remaining diamonds will become cashable.

The identical unblocking principle is similarly applied in the following "set" situations with dummy possessing low cards consisting of either a singleton, a doubleton, or a tripleton:

(1) ♠ Q J 10 7 5

```
      N
  W       E
      S
```
(a) A 4 ... (b) K 4

(2) ♠ J 10 9 7 5

```
      N
  W       E
      S
```
(a) Q 4 ... (b) K 4

In (1), when your partner leads the Queen, you play the Ace or King, whichever you happen to have.

In (2), when your partner leads the Jack, you put up the Queen or King, whichever you happen to possess.

The logic behind the unblocking in the two above cases is apparent: partner is leading from a sequence in his long suit, and you must make haste to get out of his way, so that he can get to establish and cash his suit. If you do not unblock, here is what will generally happen:

```
              ♠ 9 3 2
                  N
♠ Q J 10 7 5   W       E   ♠ K 4
                  S
              ♠ A 8 6
```

Partner opens the Queen of Spades against a notrump contract, and let us assume that you play low and declarer takes the trick with his Ace. Can you see that if either of you obtains the lead that the spade suit is blocked? If declarer does not take the first trick — employing the hold-up play — then presumably he knows enough not to take your King on the second round of that suit — and now the spade suit will never become established, for you will have no spade to return.

If, however, on the lead of the Queen, you properly unblock by playing your King, partner's suit will easily become established whether declarer holds up his Ace or not.

An obvious exception to "unblocking" occurs when the play will create a trick for declarer, as in the following situation:

$$\Diamond \ 9\ 8\ 5\ 2$$

$$\Diamond \ Q\ J\ 10\ 7\ 6 \qquad \begin{array}{c} N \\ W \quad E \\ S \end{array} \qquad \Diamond \ K\ 4$$

$$\Diamond \ A\ 3$$

Partner opens the Diamond Queen. If you play your King, dummy's nine-spot will be promoted into a trick. So you play low and hope for the best.

B.   Elementary Defense *Against A Suit Contract* by Third Hand.

The greater part of this subject has already been covered in the chapter on "signals." Much of what applies to third hand defending against notrump also applies to his defense against a suit contract. That is, third hand will, on the opening lead of an honor, give either a positive, negative, or temporizing signal; he will play "third hand high" on the lead of a low card from partner unless his judgment dictates otherwise; he will "unblock" when necessary, although the necessity for the use of this play occurs far less frequently against a suit contract than it does against notrump (partner can very seldom cash a long suit against a trump contract, since declarer's trumps become the controlling factor; so, to "unblock" to help partner establish his suit loses most of its efficacy).

The major point of divergence between third hand's defense against a suit contract as opposed to his defense against a notrump contract is the question of the "automatic" return of partner's suit. In notrump, partner usually opens his long suit, and third hand cooperates in trying to establish that suit by playing it back at the first opportunity. As was mentioned in the preceding paragraph, it is generally futile to try to establish a long suit against a suit declaration, for by the time you get it established declarer will get around to trumping it.

So, when partner opens what appears to be his fourth-highest, and you as third hand obtain the lead, you do not categorically return your partner's suit. Your clue as to what to play back will usually be determined by looking at dummy and your own hand. Before presenting illustrations of this point of not mechanically returning partner's suit, I should like to say a few general words about this subject.

In a suit contract, the time element tends to militate against the defending side. At notrump, on the other hand, the defenders are willing and happy to sacrifice a trick earlier in the play to establish their "cashable" suit. At a suit contract, of course, there is a natural reluctance to give away a trick in order to develop a suit which will not become cashable, since declarer's trumps will control the entire hand. An immediate shift to a suit other than partner's therefore often becomes necessary, since any postponement of the play is apt to lose "time," and is apt to give declarer that time for him to establish his own side suit. Let us look at three deals covering this matter of not returning partner's suit against a trump declaration:

1.

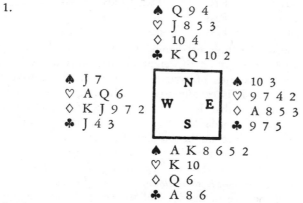

South has arrived at a *four spade* contract, and West elects to open the seven of diamonds which you win with the Ace. Had the contract been notrump, you would naturally return your fourth-best diamond. But in this case such a return would be futile even if partner held the diamond King, for it is obvious that the defenders can never make more than two diamond tricks. Should you return a diamond, and partner wins with the King, he will have to lead to trick three and will not be able to lead any card which can further your combined cause. So, upon winning the first trick, East is compelled to look for new worlds to conquer.

Glancing at the dummy, third hand can perceive that if partner has either a trump trick or the Ace of Clubs (or both), he cannot be done out of them. By elimination then, the heart suit offers the best hope, for it appears to be declarer's weakest suit. Therefore, you lead a heart — and the defenders take two hearts and two diamonds. Had diamonds been continued at trick two declarer would have fulfilled his contract.

2.

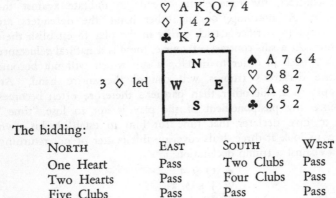

```
                    ♠ 8 5
                    ♡ A K Q 7 4
                    ◇ J 4 2
                    ♣ K 7 3
                              ♠ A 7 6 4
                  N           ♡ 9 8 2
  3 ◇ led    W        E       ◇ A 8 7
                  S           ♣ 6 5 2
```

The bidding:

NORTH	EAST	SOUTH	WEST
One Heart	Pass	Two Clubs	Pass
Two Hearts	Pass	Four Clubs	Pass
Five Clubs	Pass	Pass	Pass

Your partner opens the three of diamonds, which you take with the Ace. If you have your finger on the eight of diamonds to lead back, take it off quickly! It is true, of course, that partner might have the King of Diamonds, but it is equally true that he might not. And, if declarer happens to have that King, you are lost, for declarer will eventually get rid of his spade losers on dummy's hearts. Surely he figures to do the latter, since in the bidding he has repudiated hearts. What to return, a diamond or a spade? The proper play is to lay down the Ace of Spades. Why, you may ask? *Because partner can then give you a signal as to whether spades or diamonds should be continued.*

Suppose you lead the Ace of Spades and partner plays the ten on it, a most encouraging high-card. He will then be asking for a spade continuation. Suppose on your Spade Ace he plays the most discouraging two of spades (or some similarly discouraging low-card). He would then be renouncing any interest in the spade suit. In this latter case, you would then return his diamond suit. What is his hand? Take your choice of these two:

(1)	(2)
♠ K 10 9 2	♠ Q 10 9 2
♡ 10 6 5 3	♡ 10 6 5 3
◇ Q 10 5 3	◇ K 10 5 3
♣ 8	♣ 8

The actual deal was:

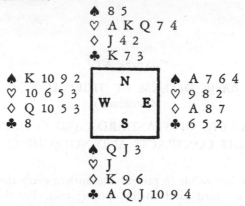

```
                    ♠ 8 5
                    ♡ A K Q 7 4
                    ◇ J 4 2
                    ♣ K 7 3
    ♠ K 10 9 2      ┌─────────┐      ♠ A 7 6 4
    ♡ 10 6 5 3      │    N    │      ♡ 9 8 2
    ◇ Q 10 5 3      │  W   E  │      ◇ A 8 7
    ♣ 8            │    S    │      ♣ 6 5 2
                    └─────────┘
                    ♠ Q J 3
                    ♡ J
                    ◇ K 9 6
                    ♣ A Q J 10 9 4
```

3. The final illustration on the return or non-return of partner's suit:

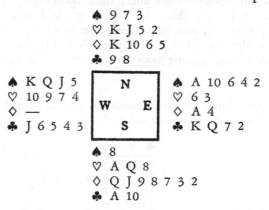

```
                    ♠ 9 7 3
                    ♡ K J 5 2
                    ◇ K 10 6 5
                    ♣ 9 8
    ♠ K Q J 5       ┌─────────┐      ♠ A 10 6 4 2
    ♡ 10 9 7 4      │    N    │      ♡ 6 3
    ◇ —            │  W   E  │      ◇ A 4
    ♣ J 6 5 4 3     │    S    │      ♣ K Q 7 2
                    └─────────┘
                    ♠ 8
                    ♡ A Q 8
                    ◇ Q J 9 8 7 3 2
                    ♣ A 10
```

South has arrived at a *five diamond* contract, against which your partner opens the King of Spades. You are sitting East, and you feel reasonably sure that you can defeat declarer's contract by cashing a spade, a club and a diamond — if you can establish a club trick. So you overtake partner's Spade King with your Ace, and shift to the King of Clubs. And that's that.

If you let partner's spade King win, there is no way on earth (and no reason on earth) for him to know that a club shift is desired. Why then not take control and defeat declarer all by yourself? Your partner will not be offended because you took his King with your Ace. After all, he gets paid just as much as you do when declarer suffers a penalty.

BASIC DEFENSE BY THIRD HAND
(Continued)

THE HANDLING OF STANDARD CARD COMBINATIONS
AGAINST SUIT CONTRACTS AND NOTRUMP CONTRACTS

I T is obviously impossible to present and analyze every specific situation
that will confront third hand on the opening lead. For this to be done
a volume would have to be written introducing the varying "external"
situations which influence and affect third hand's play (the bidding,
the dummy, etc.). But there are certain standard card combinations
that come up time and time again, which are in reality "pat" situations.
These the reader should learn as principles. Let us look at these
situations, defending against both suit contracts and against notrump
contracts.

1. You are sitting East, and South has arrived at a *heart* contract.
Your partner opens the *three of spades*.

♠ K 8 2

3 ♠ led ┌─────┐ ♠ A J 5
        │ N │
        │W   E│
        │ S │
        └─────┘

On partner's lead of the spade three, the deuce is played from dummy.
Your correct play is to put up the *Jack*. Partner's lead of the three-spot
is his fourth-best, and seeing the deuce in dummy, you know that
declarer started with exactly three spades. Where is the spade Queen?
Either partner has it or declarer does. If partner has it, then your play
of the Jack has gained a trick. If declarer has the Queen, then your
play of the Jack has not lost a thing, although declarer's Queen will
capture your Jack. Assuming declarer had the Queen, had you taken
your Ace at trick one, would you not have created *two future tricks* for
declarer, one with dummy's King and one with declarer's Queen? Putting
both of these situations in diagram form:

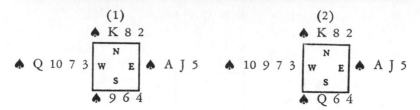

In (1), if you put up your Ace, you are giving declarer a present of dummy's King. If you correctly play the Jack, dummy's King will never win a trick.

In (2), if you put up your Ace, declarer will win two future tricks with the Queen and King. If you put up your Jack, he will make just one trick, since your Ace will capture dummy's King. In this situation you can never prevent declarer from winning *one* spade trick. But you can stop him from winning two tricks.

The identical situation is the following, the Queen being substituted for the King:

$$\spadesuit \text{ Q 8 2}$$

3 ♠ led   [N / W E / S]   ♠ A J 5

Your partner leads the three of spades, a low one is played from dummy, and, as before, your correct play is the Jack. No matter who has the King, your play of the Jack cannot be a losing play. If your partner has the King, the play of the Jack has gained a trick. If declarer has the King, your play of the Jack will probably have held declarer to just one winner in the suit, instead of the two he would automatically have secured had you played your Ace. Here is the specific situation, as it might have been:

$$\spadesuit \text{ Q 8 2}$$

♠ K 10 7 3   [N / W E / S]   ♠ A J 5

$$\spadesuit \text{ 9 6 4}$$

In the above diagram, if you put up the Jack, will you not make three tricks? If you put up your Ace, have you not lost a trick, since dummy's Queen has just been promoted into a winner?

A deal that arose a few years ago will vividly illustrate why the finesse against dummy's Queen (or King) is proper:

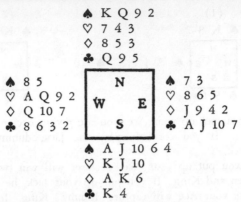

Against South's *four spade* contract West elected to open the two of clubs, the five-spot was played from dummy, and East took his Ace. Declarer's contract was now guaranteed, for he was later able to discard his losing diamond on dummy's Queen of Clubs. Had East correctly put up his ten of clubs, declarer's King would have captured the trick, but there would then have been no way for him to avoid the loss of a club trick, a diamond, and two heart tricks.

An analogous situation is the following, which is a little rougher to handle:

Your partner leads the *spade two* against a *heart* contract by South, and the four is played from dummy. Should you play the Ace or Jack?

Well, assuming that partner is leading his fourth-best, you know that partner has exactly four spades and that declarer has a singleton. *That singleton may or may not be the King.* What do you have to guide you? Only mathematics and a business instinct. Take the four remaining spades, shuffle them up, and give your partner three of them and give declarer the remaining spade. Who was given the King? The odds are three to one that your partner has it. And so, in the above situation, by putting up the Jack you will win the trick three times out of four.

Pitted against mathematics, however, is the question of the "business instinct." The play of the Jack is risky against a suit contract, for if it loses to declarer's singleton King, you will never win a trick in the spade suit, since declarer will trump away your Ace on the next round of the suit. If, however, you play your Ace (instead of the Jack), and it captures only a low card (assuming declarer's singleton was not the King), you have not lost much for you never could have secured more than one trick in the suit. By playing the Ace, you assure yourself of at least one trick.

What is the principle, then, in this situation against a *suit contract.* The expert player says: "Take your Ace!" Against a notrump contract, the play of the Jack would be the only proper play, for you are interested in developing your suit and you are willing to concede a trick to further that end.

2. Another situation which occurs quite regularly is the following:

Against a *diamond* contract your partner opens the *four of hearts,* and you are viewing this set-up:

♡ Q 8 3

4 ♡ led
```
        N
    W       E    ♡ K 10 2
        S
```

On your partner's lead of the four of hearts, the three is played from dummy. What do you play? The answer is the *ten-spot!* The King would be 100% wrong!

Let us look at the various situations that might exist in the heart suit, based on his opening lead of the four-spot. Seeing the two in your own hand, and the three in dummy, you know that partner's fourth-best lead was based on precisely four hearts (he had three higher, and none lower). Suppose declarer has the A x x. Will not your ten-spot force his Ace, and will not your King eventually capture dummy's Queen?

♡ Q 8 3

♡ J 9 6 4
```
        N
    W       E    ♡ K 10 2
        S
```
♡ A 7 5

If you play the King in the above situation, you will create a winner out of dummy's Queen.

Suppose declarer has the A J x. By playing the King you are giving declarer *three* heart tricks where he is entitled to but two:

♡ Q 8 3

♡ 9 7 6 4
```
        N
    W       E    ♡ K 10 2
        S
```
♡ A J 5

Or suppose declarer had the J x x (most unlikely, since your "learned" partner would not be leading the four-spot from the A x x x against a suit contract). Even in this almost impossible situation would you not make your two heart tricks later on with the Ace and King? And, should you incorrectly play your King, would you be able to prevent declarer from ultimately winning a heart trick if he has the J x x? Therefore it just cannot be right to play the King from the above combination, for it stands only to lose, never to gain.

If your "learned" partner is of the type who is wont to lead away from Aces against suit contracts, he probably also erroneously leads away from A J x x on occasion. Can you see in the following illustration that if you play the King it will cost you a trick, whereas if you put up the ten-spot you will pick up the entire suit?

♡ Q 8 3

♡ A J 6 4
| N |
| W   E |
| S |
♡ K 10 2

♡ 9 7 5

The play of the ten-spot is equally applicable — if not more so — in defending against notrump contracts. By playing the ten-spot you put yourself in the position where you stand to gain, and cannot lose. The worst that can happen is that you will break even.

3.   There are two other similar situations which occur quite often:

(a)   The contract is, let us say, four diamonds, and your partner opens the *three of clubs:*

♣ Q 10 9

3 ♣ led
| N |
| W   E |
| S |
♣ K 8 7

On the lead of the three of clubs the nine-spot is played from dummy. The normal reaction would be to play the King — and this would cost the "normal reactor" a trick!

Surely your partner is not underleading the club Ace against a suit contract? Is it not true, then, that declarer has the Ace of Clubs? (Either A x, or A x x, by the Rule of Eleven). If you play the King, will declarer not take it with the Ace after which he later will be able to finesse your partner for the Jack and make three club tricks? Your correct play is to put up the *seven-spot.* Here are the actual hands, as they might have been:

♣ Q 10 9

♣ J 6 4 3   ♣ K 8 7

♣ A 5 2

If you play the seven-spot, all declarer can make is two club tricks.

Incidentally, if your partner does not have the Jack, then declarer will have the A J x, in which case it makes no difference whether you play the King or not — declarer will in this situation always be able to make three club tricks by finessing you for the King.

(b)   The contract is *four hearts,* and your partner opens the three of spades:

♠ A 10 6

3 ♠ led   ♠ J 8 2

On the three, the six-spot is played from dummy. What do you play? Much as you may dislike it, you should play the *eight-spot,* not the Jack.

A moment's reflection will make you realize that partner could not have the K Q of spades, for if he did he would have opened the King. Therefore declarer has either the King or Queen. Should you put up the Jack, declarer will capture it with the King or Queen (whichever he has), after which he will be able to finesse dummy's ten-spot and make three spade tricks. For instance:

(1)	(2)
♠ A 10 6	♠ A 10 6
♠ Q 9 5 3 ♠ J 8 2	♠ K 9 5 3 ♠ J 8 2
♠ K 7 4	♠ Q 7 4

All the illustrations presented thus far have been situations where your partner has opened his fourth-highest from what was obviously a four-card suit. Also, in all situations, the final contract has been in a *suit declaration* with just a brief mention of notrump. Let us take a glance at what third hand's play would be if the final contract were notrump; or if the leader had led from what might have been a five-card suit against both a suit declaration and notrump.

With respect to third hand's plays against *notrump* in the identical situations previously presented, *they would be exactly the same,* but with even more assurance. For example:

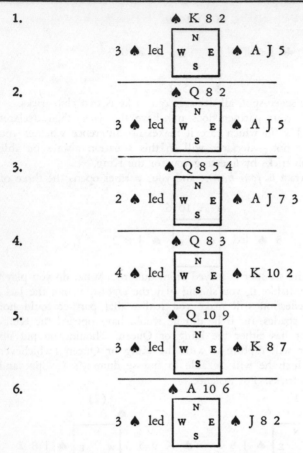

1.
♠ K 8 2

3 ♠ led [N W E S] ♠ A J 5

2.
♠ Q 8 2

3 ♠ led [N W E S] ♠ A J 5

3.
♠ Q 8 5 4

2 ♠ led [N W E S] ♠ A J 7 3

4.
♠ Q 8 3

4 ♠ led [N W E S] ♠ K 10 2

5.
♠ Q 10 9

3 ♠ led [N W E S] ♠ K 8 7

6.
♠ A 10 6

3 ♠ led [N W E S] ♠ J 8 2

In five of the above six illustrative situations, had the contract been notrump, East would make the same play as he did against a suit contract. That is, in (1) and (2), upon the lead of the low spade from partner, with dummy playing low, East would put up the Jack. In (4), he would play the ten-spot; in (5), the seven; and in (6), the eight-spot. In (3), he would automatically put up the Jack, whereas against a suit contract he would have tended to play the Ace, for fear that if he did not, declarer might make a singleton King. Against a notrump contract, however, if declarer happened to have a singleton King, there would be no way of preventing him from making a trick in that suit; and, if he did, the rest of the suit would belong to the defenders. To repeat a point that was made earlier: when the contract is notrump, the defenders are willing to give up a trick early in the play if in so doing they can establish their suit.

Let us now take the same six types of situations and see what third hand would have done if partner had led from what might have been a five-card suit *against a suit declaration.* (Against a notrump declaration, if partner had led from what might have been a five-card suit, third hand would have made the same six plays which were given in the preceding paragraph).

(1)

♠ K 8 2

4 ♠ led

```
     N
 W       E
     S
```

♠ A J 5

The contract is *four hearts,* and your partner opens the four of spades upon which the deuce is played from dummy. As before, you will play your Jack. Even if partner has five spades (he might have led the four-spot, as his fourth-best, from 10 9 7 4 2), declarer would have to have at least two spades, and your Ace could not be lost.

(2)

♠ Q 8 2

4 ♠ led

```
     N
 W       E
     S
```

♠ A J 5

This is exactly the same as (1). Your Ace cannot be lost, and if your partner is leading from the King, you will then be able to cash the maximum possible number of tricks.

(3)

♠ Q 8 5 4

6 ♠ led

```
     N
 W       E
     S
```

♠ A J 7 3

Your partner leads the six of spades, which may mean any one of three things; (1) a doubleton; (2) fourth-best of four spades; (3) fourth-best of five spades. NO MATTER WHICH OF THE THREE THE SIX-SPOT COMES FROM, THE PLAY OF THE JACK IS THE CORRECT PLAY.

If it came from a doubleton 6 2, then by putting up the Jack communication between the two hands is maintained, and if either partner can obtain the lead before trumps are drawn, West will be able to ruff the third round of that suit after East cashes his Ace of Spades and then plays another spade.

If the lead of the six-spot is fourth best from either four or five spades, then the Jack cannot be beaten by a higher spade in declarer's hand. By the Rule of Eleven, declarer can have no spade higher than the six-spot.

The reader, incidentally, may raise the question of the six being a singleton, in which case the winning play would be to take the Ace and return a spade for partner to ruff. In most cases the bidding will prove that it could not have been a singleton — if it were, declarer would have held the K 10 9 3 of the suit, and he would have bid it somewhere along the line. And, if some year it turns out that declarer failed to bid the aforementioned four-card spade suit, then you pay off to what did not figure to be.

(4)

♠ Q 8 3

N
W   E
S

4 ♠ led

♠ K 10 2

No matter whether West is leading the four-spot from a four-card suit or anything else, the play of the ten-spot on dummy's low one has to be the proper play. By playing the King you can only stand to lose, never to gain. Again, the four could not be a singleton lead: if it were, declarer would be holding a suit of A J 9 x x x, which is an impossibility since the suit has never been bid.

(5)

♠ Q 10 9

N
W   E
S

4 ♠ led

♠ K 8 7

Partner leads the four-spot, the nine is played from dummy, and your correct play is automatically to play the seven-spot. As in (3) and (4), the low card could not be from a singleton or a doubleton. If it is from a worthless tripleton (4 3 2), then your King is lost whether you play it or not (declarer would then have held the A J x x).

(6)

♠ A 10 6

N
W   E
S

5 ♠ led

♠ J 8 2

On the play of a low spade from dummy you will again play the eight-spot. The play of the Jack can never be the winning play.

4. Another "stock" situation, of frequent occurrence:

Your partner leads the four of clubs against South's *heart* contract:

♣ Q 8 6 5

4 ♣ led

| N |
| W E |
| S |

♣ A J 10 3

If partner is leading his fourth-best, he had three cards higher than the four-spot. Only one card is unaccounted for: *the deuce.* Either declarer has that card, or partner has it, in which case declarer is void of clubs. So whatever low card dummy plays, you put up the ten.

♣ Q 8 6 5

♣ K 9 7 4

| N |
| W E |
| S |

♣ A J 10 3

♣ 2

♣ Q 8 6 5

♣ K 9 7 4 2

| N |
| W E |
| S |

♣ A J 10 3

♣ —

If partner's four-spot were a singleton, then it may appear that the winning play would be to take the Ace and return a club for him to trump. Actually, this will not gain you a trick, for by playing the ten-spot, you would still make two club tricks. To illustrate:

♣ Q 8 6 5

♣ 4

| N |
| W E |
| S |

♣ A J 10 3

♣ K 9 7 2

Should you take your Ace and return a club for partner to trump, will not declarer make two club tricks with his King and Queen?

And, if partner's four of clubs is part of a doubleton (say 4 2), by playing the ten you assure yourself of two club tricks. If you take the Ace and return a club, you will never make more than one trick.

So, in this situation, as in the others, by playing the Ace at trick one you can never be making the winning play. By playing the ten, you can never be making the losing play.

5. The final "pat" situation: The contract is *four spades* and your partner leads the two of hearts:

♡ A Q 5

```
          N
2 ♡ led  W   E   ♡ K 10 4
          S
```

On the lead of the two of hearts, the five is put up from dummy. What do you play?

If you play the King you are making a "normal" play — *but it is wrong!* How do you interpret partner's lead? Is it not the fourth-best? Does he not have exactly four hearts. Must not one of these two situations exist:

(1)   ♡ A Q x   **(2)**   ♡ A Q x

```
               N                          N
♡ x x x x_  W   E  ♡ K 10 x  ♡ J x x x_ W   E  ♡ K 10 x
               S                          S
        ♡ J x x                      ♡ x x x
```

Is it not true that if you play the King, declarer will always make two heart tricks? But if you put up the ten-spot, and situation (2) exists, do you not hold declarer to one heart trick? In other words, knowing that declarer has three hearts, one of which may (or may not) be the Jack, is not the ten-spot the proper play?

Had your partner led the *three* of hearts, then you would have had a problem, for the three of hearts might have been from a five-card suit (9 8 6 3 2). In this case, declarer would have held the J x, and you might then never make your King of Hearts. What to do in this case, no expert could say with absolute certainty. But in the first situation presented, where partner leads what is obviously his fourth-best of just four of the suit, then the ten-spot must be the only proper play.

A word of advice with reference to the contents of this chapter:

Try to learn the specific situations presented, so that when the occasion for their use arises, you will not have to stop and think about what to do. The reason for this statement can be evidenced from the last illustration. If you hesitate, and then reluctantly play the ten-spot, it may cost you a trick; if you play the ten-spot quickly, you may well pick up a trick. Suppose declarer happened to have the J x (when your partner led from a five-card suit). When he would capture your quickly-played ten-spot with the Jack, would he not possibly assume that your partner held the King? And would he not then finesse your partner for the King, enabling you to capture dummy's Queen?

CHAPTER XV

THIRD HAND DEFENSIVE PLAY IN ACTUAL COMPETITION [1]

T HE following deals were all either observed or encountered by me in rubber-bridge games or in tournaments. The reader will do well to study each specific third hand defensive situation. In each deal South has been made the declarer to make reading easier.

1.

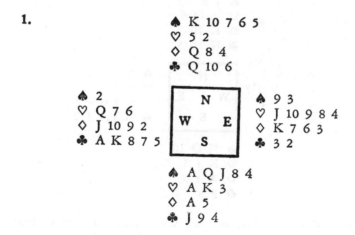

```
                    ♠ K 10 7 6 5
                    ♡ 5 2
                    ◊ Q 8 4
                    ♣ Q 10 6
      ♠ 2                            ♠ 9 3
      ♡ Q 7 6          N             ♡ J 10 9 8 4
      ◊ J 10 9 2    W     E          ◊ K 7 6 3
      ♣ A K 8 7 5      S             ♣ 3 2
                    ♠ A Q J 8 4
                    ♡ A K 3
                    ◊ A 5
                    ♣ J 9 4
```

Against South's *four spade* contract, West opened the King of Clubs, East playing the three-spot with South dropping the Jack. An unobservant West would probably have then shifted to the Diamond Jack, thereby allowing declarer to fulfill his contract.

---

[1] In this chapter "third hand" is considered to be not only the partner of the opening leader, but also, in the more all-inclusive sense, the *defender* who plays as the third hand to any given trick.

399

But our West player, John Kunkel of Miami Beach, Florida, did not become the excellent bridge player that he is by not being observant. *The two of clubs was missing!* Either declarer still had that card, or third hand had initiated a signal with the three-spot. John now led his club Ace, upon which East played the missing two. A third round of clubs was of course ruffed by East, and declarer was ultimately defeated.

From third hand's point of view, it would have been "nicer" to have held the 8 2 of clubs instead of the 3 2, so that a "violent" signal could have been given. But as you will learn, you signal with what is dealt you — and trust that your partner is looking for a signal.

2. The next deal arose in a tournament. The safety of the contract was of no concern, since it was guaranteed. What was involved was the question of an overtrick, of paramount importance in match point play.

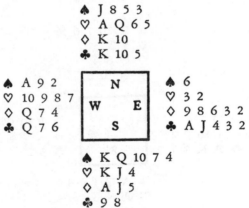

♠ J 8 5 3
♥ A Q 6 5
♦ K 10
♣ K 10 5

♠ A 9 2   ♠ 6
♥ 10 9 8 7   ♥ 3 2
♦ Q 7 4   ♦ 9 8 6 3 2
♣ Q 7 6   ♣ A J 4 3 2

♠ K Q 10 7 4
♥ K J 4
♦ A J 5
♣ 9 8

Against South's *four spade* contract West opened the ten of hearts, dummy's five was played, East followed with *the deuce,* and South captured the trick with the Jack. The King of Spades was then led, everybody following with low cards. Next came the Queen of Spades, West taking his Ace. On this trick East discarded the *two of diamonds.* West now shifted to a club and defenders took two club tricks. Had West not played a club, declarer would have discarded a club on dummy's fourth heart, thereby making an overtrick.

What motivated West to shift to a club? A simple matter, really. That East had no interest in hearts was obvious at trick one; that he had no interest in trumps was apparent at trick two; that he did not care for diamonds was evident at trick three, when East gave the negative signal of the deuce. Therefore, by elimination, West led a club.

3.

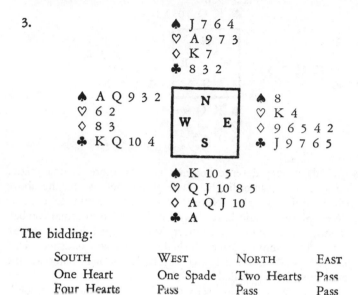

♠ J 7 6 4
♡ A 9 7 3
◇ K 7
♣ 8 3 2

♠ A Q 9 3 2
♡ 6 2
◇ 8 3
♣ K Q 10 4

♠ 8
♡ K 4
◇ 9 6 5 4 2
♣ J 9 7 6 5

♠ K 10 5
♡ Q J 10 8 5
◇ A Q J 10
♣ A

The bidding:

SOUTH	WEST	NORTH	EAST
One Heart	One Spade	Two Hearts	Pass
Four Hearts	Pass	Pass	Pass

West's opening lead was the King of Clubs, taken by declarer's Ace. Declarer now took the trump finesse, losing to East's King. [2] East then returned his eight of spades, the suit which his partner had bid, South put up his ten-spot, and West captured the trick with the Queen.

West is now faced with a serious problem. Should he cash his established Queen of Clubs, or should he cash the Ace of Spades? On the face of it — from an objective point of view, not by looking at all four hands — the Queen of Clubs seems to be the superior play, since there are more clubs left in circulation than there are spades. But, . . .

East has returned the eight of spades, denying possession of the King '(if East had the K 8 5, he would have led the five. If he had a doubleton K 8, he would have played the King). One thing is certain, therefore. Declarer still holds the King of Spades.

So West cashed his Ace — and when East showed out, West led a third spade for East to trump.

---

[2] Had declarer avoided the finesse, and drawn trumps by playing the Ace and another heart, he would have guaranteed his contract.

4.

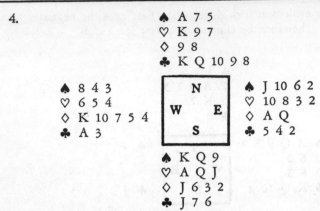

         ♠ A 7 5
         ♡ K 9 7
         ◊ 9 8
         ♣ K Q 10 9 8

♠ 8 4 3   ♠ J 10 6 2
♡ 6 5 4   N   ♡ 10 8 3 2
◊ K 10 7 5 4   W   E   ◊ A Q
♣ A 3   S   ♣ 5 4 2

         ♠ K Q 9
         ♡ A Q J
         ◊ J 6 3 2
         ♣ J 7 6

On many deals proper defense becomes nothing more than a matter
of observing and acting accordingly. Look at the defense of the above
hand, which is quite simple. Nevertheless I am certain that many
third-hand West players would have slipped had it arisen in actual combat.

Against South's *three notrump* contract, West opened his fourth-best
diamond, East's Ace winning, after which the Queen was returned. Had
West played low, waiting for East to play back another diamond, the
contract would have been fulfilled.

But an observant West, having seen the *eight and nine* of diamonds
in dummy, would overtake the Queen with the King and promptly play
the ten of diamonds back, forcing the Jack. The defenders would then
make four diamonds and one club.

Admittedly, if East had a third diamond, then West could defeat
declarer two tricks. But West, perceiving victory in his grasp, should
elect not to indulge in this dangerous wishful thinking.

5.

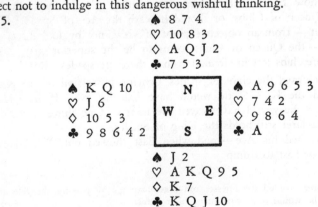

         ♠ 8 7 4
         ♡ 10 8 3
         ◊ A Q J 2
         ♣ 7 5 3

♠ K Q 10   ♠ A 9 6 5 3
♡ J 6   N   ♡ 7 4 2
◊ 10 5 3   W   E   ◊ 9 8 6 4
♣ 9 8 6 4 2   S   ♣ A

         ♠ J 2
         ♡ A K Q 9 5
         ◊ K 7
         ♣ K Q J 10

Against South's *four heart* contract, West opened the spade King, which East overtook with the Ace. Third hand then cashed the club Ace, after which he led another spade, West's Queen winning. West now played a club, and East trumped for the setting trick.

Let us examine what happened. From East's point of view, he wanted to trump a club and knew that he could do so if he could get the Ace of Clubs out of the way — and could convey that information to his partner. When he overtook West's King with his Ace, undoubtedly everybody at the table looked at him, for such things are not done, except where you are dealt a singleton Ace and have no choice. He then played the Ace of Clubs, after which he led a spade to partner's known Queen. It now became evident that East did not overtake by necessity (a singleton Ace), since he had just shown up with another spade. Therefore he must have taken the King with the Ace *for a purpose:* to lead the Ace of Clubs. Hence West played back a club, realizing that surely East did not want a spade returned, for if he did *he* could have continued spades himself. Since East must have "switched" the defense for a purpose — to play clubs — West followed this switch in defense.

6.

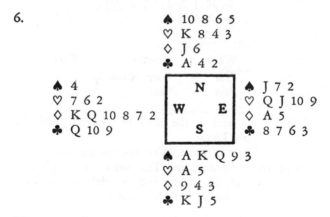

```
              ♠ 10 8 6 5
              ♡ K 8 4 3
              ◇ J 6
              ♣ A 4 2

  ♠ 4              N              ♠ J 7 2
  ♡ 7 6 2                         ♡ Q J 10 9
  ◇ K Q 10 8 7 2   W     E        ◇ A 5
  ♣ Q 10 9                        ♣ 8 7 6 3
                   S

              ♠ A K Q 9 3
              ♡ A 5
              ◇ 9 4 3
              ♣ K J 5
```

West opened the King of Diamonds against South's *four spade* contract which East overtook with the Ace, and returned the five-spot, West's Queen winning. West then played the 10 of diamonds, dummy ruffed with the ten-spot and East overruffed with the Jack. Eventually West made the Queen of Clubs, for the setting trick.

The fact that declarer should have made his contract by discarding one of dummy's clubs on the third lead of diamonds does not concern us here. What is of import is East's overtaking of partner's King with the Ace to return another diamond. This was obviously (to West) an "unblocking" play that East was making with the Ace of Diamonds. (With three diamonds, East would have given either a negative or a positive signal with respect to a diamond continuation). Hence West's return of the ten of diamonds at trick three.

7.

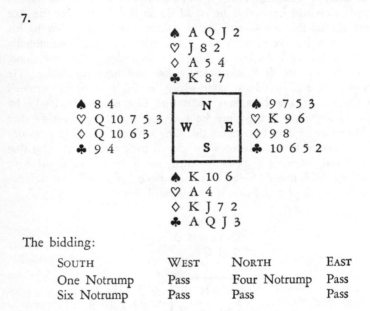

♠ A Q J 2
♡ J 8 2
◇ A 5 4
♣ K 8 7

♠ 8 4
♡ Q 10 7 5 3
◇ Q 10 6 3
♣ 9 4

N
W   E
S

♠ 9 7 5 3
♡ K 9 6
◇ 9 8
♣ 10 6 5 2

♠ K 10 6
♡ A 4
◇ K J 7 2
♣ A Q J 3

The bidding:

SOUTH	WEST	NORTH	EAST
One Notrump	Pass	Four Notrump	Pass
Six Notrump	Pass	Pass	Pass

The theme of the above deal is the Rule of Eleven — which East either forgot about or did not know.

Against South's *six notrump* contract, West opened the five of hearts, the eight was played from dummy, and East automatically played the King (third hand high). Declarer now had no difficulty in making twelve tricks, since he was able to establish dummy's Jack of Hearts as a winner.

Had East applied the Rule of Eleven, he would have played his nine of hearts instead of the King, and the slam contract would then have been defeated.

Familiarity with the rule would have yielded this information to East: West had opened the five-spot of hearts, which meant that in the North, South, and East hands there were six cards higher than the five (11 minus 5 equals 6). Five of these cards were in evidence: the J 8 in dummy and the K 9 6 in the East hand. Therefore declarer had just one card higher than the five-spot — and the card had to be the

Ace, for surely a "sane" West would not be underleading an Ace against South's six notrump contract, especially when South had opened the bidding with one notrump. On the opening heart lead, then, East should have played the nine-spot, and not the King.

8.

```
              ♠ 5 3
              ♡ A K 9 8
              ◇ Q 10 7 3
              ♣ A 9 4

  ♠ 4          ┌─────────┐       ♠ J 10 9 8
  ♡ J 7 5 2    │    N    │       ♡ Q 10 3
  ◇ A K 9 4    │  W   E  │       ◇ 8 2
  ♣ 7 6 5 2    │    S    │       ♣ K 10 8 3
              └─────────┘

              ♠ A K Q 7 6 2
              ♡ 6 4
              ◇ J 6 5
              ♣ Q J
```

West opens the King of Diamonds against South's *four spade* contract, and if third-hand mechanically plays the eight-spot, initiating the high-low signal, West will then cash his Ace, after which a third round of diamonds will be led, East ruffing. Declarer will now fulfill his contract since he will be able later to discard a club on dummy's established diamond Queen.

On the lead of the diamond King, East should play the discouraging deuce, not the eight! What does East gain by ruffing a third diamond? Not a thing, since he has a natural trump trick which can never be taken away. Observing the deuce of diamonds, and looking at the dummy, West, at trick two, would undoubtedly then shift to a club. And, once East makes his club King (as he must with the club shift) declarer will be defeated.

The reader will bear in mind that one does not give a high-low signal merely because it is the orthodox thing to do. A high-low signal is given to get partner to continue the suit led only if it will attain an objective for the defenders.

9. The following deal presents a third-hand play which years ago was deemed to be unorthodox defense, but which currently is considered to be a standard "set" play:

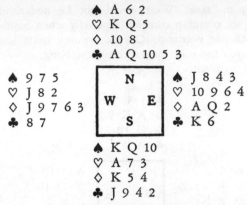

```
              ♠ A 6 2
              ♡ K Q 5
              ◊ 10 8
              ♣ A Q 10 5 3

  ♠ 9 7 5        N        ♠ J 8 4 3
  ♡ J 8 2                 ♡ 10 9 6 4
  ◊ J 9 7 6 3  W   E      ◊ A Q 2
  ♣ 8 7          S        ♣ K 6

              ♠ K Q 10
              ♡ A 7 3
              ◊ K 5 4
              ♣ J 9 4 2
```

South is declarer at *three notrump,* against which West opens his fourth-best diamond, the eight-spot being played from dummy. Third hand's normal reaction is to put up the Ace, and return the Queen. If this is done, declarer will hold up the King, and take the third round of the suit, thereby eliminating diamonds from the East hand. When declarer subsequently takes the losing club finesse, East will then have no diamond to return, and declarer will romp home with his contract.

East's "set" play in this A Q x situation (against notrump) is to play the *Queen,* which declarer takes with the King. When East obtains the lead via the club King, he then plays the Ace of Diamonds, followed by the deuce of diamonds, enabling West to cash all his diamonds.

The reader might say that if East puts up the diamond Queen, declarer can decline to take the King, employing the hold-up play to break the communication between the adverse hands. Yes he can, but he will look downright silly (or, shall we say, "stupid") if this happens to be the situation:

```
              ◊ 10 8
                N
  ◊ A J 9 6 3  W   E   ◊ Q 7 2
                S
              ◊ K 5 4
```

In the above case — which is more likely to exist than the specific A Q x in the East hand — if declarer did not capture the Queen with the King, the defenders would rattle off the first five tricks! And the screaming that would take place if West had the *club King* defies description!

By playing the Queen in the specific A Q x situation against notrump, [3] third hand prevents declarer from employing the hold-up play with the King. Incidentally, if partner happens to be leading from the King (rather than from the Jack), then your Queen will win, after which you will cash your Ace, and lead your remaining diamond to partner's King and the rest of the suit.

10. This last illustration is a classic as far as the tournament world is concerned. About 15 years ago, the National Open Pair Championships was lost because third hand played automatically to trick one, and really "fixed" himself as a result. This is not a simple hand. The key play is actually a difficult one to make for everybody except the top-flight expert. And yet, in retrospect, the proper play becomes quite easy to see. To make the play at the table, however, is another matter.

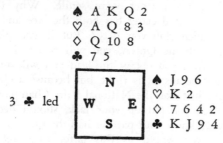

The bidding:

NORTH	EAST	SOUTH	WEST
One Spade	Pass	Two Hearts	Pass
Four Hearts	Pass	Six Hearts	Pass
Pass	Pass	Pass	

Your partner, West, opens the *three* of clubs against South's six heart contract, the five is played from dummy, you put up your King which declarer captures with the Ace. Declarer then takes a heart finesse, losing to your King. Now, gentle reader, what do you return — a club or a diamond?

Permit me to make an attempt to delve into the thoughts that may be running through your mind. Your immediate reaction will probably be to return a club, on the very sound assumption that your partner may hold the Queen of Clubs. You remember, of course, that partner had opened the three of clubs, which was either from a five-card suit, possibly

---

[3] Against a suit contract, you cannot gain by putting up the Queen. If you do not take your Ace, there will be those days when you will never make it.

from a four-card suit, or maybe from a three-card suit, etc. Then you probably give at least a passing thought to leading a diamond, but an echo haunts you: "Partner, why didn't you return *the suit I opened?* Why do you always make decisions which turn out to be wrong?" So, not wishing to incur (or perpetuate) the everlasting enmity of partner — and really not having anything intelligent to guide you — you dutifully play back a club. You have just lost the National Open Pair Championships!

Did you defend badly when you returned a club? Actually not. The club return could easily have been the winning play. Your mistake did not come at trick three when you played back a club. It came at trick one, *when you incorrectly put up the King of Clubs!*

Let us go back. Is it conceivable that on the given bidding, your partner would have opened a low club *away from the Ace?* This is an impossible lead unless partner were senile. Why then not put up your Jack of Clubs? If declarer has both the Ace and Queen of Clubs, what difference which club you play? But if you play your Jack and declarer wins it with the Queen, you will realize he still has the Ace of Clubs — and when you obtain the lead you will automatically switch to a diamond, not because it is right, but because a club return *must be wrong.* You have just won the National Pairs Championship.

Of course, when you put up your Jack, should declarer win it with his Ace, you would know your partner had the Queen. So, upon winning the heart King, you would in this latter case, return a club. The complete deal:

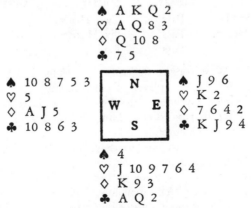

```
                    ♠ A K Q 2
                    ♡ A Q 8 3
                    ◇ Q 10 8
                    ♣ 7 5
  ♠ 10 8 7 5 3         N          ♠ J 9 6
  ♡ 5                             ♡ K 2
  ◇ A J 5        W        E       ◇ 7 6 4 2
  ♣ 10 8 6 3         S          ♣ K J 9 4
                    ♠ 4
                    ♡ J 10 9 7 6 4
                    ◇ K 9 3
                    ♣ A Q 2
```

If East returns a club at trick three, declarer wins it with the Queen (assuming the King and Ace have been played to the first trick).

He then trumps his remaining club, after which he plays all his trumps. This would be the situation just prior to declarer playing his last trump:

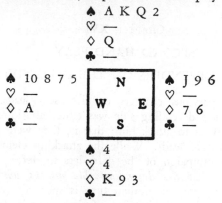

♠ A K Q 2
♡ —
◊ Q
♣ —

♠ 10 8 7 5   ♠ J 9 6
♡ —   ♡ —
◊ A   ◊ 7 6
♣ —   ♣ —

♠ 4
♡ 4
◊ K 9 3
♣ —

South now leads his last trump — and poor West has become the victim of a "squeeze." If he discards a spade, dummy's deuce of spades will be promoted into a winner (dummy discarding the Queen of Diamonds) ; if West elects to discard the Ace of Diamonds instead, then declarer's diamond King will become a winner, after which dummy's A K Q of spades will yield declarer his slam.

SECOND HAND PLAY

(THE DEFENDERS ON THE DEFENSIVE)

In each of the previous chapters on defense — leads, signals and third-hand play — the defending side was either attacking the declarer or making preparations to attack him: that is, they were either leading or preparing for future leads. While the attacking element is a most vital factor in the campaign of the defenders to defeat declarer, it is nevertheless a fact that *the defending side attacks with comparative rarity*. The major proportion of their time is spent in either following suit to declarer's leads, winning or refusing to win tricks, and, in general, parrying the thrusts of the declarer.

Before presenting the defensive maneuvers of the defenders, let me define what is meant by "Second Hand." "Second Hand" is *the defender* who plays second to a trick. That is, let us assume that South has become the declarer:

```
    N
W       E
    S
```

If the lead is made from the North hand, *East* becomes "second hand" to this specific trick. If, to a succeeding trick, South leads initially, then *West* has become "second hand" to this trick. In other words, which *defender* becomes second hand to each trick is determined simply by whether declarer or dummy led first to that trick.

Second hand's defensive play, therefore, resolves itself into a two-part classification:

1. Correct play when he plays *before the dummy,* and
2. Correct play when he plays *before the declarer.*

Superficially, it may appear that playing before the dummy (whose cards are exposed) would be easier than playing before the declarer, whose cards are concealed. Actually it is six of one and half-a-dozen of the other. Probably a bit more often than not, where second hand plays before dummy, he will generally tend to have a few more problems than when he is playing "blind" before the declarer.

The veteran bridge player is quite familiar with one of the slogans which has been handed down through the generations, to wit, "second hand plays low." While there is a great deal of truth in this slogan, unfortunately as with all slogans it was applied indiscriminately, and, as a result, developed into virtually an automatic principle. Whenever second hand played incorrectly, he felt that he had the right to justify his position by merely stating, "But, partner, I didn't do anything wrong. I played 'second hand low.' "

Actually, "second hand low" is the guiding principle for second hand's defensive play, but there are so many exceptions to this guide, that to treat it as a dogmatic principle must inevitably lead to incorrect defense. The reader will do well to use as his guide this modified principle for second hand play:

> "Second Hand" will play low when a low card is played by first hand unless there is a positive reason for doing otherwise. That is to say, when you do not play "second hand low," the burden of proof is on you to justify your play.

I.   Second Hand Play *Before* Dummy.

Let us look at some illustrations of "second hand playing low." In each of these situations second hand is playing before the exposed dummy, and in each case *a low card has been led* (not an honor card) by declarer:

(1)   The contract is 3 NT and declarer (South) leads the seven of diamonds:

♦ K 6 5 2

♦ Q 4 3

7 of ♦ led

As is obvious, for you to put up the Queen is absurd. When declarer led the seven of diamonds was it not his intention to play dummy's King? Incidentally, a large number of people still play the Queen in the given situation, stating "I wanted to force out dummy's King." That remark is perhaps analogous to burning up a twenty-dollar bill and, as justification for your irrational conduct, you say: "Well, I thought somebody was going to steal it, and I didn't want to be aggravated until it was stolen." First of all, why should you want to force dummy's King, unless some potential gain can be made thereby? And, second, if you do not "force" dummy's King, will declarer not be compelled to play it himself? If he does not, your partner (fourth hand) will capture the trick. Here is the diamond situation, as it might have been:

$\Diamond$ K 6 5 2

$\Diamond$ Q 4 3 [N / W E / S] $\Diamond$ J 10

$\Diamond$ A 9 8 7

If you put up your Queen, I think it is quite evident that you will be presenting declarer with an extra diamond trick. To play the Queen to force the King will succeed only in foolishly losing the Queen.

(2)   The contract is spades, and declarer leads the three of clubs:

♣ K 8 5

♣ A J 4 [N / W E / S]

3 of ♣ led

As second hand, your proper play is to follow low with the four-spot. Will not declarer, who is attacking in this suit, play the King, recognizing that if he does not East will capture the trick? To play the Jack to force dummy's King is absolutely wrong, since it is obvious that it is declarer's *intention* to play the King anyway. The suit might have been distributed:

♣ K 8 5

♣ A J 4 [N / W E / S] ♣ 9 7 2

♣ Q 10 6 3

(3)   The contract is no trump, and declarer leads the deuce of hearts:

♡ Q 8 5

♡ A J 4 [N / W E / S]

2 of ♡ led

Here, as in (2), you will play low. In this case you will be 100% right, as opposed to (2), where you were just 99% right. In (2) there was the ever-so-slight possibility in theory that declarer held a singleton club, in which case your Ace would have been lost. In this situation, however, either declarer has the King, in which case your

Ace will ultimately capture it; or your partner has the King, in which case he will capture dummy's Queen.

(a) ♡ Q 8 5   (b) ♡ Q 8 5

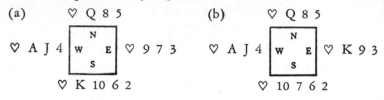

♡ A J 4 (W E) ♡ 9 7 3   ♡ A J 4 (W E) ♡ K 9 3

♡ K 10 6 2   ♡ 10 7 6 2

(4) The contract is notrump, and declarer leads the six of spades. Let us look at all four hands:

♠ K J 9 2

♠ A 10 7 3 (W E) ♠ 5 4

♠ Q 8 6

As you can see, if you play either the Ace or ten you will give declarer *three tricks* in this suit. We, of course, are looking at all four hands, and it is quite obvious to us that declarer can always make three spade tricks if he puts up dummy's nine-spot on your play of a low one. ALWAYS REMEMBER, HOWEVER, THAT DECLARER DOES NOT SEE ALL FOUR HANDS. If you keep this in mind, then you will not be assuming that declarer will always diagnose the existing situation and come up with the right answer. Unless you give him a clue, or help him even more directly, he will misguess the situation as often as he guesses it.

In the given illustration, if you correctly play the three-spot, declarer will capture the trick with the Jack. Then he will probably play the deuce off dummy, putting up the Queen, which your Ace will capture. Again, if he "guesses" that you have the ten-spot, he can successfully finesse through it. In all probability, however, he will lay down dummy's King on the third lead of the suit hoping that spades are divided 3-3. When it is revealed that they are not, he cannot make more than two spade tricks. Putting it another way, how can declarer ever know (unless you tell him) which of the following spade distributions exists:

(a)   (b)

♠ K J 9 2   ♠ K J 9 2

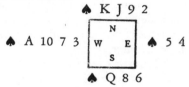

♠ A 10 7 3 (W E) ♠ 5 4   ♠ A 7 3 (W E) ♠ 10 5 4

♠ Q 8 6   ♠ Q 8 6

(5)   The contract is spades, and the following is the distribution of spades around the table: (You and I know it, but declarer does not).

♠ A Q 10 3

♠ K J 9   ♠ 7 2

♠ 8 6 5 4

Declarer leads the four of spades. If you put up your Jack, declarer will undoubtedly finesse the Queen, which will win the trick. Realizing then that you still possess the King, he will return to his hand to lead another spade. By finessing dummy's ten-spot, he will now bring in the entire suit without losing a trick. So you wind up with nothing except perhaps the appreciation of declarer.

But suppose that when declarer led the four-spot, you had played your nine. Is declarer so gifted that he will automatically finesse dummy's ten-spot? No bridge player is that clairvoyant. If he elects to finesse the Queen, he will win the trick, *but now you cannot be prevented from winning a spade trick, since you still possess the K J against dummy's A 10!*

Again, as we look at all four hands, you and I know that declarer has it in his power to avoid the loss of any spade tricks. Let him guess how to play the suit. Do not help him by departing from the principle of "second hand low."

(6)   Where you possess a sequence of high cards, and where observation of dummy indicates that you tend to promote a trick for yourself or partner by playing *high* as second hand, or that you may lose a trick by playing low as second hand, then of course you will not play low. The following is a very frequent occurrence:

♣ A 10 5

♣ Q J 3   ♣ 9 8 4

♣ K 7 6 2

Declarer leads the deuce of clubs towards dummy, and you should put up the Jack *to force dummy's Ace, and to simultaneously develop a potential winner out of your Queen.* If instead, you play low, declarer may well put up dummy's ten-spot (taking what we call a "deep finesse") which will capture the trick.

The play of the Jack, by the way, cannot be a losing play; the play of the low card, on the other hand, gives declarer a play "on the house"; if he guesses right, he wins; if he guesses wrong he does not lose (since by normal defensive play he could not avoid losing a trick).

Should your partner have the King of Clubs, incidentally, then your play of the Jack would neither have lost nor gained, since your partnership in this case would always have made two club tricks, no matter what you played. That is:

♣ A 10 5

♣ Q J 3   N / W   E / S   ♣ K 9 8

♣ 7 6 4 2

Actually the direct cause of your deviating from the principle of "second hand low" in the above illustration was the presence of the threatening ten-spot in dummy. Had dummy held, let us assume, the A 6 5 4, instead of the A 10 5, your correct play would have been to play your three-spot, for if you did not you might have run into something like this:

♣ A 6 5 4

♣ Q J 3   N / W   E / S   ♣ K

♣ 10 9 8 7 2

As you can see, if you had put up your Jack, dummy's Ace would have caught both your Jack and partner's King, thereby decreasing your winners in this suit from two to one.

Putting it another way, as you view the above dummy, the odds that your partner has either the seven, eight, nine, ten, or King are pretty good. And, if he holds any *one* of these cards, then your play of the three-spot must be the right play.

(7)   A rather automatic, and most simple situation, is the following. The contract is *notrump*.

♣ Q J 2

♣ A K 5   N / W   E / S

♣ S

4 of ♣ led

Declarer leads the four of clubs, on which you play *high,* the King. If you do not, dummy's Jack will win the trick. It is apparent that you cannot prevent dummy's Jack from ultimately winning a trick, but if you play low, you will be giving declarer "time" to develop his suit or suits. If you properly take your King, you can continue working on the suit which you started; or you might have found that declarer had a weakness elsewhere, and you could now shift to the "elsewhere."

If we modify the above illustration slightly, whether second hand should play low or high becomes problematical:

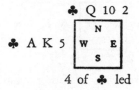

4 of ♣ led

Again the contract is notrump and declarer leads the four of clubs. As we can both see, declarer will always be able to develop a winner out of dummy's Queen of Clubs *if he knows how to do it.* But does he know?

Suppose you were sitting South, as declarer, and you (not seeing West's hand) led the four of clubs upon which West played the *five-spot.* What would you play in the following instance:

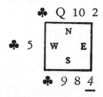

Would you not in all likelihood put up the ten-spot from dummy, on the 50-50 chance that West held the Jack? Mathematically it is the proper play. If you put up the Queen, and East happens to have *either* the Ace or King, you will never win a club trick. But if you put up the ten-spot, and East does *not* have the Jack, then you will always make a club trick.

So bear in mind that when you play high as second hand, the burden of proof will be on you to justify your deviation from the principle of "second hand low."

(8) Another standard situation is the following, in which second hand's pessimistic approach often leads him to making an incorrect play:

♡ A K 10

♡ Q J 7

♡ 3

South leads the three of hearts towards the A K 10 in dummy. As should be readily apparent *declarer can make three heart tricks*, by putting up the ten-spot if you play low. But if you put up the Jack, he will always make three heart tricks, taking your Jack with the King, returning to his own hand, and then leading another heart, finessing dummy's ten. So, as you view it, you are lost, owing to circumstances beyond your control. Therefore you play your three-spot. If declarer now puts up the ten-spot from dummy, then, if you wish, you might take a moment off to shrug your shoulders in resignation. However, *if* declarer decides to put up the King instead of the ten, you have just "found" a heart trick, for you now retain the Q J in the face of dummy's A 10.

(9)   There is one other frequently-occurring situation where the average player, sitting in second position, feels that all is lost, and to avoid prolonging the agony, he tries to get it over with as soon as he can. In so doing, he thereby creates two new friends for himself (the opponents); and he creates one enemy (his partner).

♣ A Q 9 4 3

♣ K 8 7

♣ 5

South leads the five of clubs, and West distraught with anxiety about his King, which is trapped, promptly plays it. And the story then invariably has a most unhappy ending — for the defenders.

♣ A Q 9 6 3

♣ K 8 7   ♣ J 10

♣ 5 4 2

It is true that West was not happy about the position of his King, but why sacrifice him to appease one's emotions? Had West properly played low, the defenders would have made a club trick. With the King

being played, however, dummy's Ace captured it, after which the Queen
felled East's Jack. The nine-spot then picked up West's eight-spot.
Dummy's six and three of clubs were now the highest surviving clubs in
the suit.

(10) The following situation is very frequently encountered by
second hand. Before presenting it, let me transpose you from the
defender's seat into the declarer's seat. You are South, playing a three
notrump contract and you are confronted with the question of the best
way of playing this combination to make two tricks:

$$\heartsuit \text{ A J 9}$$

	N	
W		E
	S	

$$\heartsuit \text{ 7 4 3}$$

You lead the three of hearts and West follows with the six-spot.
Your proper play is to put up dummy's *nine-spot*. This is a simple 50-50
finesse against the ten-spot, and will produce two tricks when West has
the Q 10 or K 10. It will fail to produce two tricks only when West has
the K Q without the ten-spot. So, mathematically, the superior play is to
put up dummy's nine-spot, and if it loses to the King or Queen, next
time you finesse dummy's Jack.

Let us now swing back to defense — you are West, the contract is
either in a suit or in notrump.

$$\heartsuit \text{ A J 9}$$

$$\heartsuit \text{ K Q 6}$$

	N	
W		E
	S	

3 of $\heartsuit$ led

*As of right now, whenever declarer leads a low card to dummy's
A J 9, play low.* At least three out of four times declarer will finesse
against the ten-spot — and dummy's nine-spot will be captured by your
partner's ten (if declarer happens to have the ten, then he can always
make two tricks in this suit, whether you split your honors or not).

(11) Let us look at the final "judgment" situation, where a
second-hand defender either suspects that declarer is trying to trick him,
or where a defender comes to the conclusion that if he does not take
a trick which is being proffered him, he may never get it. In both
cases our suspicious defender loses a trick.

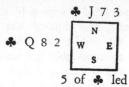

5 of ♣ led

Let us assume South has rebid clubs, and winds up in a notrump contract. He then leads the five of clubs at trick two. An average West player now usually says this to himself "South probably has the A K x x x of the suit and is trying to talk me out of taking my Queen . . . and, if I don't take it now, I won't get it. So I'll take it."

Very bad reasoning by West. Surely if South had the A K x x x of clubs, he would have played the A K in the hope (and a decent hope) of catching a doubleton Queen, thereby avoiding the loss of a club trick. Does it not follow therefore, that *East* has either the Ace or King? If West properly plays low on declarer's club lead, the Queen is bound to win a trick on the second or third round of this suit.

In my experience, here are three of the situations that existed more often than not when West put up his Queen:

(1)

♣ J 6 2

♣ Q 8 3   N
          W   E   ♣ K 10
            S

♣ A 9 7 5 4

(2)

♣ J 6 2

♣ Q 8 3   N
          W   E   ♣ A K
            S

♣ 10 9 7 5 4

(3)

♣ J 6 2

♣ Q 8 3   N
          W   E   ♣ A
            S

♣ K 10 9 7 5 4

In each of the above three situations, West's play of the Queen cost the defenders a trick.

With reference to the eleven situations which have just been presented, the theme (and principle) has been that second hand plays low when first hand leads a low card, and dummy has one or two honor cards, except where second hand can visually determine that it is incorrect to do so.

Let us now examine second hand's approach to the proper play when first hand leads an honor, and dummy has an honor or two, second hand being "caught in the middle" as it were. In bridge, as in anything one does, it is always an unenviable and uncomfortable position to be caught in the middle. But a fact is a fact — and in a bridge game you are often going to find yourself in a position where you might well be ambushed by enemies who are waiting for you to make your move before they make theirs. Being realistic about it, you have an option of either surviving or not. There is no middle road. The purpose of this section is to equip you for survival.

Just as the principle of "second hand low" has been carried over from ancient times, so another slogan that has persisted throughout the year has unfortunately become permanently ingrained in the minds of too many veteran bridge players. This slogan is "always cover an honor with an honor." By this is meant that when first hand leads an honor card, if second hand has an honor card he should play it, to force third hand to also play an honor card. The theoretical effect of this is that in so doing second hand forces declarer to waste two honor cards to capture one.

While this slogan has much merit, there is one *major* factor against its efficient application: it contains the word "always." No principle in bridge is ever properly prefaced by the word "always." As far as this specific slogan is concerned, the use of the word "always" has created a tremendous number of "bad" bridge players.

Allow me to present an example of a bridge player who played by slogans, and whose especial love was to "always cover an honor with an honor." He was once a neighbor of mine and we occasionally played bridge. Let us say this neighbor of mine was sitting West, and I, sitting South, was confronted with the following:

♠ A 8 5 2

♠ K J 10 9

This situation, or one almost exactly like it, would arise quite often, especially in the trump suit. And I would always be able to locate the Queen! I would simply lead the Jack from the South hand. If my friend had the Queen, he would always "cover" my honor with his honor, the Queen (or should it be her Honor). If, on my Jack, he failed to play the Queen, I would know that *he did not have it*. I then would capture my own Jack with dummy's Ace, after which I would finesse East for the Queen. And, as I stated, I just never guessed wrong. Although it is said that "you can't teach an old dog new tricks," my friend finally relegated the word "always" to the scrap-heap — and he became a better player as a result.

As far as second hand "covering an honor with an honor" is concerned, it is often a rough problem when dummy has an honor which is higher than both the honor that first hand has played and the one which second hand possesses. For instance, take the situation just presented from the viewpoint of West:

Spades are trumps:

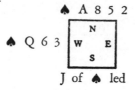

♠ A 8 5 2

♠ Q 6 3

J of ♠ led

Do you cover the Jack with the Queen? Do you play low? Are you uncertain as to what to play? What you do in these various stock situations that arise quite frequently will now be presented, going from the simple to the complex.

Let us first look at the different situations where second hand possesses the *King*, dummy has one or more honors, and declarer leads an honor card:

1. Here is an elementary illustration. The contract is either in a suit or notrump:

♠ A J 10 9

♠ K 3 2

♠ Queen led

Declarer leads the Queen of Spades, and, of course, West should play a low card, not the King. To play the King would be to give declarer four spade tricks — and it would also serve to ostracize you as far as future games are concerned.

Admittedly your King is hopelessly trapped, and if declarer had two or more spades originally, he will make four spade tricks. But suppose he had just one spade? Either you will make your King, or declarer will not be able to take more than two spade tricks.

2. Another elementary and rather obvious situation. The contract is either in a suit or notrump.

◇ A 7 5

◇ K J 10   [N / W E / S]

Q of ◇ led

If South leads the Queen of Diamonds, you will of course cover with the King, which dummy will capture with the Ace. Your Jack and ten are now the highest ranking cards in the suit.

3.   ♣ A 6

♣ K 7 5   [N / W E / S]

Q of ♣ led

(a) If the contract is *notrump,* do *not* cover the Queen with the King. By not covering, the King will win a trick on the third round of the suit.

(b) If the contract is in *a suit, cover* the Queen with the King (except when the Queen is the Queen of trumps). Should you not cover, you will never make your King, since dummy will trump it on the third round. Let me add, however, that as you cover, do not be disappointed if your side does not win a trick. Declarer figures to have the Jack; yet, there is just an outside possibility that your partner may have the Jack. But the point is that if you do not cover, your side will *never* win a club trick.

4. Suppose now that this is the situation:

♠ A 6 2

♠ K 10 5   [N / W E / S]

Q of ♠ led

You will, in this case, cover the Queen with the King, thereby forcing dummy's Ace. In so doing, you automatically promote your ten-spot into a winner on the third round. Actually, you can always make a trick in this situation, even if you play low on the lead of the Queen, provided that when the Jack is led next time, you put up your King, forcing dummy's Ace, and promoting your ten-spot into the highest-ranking spade. However, I think you will be better off in the long run if you acquire the habit of covering in this situation, rather than waiting for the next round, just in case you some day run into this:

♠ A 6 2

♠ K 10   N   ♠ 7 5 4 3
        W   E
          S

♠ Q J 9 8

If West fails to cover, then whatever South plays next, he will make four spade tricks; if West does cover the Queen with the King, here is the situation that will confront declarer on the second lead of the suit:

♠ 6 2

N
W   E
S

♠ J 9 8

In all probability South will now finesse East for the ten of spades — and West will make his unprotected ten-spot, which he could not have made if he failed to cover the Queen with the King. There is, of course, no guarantee that West will make his ten-spot — declarer might play the Jack next, and drop the ten-spot. But there is the guarantee that if West does not cover, the defenders will *never* make a trick in the suit.

5.   ♠ A 6 2

                              N
♠ K 9 5   W   E
                S

                        Q of ♠ led

This situation is somewhat comparable to the preceding one, where you held the K 10 x. In this case, however, if South possesses the Q J 10, you will never make a spade trick, for by repeated finesses, declarer will trap your King. But if your partner has the ten-spot, then your nine will be promoted into a winner on the third round:

♠ A 6 2

♠ K 9 5   N W E S   ♠ 10 3

♠ Q J 8 7 4

Here again, as in the preceding illustration, it makes no difference whether you cover the Queen or you do not, just so long as you cover the Jack on the next lead of the suit, thereby promoting your nine-spot into a winner. But, to make it easier for yourself so that you will not have to spend time working out standard situations, it would be better if you developed the habit of covering in the above case.

Actually, the two above situations (K 10 x, K 9 x) can be incorporated into a principle: WHENEVER YOU HOLD THE KING *AND* THE NINE OR TEN, COVER THE QUEEN IN THE FACE OF DUMMY'S A x x or A x x x. Paradoxically, perhaps, this principle is not presented primarily to illustrate the importance of covering with K 10 x or K 9 x (since the same result could be achieved by covering on the next round) but rather to make it simpler for the reader to recognize the *much more frequent situations when the Queen should not be covered by the King.* Putting it negatively, whenever you have *the King without the nine or ten, you should lean towards not covering.* Let me show you why:

♣ A 7 4 2

♣ K 6 3   N W E S   ♣ 10 8 5

♣ Q J 9

If declarer leads the Queen, and you cover with the King, dummy's Ace will win. A low club will then be played off dummy, East will follow with the eight-spot — and declarer will then successfully finesse his nine. As you can see, the defenders will make no tricks in this suit.

But if you do not cover the Queen with the King, declarer's Queen will win. Now, no matter what South leads, the defenders will win one trick: if South leads the Jack, West *will* cover with the King which will be taken by dummy's Ace — and East's ten-spot will become the highest surviving club; if, instead, South leads the nine-spot, West will play low, and either he or his partner will win a club trick.

In these situations — holding the K x x — you will discover that the winning play is to *not cover the Queen with the King, and, instead, to wait for the Jack to be led, which will be covered.*

6.

◇ A 5 2

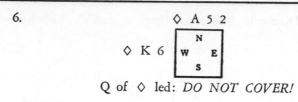

◇ K 6

N
W   E
S

Q of ◇ led: *DO NOT COVER!*

Most bridge authorities have stated that when the Queen is led, second hand, holding K x, should cover. The reason for this has been given as: "If you do not cover, declarer is apt to lead a low card next, catching your King with dummy's Ace, thereby bringing in the entire suit." The illustration that is used is generally this:

◇ A x x x

◇ K x

N
W   E
S

◇ 10 9 x

◇ Q J x x

It is specious reasoning that results in covering the Queen with the King, although at a superficial glance it may appear that if you do not cover, declarer *will* make all the tricks.

Let us look at the general situation re: K x

◇ A x x x

◇ K x

N
W   E
S

Q of ◇ led

If declarer has the Q J *and 10,* it makes no difference whether West covers or does not. Should partner have the ten, and you cover the Queen with the King, then in all probability declarer will finesse your partner for the ten-spot and not lose any tricks in that suit:

◇ A x x x

◇ K x

N
W   E
S

◇ 10 8 6

◇ Q J 9 7

But if you correctly *do not cover,* then your partner can cooperate with you by dropping the *eight-spot.* Now should declarer lead the Jack, East will be able to win the third round with the ten-spot. To illustrate declarer's attitude, what would you do as declarer in the above case, if

your Queen of Diamonds finesse had been successful, East having
dropped the eight?

◊ A 5 2

	N	
W		E
	S	

Eight-spot fell on
the Queen.

◊ J 9 7

Would you not have the feeling that East might well have started
with the 10 8 doubleton, in which case your lead of the Jack would now
simultaneously finesse West's King and drop East's ten? That is,
based on the play to the first trick would it not seem reasonable that the
following was the original distribution:

◊ A 5 4 3

◊ K 6 2

	N	
W		E
	S	

◊ 10 8

◊ Q J 9 7

In all situations, except one, by not covering the Queen, the possessor
of the K x will stand to gain. The one exception occurs when partner
holds the 10 9 x specifically. If this one situation exists, then by West's
refusal to cover the Queen with the King, declarer has the opportunity
of picking up the entire suit without loss of a trick. This will be
accomplished by him only if he elects to lead low to dummy at trick two.
But, first, it is most unlikely for East to have, specifically, the 10 9 x;
and even if he does have it, then on the play of the Queen (with
West playing low), East should drop *the nine-spot*. I will wager that
declarer will now feel that East started with a doubleton 10 9, and
again he will play the Jack to trick two, thereby establishing East's
ten-spot.

Incidentally, on the illustration just presented:

◊ A x x x

	N	
W		E
	S	

◊ Q J x x

If declarer is missing the K 10 9 x x, it would be incorrect to lead
the Queen, for in so doing he might well lose two tricks; whereby by
correct play, he might restrict his losses to but one trick.

(1)   ◇ A x x x   (2)   ◇ A x x x

```
                N                              N
◇ K 10 9 x  W     E   ◇ x     ◇ x   W     E   ◇ K 10 9 x
                S                              S
```

        ◇ Q J x x   ◇ Q J x x

Proper declarer's play in the above cases is to take the original diamond lead with the Ace, and then lead off dummy towards the Queen-Jack. This will lose only one trick whenever *East* holds the K 10 9 x. When West holds the K 10 9 x, there is no way to avoid the loss of two tricks.

Consequently, even in the one case where West holds the K x and East the 10 9 x, the defenders do not figure to lose a trick against a declarer who should know better than to lead the Queen.

If this is the situation:

        ◇ A x

```
                N
◇ K x    W     E
                S
```

        Q of ◇ led

This is an "automatic" cover of the Queen by the King. If you do not cover, the Queen will win, after which a low diamond led to the Ace will fell your King. By covering, you force declarer to waste the Ace and Queen to capture your King, thereby tending to create a winner in partner's hand. By covering you cannot lose — and you may well gain.

SUMMARY: DO NOT COVER THE QUEEN WHEN YOU HOLD THE K x IN FRONT OF EITHER THE A x x OR THE A x x x IN DUMMY; WHERE YOU HOLD THE K x IN FRONT OF DUMMY'S A x, COVER.

7. This is the final situation where second hand holds the K x, K x x, or the K x x x in the face of dummy's Ace. In my experience more defenders go wrong here than in any other "stock" situation — through either stubbornness or ignorance. In illustrating this, I hope to get rid of the ignorance, after which the stubbornness should wither away:

          ♡ A J 3

```
♡ K x          N
♡ K x x    W     E
♡ K x x x      S
```

       10 of ♡ led

Let us say the contract is spades (the defensive play would be exactly the same at notrump). South leads the ten of hearts. Do you normally cover with the King? If you do not, *you should.*

First of all, let us eliminate a few situations: (1) if South has both the ten *and the Queen,* he will make three heart tricks whether you cover or not; (2) if he happens to have the ten *and the nine,* he will make two hearts whether you cover or not.

(1)	(2)
♡ A J 3	♡ A J 3

♡ K 8 5 | N / W E / S | ♡ 9 7 6 2   ♡ K 8 5 | N / W E / S | ♡ Q 7 6 2

♡ Q 10 4   ♡ 10 9 4

In (1), if you do not cover, he will next play the Queen, again finessing through your King.

In (2), if you do not cover, your partner's Queen will win, but next time South obtains the lead, he will play another heart, finessing dummy's Jack.

The discussion of what to do when the ten is led therefore assumes first that *declarer does not have the Queen;* and second, that declarer *does not have the nine-spot.* If he has either of these two cards, whether or not you cover is immaterial, for whatever develops can be attributed to "circumstances beyond your control." WHEN THE TEN-SPOT IS LED, SECOND HAND SHOULD COVER WITH THE KING, HOLDING K x, K x x, or K x x x.

In a certain sense, covering with the King might be called "wishful thinking," hoping that your partner has the Queen and nine; but in a greater sense, it is the creation of a "fact" which must exist if you are to be successful. Let me illustrate why second hand must cover with the King if he is to gain a trick

♡ A J 3

♡ K 8 5 | N / W E / S | ♡ Q 9 6 4

♡ 10 7 2

When South leads the ten, should you not cover, dummy will play low and East's Queen will win. And, when declarer next obtains the lead, he will finesse through your King, dummy's Jack and Ace winning two tricks.

But if you cover the ten-spot with the King, dummy's Ace will capture the trick — and your partner will then possess the Q 9 over dummy's J 3, which will give him two winners.

The same principle — of covering — applies when the Jack and ten are interchanged between dummy and declarer:

$$\heartsuit \ A \ 10 \ x$$

$$\heartsuit \ K \ x \ x \quad \boxed{\begin{array}{c} N \\ W \qquad E \\ S \end{array}}$$

J of $\heartsuit$ led

Cover the Jack with the King — and hope your partner has the Q 9. If he does not, you have not lost a thing.

In the two situations that follow — which are identical to the previous illustration — you will also cover:

(1)	(2)
$\heartsuit$ A J x	$\heartsuit$ A 10 x
$\heartsuit$ Q x x $\boxed{\begin{array}{c} N \\ W \ \ E \\ S \end{array}}$	$\heartsuit$ Q x x $\boxed{\begin{array}{c} N \\ W \ \ E \\ S \end{array}}$
10 of $\heartsuit$ led	J of $\heartsuit$ led

In (1) and (2), your hope is that partner has both the King and nine. If he does not, you have not lost a thing. To illustrate:

(1)	(2)
$\heartsuit$ A J 3	$\heartsuit$ A J 3
$\heartsuit$ Q 7 6 $\boxed{\begin{array}{c} N \\ W \quad E \\ S \end{array}}$ $\heartsuit$ K 9 5 2	$\heartsuit$ Q 7 6 $\boxed{\begin{array}{c} N \\ W \quad E \\ S \end{array}}$ $\heartsuit$ K 8 5 2
$\heartsuit$ 10 8 4	$\heartsuit$ 10 9 4

Let us now discuss the various situations where second hand possesses the *Queen* (Q x; Q x x; Q x x x), and first hand leads the Jack or Ten, with one or two honor-cards being in dummy. What one does in most of these cases is quite difficult to determine, for very often it is a pure guess. But you will discover that when you play quickly or unhesitatingly you will be helping yourself by not giving declarer any tell-tale clue. For instance, let us assume that South has bid and *rebid* spades, which has become the trump suit. You, sitting West, get off to a lead which declarer wins. You find yourself gazing at dummy's trump holding:

♠ A x x x

♠ Q x x [N W E S]

You realize immediately that declarer has at least five spades, and at *that precise moment*, you make up your mind that whatever spade declarer leads, you will *not cover*. And, at trick two declarer leads the Jack of Spades:

(1)

♠ A x x x

♠ Q x x [N W E S] ♠ x

♠ K J 10 9 x

(2)

♠ A x x x

♠ Q x x [N W E S] ♠ K

♠ J 10 9 x x

In (1), the astute declarer's play of the Jack was to entice West, if he had the Queen, to cover. I can assure you that if West nonchalantly plays low, declarer will capture the trick with dummy's Ace, playing for a 2-2 break in trumps. And now you have a sure trick in spades.

In (2), if you cover the Jack with the Queen, neither you nor your partner will forget it for a long time to come.

Let us now proceed from the general to the specific with respect to second hand's play holding the Q x, Q x x, or Q x x x.

1.   Where no clues have been divulged in the bidding, no inviolable principle can be followed. But much more often than not, best results will be obtained if you cover the Jack (or ten) with the Queen whenever dummy has *two honors*, but to refrain from covering whenever the dummy holds but one threatening card. That is:

(a)   ♠ A J x

♠ Q x [N W E S]

10 of ♠ led

(b)   ♠ A 10 x

♠ Q x x x [N W E S]

J of ♠ led

(c)

♠ A x x x

♠ Q x x [N W E S]

J of ♠ led

In (a) and (b), West should properly cover with the Queen; in (c), he should unhesitatingly play low.

2. Where dummy has just one honor, *the Ace*, it is proper *not* to cover:

$$\heartsuit \ A \ 7 \ 4$$

$$\heartsuit \ Q \ 8 \ 3 \quad \boxed{\begin{array}{c} N \\ W \quad E \\ S \end{array}} \quad \heartsuit \ K \ 9 \ 6 \ 2$$

$$\heartsuit \ J \ 10 \ 5$$

If you cover the Jack with the Queen, your side will win but one trick, for declarer will capture this trick with dummy's Ace, and lead towards his ten-spot. Your partner's King will then be your only winner.

But if you do not cover, partner's King will win the trick. When the ten-spot is subsequently led, you will cover with the Queen — and partner's nine-spot will be promoted into a second winner.

3. Where dummy has just one honor, *the King*, whether you cover or not depends on your "intuition"; if you think your partner has the Ace, you cover; if you think declarer has the Ace, you do not. But try to make up your mind quickly. If you hesitate, declarer will "guess" that you hold the Queen.

(1)	(2)

♣ K 9 5 4   ♣ K 6 5 4

♣ Q 7 3 $\boxed{\begin{array}{c} N \\ W \quad E \\ S \end{array}}$ ♣ 8 6   ♣ Q 9 3 $\boxed{\begin{array}{c} N \\ W \quad E \\ S \end{array}}$ ♣ A 10 8

♣ A J 10 2   ♣ J 7 2

In (1), if you cover, declarer has no problem — he makes four tricks.
In (2), if you cover, your side will make three club tricks; if you do not cover, you will win only two tricks.

On occasion, the adverse bidding will furnish you with a clue as to the location of the Ace. But where such information is not available, your approach will be quite unscientific: you have to guess as to the whereabouts of the Ace.

4. As was mentioned, where dummy has two honors, it is *usually* good policy to cover. On occasion, however, whether to cover or not will depend on whether you think your partner has the Ace (in which case you cover), or whether declarer has it (in which case you do not cover).

♡ K 10 5

♡ Q 7 2

```
     N
   W   E
     S
```

J of ♡ led

The Jack of Hearts is led, and there you are deciding as to whether to cover or not. If only you knew which of these two types of hands declarer possesses:

(1)   (2)

♡ K 10 5   ♡ K 10 5

♡ Q 7 2   `W   E`   ♡ 8 6 3   ♡ Q 7 2   `W   E`   ♡ A 9 8 4

♡ A J 9 4   ♡ J 6 3

If declarer has Hand (1), you will look downright silly if you cover; if he has Hand (2), you will look downright silly if you do not cover, for now declarer will make two heart tricks by playing low from dummy; whereas, if you had put up your Queen, he would have made but one trick. What to do in this case? Live cleanly, get to bed early, do a good deed every day — and hold Aces and Kings so that you can become a declarer instead of a second-hand defender.

In conclusion, then, the question of what to do second-hand in the above situations is not a simple matter to resolve. As yet, no principles have been designed to cover these "Queen" situations — and there never will be.

II. Second Hand Defense When Playing *After* the Dummy

The contents of this chapter, up to this point, have been devoted exclusively to second hand playing *before* the exposed dummy plays. The basic principles which have been presented to cover these situations apply equally to second hand when he plays *after* the dummy. The difference is a visual one: you can see the cards in the dummy, but you cannot see the cards in declarer's hand. Peculiar though it may appear to be, this lack of visibility usually makes second hand's decision easier to make, as will be observed.

The governing principle here is the same: "cover an honor with an honor." That is:

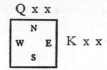

North being the dummy when the Queen is led, you cover with the King. This will create a winning trick for your partner if he has the ten or Jack. If he has neither of these two cards, then no matter whether you cover or not, all is lost:

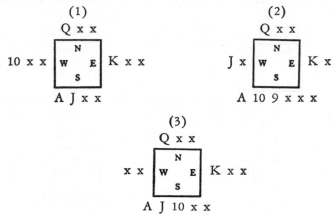

(1)

Q x x

10 x x [N W E S] K x x

A J x x

(2)

Q x x

J x [N W E S] K x

A 10 9 x x x

(3)

Q x x

x x [N W E S] K x x

A J 10 x x

In (1), when you cover the Queen with the King, you promote your partner's ten-spot into a winner. If you do not cover, declarer will lose no tricks in this suit.

In (2), if you do not cover, declarer brings home the suit without losing a trick; if you cover, your partner's Jack will capture a trick.

In (3), it makes no difference whether you cover or you do not, for declarer will lose no tricks.

There will be many situations such as the above where by covering you create the possibility or probability of winning a trick for your side; whereas, by not covering you will never win a trick. Such a situation is the following:

Q 7 2

10 5 [N W E S] K 6 3

A J 9 8 4

If you cover the Queen with the King, declarer's Ace will win. Now, in all probability, instead of then playing the Jack to drop partner's ten, declarer will return to dummy to finesse you for the ten-spot (the mathematically-sound play). In covering, you create a potential trick for your partner. If you do not cover, declarer will lead a low one from dummy at trick two, simultaneously finessing your "marked" King and dropping partner's ten-spot. He will now avoid the loss of any tricks.

As far as "covering an honor with an honor" is concerned, it is a general rule. However, there is a major exception: when the dummy holds a sequence of two honors, and one of these is led, you should practically never cover the first lead. Consider these illustrations. You are East:

(1)   Q J 8   (2)   J 10 8

	N	
W		E
	S	

K 5 2

	N	
W		E
	S	

K 5 2

In (1) and (2) when one of dummy's honors is led, you do not cover with the King. When the remaining honor is led, you *do* cover.

(1)   Q J 8   (2)   J 10 8

10 7 6

	N	
W		E
	S	

K 5 2

Q 9 6

	N	
W		E
	S	

K 5 2

A 9 4 3   A 7 4 3

In (1) if you cover the Queen with the King, declarer will encounter no difficulty in avoiding the loss of a trick, since he will finesse your partner for the ten-spot at trick two. If you properly do not cover the Queen, but cover the Jack when it is next led, your partner's ten-spot will become established (if West does not possess the ten-spot all is lost regardless of what you do).

In (2) if you cover the Jack with the King, declarer's Ace will win, after which he will lead towards dummy's ten-spot, your partner's Queen winning. The defense will then have made but one trick. But if you do not cover, declarer will let the Jack ride, your partner's Queen winning. Now the defenders must obtain another trick.

Just one more illustration as far as second hand's defense is concerned. This is a situation that occurs quite regularly:

♣ K Q x x

	N	
W		E
	S	

♣ A x

♣ J

South leads the Jack, and very often West tends to let it win. Another club is then led, West being forced to take his Ace. West has just lost a trick:

♣ K Q x x

	N	
♣ A x	W E	♣ 10 x x x
	S	

♣ J x x

Had West captured South's Jack, East's ten would have become a potential winner, and declarer would have made but two club tricks. But when West declined to win the Jack with the Ace he was later forced to capture a low club, thereby giving declarer three club tricks.

As a principle, the above situation might be stated this way:

Whenever an honor is led, and you as second hand have the Ace of that suit, take your Ace — or have a good excuse ready when your partner asks you why you did not take it. And a good, acceptable, excuse would be the following "pat" situation:

♣ K 10 x x

	N	
♣ A x	W E	
	S	

♣ J

Declarer leads the Jack of Clubs, and unless you are reasonably certain that he has only the singleton Jack, you should play low. Declarer will now probably play low from dummy, finessing you for the Queen. This could easily be the situation:

♣ K 10 x x

	N	
♣ A x	W E	♣ Q x x x x
	S	

♣ J x

If you take your Ace at trick one, declarer's King will capture the second round of the suit. Whereas, if you play low, and declarer does likewise from dummy, your side will be sure of the first two tricks in the suit. Even if declarer guesses correctly at trick one, and puts up the King, you will always win a trick with your Ace. By playing low on the lead of the Jack you stand to gain without risking anything.

SECOND HAND DEFENSE IN ACTUAL COMPETITION

1. "COVER AN HONOR WITH AN HONOR"

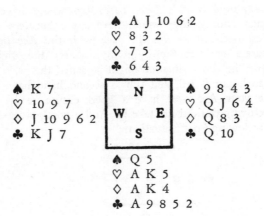

$\spadesuit$ A J 10 6 2
$\heartsuit$ 8 3 2
$\diamondsuit$ 7 5
$\clubsuit$ 6 4 3

$\spadesuit$ K 7
$\heartsuit$ 10 9 7
$\diamondsuit$ J 10 9 6 2
$\clubsuit$ K J 7

$\spadesuit$ 9 8 4 3
$\heartsuit$ Q J 6 4
$\diamondsuit$ Q 8 3
$\clubsuit$ Q 10

$\spadesuit$ Q 5
$\heartsuit$ A K 5
$\diamondsuit$ A K 4
$\clubsuit$ A 9 8 5 2

T HERE is nothing complicated about this deal which was played a few years ago. However, I have used it very frequently for teaching purposes, and second hand too often defends incorrectly.

The contract is *three notrump,* against which West opens the Diamond Jack, taken by declarer's King. Declarer then leads the spade Queen — and West tends to play low almost as often as not. Declarer now has a snap, leading his remaining spade and bringing in the entire suit.

From West's point of view, not to cover the Queen with the King shows poor judgment, since West knows that declarer's Queen will win the trick, after which dummy's Ace will fell West's King. In not covering, West gives declarer one trick with the Queen and another with the Ace; in covering, he forces declarer to expend the Ace and Queen to capture his King. In neither case can West make his King, but in forcing declarer to use the Ace and Queen to get his King, West promotes partner's nine-spot into a winning trick.

From declarer's point of view, if West plays the King on the Queen, he should be permitted to hold the trick. Now no matter what the defense returns, South makes four spade tricks and his contract.

2.   "COVER AN HONOR WITH AN HONOR"

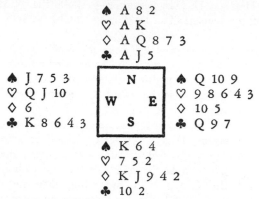

```
                 ♠ A 8 2
                 ♡ A K
                 ◊ A Q 8 7 3
                 ♣ A J 5
♠ J 7 5 3            N          ♠ Q 10 9
♡ Q J 10       W         E      ♡ 9 8 6 4 3
◊ 6                            ◊ 10 5
♣ K 8 6 4 3         S          ♣ Q 9 7
                 ♠ K 6 4
                 ♡ 7 5 2
                 ◊ K J 9 4 2
                 ♣ 10 2
```

West, on lead against South's *six diamond* contract, opened the Queen of Hearts which was taken by North's King. The Ace of Diamonds was then played, followed by a diamond to the King, drawing the adverse trumps. Now the ten of clubs was led. If West had made the "normal" play of refusing to part with his King, North would also have played low, East's Queen winning. Upon obtaining the lead again, South would then have successfully finessed dummy's Jack of Clubs, and on the Ace of Clubs declarer's losing spade would have been discarded.

But West put his King of Clubs on the ten-spot, and declarer could never win more than one club trick. He ultimately lost both a club and a spade, for a one-trick set.

3.   "SECOND HAND LOW — OR HIGH?"

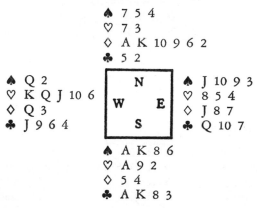

```
                 ♠ 7 5 4
                 ♡ 7 3
                 ◊ A K 10 9 6 2
                 ♣ 5 2
♠ Q 2               N          ♠ J 10 9 3
♡ K Q J 10 6   W         E      ♡ 8 5 4
◊ Q 3                          ◊ J 8 7
♣ J 9 6 4           S          ♣ Q 10 7
                 ♠ A K 8 6
                 ♡ A 9 2
                 ◊ 5 4
                 ♣ A K 8 3
```

South arrives at a *three notrump* contract, against which West opens the King of Hearts. This is permitted to hold the trick, as is the continuation of the Queen. The third round of hearts is then captured by declarer's Ace.

The five of diamonds is now led from the South hand and if West mechanically plays low, declarer makes his contract by putting up dummy's nine-spot. East, upon winning this trick with the Jack, has no heart to play back, and whatever else he elects to return, declarer will win and cash the entire diamond suit, West's Queen falling.

When this deal was played a few years ago, our West defender was John Gerber of Houston, Texas. On declarer's lead of a low diamond, Johnny put up his Queen — and declarer was a "dead duck." If the Queen were permitted to hold the trick West would cash his hearts; if declarer captured the Queen with the King, then he could never establish and cash the diamond suit, for there was no entry to dummy.

Why second hand's "sacrificial" play of the diamond Queen? To a top-notch player — one who is thinking all the time — it is not too complicated. The reason can be found in answering the query: *Who has the Jack of Diamonds?*

If South has the Jack, reasons West, then South will make six diamond tricks, whether he's the world's best player or the world's worst player. That is, should West play low, whether declarer puts up dummy's nine-spot or the King, the Ace will drop West's Queen on the next round. Therefore, West properly assumes that South does not have the Jack, for if he does there is no hope for the defenders. So West figuratively places the Jack with East — and he puts up the Queen on the original diamond lead to prevent declarer from "passing by" a diamond to East.

4. "UNBLOCKING"

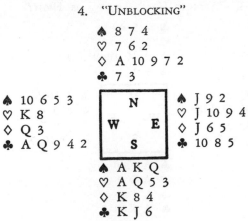

```
                 ♠ 8 7 4
                 ♡ 7 6 2
                 ◇ A 10 9 7 2
                 ♣ 7 3
  ♠ 10 6 5 3          N          ♠ J 9 2
  ♡ K 8                           ♡ J 10 9 4
  ◇ Q 3          W       E        ◇ J 6 5
  ♣ A Q 9 4 2        S           ♣ 10 8 5
                 ♠ A K Q
                 ♡ A Q 5 3
                 ◇ K 8 4
                 ♣ K J 6
```

When this hand was actually played, West opened his fourth best club against South's *three notrump* contract, East's ten being taken by South's Jack.

Declarer's play at trick two was to lead the King of Diamonds — on which West dropped the Queen! Our West player happened to be Mary Jane Kauder of California, one of the nation's top players. Although the play of the Queen smacks of the spectacular, it was actually fundamentally sound.

One thing was certain. West wanted East to have the lead, to play a club through declarer. If declarer had the Jack of Diamonds in addition to the King, then West's Queen would fall on the next round and dummy's entire diamond suit would be brought in. So Mary Jane properly assumed (hoped) that her partner held the Jack.

With the Queen falling on the King, there was no way for declarer to bring in the suit without relinquishing the lead to East. And, when East won the second round of diamonds with the Jack, a club return defeated declarer.

Had West not dropped the Queen on the King, declarer would then have played a second round of diamonds, and West's Queen would have been permitted to hold the trick. Now no matter what West returned, declarer would have had no worry about the club suit, and dummy's diamonds would have yielded her the contract.

5. "THE PRESERVATION OF PARTNER'S ENTRY CARD"

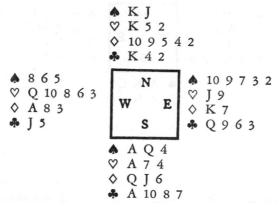

        ♠ K J
        ♡ K 5 2
        ♢ 10 9 5 4 2
        ♣ K 4 2

♠ 8 6 5   ♠ 10 9 7 3 2
♡ Q 10 8 6 3   N   ♡ J 9
♢ A 8 3   W   E   ♢ K 7
♣ J 5   S   ♣ Q 9 6 3

        ♠ A Q 4
        ♡ A 7 4
        ♢ Q J 6
        ♣ A 10 8 7

Against South's *three notrump* contract, West opened the six of hearts, dummy's King winning. [1] The deuce of diamonds was then led

[1] The fact that declarer could have made his contract by not winning the first heart lead is of no importance here.

— and East hopped up with the King! A heart was then returned, dooming declarer to defeat, for he could not establish the diamonds without giving West the lead. And, once West obtained the lead, of course, he would cash his good hearts.

Actually, East's second hand play of the King was, from the expert point of view, the only correct play. The point of the play was to conserve West's diamond entry — if he had one — so that West could obtain the lead after his hearts were established. If West did not have a diamond entry, then East's play of the King cost nothing (assuming, let us say, that declarer had A Q x, or A Q x x, in which case declarer would have successfully finessed through East's King had East not put up the King).

Had East automatically played low on the diamond lead, West's Ace would have won the trick, and he would then have continued hearts. But later, when East got in with the diamond King, he would have had no heart to return, enabling declarer to fulfill his contract.

6. "DECEPTION"

(A False Card)

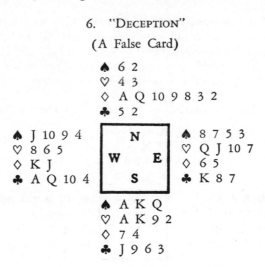

```
              ♠ 6 2
              ♡ 4 3
              ◇ A Q 10 9 8 3 2
              ♣ 5 2

♠ J 10 9 4        N        ♠ 8 7 5 3
♡ 8 6 5                    ♡ Q J 10 7
◇ K J        W      E      ◇ 6 5
♣ A Q 10 4        S        ♣ K 8 7

              ♠ A K Q
              ♡ A K 9 2
              ◇ 7 4
              ♣ J 9 6 3
```

The heroine of this deal was "Jackie" Begin, one of Canada's top-ranking women players.

Against South's *three notrump* contract, she elected to open the Jack of Spades, declarer's Queen winning. A diamond was promptly led — and Jackie just as promptly played *the King!* Declarer started to reach for the Ace — and then paused for reflection.

If the King were a singleton — and it certainly appeared to be, for who would dare voluntarily to play the King into the jaws of the

exposed A Q — then East would have started with the J x x originally.
Should this be so, then the diamond suit could not be brought home
if the Ace captured West's "singleton" King. On this assumption
declarer allowed the King to hold the trick, hoping that West would
not shift to a club. But West did shift to the Ace of Clubs, and
followed with a low club, resulting in the defeat of the contract.

Had second hand automatically played "low" (the Jack) on the
diamond lead, declarer would have put up dummy's Queen, winning the
trick. It would then have been routine play. No matter what declarer
did from here in, he could not help making seven diamonds, three
spades, and two hearts, for a total of twelve tricks.

7. "DECEPTION"
(A False Card)

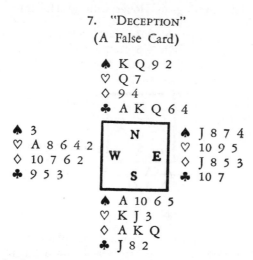

```
          ♠ K Q 9 2
          ♡ Q 7
          ◇ 9 4
          ♣ A K Q 6 4

♠ 3                      ♠ J 8 7 4
♡ A 8 6 4 2    N         ♡ 10 9 5
◇ 10 7 6 2   W   E       ◇ J 8 5 3
♣ 9 5 3         S        ♣ 10 7

          ♠ A 10 6 5
          ♡ K J 3
          ◇ A K Q
          ♣ J 8 2
```

South arrived at a *six spade* contract, against which West opened
the Ace of Hearts, after which he continued with a heart, dummy's
Queen winning. Dummy's King of trumps was now laid down, and
second hand (Charlie Solomon, of Philadelphia) dropped the eight-spot,
West following with the three. Declarer then led a low spade to his
Ace, and East played the seven. When West showed out the slam was
doomed to defeat, since Charlie's Jack of Spades had become a sure
winner.

From declarer's point of view, his sole "worry" was that one of the
opponents' might be holding the J x x x of spades. When he led
dummy's King, and East dropped the eight, assuming the eight-spot to
be East's lowest spade, it surely seemed that if anyone had four spades
to the Jack, it would be West.

From Charlie's point of view, he realized that if declarer located the Jack of Spades, the contract would be made. Hence the eight-spot, designed to deceive declarer — and it did.

Had East played the four-spot and West the three, there is no telling what declarer's next play would have been. If dummy's Queen were played next, the slam would be fulfilled since East's Jack would now be located, and successfully finessed. If instead, the Ace was played (as it was), then defeat. The play of the eight-spot was a terrific play — and the reward was well-deserved.

8. "DECEPTION"

(Not Covering an Honor with an Honor)

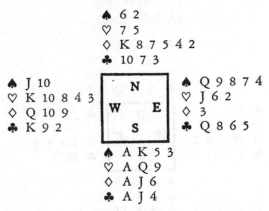

```
              ♠ 6 2
              ♡ 7 5
              ◇ K 8 7 5 4 2
              ♣ 10 7 3

♠ J 10                         ♠ Q 9 8 7 4
♡ K 10 8 4 3      N            ♡ J 6 2
◇ Q 10 9      W     E          ◇ 3
♣ K 9 2          S            ♣ Q 8 6 5

              ♠ A K 5 3
              ♡ A Q 9
              ◇ A J 6
              ♣ A J 4
```

One of the most imaginative second hand plays that I have ever seen took place on this deal. The hero was Howard Schenken, of New York City, who needs no introduction. In a poll taken some years ago, Howard was voted the "favorite bridge partner" of the expert bridge players.

Against South's *three notrump* contract, he opened the four of hearts, East's Jack being taken by declarer's Queen. The Ace of Diamonds was then led, everybody following suit. Then came the Jack of Diamonds on which Howard played *the ten-spot!* Our declarer now became a psychologist.

South reasoned that if West held the Q 10, he would automatically have covered the Jack with the Queen, for in so doing, he would be promoting his ten-spot into a winner. Therefore, declarer concluded, West did not have the Queen, which was the only diamond missing. So he put up dummy's King to drop East's Queen. When the Queen did not drop, declarer was defeated, for he had no entry to dummy to cash the diamonds.

From West's point of view, the play of the ten-spot was not a "blunder." He knew on the second diamond lead that declarer had started with either the A J x or A J doubleton of diamonds. If declarer had the A J doubleton of diamonds then by West's not covering the Jack with the Queen, declarer could never make dummy's King of Diamonds unless he overtook the Jack with the King. But if declarer had the A J x of Diamonds, then should West cover the Jack with the Queen, he would be permitted to hold the trick, since declarer would need his low diamond as a re-entry to the then-established diamond suit. West's hope, therefore, was to throw declarer off the track, which he certainly did.

9. "UNBLOCKING"

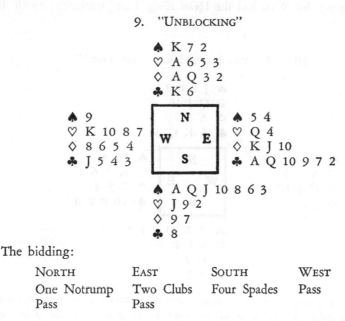

```
              ♠ K 7 2
              ♡ A 6 5 3
              ◇ A Q 3 2
              ♣ K 6
♠ 9              N              ♠ 5 4
♡ K 10 8 7    W     E          ♡ Q 4
◇ 8 6 5 4                       ◇ K J 10
♣ J 5 4 3         S            ♣ A Q 10 9 7 2
              ♠ A Q J 10 8 6 3
              ♡ J 9 2
              ◇ 9 7
              ♣ 8
```

The bidding:

NORTH	EAST	SOUTH	WEST
One Notrump	Two Clubs	Four Spades	Pass
Pass	Pass		

West opened a club, dummy's King being captured by East's Ace, after which another club was played, declarer ruffing. Two rounds of trumps followed, drawing the outstanding trumps. Dummy's Ace of Hearts was then laid down, on which East dropped the Queen! When declarer played another heart, West was able to cash two heart tricks. West then led a diamond and East ultimately made the King for the setting trick.

Had East not thrown the Queen of Hearts, he would have won the second heart trick. He would then have been compelled to lead either a diamond, which would give declarer two diamond tricks; or a club, which would enable declarer to discard his losing diamond while simultaneously trumping the trick in dummy.

How did East know enough to toss away the Queen of Hearts? Well, first, he foresaw the untenable position he would be in if he won the second heart lead with the Queen. And, secondly, East was "counting." He knew that South had started with seven sure spade tricks (West having failed to follow to the second round of the trump suit); and he saw the Ace of Hearts and the Ace of Diamonds in dummy. All of which added up to nine tricks. If South also had the King of Hearts, then he had a guaranteed contract.

So, hoping that West had the Heart King, East "unblocked" with the Queen.

10.   "SECOND HAND HIGH — OR LOW?"

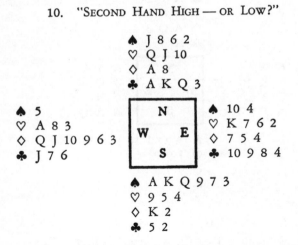

♠ J 8 6 2
♡ Q J 10
◇ A 8
♣ A K Q 3

♠ 5
♡ A 8 3
◇ Q J 10 9 6 3
♣ J 7 6

♠ 10 4
♡ K 7 6 2
◇ 7 5 4
♣ 10 9 8 4

♠ A K Q 9 7 3
♡ 9 5 4
◇ K 2
♣ 5 2

That the six spade contract South arrived at was a most unhappy one, is of no concern. What is of consequence is that he made it because East mechanically followed the principle of "second hand low."

The opening lead was the diamond Queen, captured by dummy's Ace. The Ace of Spades was then played, followed by a spade to dummy's Jack. Now came the Queen of Hearts, East followed with a low card, and West's Ace won the trick. West then continued with a diamond, South's King winning. Declarer now ran his trumps, and the situation before playing his last trump was this:

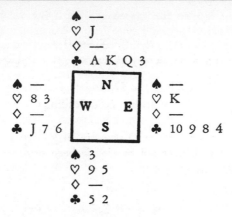

South now led his remaining trump, discarding the heart Jack from dummy — and East was squeezed. If he discarded the King of Hearts, declarer's nine-spot would be good; if, instead, he discarded a club, all of dummy's clubs would become winners.

East (who will remain anonymous) was a top-notch player, and as such, we can say he slipped. He should have covered the Queen of Hearts with the King. From East's point of view, he should have known that South had started with six spades; also that South had two diamond tricks (West had opened the Queen) ; and dummy had three club tricks. This totalled to eleven. If South also had the heart Ace, then he had twelve tricks. Therefore, was it not proper for East to put up his King of Hearts? When this would have won the trick, a lead of another heart would have become automatic.

CHAPTER XVIII

CONVENTIONAL AND STANDARD DEFENSIVE PLAYS

(While the Defenders are either
attacking or defending)

IN this chapter there are presented six major types of defensive plays and situations which have not previously been presented. They are:

1. The hold-up play.
2. "Ducking" in defensive play.
3. Discarding in a suit which partner has bid.
4. What to play when partner opens an Ace against a notrump contract.
5. The Trump Echo.
6. The "Uppercut."

1. The Hold-up Play.

This is a standard play by declarer in notrump contracts.[1] The purpose of it is to break the communication between the two defenders by rendering one of them void of the suit which they are trying to establish.

The hold-up play is also utilized by the defenders, although the defensive occurrence of this play is not so frequent. The reason for the employment of the play is to break the communication between declarer's hand and the dummy: specifically, to prevent declarer from cashing dummy's established or to-be-established suit.

How often have you been confronted with this situation, defending against South's *three notrump* contract:

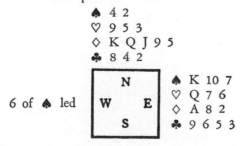

```
              ♠ 4 2
              ♡ 9 5 3
              ◇ K Q J 9 5
              ♣ 8 4 2
                  ┌─────────┐        ♠ K 10 7
                  │    N    │        ♡ Q 7 6
  6 of ♠ led      │  W   E  │        ◇ A 8 2
                  │    S    │        ♣ 9 6 5 3
                  └─────────┘
```

_____
[1] See Chapter V.

Your partner, West, opens a low spade against South's three notrump contract, your King being taken by declarer's Ace. Declarer then leads the *ten of diamonds,* a low one is played from dummy, and you probably say to yourself, "I won't take it. If I do, I'll enable declarer to cash all of dummy's diamonds." So, with his ten-spot winning, declarer leads another diamond, putting up dummy's nine-spot. Now you hesitate a little more, being quite dubious about what to do. If you take it, declarer may have another diamond; if you do not take it, declarer may have no more diamonds, and you have given him a present of a trick. The average bridge player, confronted with the above situation, simply takes a guess — which is sometimes right and sometimes wrong. Actually, the guesswork has been eliminated by the better players, for there is a signalling convention employed by second hand or fourth hand to tell his partner when to take his Ace.

It is rather a simple convention, although it may appear difficult at first glance. When it is obvious that declarer is trying to establish a long suit in dummy (which has no outside entries), and that second hand's partner is going to have a problem as to when he should take his Ace, second hand gives *a high-low signal* holding two cards or four cards of that suit; where second hand has three of that suit (say 8 5 2), he plays his lowest card on the first lead (the deuce) and then follows up by playing the five-spot. Fourth hand, perceiving the failure to give a high-low signal in the latter instance, will then *know* that his partner had three cards in that suit, and by subtraction, can determine how many declarer held. Let us take a look at a practical application of this convention:

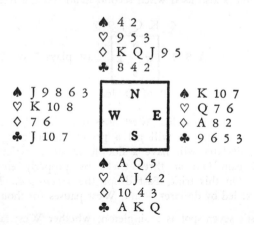

Against South's three notrump contract, West opened the six of spades,

East's King falling to declarer's Ace. South then led the ten of diamonds, West played the *seven-spot,* North and East following with low diamonds. Declarer then played the four of diamonds, West put up the *six-spot,* and dummy's nine captured the trick when East properly declined to take his Ace. Declarer now went down a trick, being unable to establish and cash dummy's diamonds.

West's *high-low* signal (7, 6) had told East that West had either two or four diamonds. That he had four became an impossibility when South led a second diamond, for if West had four diamonds, then there were 14 diamonds in the deck. Therefore East *knew* that West originally had held precisely two diamonds, and that declarer still had a diamond left. But suppose this had been the situation:

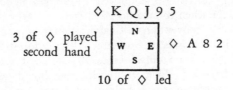

◇ K Q J 9 5

3 of ◇ played
second hand

◇ A 8 2

10 of ◇ led

Had the ten of diamonds been led, West following with the *three-spot,* the ten-spot would win the trick. Then when South would lead the four of diamonds, upon which West would follow with the *six-spot,* East would know that West had started with *exactly three diamonds,* for otherwise he would have given a high-low signal. East would now take his Ace, and not allow South to "steal" a diamond trick.

This convention is also used when second hand has the Ace.

◇ K Q J 9 5

◇ A 8 2

East plays 7 of ◇

10 of ◇ led

When the diamond ten is led, West does not take his Ace (whenever declarer has a singleton, he will get a present of a trick; but twenty times as often, declarer will have a doubleton or a tripleton, and the defenders will gain two or three tricks by properly employing the hold-up play). On this trick, East drops the *seven-spot.* The four of diamonds is next led by declarer — and West pauses for thought.

(1)   If East's seven-spot is a singleton, whether West takes his Ace or not becomes immaterial, for in this case declarer started with four

diamonds and will be able to establish and cash dummy's diamonds. Therefore West properly assumes that the seven-spot is not a singleton.

(2)   The seven-spot could not be from a four-card suit, for if it were, then the diamond distribution (on South's second diamond lead) would be 5-4-3-2, which adds to 14.

(3)   The seven-spot, therefore, must be from a doubleton or tripleton. And, since only the six and three of diamonds are missing, the seven-spot had to be the initiation of a high-low signal. Consequently, West knows that East started with precisely two diamonds (7, 6 or 7, 3). So West declines to capture the second diamond lead, knowing that South still has a diamond remaining.

Let the situation now be:

$\Diamond$ K Q J 9 5

$\Diamond$ A 8 2 | N | East plays the 3 spot
| W   E |
| S |

10 of $\Diamond$ led

Again, declarer leads the ten-spot which is permitted to win, East dropping the three-spot. South then plays the four of diamonds. Should West take his Ace, or hold up for another round? Had East held two diamonds (four becomes impossible when South leads a second diamond), he would have initiated the high-low signal at trick one. But the three-spot that East had played was the lowest in circulation. Therefore it was either a singleton (in which case declarer had started with four diamonds) or from a three-card suit, in which case no high-low signal would be given. By elimination then, West knows that East started with three diamonds — and he therefore captures South's second diamond lead.

There will be situations where second hand has the Ace, and he will be uncertain as to whether his partner's first play was made from a doubleton or a tripleton. In these cases, he will simply have to guess as to what to do. But what it boils down to is this: when the convention is used, the defenders will *not* have to guess *all* the time — seventy-five percent of the time they will know with certainty; twenty-five percent of the time they will still be guessing. And that is how "average" players become good bridge players; by being right not all the time, but a higher percentage of the time than their competitors.

A "judgment" application of the defensive hold-up play can be observed from the deal which follows. In this deal the hold-up was employed by a defender who held a double-stopper in the suit that declarer was attempting to establish.

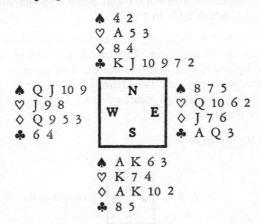

♠ 4 2
♡ A 5 3
◇ 8 4
♣ K J 10 9 7 2

♠ Q J 10 9   ♠ 8 7 5
♡ J 9 8   ♡ Q 10 6 2
◇ Q 9 5 3   ◇ J 7 6
♣ 6 4   ♣ A Q 3

♠ A K 6 3
♡ K 7 4
◇ A K 10 2
♣ 8 5

Against South's *three notrump* contract, West opened the Spade Queen, which was taken by Declarer's Ace. South then led the eight of clubs, and finessed for the Queen. If East had taken his Queen, declarer would have fulfilled his contract, for there would be no way of preventing declarer from establishing and cashing dummy's club suit.

East, recognizing that he must try to prevent the establishment of the club suit, properly did not take the Queen on the first club lead. He lost nothing in so holding up, for he would always either make the A Q, or declarer would be unable to establish dummy's clubs. Declarer then led another club, East capturing the trick with the Queen. No matter what declarer did from here in, his position was a hopeless one, since he had but one entry to dummy, the Heart Ace. If he used that card as an entry to establish the club suit, he would have no entry to get to dummy to cash the suit.

2. "Ducking" in Defensive Play:

By "ducking" is meant the refusal to win a trick which is being proffered. This play is somewhat analogous to the defender's hold-up play, except that it is made while the defending side is attacking as opposed to defending.

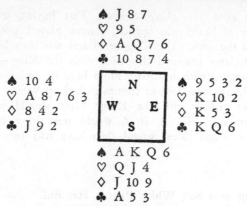

West opens the six of hearts against South's *three notrump* contract, East's King winning. East promptly returns the ten of hearts, and declarer plays the Jack.

If West takes his Ace of Hearts and returns a heart, he will establish the suit — but he will never obtain the lead to cash it since he has no entry.

So, at trick two, when declarer puts up the Jack of Hearts, West "ducks" it, with the hope that partner has another heart plus the ability to obtain the lead (an "entry").

As is apparent, sooner or later East must obtain the lead with the King of Diamonds. When he does. he will return his remaining heart, West capturing declarer's Queen, and then going on to run the rest of the suit. All in all the defenders make four hearts and a diamond.

The following situation bears a resemblance to the "ducking" play just described, and is very often misplayed by the average defender.

South arrived at a *four-spade* contract, East having overcalled in hearts. The nine of hearts was opened, dummy played low, and East's ten-spot captured the trick. The King of Hearts was then led, followed by the Ace. Declarer trumped this trick with the King — and West promptly overtrumped with his Ace. From here in declarer's path was smooth, for his Queen and Jack of trumps picked up West's six and ten.

When declarer ruffed with the King, West should simply have discarded a diamond. His A 10 6 would now have been behind declarer's Q J x — and West would then have had two sure trump winners.

3. Discarding in a Suit Which Partner Has Bid.

Whenever you have three low cards in partner's suit, you lead your highest — that is, with 8 7 2, you would lead the eight-spot. When that suit is led the next time, conventionally you will *discard downwards* — having opened the eight, your next play will be the seven-spot; and the third time the suit is led, you will play the deuce. Played in this manner, you will very often give your partner a complete "count" of your hand. If you do not discard downwards, partner will perpetually be guessing as to what you have. The importance of this "downward discard" convention can be observed from the following deal:

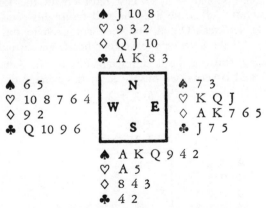

```
              ♠ J 10 8
              ♡ 9 3 2
              ◇ Q J 10
              ♣ A K 8 3

♠ 6 5           ┌─────────┐      ♠ 7 3
♡ 10 8 7 6 4    │    N    │      ♡ K Q J
◇ 9 2           │ W     E │      ◇ A K 7 6 5
♣ Q 10 9 6      │    S    │      ♣ J 7 5
                └─────────┘
              ♠ A K Q 9 4 2
              ♡ A 5
              ◇ 8 4 3
              ♣ 4 2
```

North-South arrived at a *four spade* contract after East had opened the bidding with one diamond. West dutifully opened his nine of diamonds, East winning the trick with the King. On this trick South dropped the *four-spot*. The diamond Ace was then continued, declarer

playing the *eight-spot*, West following with the *deuce*. At this point
if West had not discarded downwards in conventional fashion, East
would have had a problem as to whether to switch to hearts, or whether
to play another diamond. In the abstract it seemed that South had no
more diamonds, having played the eight-spot to the previous trick.

But the three of diamonds was missing — and East knew that if West
had held the 9 3 2, he would have played the three-spot to the second
lead of diamonds. Since he had played the deuce, however, South was
known to still possess the three. So East played another diamond,
West ruffing. South ultimately had to lose a heart trick, and suffered a
one-trick set.

4.   What to Play When Partner Opens An Ace Against a Notrump
      Contract.

It is a very rare case when an Ace is the opening lead against a
notrump contract. When it is done, it denotes a specific type of suit in
the leader's hand: long and almost solid (A K J 10 x x; A K Q x x x).

It is standard procedure that when your partner opens an Ace against
a notrump contract that you follow with your *highest card in that suit*,
regardless of its denomination. In so doing, you will very often convey
most important information to him. Let us look at two illustrations:

```
                      ♠ K 8 7 2
                      ♡ 7 4
                      ◇ A Q J 6
                      ♣ K J 3
  ♠ 6                                      ♠ Q 10 9 5
  ♡ A K J 10 6 3         N                 ♡ Q 2
  ◇ 8 5 2            W        E             ◇ 9 7 4
  ♣ 9 5 4                S                  ♣ 10 8 7 2
                      ♠ A J 4 3
                      ♡ 9 8 5
                      ◇ K 10 3
                      ♣ A Q 6
```

The bidding:

NORTH	EAST	SOUTH	WEST
One Diamond	Pass	Two Notrump	Pass
Three Notrump	Pass	Pass	Pass

If you do not approve of South's two notrump bid, you have a point. But the fact remains that bids such as these are made every day — and very often produce good results.

West opens the Ace of Hearts, and if East plays the discouraging deuce, West will undoubtedly shift to some other suit, for fear that if he next leads the heart King, he will establish declarer's theoretical Queen.

But, following convention, on West's lead of the Ace, East plays the Queen — and West promptly cashes six heart tricks.

Another illustration:

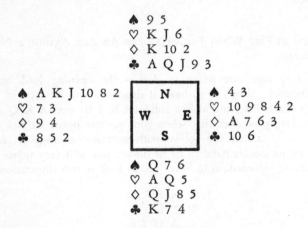

```
               ♠ 9 5
               ♡ K J 6
               ◇ K 10 2
               ♣ A Q J 9 3
♠ A K J 10 8 2    N        ♠ 4 3
♡ 7 3          W     E     ♡ 10 9 8 4 2
◇ 9 4             S        ◇ A 7 6 3
♣ 8 5 2                    ♣ 10 6
               ♠ Q 7 6
               ♡ A Q 5
               ◇ Q J 8 5
               ♣ K 7 4
```

Against South's *three notrump* contract, West opens the Ace of Spades, on which East plays the four. Knowing that East has played his highest spade, West recognizes that to play the King would make a winner out of South's Queen, since South is marked with at least the Q 7 6 (who has the three-spot is unknown). West therefore discontinues the spade suit — and whatever he leads, South will now go down, for sooner or later East will obtain the lead via the Ace of Diamonds, and will play back his remaining spade, trapping declarer's Queen.

Had West cashed his King of Spades at trick two, the Queen of Spades would have produced declarer's ninth trick.

5. The Trump Echo.

The trump echo is a "high-low" signal made within *the trump suit.* Whenever one of the defenders plays high-low in trumps, he is stating:

"Partner, I have three trumps *and* I am void in some suit." Another situation where it becomes apparent that the trump echo is being applied is when one of the defenders ruffs a trick with a trump that is not the lowest. When he later plays a lower trump, his partner knows that the "echoer" still has a trump left, and still possesses the ability to trump a trick. To illustrate:

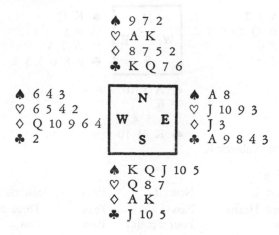

```
              ♠ 9 7 2
              ♡ A K
              ◊ 8 7 5 2
              ♣ K Q 7 6

♠ 6 4 3          N          ♠ A 8
♡ 6 5 4 2                   ♡ J 10 9 3
◊ Q 10 9 6 4   W   E        ◊ J 3
♣ 2                         ♣ A 9 8 4 3
                 S
              ♠ K Q J 10 5
              ♡ Q 8 7
              ◊ A K
              ♣ J 10 5
```

Against South's *four spade* contract West opened the deuce of clubs, East winning with the Ace and returning a club. West trumped this trick with *the four* of spades.

He now returned a low diamond, East's Jack being taken by declarer's Ace. South then laid down the King of Trumps, West followed with *the three,* and East's Ace won.

Without the use of the trump echo, East would now have had a problem: a club return would be bad if West had no more trumps, and a diamond return would then be proper, in the hope that West had the diamond King.

But, since West had "echoed" in trumps (playing the four-spot first and then following with the three), East knew that West had another trump. He therefore led a club, which West trumped for the setting trick.

Bear in mind that this trump echo is not used promiscuously. It is applied *only* when the user has three trumps *plus the ability to trump something.* If used on every deal, the information thereby imparted will assist declarer more than the signaller's partner.

Let us look at another illustration of the three-card "trump echo":

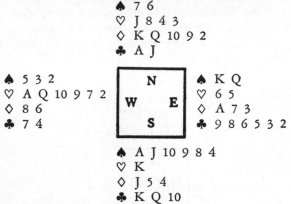

♠ 7 6
♡ J 8 4 3
◇ K Q 10 9 2
♣ A J

♠ 5 3 2   ♠ K Q
♡ A Q 10 9 7 2   ♡ 6 5
◇ 8 6   ◇ A 7 3
♣ 7 4   ♣ 9 8 6 5 3 2

♠ A J 10 9 8 4
♡ K
◇ J 5 4
♣ K Q 10

North-South vulnerable.

The bidding:

WEST	NORTH	EAST	SOUTH
Three Hearts	Pass	Pass	Three Spades
Pass	Four Spades	Pass	Pass
Pass			

West opened the eight of diamonds, East taking the trick with his Ace, and returning a diamond, West dropping the six-spot. On these two tricks declarer played the four and Jack of Diamonds.

Dummy was then entered via the club Jack, and a spade led, East's Queen falling to declarer's Ace. The Jack of Spades was now led, East's King winning. On the first spade lead West dropped *the three-spot,* and on the second, *the deuce.*

East now knew that West had started with three trumps, and promptly returned his remaining diamond, West trumping, after which the Ace of Hearts was cashed, for the setting trick. Without the use of the trump echo, East would not have known whether or not West possessed a third trump — and East might then have shifted to a heart. With the trump echo, certainty replaced uncertainty.

The following is a classic illustration of the misuse of the trump echo. West, the offender, was one of the nation's best players, but by force of habit he mechanically played high-low in trumps, thereby sealing his doom. The South declarer was Waldemar von Zedtwitz, and North was Lee Hazen.

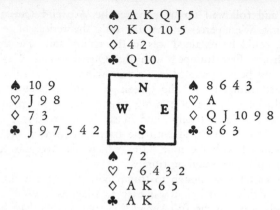

Against South's *six heart* contract, West opened a small club declarer's Ace winning. A heart was then led, dummy's King being captured by East's Ace. On this trick West played the *nine of hearts*. East then returned a club, declarer's King taking the trick.

Von Zedtwitz now led another trump, West following with the *eight-spot*. At this point it was a guess; to play the Queen to drop the sole missing trump, the Jack; or to finesse against the Jack. Choosing to believe West's high-low signal showing three trumps, declarer finessed for the Jack and fulfilled his slam contract.

6. The "Uppercut."

A defensive play which arises frequently enough to warrant its presentation as a standard defensive play is the "uppercut." Let us look at this play in action prior to describing its technical aspects:

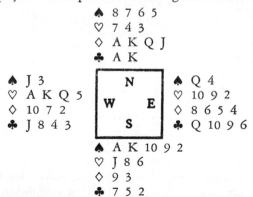

On lead against South's *four spade* contract, West opened the King of Hearts, and followed up by playing the Ace and Queen. Looking at the dummy, West perceived that the only theoretical place where the setting trick could be obtained was in the trump suit. He then led the thirteenth heart, East trumped with the Queen — and West's Jack of Spades had just been promoted into a sure winner!

When East trumped with the Queen of Spades, he was performing the play called an "uppercut": using one of his high trumps to force one of declarer's higher trumps, and in so doing creating a trump trick for partner. Had he trumped with the four-spot instead, declarer would have overtrumped with the nine, after which his Ace and King would have picked up the outstanding trumps.

How did East know enough to trump with the Queen instead of the four-spot? In this situation it was easy to diagnose: West was leading the thirteenth heart, in the full knowledge that neither East nor declarer had any more hearts. Therefore, as West was making this play he knew that declarer would overtrump East. The only purpose of the lead of the thirteenth heart — putting East in the middle — had to be to force declarer to use up a high trump. Otherwise West's play was tantamount to committing partnership suicide. So East trumped with the Queen of Trumps . . . and if your partner ever leads the thirteenth card of a suit, reach for your highest trump and put it on the table.

"Uppercutting" situations are not always as easy to recognize as in the preceding deal. As you play, however, you will become familiar with them, from both a sending and receiving point of view.

Let us look at another illustration:

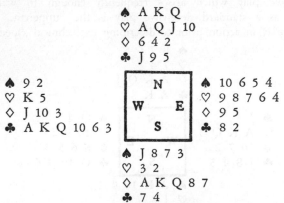

```
               ♠ A K Q
               ♡ A Q J 10
               ◇ 6 4 2
               ♣ J 9 5
♠ 9 2                              ♠ 10 6 5 4
♡ K 5           N                  ♡ 9 8 7 6 4
◇ J 10 3     W     E                ◇ 9 5
♣ A K Q 10 6 3     S                ♣ 8 2
               ♠ J 8 7 3
               ♡ 3 2
               ◇ A K Q 8 7
               ♣ 7 4
```

Against South's *five diamond* contract West opened the King of Clubs and followed up with the Queen, East giving a high-low signal. West then led the three of clubs and East ruffed with the nine-spot, declarer overruffing with the Queen. West's Jack of Diamonds now became the setting trick.

Again, how did East know enough to ruff with the nine-spot and not with the five? Well, it was perfectly apparent from the play to the first two club tricks that West had the club Ace. Why was he not cashing that card at trick three instead of leading a low one towards dummy's Jack? It had to be to get East to "uppercut." So East ruffed with the nine-spot.

The final illustration:

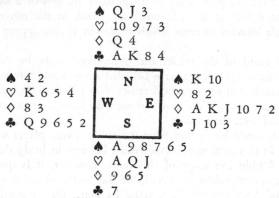

♠ Q J 3
♡ 10 9 7 3
◇ Q 4
♣ A K 8 4

♠ 4 2
♡ K 6 5 4
◇ 8 3
♣ Q 9 6 5 2

♠ K 10
♡ 8 2
◇ A K J 10 7 2
♣ J 10 3

♠ A 9 8 7 6 5
♡ A Q J
◇ 9 6 5
♣ 7

With East having opened the bidding with one diamond, South arrived at a *four spade* contract. The opening lead was the eight of diamonds, dummy played low, and East's ten captured the trick, after which East cashed the diamond Ace. South played the five of diamonds to the first trick, and he dropped the nine on the second diamond lead.

East, however, knew that South still held the diamond six, for West, discarding downwards, had played the eight and three, respectively (had he held the 8 6 3, he would have led the eight, and then played the six-spot).

The *deuce* of diamonds [2] was led next — and West "uppercutted" with the four-spot of spades! Dummy now had to win the trick with the Jack, and East had "found" a spade trick. Since declarer eventually had to lose a heart trick, he went down one. The four of spades sure was a little pain-in-the-neck as far as declarer was concerned.

---

[2] As the reader can observe, East deliberately avoided leading the King of Diamonds on the third diamond lead. Had he led the latter card, West might not have trumped, figuring that East was merely making a safe exit. By leading the two of diamonds, upon which declarer played the six-spot, East *forced* West to trump declarer's six of diamonds.

III. 50 Classic Deals Played by Famous Experts

In each of these 50 deals, there is presented a fleeting moment in the life of the top-flight expert in action: a hand played magnificently, an inspired defensive play, a highly-imaginative analysis of a situation which led to the defeat of his adversary, etc.; and, at the other extreme, an inexcusable blunder or error which made our expert appear to be a mere mortal.

In the mind of the reader the impression might be created that in a few of these episodes, I have belittled some world-famous player, that I have accentuated his weakness rather than his strength, and that I have painted a portrait of "the evil that men do lives after them; the good is oft interred with their bones."

Nothing could be further from the truth. Every player whose name is included in this section on classic deals belongs in bridgedom's "Hall of Fame." Within the scope of this book, however, it is quite impossible to depict in comprehensive detail, the day-to-day skirmishes and victories of each of these experts. If it could be done, their magnificent achievements at the bridge table would far outweigh their occasional mistakes. So, if any particular deal seems to diminish the stature of the expert involved, it is only because I wanted to illustrate that every bridge player is human, and, as such, will blunder and err at times.

When, someday, history will record the sum total of the thousands of accomplishments of these experts, it will be demonstrated that they all are, in fact, the world's greatest bridge players.

RUBBER BRIDGE:
MAYFAIR BRIDGE CLUB

NORTH
♠ J 7 6 4
♡ Q J 4
♢ K 9 3
♣ 10 6 3

WEST
♠ Q 2
♡ 6 5 3
♢ A Q J 10 6 4
♣ Q 5

EAST
♠ 10 3
♡ 10 9
♢ 8 7 5 2
♣ A K 9 7 2

SOUTH
♠ A K 9 8 5
♡ A K 8 7 2
♢ —
♣ J 8 4

North-South vulnerable.

The bidding:

SOUTH	WEST	NORTH	EAST
	H. Fishbein		
1 ♠	2 ♢	Pass	3 ♣
3 ♡	Pass	4 ♠	Pass
Pass	Pass		

Harry Fishbein is famous not only for his flawless technique, but also for his imagination. This deal serves to illustrate the latter.

Harry opened the Queen of Clubs against declarer's four-spade contract. He followed up by playing another club, taken by East's King, after which East cashed the Ace of Clubs. Fishbein now had to make a discard.

If he threw a low heart, East would certainly return a diamond, which suit Harry had bid. And Harry felt — from the bidding — that South was void of diamonds. If, instead, he discarded a low diamond, East might well return a heart. He solved his problem by discarding the Ace of Diamonds!

To say that East was amazed by this discard would be the understatement of the year. Glancing at the dummy, East became aware of the fact that Fishbein wanted neither a heart nor a diamond return. So he returned a club, and Fishbein's Queen of Spades took the setting trick. As is apparent, any return but a club would have given declarer his contract.

MASTERS-TEAM-OF-FOUR
CHAMPIONSHIPS:
1955

NORTH
♠ 6 4
♡ 8
♢ A K Q J 10 8 5
♣ Q 8 4

WEST
♠ K Q 10 9 7 3
♡ A Q 7 6
♢ 9
♣ 10 5

EAST
♠ J 8 2
♡ J 9 5 3
♢ 7 6 4 2
♣ K 3

SOUTH
♠ A 5
♡ K 10 4 2
♢ 3
♣ A J 9 7 6 2

Neither side vulnerable

The bidding:

NORTH	EAST	SOUTH	WEST
	D. Weld		P. Allinger
1 ♢	Pass	2 ♣	2 ♠
3 ♢	Pass	3 ♡	Pass
4 ♣	Pass	6 ♣	Pass
Pass	Pass		

This deal serves as a splendid example of steering declarer away from the proper way of playing the hand.

West opened the King of Spades, which was captured by declarer's Ace. Declarer now surveyed the possibilities. First, East had to have the King of trumps, for otherwise the contract was doomed to defeat. So, declarer promptly led his singleton diamond to dummy's Ace, after which he led the Queen of trumps. The defenders now cooperated beautifully: East played low and West dropped the *ten-spot*. This play "convinced" declarer that West had no more trumps, and that East had started with the K-5-3 of trumps. Hoping to "coup" East, declarer then prepared to cash as many diamonds as he could — but West "ruined" declarer by trumping the King of Diamonds (upon which declarer discarded his spade), and cashing the Ace of Hearts for the setting trick.

Of course if declarer were clairvoyant, he could have made his contract by drawing trumps. But how many South declarers would have correctly diagnosed the true situation?

NATIONAL OPEN TEAM-OF-FOUR CHAMPIONSHIPS:
1951

NORTH
♠ A K 8 2
♡ A K 4 2
◇ Q 6
♣ 6 5 2

WEST
♠ 6 5
♡ J 8 6
◇ A K J 8 7 3
♣ A 9

EAST
♠ 10 9 4 3
♡ 10 3
◇ 9 2
♣ K J 10 7 3

SOUTH
♠ Q J 7
♡ Q 9 7 5
◇ 10 5 4
♣ Q 8 4

Both sides vulnerable

The bidding:

WEST H. Sobel	NORTH	EAST C. Goren	SOUTH
1 ◇	Double	Pass	1 ♡
Pass	2 ♡	Pass	Pass
Pass			

This deal is offered in evidence as to why Charles Goren and Helen Sobel are considered two of the world's finest players. Their defense against South's two heart contract was magnificent.

Mrs. Sobel opened the King of Diamonds, Goren playing the nine-spot, after which the Ace of Diamonds was cashed, Goren completing the echo by following with the deuce. The Jack of Diamonds was then led, a small club being discarded from dummy, with Goren discarding the seven of clubs.

Had Mrs. Sobel now cashed the Ace of Clubs, followed by a club to Goren's King, declarer would have made the remainder of the tricks. But Mrs. Sobel perceived that if her partner held as good as the ten of trumps, she could defeat the contract (provided, of course, that Goren had the King of Clubs, which his discard seemed to indicate he had). So instead of playing the Ace of Clubs, she led the nine-spot, Goren's King winning. Goren now returned a club to Mrs. Sobel's Ace. Mrs. Sobel then led a diamond, Goren "upper-cutting" with the ten-spot of trumps, declarer's Queen winning. Mrs. Sobel now had a sure trump trick, to inflict a one-trick set on declarer.

ANGLO-AMERICAN MATCH:
1949

NORTH
♠ K J 5
♡ 10 8 3
◇ A Q 10 9 8 2
♣ 7

WEST
♠ 10 7 6
♡ A 7 5
◇ J 5
♣ A Q J 10 6

EAST
♠ 4 3
♡ K J 9 6 4 2
◇ K 4
♣ K 8 3

SOUTH
♠ A Q 9 8 2
♡ Q
◇ 7 6 3
♣ 9 5 4 2

Neither side vulnerable

The bidding:

WEST	NORTH	EAST J. Crawford	SOUTH
1 ♣	1 ◇	1 ♡	1 ♠
Pass	2 ♠	4 ♡	4 ♠
Pass	Pass	Double	Pass
Pass	Pass		

John Crawford is well-known for his "dangerous living" at the bridge table. Nevertheless, despite the frequent condemnation of dangerous living at the bridge table, it is often the proper way to live. The reader can determine this for himself after observing Crawford's defense.

West opened the Ace of Hearts, after which another heart was played, South ruffing. A low diamond was then led, dummy's ten-spot being put up. With no hesitation whatsoever, Crawford played the four-spot!

Declarer then drew three rounds of trumps, after which he led another low diamond, covered by West's Jack, dummy's Queen, — and Crawford's King. The defenders then took four club tricks, inflicting a three-trick set on declarer.

Dangerous play by Crawford? Well, it might have cost him a trick. But is there a declarer who would have played Crawford for the diamond King after the original diamond finesse had been "successful"?

CULBERTSON-SIMS MATCH:
1935

NORTH
♠ K J 3
♡ 7
♢ A Q 7 4
♣ K Q 9 4 2

WEST
♠ A 5 4
♡ 8 4 3 2
♢ K 9 6
♣ A 10 7

EAST
♠ Q 10 7 6
♡ 10 5
♢ J 10 5 3 2
♣ 6 3

SOUTH
♠ 9 8 2
♡ A K Q J 9 6
♢ 8
♣ J 8 5

Both sides vulnerable

The bidding:

WEST	NORTH	EAST	SOUTH
Mrs. Cul'tson	Mrs. P Sims	E. Cul'tson	P. Hal Sims
Pass	1 ♣	Pass	1 ♡
Pass	2 ♢	Pass	3 ♡
Pass	3 NT	Pass	4 ♡
Pass	Pass	Pass	

Deciding from the bidding that a spade lead seemed to be indicated Mrs. Culbertson opened the four of spades. After some thought, Hal Sims played low from dummy, and East's ten-spot captured the trick. A club was then returned, West's Ace winning. Now Mrs. Culbertson returned the five of spades.

As is rather apparent, if Sims had put up dummy's King, he would have taken the remainder of the tricks. But he could not bring himself to believe that Mrs. Culbertson would have underled the Ace of Spades twice in a row, so he played the Jack from dummy. Upon winning with the Queen, Mr. Culbertson played back a spade, Mrs. Culbertson's Ace taking the setting trick.

The result of this deal gave the Culbertsons a tremendous psychological advantage during the balance of the match, for P. Hal Sims was an expert who (almost) invariably made the correct guess in situations comparable to the above. Yet, who could criticize him for going wrong?

MASTERS' TEAM-OF-FOUR CHAMPIONSHIPS:
1955

NORTH
♠ 9 5
♡ 10
♢ A Q 8 6 5 3
♣ A 9 8 7

WEST
♠ J 10 6 3
♡ Q J 9 6 5
♢ 10 7 2
♣ 6

EAST
♠ K 7 4 2
♡ 4 2
♢ K J
♣ K 10 5 4 2

SOUTH
♠ A Q 8
♡ A K 8 7 3
♢ 9 4
♣ Q J 3

Both sides vulnerable

The bidding:

SOUTH	WEST	NORTH	EAST
			L. Mathe
1 ♡	Pass	2 ♢	Pass
2 NT	Pass	3 NT	Pass
Pass	Pass		

Against South's three notrump contract, West opened the three of spades and East played the King, which was permitted to hold the trick. A spade was then continued, declarer's Ace winning. South then led a diamond, and finessed the Queen, losing to East's King. East, Lew Mathe, now led the only card that could defeat the contract — the King of Clubs!

If dummy's Ace won the trick, it would become impossible to both establish and cash the diamond suit. And if South permitted the King of Clubs to win, a spade return would defeat declarer. Once the King of Clubs is led, South can make but eight tricks.

How come East returned the King of Clubs, when, from the bidding, South figured to have at least the Queen of Clubs? From East's point of view, if South held three diamonds, then the contract was unbeatable, since declarer could always bring home the diamond suit without the Ace of Clubs as an entry. Hence East correctly assumed that South held only two diamonds originally — and it became necessary to "kill" dummy's Ace of Clubs entry before the diamond suit became established.

VANDERBILT TEAM-OF-FOUR CHAMPIONSHIPS:
1957

NORTH
♠ 6 2
♡ Q 10 9 6 3
♢ A 5
♣ A K 6 5

WEST
♠ 8 7 3
♡ K
♢ 10 6 2
♣ Q J 9 8 4 2

EAST
♠ Q J 5
♡ A J 8 5 2
♢ 7 4
♣ 10 7 3

SOUTH
♠ A K 10 9 4
♡ 7 4
♢ K Q J 9 8 3
♣ —

Both sides vulnerable

NORTH	EAST R. Hirschberg	SOUTH	WEST E. Kaplan
1 ♡	Pass	1 ♠	Pass
1 NT	Pass	3 ♢	Pass
3 NT	Pass	4 ♢	Pass
4 ♠	Pass	4 NT	Pass
5 ♡	Double	6 ♢	Pass
Pass	Pass		

The fact that the final contract was a bad one is unimportant. Without East's keen analysis, it would have been fulfilled.

In response to East's double of North's five heart bid, Edgar Kaplan opened the King of Hearts which Hirschberg overtook with the Ace. He then returned a heart which West ruffed for the setting trick. How did Hirschberg know that the King of Hearts had to be overtaken?

From the bidding, South was marked with at least five spades and at least five diamonds. South therefore had, at most, three cards in hearts and clubs combined. If he had one heart and two clubs, then the slam could not be defeated, reasoned Hirschberg. But if he had two hearts, then Kaplan's lead of the King was a singleton, in which case it became imperative to overtake the King with the Ace in order to give West a heart ruff.

Had East not overtaken the King, declarer would have made his contract by establishing his spades (and, of course, discarding his heart loser on the Ace of Clubs).

MASTER'S PAIRS:
1955

NORTH
♠ Q 7 5
♡ 8
♢ A Q 10 9 7
♣ A K 10 6

WEST
♠ J
♡ A J 10 9 7 6 4
♢ 6
♣ Q J 9 4

EAST
♠ 10 6
♡ K 5 2
♢ 8 4 3 2
♣ 8 7 5 2

SOUTH
♠ A K 9 8 4 3 2
♡ Q 3
♢ K J 5
♣ 3

Neither side vulnerable

The bidding:

WEST	NORTH	EAST J. Ehrlenbach	SOUTH
4 ♡	Pass	Pass	4 ♠
Pass	6 ♠	Pass	Pass
Pass			

If the reader will look at the above four hands, he will perceive that there is no way of beating declarer's six spade contract. Nevertheless, by virtue of a brilliant defensive falsecard, the East defender succeeded in creating a trend of thought in declarer's mind which led to declarer's defeat.

West opened the Ace of Hearts upon which Jack Ehrlenbach, East, dropped the King! West, of course, continued with another heart, which was ruffed by dummy's Queen (to prevent the "obvious" overruff). When East followed to the second round of hearts, South was certain that the only plausible excuse for East's falsecard was that East possessed the J-10-6 of spades. So the seven of spades was led from dummy and finessed. West's Jack took the setting trick.

Before you criticize declarer, remember one thing: East would also have made the falsecard if he *had* the J-10-6 of trumps — and declarer would then have become a temporary "genius" instead of a gullible victim.

RUBBER BRIDGE
1951

NORTH
♠ Q 9 7 2
♡ A Q J 9
◇ A K J 7
♣ 5

WEST
♠ A 5
♡ 10 3
◇ Q 8 3 2
♣ J 8 7 3 2

EAST
♠ 3
♡ K 6 4 2
◇ 10 9 4
♣ A K Q 10 6

SOUTH
♠ K J 10 8 6 4
♡ 8 7 5
◇ 6 5
♣ 9 4

Neither side vulnerable

The bidding:

NORTH	EAST *A. Sheinwold*	SOUTH	WEST
1 ♡	2 ♣	Pass	3 ♣
Double	4 ♣	4 ♠	Pass
Pass	Pass		

The theme of this deal is the "convincing" of a declarer that a certain situation existed, thereby "compelling" him to adopt a losing line of play. Without the defensive chicanery, declarer would easily have fulfilled his contract.

West opened the three of clubs, which was captured by Sheinwold's Queen. Gazing at the dummy, Sheinwold concluded that the prospects of the defenders collecting four tricks in "honest" fashion were not hopeful. So he resorted to deception.

At trick two, he led the six of hearts, West's ten-spot being captured by dummy's Jack. In declarer's mind the "fact" was created that Sheinwold had led a singleton. A trump lead was then made, West's Ace winning, after which West returned the three of hearts. Convinced that West held the King, declarer finessed dummy's Queen, East's King winning. East now returned a heart, which West ruffed for the setting trick.

Is there a declarer who, when Sheinwold led the six of hearts at trick two, would not have placed the King of Hearts in the West hand? And once he came to this conclusion, was he not a doomed man?

OPEN PAIR CHAMPIONSHIPS:
SAN FRANCISCO: 1953

NORTH
♠ A 8 6 4
♡ 10 9 5
◇ K 8 6
♣ Q 5 4

WEST
♠ 10 3
♡ A Q J 8 4
◇ A Q J 5
♣ 8 3

EAST
♠ J 7 5
♡ 7 6 3 2
◇ 9 3 2
♣ A J 6

SOUTH
♠ K Q 9 2
♡ K
◇ 10 7 4
♣ K 10 9 7 2

East-West vulnerable

The bidding:

SOUTH	WEST *D. Oakie*	NORTH	EAST *D. Steen*
Pass	1 ♡	Pass	2 ♡
2 ♠	4 ♡	4 ♠	Double
Pass	Pass	Pass	

The eight of clubs was opened, North and East playing low, South's ten-spot capturing the trick. Three rounds of trumps then followed, picking up the adverse pieces, after which a club was led to the Queen. This was permitted to win the trick, and a third round of clubs was led and captured by Steen's Ace.

Had East now "automatically" returned a heart — his partner's suit — declarer would have fulfilled his contract, for he would have been able to reach his hand to discard two of dummy's diamonds on the established club suit.

But, on the bidding, it was obvious that South could not have more than one heart, and that, therefore, a heart return was futile. So, after taking the Ace of Clubs, East switched to a diamond, and it now became impossible for declarer to avoid the loss of two diamond tricks.

Incidentally, if East had taken the second round of clubs (instead of the third) declarer would have fulfilled his contract by being enabled to re-enter his hand. The defense had to be perfect to defeat declarer — and it was.

RUBBER BRIDGE

NORTH
♠ A Q 3 2
♡ 8 6
◊ Q J 10 9 8
♣ J 7

WEST
♠ 7 6 5
♡ K 9 7 5
◊ K 4
♣ K 8 6 4

EAST
♠ 10 9 8
♡ J 10 3 2
◊ 6 5
♣ A Q 9 3

SOUTH
♠ K J 4
♡ A Q 4
◊ A 7 3 2
♣ 10 5 2

Neither side vulnerable

The bidding:

SOUTH E. Cul'son	WEST	NORTH	EAST
1 NT	Pass	2 ◊	Pass
2 NT	Pass	3 ♠	Pass
3 NT	Pass	Pass	Pass

The present generation does not know of the brilliance of Ely Culbertson, who, in the 1930's, was considered to be one of the world's greatest players. Here is an example of his technique.

West opened the five of hearts, East put up the ten-spot and Mr. Culbertson captured the trick — with his *Ace!* Dummy was then entered via the Queen of Spades, and a diamond finesse was taken, losing to West's King. Convinced that his partner had the Queen of Hearts, West now continued that suit. South, of course, won with the Queen, and walked home with ten tricks.

Had Mr. Culbertson captured the opening heart lead with his Queen, West would have known that Mr. Culbertson still possessed the Ace. After winning the diamond King, West would then have perceived the futility of continuing hearts, and by a process of elimination would have switched to clubs.

But the wool Mr. Culbertson pulled over West's eyes made it impossible for West to shift to clubs.

WORLD CHAMPIONSHIPS: 1956

NORTH
♠ A 8
♡ Q J 4
◊ K 10 8
♣ K 10 9 7 2

WEST
♠ K Q J 7 5 3 2
♡ K 8
◊ 5 4 2
♣ 4

EAST
♠ 10 9 6
♡ 9 6 5 3 2
◊ 9 3
♣ A J 5

SOUTH
♠ 4
♡ A 10 7
◊ A Q J 7 6
♣ Q 8 6 3

North-South vulnerable

The bidding:

EAST	SOUTH	WEST	NORTH
1 ♠ (a)	Double	4 ♠	5 ♣
Pass	Pass	Pass	

(a) The infrequent "psychic" opening bid.

When this deal was played, our North declarer fulfilled his five club contract. But even in victory, he looked "bad" for the fact is that he did not play the hand properly. "Luck", however, was at his side.

The opening lead of the ten of spades was captured by North's Ace, after which a spade was ruffed in dummy. A club was then played to the King, East's Ace winning, after which a heart was returned and taken by West's King. Eventually declarer guessed the location of the club Jack, and successfully finessed against it.

The proper play, after capturing the opening spade lead, is to lead the seven of trumps and when East plays low, South does likewise. Played in this manner, declarer can never lose more than two trump tricks and nothing else, for if *West* shifts to a heart (no matter where the heart King is), declarer will avoid the loss of a heart trick. The important consideration on this hand was to keep *East* out of the lead, since a heart lead by him might result in declarer losing a heart trick — as he did. And it then took a "guess" to recover.

WORLD CHAMPIONSHIPS:
1955

NORTH
♠ A 8 6
♡ A K J 3
◇ A J 8 4
♣ J 6

WEST
♠ K 7 4 2
♡ Q 10 9
◇ 7 5 2
♣ A 8 4

EAST
♠ Q 10 9 3
♡ 8 5 4
◇ K Q 10
♣ 10 5 3

SOUTH
♠ J 5
♡ 7 6 2
◇ 9 6 3
♣ K Q 9 7 2

Both sides vulnerable

The bidding:

EAST	SOUTH	WEST	NORTH
	A. Meredith		
Pass	Pass	Pass	1 ◇
Pass	1 NT	Pass	3 NT
Pass	Pass	Pass	

We, in the United States, do not often get to see European teams in action. Just how magnificent some of their players are can perhaps be learned from this deal. The South declarer was Adam Meredith of England, who found himself in a hopeless contract. With a little luck and a big imagination, he proceeded to fulfill his contract with an overtrick.

West opened a low spade, East's Queen winning, after which the ten of spades was played, covered by the Jack, King and Ace. Meredith now led the Jack of Clubs and *overtook* it with his own King! Why West grabbed this trick is unknown. Possibly it was because declarer wanted to get to the South hand, and West just was not going to let him do it. A spade was now returned, East winning with the nine-spot. The King of Diamonds was then laid down, taken by North's Ace.

Meredith now calmly led the six of clubs and successfully finessed his nine-spot. He next took four club tricks. He then finessed the Jack of Hearts, and took four heart tricks. Bridge is a simple game — for Meredith!

NATIONAL CHAMPIONSHIPS:
SWITZERLAND

NORTH
♠ K Q 2
♡ 10 5 3 2
◇ A 10 3
♣ A 8 5

WEST
♠ J 7 5
♡ 6
◇ K J 9 8 4
♣ J 9 6 3

EAST
♠ A 10 9 8 6 4
♡ 9
◇ Q 7 2
♣ Q 10 4

SOUTH
♠ 3
♡ A K Q J 8 7 4
◇ 6 5
♣ K 7 2

Neither side vulnerable

The bidding:

NORTH	EAST	SOUTH	WEST
		Dr. E. Frischauer	
1 ♣	Pass	1 ♡	Pass
2 ♡	Pass	4 NT	Pass
5 ♡	Pass	6 ♡	Pass
Pass	Pass		

This deal is significant in just one respect: it is questionable as to whether one out of a thousand players would fulfill the slam contract even if he was able to see all four hands. Yet our South declarer, Dr. Edward Frischauer, promptly came up with the winning play.

The opening lead of the three of clubs was captured by dummy's Ace, after which the deuce of spades was immediately led off dummy! When East played the Ace to this trick, declarer had smooth sailing.

From declarer's point of view, the only way he could make his contract was if he could deceive the opposition. West was known to be an excellent player, and if West had the spade Ace — reasoned South — even if a spade were led originally from the South hand, West would not take his (hypothetical) Ace. A club and a diamond trick would then be lost. South's only chance, he felt, was for East to have the Ace of Spades and not the Jack of Spades — and that East would figure declarer for the singleton Jack of Spades. And East came to the exact conclusion declarer desired.

NATIONAL TEAM-OF-FOUR CHAMPIONSHIPS:
1949

NORTH
♠ J 4
♡ Q 7 5 2
◇ A K Q 8 4 2
♣ 6

WEST
♠ K 10 5
♡ 10 6 3
◇ 6
♣ K 10 9 5 4 2

EAST
♠ 6
♡ A K 8
◇ J 10 7 5 3
♣ Q J 8 7

SOUTH
♠ A Q 9 8 7 3 2
♡ J 9 4
◇ 9
♣ A 3

North-South vulnerable

The bidding:

NORTH	EAST	SOUTH F. Hirsch	WEST
1 ◇	Pass	1 ♠	Pass
2 ◇	Pass	4 ♠	Pass
Pass	Pass		

West opened a heart, taken by East's Ace, after which East cashed the King of Hearts, and then played another round of the suit, declarer's Jack winning. Now a diamond was led to dummy's Ace, followed by the Ace of Clubs. A club was then ruffed in dummy. Next the Jack of trumps was played, and all West could make was the King of trumps.

Superficially, it looks as though there was nothing to the play of the hand. But just try ruffing the three of clubs *before* playing one round of diamonds. When declarer then takes the spade finesse, West exits with his singleton diamond, and declarer cannot get back to his hand without enabling West to make his ten of spades.

Or suppose declarer wins the third round of hearts with dummy's Queen and promptly takes the spade finesse. Again, West will capture the trick with the King, lead his singleton diamond — and his ten of spades either becomes a winner, or declarer loses a club trick.

In retrospect, the hand seems absurdedly simple — but as can be evidenced, it is not.

VANDERBILT CHAMPIONSHIPS:
1950

NORTH
♠ A
♡ K J 8 6 2
◇ A 8 5 4
♣ Q 4 3

WEST
♠ K Q 8 7 2
♡ 9 4
◇ K 10 2
♣ J 8 7

EAST
♠ 10 9 6 5
♡ 10 7 5 3
◇ J 9
♣ K 9 2

SOUTH
♠ J 4 3
♡ A Q
◇ Q 7 6 3
♣ A 10 6 5

Both sides vulnerable

The bidding:

SOUTH Lee Hazen	WEST	NORTH	EAST
1 ◇	Pass	1 ♡	Pass
1 NT	Pass	3 ◇	Pass
3 NT	Pass	Pass	Pass

As the reader can observe, three notrump is not in the cards against a low spade opening — which was made — but by a bold deceptive play, Hazen succeeded in bringing home his contract.

West opened the seven of spades, dummy's Ace capturing the trick. A count of the hands revealed that North-South had but eight tricks, and that if the opponents were given the lead via a club or a diamond, they might cash four spade tricks. It was equally apparent that declarer's ninth trick had to come from either the club or diamond suit.

At trick two, declarer cashed his Ace of Hearts, and then took his Queen of Hearts. He then laid down the Jack of Spades!

Upon capturing this trick, West was "convinced" that declarer had started with the J-10-9-x of spades, and was trying to create a spade trick. West, therefore, discontinued playing spades and shifted to a club. Hazen played low from the dummy — and whatever East played, South had created his ninth trick in clubs.

Had West cashed four spades, the contract would have been defeated. But Hazen's lead of the Jack of Spades "talked him out" of leading spades.

MASTERS' TEAM-OF-FOUR CHAMPIONSHIPS:
1949

```
            NORTH
            ♠ 9 8
            ♡ A Q
            ◊ A K J 9 4
            ♣ K J 3 2
WEST                      EAST
♠ 2                      ♠ K 7 5 3
♡ 7 3 2                  ♡ 9 6 4
◊ 8 7 5 3 2              ◊ 10 6
♣ A 9 6 4               ♣ Q 10 7 5
            SOUTH
            ♠ A Q J 10 6 4
            ♡ K J 10 8 5
            ◊ Q
            ♣ 8
```

North-South vulnerable

The bidding:

SOUTH S. Silodor	WEST	NORTH	EAST
1 ♠	Pass	2 ◊	Pass
2 ♡	Pass	3 NT	Pass
5 ♠	Pass	6 ♠	Pass
Pass	Pass		

The Grand Coup does not arise too frequently in actual play, but when it does, it is a beautiful thing to behold. Here it is, as handled by Sidney Silodor.

West opened the Ace of Clubs, after which he shifted to the seven of hearts, dummy's Ace winning. The nine of trumps was then led, winning the trick. This was followed by the eight of spades, which also won the trick, West discarding a low diamond. It was now obvious that East's guarded King of trumps could not be finessed again, so Sidney made preparations to surround and ambush the King.

At trick five, he trumped a club, and then re-entered dummy via the Queen of Hearts to ruff another club. Declarer now had the A-Q of trumps remaining behind East's K-7 of trumps. The Queen of Diamonds was then overtaken by dummy's Ace, and the board's high diamonds were led, declarer discarding his high hearts. When East eventually trumped with the seven-spot, South overtrumped with the Queen, laid down his Ace of trumps to fell East's King, and claimed the remainder of the tricks.

MIXED PAIR CHAMPIONSHIPS:
1939

```
            NORTH
            ♠ 7 6 5
            ♡ K 8
            ◊ J 4 3 2
            ♣ J 8 5 4
WEST                      EAST
♠ K                      ♠ 8 3 2
♡ A Q 10 7 6 5 2        ♡ 9 4 3
◊ 9 8 7                  ◊ 10 6 5
♣ 7 2                   ♣ 10 9 6 3
            SOUTH
            ♠ A Q J 10 9 4
            ♡ J
            ◊ A K Q
            ♣ A K Q
```

Both sides vulnerable

The bidding:

WEST O. Jacoby	NORTH	EAST	SOUTH L. Hazen
3 ♡	Pass	Pass	4 ♡
Pass	4 NT	Pass	6 ♠
Pass	Pass	Pass	

The moral of this deal was aptly expressed by Lee Hazen when he stated: "What a pleasure it was to be able to trust an opponent to do the right thing. I had arrived in fast company."

On the bidding, Mr. Hazen frankly stated that his six spade bid was just a stab in the dark, but that he could not figure out any way of discovering scientifically whether North had the needed card.

The Ace of Hearts was opened, followed by another heart, dummy's King winning, South discarding a diamond. A trump was then led, with the intention of finessing for the King, when suddenly a thought struck Mr. Hazen. Why was Jacoby leading a second round of hearts when he knew darned well that Hazen had but one heart? (Hazen would not have bid a slam all by himself with two low hearts).

The only reason, Hazen concluded, could be that Jacoby wanted him to be in dummy to take the trump finesse. So Hazen went up with his Ace of trumps — spurning the finesse — and dropped West's singleton King.

MIXED-TEAM-OF-FOUR CHAMPIONSHIPS: 1950

NORTH
♠ 9 5
♡ A Q 10
◇ Q J 10 9 8 7 4
♣ 4

WEST
♠ A K Q J 6 3
♡ 8 7 3
◇ —
♣ 10 6 3 2

EAST
♠ —
♡ K J 6 5 4
◇ K
♣ A K Q J 9 8 7

SOUTH
♠ 10 8 7 4 2
♡ 9 2
◇ A 6 5 3 2
♣ 5

North-South vulnerable

The bidding:

EAST A. *Landy*	SOUTH	WEST	NORTH
1 ♣	Pass	1 ♠	2 ◇
2 ♡	3 ◇	4 ◇	Pass
5 ♣	Pass	6 ♣	Pass
Pass	Pass		

On the above deal, most pairs arrived at a six spade contract, which was defeated owing to the bad spade break. There was justification in bidding six spades as opposed to the guaranteed six club contract: it was a duplicate game, and spades counted more than clubs.

Against Landy's six club contract, the Ace of diamonds was opened and ruffed in dummy. If a trump is then led, only 12 tricks will be made, since declarer will be able to get rid of only four hearts on dummy's spades, and will have to concede a heart trick at the end.

After ruffing the opening diamond lead there is just one proper play to make, in either rubber bridge or duplicate bridge — to lead a low spade off the board and ruff it high. Then follows the Ace of trumps, after which a trump is led to dummy's ten-spot. Now declarer can discard his five hearts on dummy's five spades. And that is just the way Landy played it, to make all 13 tricks. A simple hand — and yet I wonder how many bridge players would have played it properly.

MIXED-TEAM-OF-FOUR CHAMPIONSHIPS: 1952

NORTH
♠ Q 8 5
♡ 10
◇ A K 5 4
♣ A K 7 5 4

WEST
♠ 10 6 2
♡ 9 8 2
◇ J 8 7 2
♣ 9 8 3

EAST
♠ K J 9 4
♡ A Q J 6 4 3
◇ 10 3
♣ 2

SOUTH
♠ A 7 3
♡ K 7 5
◇ Q 9 6
♣ Q J 10 6

East-West vulnerable

The bidding:

NORTH	EAST	SOUTH Ann Burnstein	WEST
1 ♣	Double	Redouble	Pass
Pass	1 ♡	Pass	Pass
2 ◇	Pass	2 NT	Pass
3 NT	Pass	Pass	Pass

West opened the nine of hearts, which East captured with his Ace, and returned the Queen of Hearts, declarer's King winning. On this trick, West, following the accepted custom of playing the second-highest of partner's bid suit, played the eight-spot instead of the deuce, a play that was to cost him dearly. Dummy discarded a spade.

Mrs. Burnstein now proceeded to run five club tricks and three diamond tricks, ending up in the North hand. At this point, dummy had the Q-8 of spades and the five of diamonds; and declarer had the A-7 of spades and the seven of hearts. Dummy's five of diamonds was then led to be won by West's known Jack (East had failed to follow suit to the third round of diamonds). On this trick East was "squeezed." If he discarded the Jack of Spades, dummy's Queen of Spades would be promoted into a winner; if, instead, he discarded the Jack of Hearts, declarer's Ace of Spades and seven of hearts would win the last two tricks.

The eleven tricks which she made gave her a "top" on the board, since no one else made 11 tricks at notrump.

NATIONAL MIXED PAIRS: 1955

NORTH
♠ 8 6 2
♡ J 8
♢ A K 4 2
♣ K 9 6 3

WEST
♠ Q 10 5 4
♡ K 7 4 2
♢ Q 9
♣ 10 8 5

EAST
♠ 9 7
♡ 10 9 5 3
♢ 8 7 6 3
♣ A Q J

SOUTH
♠ A K J 3
♡ A Q 6
♢ J 10 5
♣ 7 4 2

North-South vulnerable

The bidding:

SOUTH	WEST	NORTH	EAST
			M. Cohn
1 NT	Pass	2 NT	Pass
3 NT	Pass	Pass	Pass

Had West not opened a spade, declarer would have had little chance for his contract. But West chose to open a low spade, which was won by declarer's Jack. The Jack of Diamonds was now led, covered by the Queen, and taken by dummy's King. A low club was then played off the board, captured by East's Jack, after which East returned a spade, declarer's Ace winning.

Another club was now led, dummy's King falling to East's Ace. Out of spades, East then shifted to a heart. At this point, declarer could have made his contract by going up with the Ace of Hearts and leading a club, establishing dummy's fourth club. But he elected to play low, the trick being taken by West's King. West next played his Queen of Spades, upon which East discarded his Queen of Clubs! West's ten of clubs now became an entry to cash the fourth spade, thereby holding declarer to eight tricks.

In retrospect, East's discard of the club Queen does not seem to be so spectacular. But at the table it is a tough play to make.

RUBBER BRIDGE: 1937

NORTH
♠ 8 4 3
♡ 10 8 7 2
♢ K J 6 4
♣ K 2

WEST
♠ Q 7 6 2
♡ J 6 5 4
♢ 3
♣ 9 8 7 6

EAST
♠ J 10 5
♡ A Q 9 3
♢ Q 10 2
♣ J 10 5

SOUTH
♠ A K 9
♡ K
♢ A 9 8 7 5
♣ A Q 4 3

North-South vulnerable

The bidding:

SOUTH	WEST	NORTH	EAST
			W. Malowan
1 ♢	Pass	2 ♢	Pass
3 NT	Pass	Pass	Pass

That "defense" is the most difficult aspect of the game to master is an accepted fact. And when someone comes up with a highly-imaginative defense play, one often has the urge to stand up and applaud. This deal illustrates one of these defensive gems.

Against South's three notrump contract, West opened the two of spades, East's ten-spot being taken by declarer's Ace. Declarer then laid down the Ace of Diamonds, which was followed by another diamond. When West showed out — discarding a club — East's Queen was permitted to win the trick.

East, Walter Malowan, now did some "counting." It quickly became apparent that West, who had started with precisely four spades and one diamond, had eight cards in hearts and clubs. It was highly improbable that West had a five-card suit, since he would have opened a five-card suit against the three notrump contract. Therefore, West's distribution had to be 4-4-4-1 — and declarer had to have *a singleton heart!*

So Mr. Malowan laid down the Ace of Hearts and caught declarer's singleton King. The defenders then took three more heart tricks.

PACIFIC PAIR CHAMPIONSHIPS:
1952

NORTH
♠ 10 9 7 5
♡ A 5 4
◇ Q J 7 6
♣ 6 5

WEST
♠ 2
♡ 10 6
◇ A K 10 9
♣ Q J 10 9 8 3

EAST
♠ K J 4 3
♡ 9 8 7 3
◇ 8 5 3
♣ 4 2

SOUTH
♠ A Q 8 6
♡ K Q J 2
◇ 4 2
♣ A K 7

Neither side vulnerable

The bidding:

SOUTH	WEST	NORTH	EAST
			A. Okuneff
1 ♣	Pass	1 ◇	Pass
1 ♠	Pass	2 ♠	Pass
3 NT	Pass	4 ♠	Pass
Pass	Pass		

The opening lead of the Queen of Clubs was captured by declarer's Ace, after which he played the King of Clubs, and another club which was ruffed in dummy with the five-spot. Albert Okuneff, East, overruffed this trick with his King!

This play firmly established in declarer's mind the fact that West held the Jack of trumps, for surely East would have otherwise overruffed with the Jack instead of the King.

East returned a diamond, West cashing his King and Ace of that suit. He then played another diamond, dummy winning. "Knowing" that West possessed the Jack of trumps, declarer then took his Ace and Queen of trumps, hoping to drop West's (hypothetical) Jack. When West showed out on the lead of the Queen, declarer belatedly found out that he had been duped.

Had East ruffed with the Jack of Spades, declarer would have subsequently made the normal play of finessing East for the King of Spades.

VANDERBILT TOURNAMENT:
1945

NORTH
♠ 8
♡ 10 3
◇ A K J 9 4
♣ K J 10 9 3

WEST
♠ 10 9 5 3 2
♡ 8 6 2
◇ Q 8 3
♣ A 2

EAST
♠ K Q 7
♡ K Q
◇ 10 7 2
♣ Q 7 6 5 4

SOUTH
♠ A J 6 4
♡ A J 9 7 5 4
◇ 6 5
♣ 8

Neither side vulnerable

SOUTH	WEST	NORTH	EAST
	Mrs. Sobel		*B. J. Becker*
1 ♡	Pass	2 ◇	Pass
2 ♡	Pass	3 ♣	Pass
3 ♡	Pass	4 ♡	Pass
Pass	Pass		

Mrs. Sobel, West, opened the Ace of Clubs, after which she led the deuce, dummy's King winning, with South discarding a spade. The Ace of Spades was then cashed, and a spade was next ruffed in dummy.

Declarer now had a problem as to how to get back to his own hand in order to trump another spade. Apprehensive of an overruff if he led a club, he decided to get back to his own hand via a ruff of the third round of diamonds. So he cashed the board's Ace of Diamonds, and then the King of Diamonds. On this trick, Mrs. Sobel dropped the Diamond Queen!

Declarer now paused to examine this new development. And, after due deliberation, he decided to "trust" Mrs. Sobel's play of the diamond Queen. He then led a club off the board, and trumped with the seven-spot (saving the nine and Jack to re-enter his hand later). Mrs. Sobel overtrumped with the eight-spot, returned a trump, and declarer had to lose a spade and a trump, for a one trick set.

If Mrs. Sobel had not false-carded with the Queen of Diamonds, declarer would have trumped a diamond after which dummy's ten of hearts would have been used to ruff declarer's losing spade.

CAVENDISH BRIDGE CLUB: DUPLICATE

NORTH
♠ Q 10 4
♡ A K 8 3
◇ K J 7 3
♣ J 8

WEST
♠ K 3
♡ J 5 4 2
◇ A 9 2
♣ 10 5 3 2

EAST
♠ J 7 2
♡ 10 9 7
◇ Q 6 5 4
♣ 9 6 4

SOUTH
♠ A 9 8 6 5
♡ Q 6
◇ 10 8
♣ A K Q 7

Both sides vulnerable

The bidding:

NORTH C. Lockridge	EAST Mrs. Lockridge	SOUTH L. Hazen	WEST Mrs. Hazen
1 ♡	Pass	1 ♠	Pass
2 ♠	Pass	4 ♠	Pass
Pass	Pass		

Precisely how important "guessing" is can be evidenced from this deal. The defenders timed their plays perfectly, and the declarer misguessed in every critical situation. Had declarer guessed right in these situations, Charles Lockridge and Lee Hazen would have won the duplicate game instead of finishing fourth. The reader will note that East and West were married to North and South, respectively.

West opened the deuce of diamonds, declarer played low, and East's Queen captured the trick. East returned a diamond to West's Ace, after which a third diamond was led, dummy winning, with South discarding a heart.

A low heart to declarer's Queen was then played, followed by a low trump toward the dummy. Without a flicker of an eyelash, Mrs. Hazen played the three of spades. Mr. Hazen then put up dummy's ten-spot, East's Jack winning. East now returned her fourth diamond, and declarer could not prevent West's King of trumps from taking the setting trick.

After the game was over, Mrs. Hazen remarked: "Well, we sure gave you every chance to make a top-on-the-board!"

NATIONAL MIXED TEAM-OF-FOUR CHAMPIONSHIPS: 1952

NORTH
♠ 6
♡ Q J 8 3
◇ —
♣ A Q J 9 8 6 5 3

WEST
♠ K 10 8 7 5 2
♡ 7 5 2
◇ 4
♣ K 7 2

EAST
♠ A J 9
♡ A K 4
◇ Q J 9 8 6 5
♣ 10

SOUTH
♠ Q 4 3
♡ 10 9 6
◇ A K 10 7 3 2
♣ 4

Neither side vulnerable

The bidding:

NORTH D. Oakie	EAST S. Rebner	SOUTH	WEST
Pass	1 ◇	Pass	1 ♠
2 ♣	3 ◇	Double	Pass
4 ♣	Pass	Pass	4 ♠
Pass	Pass	Double	Pass
Pass	Pass		

North opened the Ace of Clubs, and followed up by then leading the three-spot. Had West been a good guesser, he would have trumped with dummy's Ace, and then finessed South for the Queen of Spades. But, instead, he elected to discard the four of hearts, with Mrs. Rebner trumping the trick.

Mrs. Rebner, noting her partner's lead of the three-spot, (she knew Mr. Oakie could have played any one of five or six other clubs), properly interpreted his three of clubs as a "suit-preference" signal, directing her to return the lower of the two obvious suits (excluding trumps and clubs). So she calmly underled her A-K of Diamonds, and Oakie won the trick by ruffing. Another club was then led, dummy trumping with the Ace, while Mrs. Rebner discarded a heart. It was now impossible for declarer to avoid losing a heart trick, and he went down.

If Mrs. Rebner had led the King of Diamonds, even if Oakie ruffed it, the contract would have been fulfilled, since declarer would then have been able to establish a diamond for a heart discard.

NATIONAL TEAM-OF-FOUR CHAMPIONSHIPS: 1953

NORTH
♠ K 3
♡ A 6
◇ K 10 9 7 4 3
♣ 10 5 3

WEST
♠ A 10 8 4
♡ Q 10 7 2
◇ J 5
♣ A J 9

EAST
♠ 9 7 6 2
♡ 5 4
◇ Q 6 2
♣ K 8 6 2

SOUTH
♠ Q J 5
♡ K J 9 8 3
◇ A 8
♣ Q 7 4

Both sides vulnerable

SOUTH	WEST	NORTH	EAST
H. Harkavy			W. von Zedtwitz
1 ♡	Pass	2 ◇	Pass
2 ♡	Pass	3 ♡	Pass
3 NT	Pass	Pass	Pass

That the experts live in a different world can be evidenced from the above deal, on which Harkavy pointed out that he made a "mistake" in his defense. I am reasonably certain that 99 out of every 100 players, if they were asked to find the play that Harkavy called a "mistake" would be unable to do so.

Harkavy opened the four of spades, which was taken by dummy's King. A low diamond was then led, declarer "finessing" his eight-spot, which lost to West's Jack. West now switched to a low club, taken by von Zedtwitz's King, and von Zedtwitz returned a spade, West's Ace winning. All the defenders could now take was the Ace of Clubs, and the three notrump contract was fulfilled. Had von Zedtwitz returned a club instead of a spade (when he took the club King), declarer would have gone down.

Harkavy later pointed out that his "mistake" was in not cashing the Ace of Spades *before* leading the club nine. Then his partner would have known not to play back a spade, but instead to play back a club. In other words, by cashing the Spade Ace, he would have eliminated von Zedtwitz's guess as to which black suit to play back.

NATIONAL PAIR CHAMPIONSHIPS: 1932

NORTH
♠ 9 8 2
♡ Q 9 2
◇ K 3
♣ A Q 10 9 5

WEST
♠ Q 4 3
♡ A K 5
◇ 7 6 2
♣ K J 7 4

EAST
♠ 6
♡ J 8 7 3
◇ Q J 10 9 8 4
♣ 8 6

SOUTH
♠ A K J 10 7 5
♡ 10 6 4
◇ A 5
♣ 3 2

Both sides vulnerable

The bidding:

SOUTH	WEST	NORTH	EAST
H. Schenken			
1 ♠	Pass	2 ♣	Pass
2 ♠	Pass	2 NT	Pass
4 ♠	Pass	Pass	Pass

Just how important it is to "listen" to the bidding of the opponents can be observed from this deal. The West defender was Howard Schenken.

Normally, the King of Hearts would be the technically correct opening lead. But North's bid of two notrump seemed to indicate that North possessed the Queen of Hearts. And if this was true, the lead of the King of Hearts would announce that the leader also possessed the Ace, and declarer would then be able to establish dummy's Queen as a winner.

The above reasoning is what motivated Mr. Schenken into leading the *Ace* of Hearts. East, not desiring any other suit to be led, gave a "come-on" signal by playing the eight of hearts. West now played the five of hearts, declarer mechanically put up dummy's nine-spot, and East's Jack won the trick. Another heart lead then enabled Schenken to win his King, and ultimately the Queen of Spades took the setting trick.

That declarer guessed wrong is unimportant. What is important is that if Schenken had opened the King of Hearts, no declarer in the world would have guessed wrong.

NATIONAL OPEN PAIRS:
1949

NORTH
♠ 8 5
♡ 10 7 4 2
♢ A 9 6 3
♣ K 5 4

WEST
♠ 10 9 4 2
♡ 3
♢ Q 8 5 4
♣ 10 8 7 2

EAST
♠ A K
♡ K J 9 8 6
♢ 10 2
♣ J 9 6 3

SOUTH
♠ Q J 7 6 3
♡ A Q 5
♢ K J 7
♣ A Q

Both sides vulnerable

The bidding:

EAST	SOUTH	WEST	NORTH
	H. Sobel		
1 ♡	Double	Pass	2 ♢
Pass	2 NT	Pass	3 NT
Pass	Pass	Pass	

Precisely why Helen Sobel is considered to be one of the world's greatest players can be evidenced from this deal. One cannot help but admire the brilliance of her analysis.

West opened the deuce of clubs, which declarer took with her Ace — and promptly led the three of spades, playing East for the A-K doubleton of spades! How could anybody be that clairvoyant, you might ask? Well, let us follow her trend of thought.

West's lead of the deuce, as the fourth best, showed exactly four cards in that suit. Mrs. Sobel assumed that if West had held two hearts (his partner's suit), he would have opened that suit in preference to leading from a broken-down four-card suit (East, for his opening bid, had to have the A-K of spades and the King of Hearts, since only 14 high-card points were outstanding). That West had exactly a singleton heart was apparent to Mrs. Sobel, for if West were void of hearts, he would certainly have led from the five-card suit which he must then have had. So West was "marked" with three four-card suits, and a singleton heart. Hence East had exactly two spades — the Ace and King.

MASTERS TEAM OF FOUR
CHAMPIONSHIPS:
1952

NORTH
♠ 10 9 6 5 2
♡ A J 8 4
♢ 9 8 3 2
♣ —

WEST
♠ Q 4
♡ K 10 9 7 6 3
♢ 7 6 5
♣ 9 5

EAST
♠ A
♡ 5 2
♢ K Q J 4
♣ J 10 8 7 4 3

SOUTH
♠ K J 8 7 3
♡ Q
♢ A 10
♣ A K Q 6 2

The bidding of the hand has been forgotten, except that South arrived at a *six spade* contract. Sitting South was Theodore Lightner, one of the greatest players in the world. On this deal "percentage" deserted him — and his team lost the match as a result.

The opening lead was a diamond, East's Jack being taken by declarer's Ace. The problem, of course, was to dispose of the diamond loser before touching trumps. The heart finesse offered a 50-50 proposition. A 4-4 or a 5-3 division of the eight outstanding clubs figured to exist, mathematically, 80% of the time. So Lightner naturally attacked the club suit, leading the Ace, King and Queen to get rid of dummy's three remaining clubs. But West ruffed the third club with the Queen of Spades, and Lightner went down.

When this deal was replayed with Lightner's teammates sitting East-West, South also arrived at a six spade contract, and West made the identical diamond opening, giving South the same problem Lightner had. But this South led the Queen of Hearts and finessed successfully, after which it was routine play to ruff a club, and discard a diamond on the Ace of Hearts. His only loser was the Ace of trumps.

MASTERS PAIRS CHAMPIONSHIPS:
1952

NORTH
♠ 4 2
♡ A K Q 9 8
◇ 7 6 3
♣ A 8 3

WEST
♠ J 5
♡ 10 5 4 3
◇ J 10 9 8
♣ Q 6 4

EAST
♠ 9 8 7 6 3
♡ J 6
◇ A 5 4 2
♣ 10 5

SOUTH
♠ A K Q 10
♡ 7 2
◇ K Q
♣ K J 9 7 2

Both sides vulnerable

SOUTH W. von Zedtwitz	WEST	NORTH	EAST
1 ♣	Pass	1 ♡	Pass
1 ♠	Pass	3 ♡	Pass
4 ♣	Pass	5 ♣	Pass
6 ♣	Pass	Pass	Pass

Waldemar von Zedtwitz once made a remark to me which I have never forgotten: "There is no such thing in bridge as a pure guess. There is always at least a fragment of a clue." This deal serves to illustrate his thesis.

A diamond was opened, taken by East's Ace, and a diamond returned to South's King. The problem was to avoid the loss of a trump trick.

Normal play is to lead a trump to the Ace, and finesse a trump on the way back. But Waldy had other ideas. He led a heart to the Ace, and trumped dummy's remaining diamond. He then led the Ace and King of Spades, felling West's Jack, after which he led the Queen of Spades, West discarding a diamond. Next came the Jack of Clubs, which won the trick when West played low. Trumps were now picked up and the slam fulfilled.

Von Zedtwitz's reason for his play of the trump suit was that if West held the ten of trumps, he would have ruffed the Queen of Spades to force dummy's Ace of trumps. And the fact that he had not trumped at all suggested that he held the Queen. Of course, if West had covered the Jack it would have made no difference, since East's ten-spot would have fallen on the next round.

NATIONAL TEAM-OF-FOUR CHAMPIONSHIPS:
1957

NORTH
♠ J 7 6
♡ Q 10 9 7
◇ A 7 5
♣ K Q 10

WEST
♠ K
♡ 6 5 3
◇ 3 2
♣ 9 8 7 6 4 3 2

EAST
♠ 10 5 4 2
♡ —
◇ K Q J 10 9 8 6
♣ A 5

SOUTH
♠ A Q 9 8 3
♡ A K J 8 4 2
◇ 4
♣ J

Both sides vulnerable

The bidding:

NORTH	EAST	SOUTH I. Stakgold	WEST
Pass	4 ◇	4 ♡	Pass
5 ◇	Pass	5 ♠	Pass
6 ♡	Pass	Pass	Pass

One of the rising stars in the world of bridge is Ivar Stakgold. As evidence, witness the play of this hand.

The three of diamonds was opened, North's Ace winning, East dropping the King. A diamond was then ruffed high in the closed hand after which the King of trumps was cashed, East showing out. Then came the Jack of Hearts, followed by a heart to dummy's ten-spot. West's trumps had now been removed.

Dummy's remaining diamond was then trumped, West discarding a club. East was now known to have started with seven diamonds. The Jack of Clubs was led next, taken by East's Ace. East returned a club, and declarer cashed dummy's King and Queen, discarding two spades. East's distribution was now an open book: he had started with exactly seven diamonds, two clubs, and four spades. But Stakgold "knew" that East could not have the King of Spades, for no East player in his right mind would have opened with four diamonds had he held four spades to the King, seven solid diamonds missing the Ace, and the Ace and one club. So Stakgold played his Ace of Spades — and caught West's blank King.

NATIONAL OPEN PAIRS
CHAMPIONSHIPS:
1947

NORTH
♠ K Q 8 7
♡ 7 6 4 2
♢ K 3
♣ A Q 5

WEST
♠ J 9 5 2
♡ K Q 9
♢ 8 6 2
♣ 10 4 2

EAST
♠ 10 4 3
♡ 3
♢ 10 9 7 5 4
♣ 9 8 7 6

SOUTH
♠ A 6
♡ A J 10 8 5
♢ A Q J
♣ K J 3

North-South vulnerable

The bidding:

SOUTH	WEST	NORTH	EAST
P. Abramsohn			
1 ♡	Pass	1 ♠	Pass
2 NT	Pass	3 ♡	Pass
4 ♡	Pass	6 ♡	Pass
Pass	Double	Pass	Pass
Pass			

After the dummy was put down, it was perfectly obvious to Mr. Abramsohn that West's double was based on the King and Queen of Hearts, since they were the only two picture cards outstanding (plus the Jack of Spades). Without the double, South would have double-finessed in trumps on the basis that East held either the King or Queen of trumps. With the double, this latter line of play was out of the question.

West opened the two of spades, taken by declarer's Ace, after which a spade was led to dummy's Queen. This was followed by a third round of spades, which declarer ruffed. Then came three rounds of clubs, ending up in dummy. Dummy's high Queen of Spades was then trumped in the closed hand. Then followed the King, Queen and Ace of Diamonds, the latter trick being ruffed in dummy. At this point, with the lead in dummy, declarer had the A-J-10 of trumps and West held the K-Q-9. A low heart was then led, declarer put up his ten-spot, which was taken by West's Queen — and West was endplayed, being forced to lead away from the K-9 of hearts.

NATIONAL OPEN PAIR
CHAMPIONSHIPS:
1951

NORTH
♠ 6 5 2
♡ K J
♢ A K Q 4 2
♣ J 5 4

WEST
♠ 10 9 7
♡ Q 8 7 4 3
♢ 5
♣ Q 8 7 2

EAST
♠ 4
♡ A 10 9 6 5 2
♢ J 7 3
♣ K 9 6

SOUTH
♠ A K Q J 8 3
♡ —
♢ 10 9 8 6
♣ A 10 3

North-South vulnerable

NORTH	EAST	SOUTH	WEST
		O. Jacoby	
1 ♢	1 ♡	1 ♠	4 ♡
Pass	Pass	6 ♠	Pass
Pass	Pass		

Had West opened a low heart, declarer, by putting up the Jack, would have made all 13 tricks. But Oswald Jacoby received the opening of the ten of spades instead — and he had his work cut out for him to make 12 tricks.

The opening trump lead was won with the Queen and trumps were then picked up. A diamond was next led to the Ace, followed by the King of Diamonds. When the Jack of Diamonds failed to drop, the diamond suit was blocked. If the Queen of Diamonds were now cashed, South's fourth diamond would be high and there would be no way of cashing dummy's fifth diamond.

Jacoby solved this problem in neat fashion. After cashing the King of Diamonds, he led the Jack of Hearts, upon which he discarded a diamond. West won the trick with the Queen, and shifted to a club, South's Ace winning. South then led his remaining diamond to dummy Queen, and on the deuce and four of diamonds, Jacoby discarded his two losing clubs.

The interesting aspect of this deal is that Jacoby received a pretty poor score, for at most tables a heart was opened, the various declarers all guessed right, and romped in with all 13 tricks.

VANDERBILT TEAM-OF-FOUR CHAMPIONSHIPS:
1954

NORTH
♠ Q 9
♡ 5 4 2
◇ A Q 8 7
♣ 10 8 3 2

WEST
♠ 10 3
♡ A Q 10 9
◇ 10 6 5 4 2
♣ 9 5

EAST
♠ A J 7 6 5 2
♡ K J 3
◇ J 9 3
♣ K

SOUTH
♠ K 8 4
♡ 8 7 6
◇ K
♣ A Q J 7 6 4

Both sides vulnerable

The bidding:

EAST	SOUTH *M. Moss*	WEST	NORTH
1 ♠	2 ♣	Pass	3 ♣
Pass	3 NT	Pass	Pass
Pass			

West opened the ten of spades, and Milton Moss saw that he could get two spade tricks by putting up dummy's Queen (with the ten of spades lead East was "marked" with the A-J of spades). But Moss knew that East would then also surmise that South had two spade tricks, and that East would therefore probably shift to hearts.

Hoping to prevent the disastrous heart shift, South put up dummy's nine of spades on the opening lead. East, recognizing that he could now prevent declarer from winning two spade tricks, played the encouraging seven-spot, South's King winning.

Declarer then led his King of Diamonds which he overtook with dummy's Ace, and led a club. When East put up the King, nine tricks became guaranteed.

It is, of course, quite obvious that had East won the opening lead with the Ace of Spades, a shift to hearts would have defeated declarer. But who can blame East for his failure to diagnose the situation? If declarer was willing to "throw away" a spade trick, East was delighted to help him.

WORLD CHAMPIONSHIPS:
1950

NORTH
♠ Q 7 6
♡ 10 9 5
◇ A Q 10 5 2
♣ 6 2

WEST
♠ 8 3 2
♡ Q 8 6 4 3 2
◇ —
♣ A K 9 3

EAST
♠ J 10 9 4
♡ K 7
◇ J 9 8 7
♣ Q 7 5

SOUTH
♠ A K 5
♡ A J
◇ K 6 4 3
♣ J 10 8 4

Both sides vulnerable

The bidding:

SOUTH *J. Crawford*	WEST	NORTH	EAST
1 ◇	1 ♡	2 ◇	Pass
2 NT	Pass	3 NT	Pass
Pass	Pass		

A play by declarer which creates an intended impression in a defender's mind can often turn defeat into victory. This point is the theme of the above deal.

West opened his fourth-best heart, East's King falling to declarer's Ace. A low diamond was then led, and when West failed to follow suit, dummy's ten-spot was inserted, East's Jack winning. A heart was now returned, West taking the trick with the Queen.

Because of Crawford's original play of the ten of diamonds, West came to the conclusion that East still possessed the King of Diamonds. Even when he next laid down the King of Clubs and East signalled with the seven-spot, West could not shake off his belief that East had the diamond King. So he returned a heart, establishing that suit. Crawford now took his nine tricks.

Had Crawford laid down the Diamond King before finessing for the Jack, West would later have shifted to clubs and continued clubs as a desperation play, and three notrump would have been defeated.

WORLD CHAMPIONSHIPS:
1956

NORTH
♠ K 7
♡ Q 8
◇ A K J 9 7 6 4 3
♣ A

WEST	EAST
♠ Q 6 4 3	♠ J 10 8
♡ 10 2	♡ A K J 9 7 5 4
◇ —	◇ Q 5
♣ K Q J 10 6 5 2	♣ 8

SOUTH
♠ A 9 5 2
♡ 6 3
◇ 10 8 2
♣ 9 7 4 3

North-South vulnerable

The bidding:

WEST	NORTH	EAST	SOUTH
4 ♣	5 ◇	Pass	6 ◇
Pass	Pass	Pass	

For those who are accustomed to the top-flight experts being perfect at all times, this deal will come as an almost unbelievable surprise. But experts are human, and, as such, err at times. The names of the offenders are withheld to protect the defenders, since to reveal them would make them "look bad" — and they happen to be very good. But they sure did slip on this one.

East opened the King of Hearts, West played the deuce, and declarer, North, dropped the Queen. East now shifted to a club, North's Ace winning. Declarer then ran all of his diamonds, West throwing his ten of hearts somewhere along the line. The location of the eight of hearts now became an open book — North had to have that card.

But, somehow or other, East developed that famous "blind spot" which we mortals develop a little too frequently and he discarded his top hearts, saving his J-10-8 of spades. And so declarer's eight of hearts won a trick, to fulfill the slam contract. Unbelievable perhaps, but absolutely a "true story."

RUBBER BRIDGE:

NORTH
♠ J 9 6 5
♡ 7
◇ Q 6 3
♣ A Q 10 6 2

WEST	EAST
♠ A 10	♠ K 8 7 4 3
♡ A 5	♡ 8 4 3
◇ K J 9 5	◇ 8 4 2
♣ K J 9 8 3	♣ 7 5

SOUTH
♠ Q 2
♡ K Q J 10 9 6 2
◇ A 10 7
♣ 4

Both sides vulnerable

The bidding:

SOUTH Dr. R. P. Greene	WEST	NORTH	EAST
1 ♡	Double	Pass	1 ♠
3 ♡	Pass	3 NT	Pass
4 ♡	Double	Pass	Pass
Pass			

Simple "carelessness" is probably responsible for the loss of more points than any other single factor. Here is an example of how an alert declarer capitalized on a defender's carelessness.

West opened the Ace of Spades, and upon observing East's come-on signal of the eight-spot, he continued the suit, East's King winning. A third round of spades was now led, declarer ruffing with the King, and West overruffing with the Ace.

A low club was now returned, declarer successfully finessing dummy's Queen. On the Ace of Clubs, declarer then discarded the ten of diamonds. Now came the seven of hearts, and when East followed with the three-spot, declarer played his deuce. As is apparent, the seven-spot won the trick while extracting West's last trump. On dummy's established Jack of Spades, Dr. Greene now discarded his losing seven of diamonds.

All East had to do was to cover the seven of hearts with the eight-spot and declarer would have been shut out of dummy forever, with the result that declarer would have had to lose a diamond trick. But East "forgot" — and it cost him the rubber.

VANDERBILT TOURNAMENT: 1945

NORTH
♠ A 10 6 4 3 2
♡ 8 7
♢ A 10 9 2
♣ 6

WEST
♠ Q 8
♡ 9 5
♢ Q J 5
♣ A K Q 9 8 2

EAST
♠ K 9 5
♡ K 6 2
♢ K 7 6
♣ J 10 7 3

SOUTH
♠ J 7
♡ A Q J 10 4 3
♢ 8 4 3
♣ 5 4

Neither side vulnerable

EAST S. Silodor	SOUTH T. Lightner	WEST C. Goren	NORTH W. von Zedtwitz
Pass	3 ♡	Pass	Pass
Pass			

On this hand there is no hero and there is no goat. The deal is an illustration of brilliant all-around defenders' play and declarer's play, with the victory ultimately going to the defenders.

The King of Clubs was opened, after which West shifted to the nine of trumps, declarer's ten-spot winning. If declarer now ruffed his remaining club, he figured to go down, since he would lose one club, two diamonds, one heart and one spade. So he tried to develop the spade suit by leading the seven of spades and putting up dummy's ten-spot.

East won this trick with the King and promptly banged down the King of Diamonds! When this was permitted to win, East continued the diamond suit. Once again, South permitted the defenders to win, hoping that the diamond suit was now established, which would permit him to discard his losing club, while still possessing a trump in dummy to finesse for the King.

But West ruined South's plans by laying down his Ace of Clubs, forcing dummy to trump. Eventually East's King of Hearts took the setting trick.

It has often been said that the top-flight experts play their cards as if they had seen all four hands. The above deal is submitted in evidence of this statement.

MASTERS PAIRS CHAMPIONSHIPS: 1952

NORTH
♠ 10 4
♡ Q 6 3
♢ 4
♣ A K Q J 6 5 2

WEST
♠ 8 7 6 3 2
♡ 8 4
♢ Q 10 8 5 3
♣ 7

EAST
♠ J
♡ A K 10 9 5
♢ J 7 2
♣ 10 9 8 3

SOUTH
♠ A K Q 9 5
♡ J 7 2
♢ A K 9 6
♣ 4

Neither side vulnerable

The bidding:

NORTH D. Steen	EAST	SOUTH W. Hanna	WEST
3 NT	Pass	6 NT	Pass
Pass	Double	7 ♣ (!)	Pass
Pass	Double	Pass	Pass
Pass			

Probably the most imaginative bid ever made in any bridge game occurred in the Masters' Pair Championships of 1952. The first suit bid made in the entire auction came at the seven-level — and the bid suit was on a singleton! Although this deal has nothing to do with the play of the cards, it is my opinion that no bridge book would be complete without this example of the heights to which imagination can soar.

The opening three notrump bid was a gambling, pre-emptive bid made on a long, solid suit. Hanna's jump to six notrump was strictly a gambling bid, based on the hope that the opponents would not find the proper defense. But when East doubled, South was reasonably certain that East, who was on lead, held the Ace and King of Hearts. Since North's bid had denoted a solid suit, South figured it to be clubs. So South now bid seven clubs, making West the leader.

West did not know what to lead. He finally chose a spade — and dug his own grave with it. As is evident, declarer romped in with all 13 tricks.

VANDERBILT CHAMPIONSHIPS:
1942

NORTH
♠ A K Q 9 5 4
♡ 8 4
◇ K 4
♣ 10 7 3

WEST
♠ J 10
♡ A K J 10 5 3
◇ J 8 7 3
♣ 9

EAST
♠ 7 2
♡ 6 2
◇ 6 5 2
♣ A K Q 8 5 2

SOUTH
♠ 8 6 3
♡ Q 9 7
◇ A Q 10 9
♣ J 6 4

North-South vulnerable

The bidding:

NORTH	EAST	SOUTH	WEST
1 ♠	Pass	1 NT	2 ♡
2 ♠	Pass	2 NT	Pass
3 NT	Double	Pass	Pass
Pass			

Within the realm of classic hands, the above is what might be described as a "nightmarish" hand. The names of the participants are unimportant — each of the four was — and is — a top-flight expert. But, in the best of circles, as in the worst, the most amazing things happen sometimes.

On the bidding, South, holding a near-maximum one notrump response with the adversely-bid heart suit protected (in theory), rebid two notrump with the hope that North, for his free bid, had a hand that was well above minimum. North then bid the game in notrump — which was a sad mistake.

West opened the King of Hearts, after which he shifted to a club. East now ran six club tricks, then returned a heart for West to run five more heart tricks. Declarer won the thirteenth trick, for his only winner. Down 8 tricks, for a minus 2300 score, on a hand where the opponents could make two hearts with a hundred honors.

A moral to this hand? Overbid when you can make your contract, and do not overbid when you cannot.

RUBBER BRIDGE

NORTH
♠ K J 9 8 7 4
♡ 7 4
◇ Q 3 2
♣ 7 3

WEST
♠ Q 2
♡ Q 8 3 2
◇ J 10 8 7
♣ A Q 10

EAST
♠ 3
♡ A K J 10 9 6 5
◇ 4
♣ J 8 6 5

SOUTH
♠ A 10 6 5
♡ —
◇ A K 9 6 5
♣ K 9 4 2

Both sides vulnerable

The bidding:

EAST	SOUTH	WEST	NORTH
	H. Fishbein		
4 ♡	4 NT	Double	Pass
Pass	Redouble	Pass	Pass
Pass			

This deal does not illustrate any point of play, but when one goes down 4000 points on a deal, it must be considered a "classic hand."

The South declarer was Harry Fishbein. North was a nationally-known expert (who misinterpreted a bid or two), and whose temporary alias will be Mr. Anonymous.

Fishbein's four notrump bid was a universally conventional bid demanding that partner name his best suit. The redouble was a confirmation of his earlier demand that partner bid, a demand that partner had failed to fulfill over West's double. But again North "forgot" to bid, so Fishbein became the declarer at four notrump, doubled and redoubled, vulnerable. (North-South could have made 11 tricks at a five spade contract).

When the smoke lifted, it was observed that the defenders had cashed seven heart tricks and three club tricks. Down seven, for a loss of 4000 points!

Whether it is true or not, I do not know, but the next day North was rumored to have said to a friend: "What do you think of that Fishbein? I went down 4000 points without even opening my mouth!"

NATIONAL MEN'S PAIRS CHAMPIONSHIPS:
1955

NORTH
♠ 9 3
♡ A Q
◇ A Q 10 7 6 4
♣ 10 9 8

WEST
♠ 10 4 2
♡ J 10 8 5 3 2
◇ J 3
♣ A 5

EAST
♠ A K 8 6 5
♡ 7 4
◇ 9 5
♣ K J 7 4

SOUTH
♠ Q J 7
♡ K 9 6
◇ K 8 2
♣ Q 6 3 2

Neither side vulnerable

The bidding:

NORTH	EAST E. Kaplan	SOUTH	WEST I. Erdos
1 ◇	1 ♠	1 NT	2 ♡
3 ◇	Pass	3 NT	Pass
Pass	Pass		

This deal illustrates some razzle-dazzle defense which had declarer coming and going — and he finally went the way of all flesh.

Ivan Erdos, West, opened the deuce of spades which Edgar Kaplan captured with the *Ace* (not the King). He then led the King of Clubs and continued with the four of clubs.

Our poor declarer was now in a quandary: it certainly looked as though Kaplan had the Ace of Clubs, judging by his lead of the King. So South put up the Queen of Clubs, which was taken by West's Ace. West now played another spade, East won with the King, and cashed the Jack and seven of clubs, to inflict a two-trick set on declarer.

What motivated Kaplan to defend as he did? On the bidding, South was marked with the King of Hearts (South had bid 3 NT without knowing that North had the A-Q of hearts). So Kaplan assumed (hoped) that Erdos had the Ace of clubs for his "free" two heart bid. Hence the play of the King of Clubs at trick two, which "convinced" declarer that East also held the Ace of Clubs.

NATIONAL CHAMPIONSHIPS:
1957

NORTH
♠ A 5 4
♡ 2
◇ A K 9 8 7 4 3
♣ J 8

WEST
♠ 9
♡ 9 5 3
◇ Q J 10
♣ A 10 9 7 6 5

EAST
♠ K Q J 8 3
♡ 7 6 4
◇ 6 5 2
♣ 4 3

SOUTH
♠ 10 7 6 2
♡ A K Q J 10 8
◇ —
♣ K Q 2

North-South vulnerable

WEST	NORTH	EAST	SOUTH C. Solomon
3 ♣	3 ◇	3 ♠	5 ♡
Pass	6 ◇	Pass	6 ♡
Pass	Pass	Pass	

For the top-flight experts, the play of apparently hopeless contracts is a challenge which they welcome. In these situations, it becomes essential to create the conditions which must exist if disaster is to be avoided — and the expert has learned how to create these conditions, and hope they exist.

Against Mr. Solomon's slam contract, West opened the nine of spades, which was captured by dummy's Ace. From the bidding, West's spade lead was obviously a singleton; and it was equally obvious that West possessed the Ace of Clubs. So, based on these "facts", and on the hope that the adverse six diamonds were divided 3-3, declarer found the answer to the avoidance of the loss of two tricks.

After winning the Ace of Spades declarer cashed the Ace and King of Diamonds, upon which he discarded the King and Queen of Clubs! A third round of diamonds was then trumped, declarer noting with great satisfaction that the adverse diamonds were divided 3-3. Trumps were now drawn, after which declarer led the deuce of clubs towards dummy's Jack and dummy's established diamonds. No matter whether West took the Club Ace or not, dummy's diamonds served as discards for declarer's three losing spades.

WORLD CHAMPIONSHIPS: 1956
(Great Britain vs. United States)

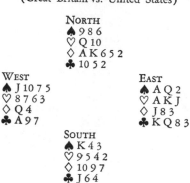

NORTH
♠ 9 8 6
♡ Q 10
◊ A K 6 5 2
♣ 10 5 2

WEST
♠ J 10 7 5
♡ 8 7 6 3
◊ Q 4
♣ A 9 7

EAST
♠ A Q 2
♡ A K J
◊ J 8 3
♣ K Q 8 3

SOUTH
♠ K 4 3
♡ 9 5 4 2
◊ 10 9 7
♣ J 6 4

East-West vulnerable

The bidding:

SOUTH	WEST	NORTH	EAST *C. Solomon*
Pass	Pass	1 ◊	Double
Pass	1 ♠	Pass	1 NT
Pass	2 NT	Pass	3 NT
Pass	Pass	Pass	

South opened a diamond against East's three notrump contract, and East was permitted to capture the trick with the Jack. Glancing at the East-West hands in superficial fashion, one might conclude that the proper play is to stake everything on a successful spade finesse. But actually the finesse turned out to be unnecessary.

At trick two, Mr. Solomon laid down the Ace of Hearts, and then followed by playing the King of Hearts, dropping North's Queen. The Jack of Hearts was now cashed, after which the King, Queen, and Ace of Clubs were taken. With the six adverse clubs being divided 3-3, Mr. Solomon had nine sure tricks and his contract.

Admittedly, the Queen of Hearts did not figure to drop on the second heart lead; nor did the adverse clubs figure to be divided 3-3. But surely Mr. Solomon's play was absolutely proper, for the spade finesse could always be taken as a last resort. An unspectacular, but neat, display of technique.

INTERNATIONAL MATCH:
Great Britain vs. Norway

NORTH
♠ K 9 6
♡ Q 5 2
◊ 8 4
♣ A K 8 5 3

WEST
♠ Q 5 4
♡ 10 9
◊ K 10 7 6 2
♣ 7 6 4

EAST
♠ J 10 7 2
♡ J 8 6 3
◊ A Q 3
♣ 9 2

SOUTH
♠ A 8 3
♡ A K 7 4
◊ J 9 5
♣ Q J 10

Both sides vulnerable

The bidding:

NORTH *B. Schapiro*	EAST	SOUTH *T. Reese*	WEST
1 ♣	Pass	1 ♡	Pass
2 ♡	Pass	4 ♡	Pass
Pass	Pass		

One of the world's finest players is Terence Reese, of England. An example of his technical ability can be observed in this deal, which is taken from the 1954 International Match between Great Britain and Norway.

West opened the ten of hearts — and Reese permitted him to hold the trick! From here on declarer had no problem, and no return could prevent him from making two spade tricks, three heart tricks, and five club tricks. On the face of it, it certainly seems that this deal is not what one would call evidence of Reese's "technical ability."

Yet, had Reese won the opening trump lead, and had then drawn three rounds of trumps, he would have gone down. His "ducking" of the opening heart lead was insurance against the adverse trumps breaking 4-2.

After all, technical ability is not concerned exclusively (or predominantly, for that matter) with recognizing endplays, squeezes, etc. It is the correct handling of the "little things" — such as counting tricks and employing safetyplays — that stamp the expert as a technician. And it is the proper handling of the little things that make an expert an expert.

VANDERBILT CHAMPIONSHIPS: 1954

NORTH
♠ A J 7
♡ 9 4
◇ A 6
♣ 9 8 7 6 4 2

WEST
♠ 9 5 4 2
♡ Q 10 8 7 2
◇ K 3
♣ A 3

EAST
♠ 8 3
♡ A 6 5 3
◇ 9 8 7 5 4
♣ Q 5

SOUTH
♠ K Q 10 6
♡ K J
◇ Q J 10 2
♣ K J 10

North-South vulnerable

WEST	NORTH	EAST	SOUTH
Pass	Pass	Pass	1 NT
Double	Redouble	Pass	Pass
2 ♡	Pass	Pass	2 ♠
Pass	3 ♣	Pass	3 NT
Pass	Pass	Pass	

The South declarer on this deal shall remain anonymous, since it is not the policy of your author to point a finger at an expert and say: "You played this hand badly." But the fact is, declarer could probably have made his contract if he had given a little more thought to the card he led at trick three.

West's opening heart lead was taken by East's Ace, and the heart return was captured by declarer's King. The Queen of Diamonds was then laid down, covered by West's King, and taken by dummy's Ace. Declarer now had eight sure tricks, but there was no way to obtain the ninth trick.

It is impossible to prove what *might* have happened, but suppose declarer had led the ten of diamonds instead of the Queen? In all probability West would *not* have covered with the King. The deuce of diamonds would then have been led, upon which West's King would have fallen, and declarer would have had nine tricks.

To a top-flight expert, the suggested line of play is the proper line, for the only way declarer can make nine tricks would be to bring in four diamond tricks. And this can be done if West has the K-x of diamonds — and can be "talked" into not covering the ten.

NATIONAL TEAM-OF-FOUR CHAMPIONSHIPS: 1953

NORTH
♠ J 9 7 6 2
♡ —
◇ A Q J 9 5 4
♣ J 4

WEST
♠ K 3
♡ A 4
◇ 8 7 3 2
♣ A K 6 5 3

EAST
♠ Q 10 8 5
♡ 10 6 3
◇ K
♣ Q 9 8 7 2

SOUTH
♠ A 4
♡ K Q J 9 8 7 5 2
◇ 10 6
♣ 10

Both sides vulnerable

The bidding:

SOUTH A. Roth	WEST	NORTH	EAST
1 ♡	Pass	1 ♠	Pass
2 ♡	Pass	2 ♠	Pass
4 ♡	Pass	Pass	Pass

In retrospect, Al Roth's play of this deal is simple and proper. Nevertheless, his play would not have been made by most bridge players.

The King of Clubs was opened, followed by the Ace, declarer ruffing. The King of trumps was then led, and taken by West's Ace, after which West shifted to the King of Spades which was captured by declarer's Ace. The defenders' trumps were now drawn.

Roth then led the ten of diamonds and took it with dummy's Ace. When East's King fell, the contract was guaranteed. How and why did Roth avoid taking the diamond finesse?

West had not made a bid — and he had thus far shown up with the A-K of Clubs, the Ace of Hearts, and the King of Spades. Surely it was impossible for him to also possess the King of Diamonds. Therefore East had the King of Diamonds, and the finesse had to lose. Hence the sole hope was that East's "marked" King of Diamonds was unprotected. Luck? Yup. But skill also.

FRENCH NATIONAL CHAMPIONSHIPS: 1947

NORTH
♠ 8 5
♡ J 10 7
◇ J 8 2
♣ A K 8 5 2

WEST
♠ 10 9 3
♡ Q 9 5 3
◇ 4
♣ J 9 6 4 3

EAST
♠ —
♡ 8 4 2
◇ K Q 10 9 7 6 5
♣ Q 10 7

SOUTH
♠ A K Q J 7 6 4 2
♡ A K 6
◇ A 3
♣ —

North-South vulnerable

The bidding:

WEST	NORTH	EAST	SOUTH
			B. Koytchou
Pass	Pass	3 ◇	6 ♠
Pass	Pass	Pass	

Against the slam, West opened the four of diamonds, which was taken by declarer's Ace. Declarer was quite unhappy about the situation, for it was obvious that unless he caught the Queen of Hearts, he was doomed.

Declarer then cashed the Ace and King of Trumps — and the solution dawned on him. West was marked for a singleton diamond since he had led the four-spot and the trey and deuce were in evidence (In theory, East could have had only six diamonds, rather than seven diamonds, but the opening lead of the four-spot made this impossible). Now declarer played the deuce of trumps, throwing West into the lead!

West, of course, had no option but to lead a heart or a club, either of which would enable declarer to reach dummy to shed his losing diamond on the Ace of Clubs.

Even if West had foreseen what declarer was going to do, he would have been powerless to stop declarer. Had West, on the leads of the Ace and King of Trumps, thrown his ten and nine of trumps, he still would have had the three-spot remaining. And declarer's deuce would have forced West into the lead.

RUBBER BRIDGE

NORTH
♠ 8 7 5 2
♡ A
◇ A K J 6 2
♣ Q 7 3

WEST
♠ 10 6 4 3
♡ K Q J 9
◇ 9 5
♣ K 6 2

EAST
♠ Q
♡ 8 7 5 4 2
◇ 8 7 3
♣ J 10 8 5

SOUTH
♠ A K J 9
♡ 10 6 3
◇ Q 10 4
♣ A 9 4

Neither side vulnerable

The bidding:

SOUTH	WEST	NORTH	EAST
J. Stablein			
1 ♠	Pass	3 ◇	Pass
4 ◇	Pass	4 ♡	Pass
5 ♣	Pass	6 ♠	Pass
Pass	Pass		

The key play in the above deal is much simpler to make away from the table than it is at the table. When the deal arose in actual play, John Stablein, our South declarer, came up with the right answer at the right time.

West opened the King of Hearts, which was captured by dummy's Ace. A low trump was then led, East played the Queen — and declarer permitted the Queen to win! It was now a cinch for declarer to win any return, trump two hearts, and discard his two low clubs on dummy's diamonds.

If declarer had captured the Queen of Spades, he would have been defeated no matter what he did after that. If he then ruffed his losing hearts in dummy, West would still possess his high trump to prevent effectively declarer from running dummy's diamonds; if he drew three rounds of trumps after winning the Spade Queen, there would be no way to dispose of his losers in clubs and hearts.

By conceding a trick to the Queen of Spades, declarer was able to retain control of trumps. A simple hand — in retrospect only.

THE INTERNATIONAL CODE:

LAWS OF
CONTRACT BRIDGE

Reprinted by permission of
THE JOHN C. WINSTON COMPANY
PHILADELPHIA

THE SCOPE OF THE LAWS

The Laws are designed to define correct procedure and to provide an adequate remedy in all cases where a player accidentally, carelessly or inadvertently disturbs the proper course of the game, or gains an unintentional but nevertheless unfair advantage. An offending player should be ready to pay a prescribed penalty graciously.

The Laws are not designed to prevent dishonorable practices and there are no penalties to cover intentional violations. In the absence of penalty, moral obligations are strongest. Ostracism is the ultimate remedy for intentional offenses.

The object of the Proprieties is twofold: to familiarize players with the customs and etiquette of the game, generally accepted over a long period of years; and to enlighten those who might otherwise fail to appreciate when or how they are improperly conveying information to their partners — often a far more reprehensible offense than a violation of a law.

When these principles are appreciated, arguments are avoided and the pleasure which the game offers is materially enhanced.

PART I

DEFINITIONS

THE PLAYERS —

Partner — The player with whom one plays as a SIDE against the other two. He occupies the opposite seat at the table.

Opponent — A player of the other side.

Declarer — The player who for his side first bid the denomination named in the contract.

Dummy — Declarer's partner.

Contractor — Declarer or dummy.

Defender — An opponent of declarer.

HONOR — Any Ace, King, Queen, Jack or ten.

HAND — The cards originally dealt to a player or the remaining portion thereof.

ROTATION — The order of progression applying in the game, which is from player to player clockwise.

DENOMINATION — The suit or no-trump named in a bid.

ODD TRICK — A trick won by declarer in excess of six.

CALL — A comprehensive term applicable to a bid, a double, a redouble or a pass.

BID — An offer to contract to win at least a specified number of odd tricks in a specified denomination.

PASS — A call signifying that a player does not, on that occasion, elect to bid, double or redouble.

PLAY — To contribute a card to a trick, including the first card which is the LEAD.

TRUMP — Each card of the suit, if any, named in the contract.

FOLLOW SUIT — To play a card of the suit led.

REVOKE — To play a card of another suit when able to follow suit.

OVERTRICK — A trick won by declarer in excess of his contract.

UNDERTRICK — A trick by which declarer falls short of his contract.

SLAMS: Grand Slam — the winning of thirteen tricks by one side; Little Slam — the winning of twelve tricks by one side.

VULNERABLE — Having won a game toward rubber.

The meaning of the following terms is clarified in the laws: Pack, section 1; Deal, section 8; Contract, section 22-b; Sufficient Bid, Insufficient Bid, section 23; Double and Redouble, sections 24 and 25; Trick, section 47; Penalty Card, sections 67, 68 and 69; Game, section 94; Rubber, section 95.

PART II

THE DRAW, THE SHUFFLE, THE CUT, THE DEAL

1. THE PACK — RANK OF CARDS AND SUITS

Contract Bridge is played by four players with a pack of 52 cards, comprising 13 cards, in each of 4 suits. The suits rank downwards in the order — Spades (♠), Hearts (♡), Diamonds (♢), Clubs (♣). The cards of each suit rank downwards in the order — Ace, King, Queen, Jack, 10, 9, 8, 7, 6, 5, 4, 3, 2. When practicable, two packs with distinguishable backs are used.

2. THE DRAW [1]

Before every rubber, each player draws a card from a shuffled pack spread face downwards on the table. A drawn card should not be exposed until all players have drawn. If a player exposes more than one card, or draws one of the four cards at either end of the pack, or draws a card from the other pack, he must draw again. In drawing, equal cards rank according to suit.

3. PARTNERSHIPS

The two players who draw the highest cards play as partners against the other two. The player with the highest card deals first and has the right to choose his seat and the pack with which he will deal. He may consult his partner but, having announced his decision, must abide by it. His partner sits opposite him. Thereafter, the opponents may, after consultation, determine their respective occupancy of the two remaining seats.

4. THE SHUFFLE

The pack for each deal is prepared by the player on the left of its dealer, if practicable while the other pack is being dealt. Preparing a pack consists of collecting the cards, shuffling them, and placing the shuffled pack face downwards on the left of the next dealer. The cards should be shuffled thoroughly and in full view of all players, but without exposing the face of any card.

5. A properly prepared pack should not be disturbed until its dealer picks it up for his deal, at which time he is entitled to the final shuffle. No player may shuffle a pack other than its dealer and the player on his left.

6. THE CUT

A pack must always be cut immediately before it is dealt. The dealer presents it to the player on his right, who lifts off a portion and places it on the table toward the dealer beside the bottom portion. Each portion must contain at least four cards. The dealer completes the cut by placing the bottom portion uppermost.

7. NEW SHUFFLE — NEW CUT

Before the first card is dealt, any player may demand a new shuffle or a new cut. There must be a new shuffle and cut if a card is faced in cutting, or if there is a redeal. When there is a new shuffle, only the dealer may shuffle.

---

[1] If more than four persons desire to play, it is customary to follow the Rules for Club Procedure (Part VIII) to determine which of them shall have the right to play.

8. THE DEAL

The dealer must deal the cards face downwards, one at a time in rotation into four separate hands of 13 cards each, the first card to the player on his left and the last card to himself. If he deals two cards simultaneously or consecutively to the same player, he may rectify the error, provided he does so promptly and to the satisfaction of his opponents.

9. The dealer must not allow the face of any card to be seen while he is dealing. Until the deal is completed, no player may look at the face of any card, and no one but the dealer may touch any card except to correct or preclude an irregularity.

10. CHANGING THE DEALER

The turn to deal passes in rotation unless there is a redeal, in which case the same dealer redeals.

11. CHANGING THE PACK

The packs should be used alternately unless there is a redeal. The pack originally belonging to a side must be restored if reclaimed, but a deal may not be stopped to restore a pack. A pack containing a distinguishable damaged card must be replaced.

PART III
GENERAL LAWS COVERING IRREGULARITIES

12. REDEAL

There must be a redeal:

(a) If, before the last card is dealt, a redeal is demanded because a player is dealing out of turn or with an uncut pack.

(b) If it is ascertained before the last card is dealt that the cards have not been dealt correctly, or that a card is faced in the pack or elsewhere.

(c) If it is ascertained before the first call is duly made that a player has picked up another player's hand and seen a card in it.

(d) If it is ascertained before the cards have been mixed together that one player has picked up too many cards, another too few; or that the pack, when the deal began, did not conform in every respect to the requirements of section 1.

(e) If the players have allowed their hands to be mixed together before finding a missing card, or in the belief that a redeal is in order.

There may not be a redeal except as provided above.

13. MISSING CARD

A missing card, when found, is deemed to belong to the deficient hand.

When clause (d) or (e) of section 12 applies, there must be a redeal.

When neither clause applies, the deal stands, and, if the missing card was found in a trick, the defective trick law (section 80 or 81) applies. The missing card may become a penalty card under section 26 or 67, or failure to have played it may constitute a revoke. It must be placed in the deficient hand unless it becomes a penalty card or is found in a trick that stands as played.

14. SURPLUS CARD

If a player has too many cards, there must be a redeal unless he has omitted to play to a trick, in which case the defective trick law (section 80 or 81) applies.

15. DRAWING ATTENTION TO AN IRREGULARITY

When an irregularity is committed, any player (except dummy if he has looked at another player's hand) may draw attention to it and give or obtain information as to the law covering it. The fact that the offending side draws attention to its own irregularity does not in any way affect the rights of the opponents.

16. ENFORCEMENT OF A PENALTY

Either opponent individually (but not dummy) may select or enforce a penalty. If the opponents consult as to penalty selection or enforcement, or if either opponent waives the penalty; the right to penalize is cancelled, but the rectification provisions (if any) of the applicable section still apply.

17. After attention has been called to an irregularity, no player may call or play until all questions in regard to rectification and penalty enforcement have been determined.

18. The penalty provisions of the laws apply only after agreement on the fact that an irregularity has been committed, and after specific statement of the penalty to be applied.

19. All questions as to what course to follow must be settled by the players before the game continues. A penalty once paid or other action once taken stands, even though at some later time it is discovered to have been incorrect.

20. IMPROPER REMARKS AND GESTURES

If by a remark or unmistakable gesture a player other than declarer: discloses his intentions or desires, or the nature of an unfaced hand, or the presence or absence of a card in an unfaced hand; or improperly suggests a lead, play, or line of play; or improperly directs attention to the cards on a trick to which his partner has yet to play:

(a) If the offense occurred before the auction closed, (penalty) either opponent may require the offending side to pass whenever it is its turn to call; and if the offending side become defenders, declarer may require or forbid the opening lead of a specified suit.

(b) If the offense occurred after the auction closed, (penalty) declarer or either defender, as the case may be, may require the offender's partner to withdraw any lead or play which may have been suggested by the improper remark or gesture, and to substitute a card which does not conform to the improper suggestion. This penalty may be exacted on any trick subsequent to the offense but only on one such trick. The offender's partner may not be required to withdraw his card from a trick to which an opponent has played after him. Before this penalty may be enforced, a majority of the players must agree as to what lead, play or line of play has been improperly suggested.

PART IV

THE AUCTION

21. DURATION OF AUCTION

The auction begins when the last card of a correct deal has been placed on the table. The dealer makes the first call, and thereafter each player calls in rotation. After the first call has been made, the auction continues until three players have passed in rotation. This closes the auction.

22. PROCEDURE AFTER AUCTION IS CLOSED

After the auction is closed:

(a) If no player has bid, the hands are abandoned and the turn to deal passes in rotation.

(b) If any player has bid, the last bid becomes the contract and the play begins.

23. BIDS

Each bid must name a number of odd tricks, from one to seven, and a denomination, and must supersede any previous bid by naming either a greater number of odd tricks or the same number in a higher denomination. A bid that supersedes the previous bid is sufficient; one that does not is insufficient. The denominations rank downwards in order: No Trump, Spades, Hearts, Diamonds, Clubs.

24. DOUBLES AND REDOUBLES

A player may double only if the last preceding bid was made by an opponent and no call other than a pass has intervened. A player may redouble only if the last preceding call other than a pass was a double by an opponent.

25. All doubles and redoubles are nullified by a proper subsequent bid. If there is no subsequent bid, the scoring value of the contract is increased as provided in section 98.

26. CARD EXPOSED DURING THE AUCTION

If during the auction a player faces a card on the table, or sees the face of a card belonging to his partner:

(a) If an Ace, King, Queen or Jack, or a lower card prematurely led, or more than one card; [1] (penalty) the owner's partner must pass when next it is his turn to call. Every such card must be left face up on the table until the auction closes; and if its owner is then a defender, it becomes a penalty card.

(b) If a single card, lower than a Jack and not prematurely led, there is no penalty.

IMPROPER CALLS [2]

27. IMPROPER CALL PREMATURELY OVERCALLED IN ROTATION

If a player calls before the penalty for an improper call by his right-hand opponent has been enforced (see section 17), the auction proceeds as though it had been a proper call; except that if the improper call was a bid of more than seven, or a double or redouble made when only a pass or bid could be a proper call, the auction proceeds as though the improper call had been a pass.

28. CHANGING A CALL

If a player changes a call in any way and does so practically in the same breath, his last call stands. There is no penalty unless he has changed to an improper call, in which case the appropriate "improper calls" section applies.

29. If a player changes a call in any way, and does not do so practically in the same breath, the change of call is void, and:

(a) If the first call was improper, the appropriate "improper calls" section applies.

(b) If the first call was a proper call, either the offender must allow his first call to stand, in which case (penalty) his partner must pass when next it is his turn to call; or the offender must substitute any other proper call, in which case (penalty) his partner must pass whenever it is his turn to call.

---

[1] If two (or more) cards are faced or seen at different times, clause (a) applies to both of them even though one has been picked up as provided in clause (b).

[2] All possible improper calls are listed under this heading. Calls not recognized by nor dealt with in these laws are merely improper remarks. The auction proceeds as if an improper remark had not been made, unless the remark is sufficiently informative to warrant the imposition of a penalty under section 20 (a).

30. INSUFFICIENT BID

If a player makes an insufficient bid, he must substitute either a sufficient bid or a pass [3] If he substitutes —

(a) The lowest sufficient bid in the same denomination, there is no penalty.

(b) Any other bid, (penalty) the offender's partner must pass whenever it is his turn to call.

(c) A pass, (penalty) the offender's partner must pass whenever it is his turn to call; and if the offending side become the defenders, declarer may require or forbid the opening lead of a specified suit.

31. CALL OUT OF ROTATION

A call out of rotation is void. The auction reverts to the player whose turn it is to call; and —

(a) If a player has passed out of rotation before any player has bid, or when it was the turn of the opponent on his right to call, (penalty) the offender must pass when next it is his turn to call.[4]

(b) If a player has made any call out of rotation other than a pass listed in (a), (penalty) the offender's partner must pass whenever it is his turn to call. [5]

32. A call is not out of rotation when made without waiting for the right-hand opponent to pass, if he is required to pass because of a law infringement.

33. If a player, whose turn it was to call, calls before attention has been drawn to a call out of rotation by his left-hand opponent, the auction proceeds as though that opponent had not called.

34. SIMULTANEOUS CALLS

A call made simultaneously with another player's proper call is deemed to be a subsequent call.

35. NAMING BID INCORRECTLY IN DOUBLING [6]

If a player in doubling or redoubling names an incorrect number of tricks or a wrong denomination, he is deemed to have doubled or redoubled the bid as made.

36. DOUBLING WHEN THE ONLY PROPER CALL IS A PASS OR BID

If a player doubles or redoubles a bid which his side has already doubled or redoubled, (penalty) he must substitute any proper call, and his partner must pass whenever it is his turn to call. In addition, if the offender elects to pass, either opponent may cancel all previous doubles and redoubles.

---

[3] As provided in section 18, a player is entitled to select his substituted call after the applicable penalties have been stated. Any call he may have substituted previously is void, unless his left-hand opponent has overcalled it, in which case section 27 applies.

[4] Example: North (dealer) 1 Heart, South pass. The pass is void, and the auction reverts to East. After East has called, South must pass. Thereafter, North and South may in rotation make any proper call.

[5] Example: North (dealer) 1 Heart, South 1 Spade. The 1-Spade bid is void, and the auction reverts to East. After East has called, South may make any proper call. Thereafter, North must pass whenever it is his turn to call, but South may make any proper call whenever it is his turn to call.

[6] It is improper to state the number of tricks or the denomination in doubling.

37. If a player doubles his partner's bid, redoubles an undoubled bid, or doubles or redoubles when there has been no bid, (penalty) the offender must substitute any proper call, and his partner must pass whenever it is his turn to call.

38. **BID, DOUBLE OR REDOUBLE WHEN REQUIRED TO PASS BID OF MORE THAN SEVEN**

If a player bids more than seven, or bids, doubles or redoubles when required by law to pass; the offender is deemed to have passed, and (penalty) the offending side must pass whenever it is its turn to call, and if the offender becomes a defender, declarer may require or forbid the opening lead of a specified suit.

39. **DOUBLY IMPROPER CALL**

If a player makes a call subject to penalty under two or more "improper calls" sections, either section may be applied but not both.

40. **CALL AFTER THE AUCTION IS CLOSED**

A call made after the auction is closed is cancelled. If it is a pass by a defender, or any call by a contractor, there is no penalty. If it is a bid, double or redouble by a defender, (penalty) declarer may require or forbid the other defender to lead a specified suit when first it is the latter's turn to lead.

REVIEWING THE AUCTION

41. A player who does not hear a call distinctly may forthwith require it to be repeated. There is no redress for a call based on a misunderstanding or on misinformation.

42. A player is entitled to have previous calls restated either when it is his turn to call, or after the auction closes but before the opening lead has been duly made. His request should be responded to only by an opponent. Dummy, or a player required by law to pass, should not ask to have calls restated, but may review the auction at an opponent's request and should correct errors in restatement.

43. After the opening lead, calls may not be restated, but declarer or a defender is entitled to be informed what the contract is and whether, but not by whom, it was doubled or redoubled.

PART V
THE PLAY

44. **COMMENCEMENT OF PLAY**

After the auction closes, the defender on declarer's left makes the opening lead. After the opening lead dummy spreads his hand in front of him on the table, face up and grouped in suits with the trumps on his right. Declarer plays both of the contractors' hands.

45. **DUMMY'S RIGHTS**

Dummy should refrain from all comment and from taking any active part in the play, except that he may:

   (a)   Give or obtain information as to fact or law.

   (b)   Question players regarding revokes as provided in section 71.

   (c)   Draw attention to an irregularity, or try to prevent one apparently about to be committed. [1]

---

[1] Example: He may warn declarer against leading from the wrong hand, but only when it is apparent that declarer is about to do so.

Dummy forfeits these rights if he looks at a card in another player's hand.

46. DUMMY'S LIMITATIONS

Dummy should not exchange hands with declarer, lean over to see a defender's cards, leave his seat to watch declarer play, or, on his own initiative, look at the face of a card in any other player's hand. If dummy, as a result of any such act, sees a card in any other player's hand, and thereafter:

(a) Is the first to draw attention to a defender's irregularity, declarer may not enforce any penalty for the offense.

(b) Warns declarer not to lead from the wrong hand, (penalty) either defender may choose the hand from which declarer shall lead.

(c) Is the first to ask declarer if a play from his hand constitutes a revoke, and the revoke card is consequently withdrawn, (penalty) either defender may require declarer to substitute his highest or lowest correct card.

LEADS AND PLAYS

47. THE SEQUENCE AND PROCEDURE OF PLAY

The leader to a trick may play any card in his hand. After a lead, each other hand in rotation plays a card, and the four cards so played constitute a trick.

48. In playing to a trick, each player must if possible follow suit. This obligation overrides all other requirements of the laws. If unable to follow suit, a player may play any card.

49. A trick containing a trump is won by the hand playing the highest trump. A trick that does not contain a trump is won by the hand playing the highest card of the suit led. The hand winning a trick leads to the next trick.

50. PLAYED CARD

A card in any hand is played when named as the one a player proposes to play; but a player may change his designation if he does so practically in the same breath.

51. A card in any unfaced hand is played when it touches the table face upwards after being detached from the remaining cards with apparent intent to play; a defender's card so detached is also played as soon as his partner sees its face.

52. A card in dummy or any other faced hand is played when touched unless for a purpose other than play either manifest or mentioned.

53. TAKING BACK PLAYED CARD

A played card may not be withdrawn except:

(a) To comply with a penalty.

(b) To correct a revoke.

(c) To correct the error of playing more than one card to a trick.

(d) To substitute another card after an opponent has corrected either a revoke or a failure to comply with a lead or play penalty.

54. PREMATURE LEAD OR PLAY BY A DEFENDER

If a defender leads to the next trick before his partner has played to the current trick, or plays out of rotation before his partner has played, (penalty) declarer may require the offender's partner to play:

(a) His highest card of the suit led; or

(b) His lowest card of the suit led; or

(c) A card of another specified suit.

If declarer has played from both contractors' hands, a defender is not subject to penalty for playing before his partner.

55. LEAD OUT OF TURN

A lead out of turn may be treated as a correct lead. It must be so treated if the non-offending side plays a card before attention is drawn to the irregularity. [2]

56. If either defender requires declarer to retract his lead out of turn, the card wrongly led is replaced without penalty; and if declarer has led from the wrong hand, he must lead from the correct hand and (penalty), if he can, a card of the same suit. A defender's drawing attention to declarer's lead out of turn is equivalent to requiring its retraction.

57. If declarer requires a defender to retract his lead out of turn:

    (a) If it was a contractor's turn to lead, declarer leads from the correct hand and the card led out of turn becomes a penalty card.

    (b) If it was the other defender's turn to lead, (penalty) declarer may forbid the lead of that suit, in which case the card wrongly led is picked up; or may treat the card led out of turn as a penalty card, in which case any card may be led.

58. SIMULTANEOUS LEADS OR PLAYS

A lead or play made simultaneously with another player's proper lead or play is deemed to be subsequent to it. If a defender leads or plays two or more cards simultaneously, he may play either card, and the other card becomes a penalty card.

59. INABILITY TO LEAD OR PLAY AS REQUIRED

If a player is unable to lead or play as required to comply with a penalty, either because he has no card of the required suit or because of his obligation to follow suit, he may play any correct card. The penalty is satisfied, except in the case of a penalty card, which must be played at the first legal opportunity.

60. PLAYING BEFORE PENALTY HAS BEEN ENFORCED

If declarer plays from either hand before enforcing a lead or play penalty, he is deemed to waive the penalty.

61. If a defender plays to a contractor's lead out of turn after declarer has been required to retract it, the defender's card becomes a penalty card.

62. A play by a member of the offending side, before a penalty has been enforced, does not affect the right of the non-offending side to enforce a penalty.

EXPOSED CARDS

63. DECLARER EXPOSING CARDS

Declarer is never subject to penalty for exposure of a card, and no card of declarer's ever becomes a penalty card.

64. If declarer plays more than one card he must designate which is his play, and must restore any other card to his hand.

65. If declarer exposes his hand after an opening lead by the wrong defender, and before dummy has spread any part of his hand, dummy becomes declarer.

66. If declarer intentionally exposes his hand otherwise than as provided in the preceding section, it is treated as a claim or concession of tricks and section 88 applies.

---

[2] If, after an opening lead by the wrong defender, declarer exposes his hand, see section 65.

67. DEFENDER EXPOSING CARDS

If a defender faces a card on the table, or sees the face of a card belonging to his partner before he is entitled to see it in the normal course of play or penalty enforcement; any such card becomes a penalty card, except as otherwise provided in these laws.[3]

68. DISPOSITION OF A PENALTY CARD

A penalty card must be left face upward on the table until played. A defender should not pick up a penalty card and restore it to his hand; but if he does so, and if declarer plays from his own hand or dummy before requiring that the card be faced on the table again, such card ceases to be a penalty card.

69. A penalty card must be played at the first opportunity, whether in leading, following suit, discarding or trumping. The play of a penalty card is always subject to the obligation to follow suit, or to comply with a lead or play penalty. If a defender can play two or more penalty cards, declarer may designate which one is to be played.

70. DEFENDER IMPROPERLY EXPOSING HIS HAND

If a defender improperly exposes his remaining card or cards, declarer may treat the remaining cards of either defender as penalty cards. The hand of the other defender, if exposed, may be picked up.

THE REVOKE [4]

71. INQUIRIES REGARDING A REVOKE

Any player, including dummy, may ask a player who has failed to follow suit whether he has a card of the suit led, and may demand that an opponent correct his revoke.

72. CORRECTING A REVOKE

A player must correct his revoke —

    (a)   Made in any of the first eleven tricks, if aware of it before it becomes established.

    (b)   Made in the twelfth trick, if aware of it before the cards have been mixed together. There is no penalty for a revoke made in the twelfth trick and it never becomes established.

73. To correct a revoke, the offender withdraws the revoke card and follows suit with any card. A revoke card from a defender's unfaced hand becomes a penalty card; any other revoke card may be replaced without penalty. The non-offending side may withdraw any card it played after the revoke but before attention was drawn to it.

74. ACTS THAT ESTABLISH A REVOKE

A revoke in any of the first eleven tricks becomes established when the offender or his partner leads or plays to a subsequent trick or signifies his intention of doing so by naming a card, by claiming or conceding a trick, or by exposing a hand.

---

[3] Exceptions to section 67: A card led out of turn may be treated as a correct lead (section 55) or may be picked up (section 57-b). An exposed card may not be treated as a penalty card if dummy improperly (section 46-a) draws attention to it, or to the irregularity that caused its exposure.

[4] The penalty provisions of the revoke law are subject to section 46 if dummy has forfeited his rights. A claim of revoke does not warrant inspection of turned tricks except as permitted in sections 78 and 79.

75. PROCEDURE WHEN A REVOKE IS ESTABLISHED

When a revoke is established, the revoke trick stands as played. It counts in transferring tricks as a trick won "after the revoke."

76. If a revoke becomes established, after play ceases two tricks are transferred to the non-offending side if the revoking side has won two or more tricks after the revoke. One trick only is transferred if the revoking side wins but one trick after the revoke. There is no penalty for an established revoke:

(a) If the revoking side wins no trick after the revoke.

(b) If it is a subsequent revoke in the same suit by the same player.

(c) If attention is first drawn to it after the cards have been mixed together.

(d) If it is made in failing to play any card faced on the table, including a card from dummy's hand or a penalty card.

TRICKS

77. GATHERING AND ARRANGING TRICKS

Each completed trick must be gathered and turned face down on the table by the side winning it. The cards of each turned trick should be kept together so that the trick can be readily identified. All the tricks taken by a side should be arranged together in front of declarer or of one defender in such manner that their number and sequence are apparent.

78. INSPECTING TRICKS — MIXING CARDS BEFORE A CLAIM IS SETTLED

Declarer or either defender may, until his side has led or played a card to the next trick, inspect a trick and inquire what card each hand has played to it. Except as above provided or to account for a surplus or missing card, turned tricks may be inspected before play ceases only with the other side's consent.

79. After play ceases, the tricks and unplayed cards may be inspected to settle a claim of a revoke or of honors, or the number of tricks won or lost. If, after such claim, an opponent so mixes the cards that the claim cannot be proved, it must be allowed.

80. DEFECTIVE TRICK

If a hand has played too many cards to a trick, or has omitted to play to it, and if attention is drawn to the irregularity before a player of each side has played to the next trick, the error must be rectified. A card withdrawn from a defective trick, if played from a defender's unfaced hand, becomes a penalty card.

81. If attention is drawn to a defective trick after a player of each side has played to the next trick, the defective trick stands as played, and:

(a) A hand with too few cards plays the hand out with fewer cards than the other hands, does not play to the final trick (or tricks), and if it wins a trick with its last card the lead passes in rotation.

(b) A hand with too many cards forthwith faces and adds to the defective trick (but without changing its ownership) a card it could properly have played to it.

82. TRICK APPROPRIATED IN ERROR

A trick appropriated by the wrong side must be restored on demand to the side that played the winning card, and, in any case, its scoring value must be credited to that side, subject to section 93.

FAILURE TO COMPLY WITH A LEAD OR PLAY PENALTY

83.   If a player is able to lead or play a penalty card, or a card or suit specified by an opponent in conformity with an agreed penalty, but instead plays an incorrect card:

(a)   The offender must correct his error if aware of it before he or his partner plays another card. If the incorrect card was played from a defender's unfaced hand, it becomes a penalty card. A card played from the hand on the offender's left may be withdrawn if it was played after the error and before attention was drawn to it.

(b)   After the offender or his partner has played another card, the incorrect card may not be withdrawn. After play ceases, (penalty) there is a transfer of tricks to the non-offending side as though the offense were an established revoke (section 76).

CLAIMS AND CONCESSIONS

84.   CONCESSION OF TRICK WHICH CANNOT BE LOST

The concession of a trick which cannot be lost by any play of the cards is void if attention is called to the error before the cards have been mixed together.

85.   CONCESSION OF TRICK WHICH HAS BEEN WON

If a player concedes a trick he has in fact won (as by claiming nine tricks when his side has already won ten, or conceding defeat of a contract his side has fulfilled), the concession is void. If the score has been entered it may be corrected as provided in section 93.

86.   DEFENDER CLAIMING OR CONCEDING TRICKS

A defender may show any or all of his remaining cards to declarer for the purpose of establishing a claim or concession. If a defender makes a claim or concession in any other manner, he may be liable to penalty under section 20.

87.   A concession of tricks by a defender is not valid unless his partner accedes. This provision does not preclude the enforcement of a penalty for a defender's irregularity.

88.   DECLARER CLAIMING OR CONCEDING TRICKS

If declarer intentionally exposes his hand, specifically claims or concedes one or more of the remaining tricks, or suggests that play may be curtailed, it is deemed to be a claim by declarer; and —

(a)   Play should cease; and declarer should place and leave his hand face upwards on the table and forthwith make an adequate statement of his intended line of play.

(b)   At any time after declarer's claim a defender may face his hand and may suggest a play to his partner. Declarer may not enforce any penalty for an irregularity committed by a defender whose hand is so faced.

(c)   Declarer's claim must be allowed if both defenders accede to it, or if either defender allows his hand to be mixed with other cards.

(d)   Either defender may require that play continue, in which case the section 89 applies.

89.   If either defender requires that play continue after declarer's claim, declarer must play on, leaving his hand face upwards on the table. Declarer may make no play inconsistent with any statement he may have made. Unless declarer has stated his intention to do so at the time of making his claim —

(a)   He may not lead a trump while either defender has a trump.

(b)   He may not finesse either in the suit led or in trumping the suit led.

If declarer attempts to make a play prohibited by this section, either defender may require him to withdraw it, provided neither defender has played a card after it.

PART VI

THE SCORE

90. KEEPING SCORE

Each side has a trick score and a premium score. The scores of the respective sides for each rubber should be entered in two adjacent vertical columns, the trick points in descending order below a horizontal line separating the trick and premium scores, the premium points (i.e., all points other than trick points) in ascending order above this line. A scorer should enter scores made by his side in the left-hand column. Whenever a game is scored, a line should be drawn across the trick score of both sides and underneath all trick point entries made in that game, none of which carry over to the next game. Subsequent trick points should be entered only below lines so drawn. Lines drawn prematurely should be forthwith erased.

91. RECORDING THE SCORE

When play ceases, all four players are equally responsible to see that the number of tricks won by each side is correctly determined, and that all scores are promptly and correctly entered in the score or scores, in accordance with the scoring table (section 98).

92. SCORING TRANSFERRED TRICKS

A transferred trick ranks for all scoring purposes as a trick won in play by the side receiving it.

93. CORRECTING THE SCORE

A proven or admitted error in any score may be corrected at any time before the rubber score is agreed, except that: If each player keeping score has made an error in entering or failing to enter a part score, or in omitting to score a game or in awarding one; such an error may not be corrected after the last card of the second succeeding correct deal has been dealt, unless a majority of the players consent.

94. A GAME — THE RUBBER

A game is won by the side which first scores a total of 100 or more trick points for odd tricks bid and won.

95. A rubber ends when a side has won two games, and the winners of the final game add to their score: 500 points if their opponents have won one game, 700 points if their opponents have not won a game. At the end of the rubber the trick and premium points of each side are added. The side with the larger total score wins the rubber, irrespective of the number of games (if any) which it has won. The difference between the two totals represents the number of points won.

96. EFFECT OF INCORRECT PACK

Scores made as a result of hands played with an incorrect pack are not affected by the discovery of the imperfection after the cards have been mixed together.

97. SCORING AN UNFINISHED RUBBER — PLAYER OBLIGED TO LEAVE

If for any reason a rubber is not finished, the score is computed as follows: If but one game has been completed, the winners of that game score 300 points; if but one side has a part score (or scores) in an unfinished game, that side scores 50 points; the trick and premium points of each side are added, and the side with the larger total score wins the difference between the two totals.

98. CONTRACT BRIDGE SCORING TABLE

		Odd Tricks Bid and Won in	Undoubled	Doubled
TRICK POINTS	FOR CONTRACTORS	Clubs or Diamonds, each	20	40
		Hearts or Spades, each	30	60
		No Trump { first / each subsequent	40 / 30	80 / 60

Redoubling doubles the doubled points for Odd Tricks.
Vulnerability does not affect points for Odd Tricks.
100 Trick Points constitute a game.

			Not Vulnerable	Vulnerable
PREMIUM POINTS FOR	CONTRACTORS	*Overtricks*		
		Undoubled, each	Trick Value	Trick Value
		Doubled, each	100	200
		Making Doubled or } Redoubled Contract }	50	50
	DEFENDERS	*Undertricks*		
		Undoubled, each	50	100
		Doubled { first / each subsequent	100 / 200	200 / 300

Redoubling doubles the doubled points for Overtricks and Undertricks,
but does not affect the points for making Doubled Contracts.

PREMIUM POINTS FOR	CONTRACTORS HOLDERS	*Honors in One Hand* {	4 Trump Honors	100
			5 Trump Honors or 4 Aces at Notrump	150
		Slams Bid and Won {	Little, not vulnerable 500, vulnerable	750
			Grand, not vulnerable 1000, vulnerable	1500
		Rubber Points {	Two game	700
			Three game	500

Unfinished Rubber — Winners of one game score 300 points. If but one
side has a part score in an unfinished game, it scores 50 points.

Doubling and Redoubling do not affect Honor, Slam, or Rubber points.

Vulnerability does not affect points for Honors.

PART VII

THE PROPRIETIES

(1) It is reprehensible to profit by information gained as a result of an irregularity committed by one's own side for which no penalty, or a penalty incommensurate with the information gained, is prescribed.

(2) It is improper to infringe a law deliberately, as by making an insufficient bid, whether or not a penalty is prescribed.

(3) A player should refrain from —

a. Varying the formulae used in calling; [1]

b. Calling with special emphasis, inflection or intonation;

c. Passing or doubling with exceptional haste or reluctance;

d. Making a call with undue delay which may result in conveying improper information to partner;

e. Indicating in any way approval or disapproval of partner's call or play;

f. Giving by word, manner or gesture an indication of the nature of the hand held;

g. Making a remark or gesture or asking a question from which an inference may be drawn;

h. Giving unauthorized information as to an incident of the auction or play;

i. Volunteering information which should be given only in response to a question;

j. Requesting, except for his own benefit, a review of calls or a placing of cards played to a trick;

k. An unnecessary hesitation, remark or mannerism which may deceive the opponents;

l. Attracting attention to the score, except when necessary to do so for his own information;

m. Calling attention to the number of tricks needed to complete or defeat the contract or to the fact that it has already been fulfilled or defeated;

n. Playing a card with special emphasis;

o. Playing with undue delay when the play does not need consideration;

p. Preparing to gather a trick before all four hands have played to it;

q. Detaching a card from his hand before it is his turn to lead or play;

r. Failing to keep the tricks in correct order and distinct from one another, or allowing some to be placed on the opposite side of the table;

s. Watching the place in a player's hand from which he draws a card, and drawing any inference therefrom;

t. Making gratuitous comments during the play as to the auction, the adequacy of the contract or the nature of the hand.

(4) It is improper to attempt to conceal a revoke by revoking again, or to conceal a revoke card if a hand is not played out, but there is no obligation to call attention to an established revoke or other irregularity committed by self or partner.

(5) It is improper to play out of turn, carelessly or otherwise.

---

[1] The recommended calling formulae are: "Pass" (avoid "I pass" or "no bid"); "1 heart" (avoid "I bid"); "1 notrump" (avoid "without" or "without a trump"); "double" (avoid stating the number of tricks or the denomination doubled); "6 spades" (avoid "little slam").

(6)   While it is reprehensible to allow partner's hesitation, remark or manner to influence a call, lead or play, it is proper to draw inferences from an opponent's gratuitous hesitation, remark or manner, but such inferences are drawn at one's own risk.

(7)   It is proper to warn partner against infringing a law of the game (e.g., against revoking, or against calling, leading or playing out of turn).

(8)   All four players are responsible to see that each hand plays a card, and but one, to each trick, and should forthwith correct such an irregularity.

(9)   Declarer should play out all hands in which there is any doubt as to the eventual outcome.

(10)   Bystanders or members not playing should refrain from making gratuitous remarks. They should not call attention to any irregularity or mistake, or speak on any question of fact or law except when requested to give an opinion.

(11)   It is improper to employ, without explaining its meaning to the opponents, a convention in calling or an unusual convention in play, the sigificance of which may not be clear to them. When applied to a call, the term convention covers a call designed to convey an arbitrary or artificial meaning, or used by a player with the assurance that his partner will not accept it in its natural sense. Such a call is not subject to penalty as an improper remark. It is necessary that a convention so used should be fully understood by the other side, and players using convention calls should be ready to reply fully to a proper inquiry by an opponent as to their meaning or use. Should it be necessary to make such an inquiry during the auction, the partner of the player who has made the convention call should reply. The committee of any Association, Tournament or Club, or a group of persons playing Contract Bridge, may prohibit or restrict the use of conventions which are both generally unrecognized and sufficiently intricate to cause unreasonable delay.

PART VIII

RULES FOR CLUB PROCEDURE

The following rules, governing membership in new and existing tables, have proven satisfactory in club use over a long period of years.

DEFINITIONS

Member — An applicant who has acquired the right to play at a table either immediately or in his turn.

Complete Table — A Table with six members.

Incomplete Table — A Table with four or five members.

A.   TIME LIMIT ON RIGHT TO PLAY

An applicant may not play in a rubber, unless he has become a member of a table before a card is duly drawn for the selection of players or partners.

B.   NEWLY FORMED TABLES

If there are more than six applicants, the six highest-ranking ones become members. The four highest-ranking members play the first rubber. Those who have not played, ranked in their order of entry into the room, take precedence over those who have played. The latter rank equally, except that players leaving existing tables to join the new table rank lowest.[1]

---

[1] Precedence between those of equal rank is determined by drawing cards, the drawer of the higher-ranking card obtaining precedence.

C. EXISTING TABLES

An application establishes membership in a table either forthwith or (if the table is complete) as soon as a vacancy occurs, unless applications in excess of the number required to complete a table are made at the same time, in which case precedence between applicants is established as in the preceding rule.

D. After each rubber place must be made, by the member who has played the greatest number of consecutive rubbers at that table, [1] for any member who did not play the last rubber, except that a member who has left another existing table must draw cards for the right to play his first rubber with the member who would otherwise have played.

E. If a member breaks up a game by leaving three players at a table, he is not entitled to compete against them for entry at another table.

F. MEMBERSHIP LIMITED TO ONE TABLE

No one can be a member of more than one table at the same time, unless a member consents, on request, to make a fourth at another table and announces his intention of returning to his former table as soon as his place can be filled. Failure to announce such intention results in loss of membership at his former table.

GLOSSARY OF TERMS

(Relating To the Play of the Cards)

ADVERSARY — The opponent(s) of declarer.

ATTACKING SIDE — The opener and his partner (the dummy).

BLANK SUIT — A suit of which a player has none. A void suit.

BLIND LEAD — The opening lead when leader's partner has not previously bid. Synonymous with an "opening lead in the blind."

BOARD — The exposed dummy hand.

BREAK — The division of the outstanding cards of a player's suit between the hands of his two opponents.

CASH — One "cashes" a trick when he wins the trick.

CLOSED HAND — Declarer's hand.

COME-ON SIGNAL — The play of an obviously unnecessarily high-card in any suit, as a signal to partner to lead that suit, or to continue leading it.

COMMANDING CARD — The highest remaining unplayed card of a suit.

CONTINUE A SUIT — The playing of the same suit which was played to the immediately preceding trick.

COVER — To play a card ranking higher than the one played by the immediately preceding hand (to play a King or a Queen on a Jack, etc.).

CROSS-RUFF — (See Ruffing or Trumping).

DECLARER — He who holds the closed hand and plays both partnership hands.

DEFENDER — Either opponent of the declarer.

DEFENSIVE SIDE — The opponents of the declarer.

DEUCE — The two-spot of any suit.

DISCARD — To play a card not of the suit led and not a trump.

DISCOURAGING SIGNAL — The play of a very low card in a suit by defender to discourage partner from leading that suit.

DOUBLETON — An original holding of exactly two cards in a suit.

DRAW TRUMPS — The play by declarer of playing as many trumps as necessary to eliminate all the trumps from the defenders' hands.

DUMMY — (1) Declarer's partner; (2) dummy's cards.

ECHO, OR ECHO SIGNAL — This is the play, or discard of a high card in a suit, which is followed up by the play, or discard, of a low card in the same suit. This is synonymous with a "high-low" signal.

ELIMINATE A LOSER — To get rid of a losing card by either trumping it, or discarding it on a card of some other suit.

ENCOURAGING SIGNAL — A high card played or discarded by the defenders on the first round of a suit, to direct partner to lead that suit. (See "come-on" signal).

ESTABLISHED SUIT — A suit in which the possessor can take all of the remaining tricks of that suit.

FINESSE — The attempt to win a trick with a card when there is a higher card (or cards) outstanding.

FOLLOW SUIT — To play a card of the suit that has been led.

FOURTH-BEST — The fourth-highest card that a player originally holds in a suit. The "fourth-best" is the normal lead against no trump contracts.

FOURTH-HAND — The last hand to play to any given trick.

GET IN — A player "gets in" the lead when he captures a trick.

GIVE PARTNER A RUFF — Leading a suit which partner ruffs (trumps).

HAND — The 13 cards that are dealt to one player. "Hand" is frequently used synonymously with "deal", i.e. "the following hand was played."

HOME — A player is "home" when he has fulfilled his contract, or can see that he will absolutely fulfill his contract.

HOLD-UP OR HOLDING-UP — The refusal to play a winning card — one which will win a trick — so as to use it to win a subsequent trick instead.

LEADER — The hand which leads to any trick.

LEAD FROM, THROUGH, TOWARD, UP TO — Any lead is "from" the leader's hand, "through" the hand on the left, "toward" the hand opposite, and "up to" the hand on the leader's right.

LOSE THE LEAD — To lose a trick to an opponent, thereby enabling him to lead to the next trick.

OFF THE TOP — Sure winning tricks.

OFFENSIVE PLAY — The play by declarer.

ON THE LEAD — A hand is "on the lead" when it has captured the preceding trick and must lead to the succeeding trick.

OPEN HAND — The dummy.

OPENING LEAD — The initial lead by declarer's left-hand opponent, which is made before the dummy is exposed.

OUTSTANDING CARDS — The missing cards of a player's suit which are in the possession of his opponents.

OVERTAKE — To play a higher card than partner, when such a play is unnecessary for the winning of a trick (e.g., partner plays the Queen of Spades, which you take with the King of Spades, in order to obtain the lead).

PROTECTED SUIT — A suit protected by one or more stoppers (See Stopper).

REACH — One reaches his partner's hand when he makes a lead that enables partner to win the trick.

REVOKE — The failure to follow suit by a player when he has a card of that suit. A revoke is subject to a penalty.

ROUND OF A SUIT — When a suit is led for the first time, it is called the "first round" of the suit; when it is led a second time, it is called the "second round" of the suit etc.

RUFFING — The trumping of a lead of any suit. A cross-ruff occurs when each partner leads a suit that the other can ruff (see Trumping).

RULE OF ELEVEN — When the fourth-highest is led originally, its denomination subtracted from the number 11 shows the number of high cards outstanding.

SECOND HAND — The hand to the left of the leader to any trick.

SHOW OUT — Failing to follow suit.

SINGLETON — An original holding of one card in a suit.

STACKED — The outstanding cards of any suit are considered stacked when all of them — or most of them — are in one opponent's hand (if seven hearts are outstanding, they figure to be divided 4-3 or 5-2; if they are divided 6-1 or 7-0, they are deemed to be stacked).

STOPPER — (1) At no trump, a commanding card possessed by declarer which will win a trick, thereby effectively halting the attack of the defenders. (2) at a suit contract, a trump card is also a "stopper" since it will be able to prevent the opponents from winning tricks in their suit.

SWITCH — If, after capturing a trick in one suit, you then lead another suit, i.e., "switching" suits.

TREY — The three-spot of each suit.

TRICK — Consists of 4 cards, the first being played by the leader.

TRIPLETON — An original holding of 3 cards in a suit.

TRUMPING — Synonymous with "ruffing."

UNBLOCK — To deliberately play a higher-than-necessary card to get out of partner's way, avoiding the "blocking" of a suit.

UNDERLEAD — To lead away from a "picture card"; e.g., to lead the two or the three from a holding of A 3 2.

VOID — To have none of a suit. Synonymous with "blank suit."